THE UNTOLD STORY OF
JESUS

A Modern Biography from *The Urantia Book*

THE UNTOLD STORY OF
JESUS

A Modern Biography from *The Urantia Book*

URANTIA PRESS

CONTENTS

7   ARTWORK

8   PREFACE

[CHAPTER I]

13 THE EARLY YEARS

14   GABRIEL'S ANNOUNCEMENT TO MARY

16   JOSEPH'S DREAM

16   JOSEPH AND MARY

19   THE TRIP TO BETHLEHEM FOR THE CENSUS

20   THE BIRTH OF JESUS

21   THE PRESENTATION IN THE TEMPLE

23   THE ESCAPE FROM HEROD

25   SOJOURN IN ALEXANDRIA

26   BACK IN NAZARETH

27   LIFE IN NAZARETH, AGES FOUR TO FIVE

30   LIFE IN NAZARETH, AGES SIX TO SEVEN

31   SCHOOL DAYS

34   THE INVITATION TO JERUSALEM

35   TROUBLE AT SCHOOL

36   SABBATH WALKS WITH JOSEPH

39   THE TRIP WITH JOSEPH TO SCYTHOPOLIS

40   THE TWELFTH YEAR

41   THE TRIP TO JERUSALEM

43   YOUNG JESUS TEACHING IN THE TEMPLE

47   MARY AND JOSEPH FIND JESUS

[CHAPTER II]

51 THE MISSING YEARS: FAMILY LIFE

52   THE DEATH OF JOSEPH

53   THE SON OF MAN

54   THE FINANCIAL STRUGGLE

55   HEAD OF HOUSEHOLD

59   JESUS' EIGHT SIBLINGS   (SIDEBARS)

60   REBECCA'S UNDYING LOVE

62   JESUS AND ROMANTIC LOVE

62   THE VISIT WITH LAZARUS, MARTHA, AND MARY

63   JAMES INSTALLED AS HEAD OF THE FAMILY

64   SUMMARY OF AGES 21 TO 25

65   JESUS LEAVES HIS FAMILY

68   THE WEALTHY TRAVELERS FROM INDIA

[CHAPTER III]

71 THE MISSING YEARS: TRAVEL AND MINISTRY

72   EMBARKING FROM CAESAREA

77   THE LIGHTHOUSE AT ALEXANDRIA

78   THE ALEXANDRIAN LIBRARY

79   THE YOUNG MAN WHO WAS AFRAID

82   THE SOJOURN AT ROME

85   THE THOUGHTLESS PAGAN

85   THE RETURN FROM ROME

88   THE TWO COURTESANS

90   PERSONAL WORK IN CORINTH

92   MINISTRY TO HUNGRY SOULS

95   THE CONCLUSION OF THE TOUR

98   THE THREE FRIENDS PART

[CHAPTER IV]

101 THE MISSING YEARS: THE TRANSITION

102   MANAGING A CARAVAN TO THE CASPIAN SEA

104   THE URMIA LECTURES

106   THE YEAR OF SOLITARY WANDERINGS

109   THE GREAT TEMPTATION

111   THE WAR IN HEAVEN

111   THE TIME OF WAITING

114   THE BAPTISM IN THE JORDAN

116   JOHN THE BAPTIST

117   THE RUGGED AND FIERY PROPHET

[CHAPTER V]

121 "My Hour Has Come"

122	Forty Days in the Perean Wilderness
124	The Six Great Decisions
125	Choosing the First Six Apostles
130	The Wedding at Cana
132	The Master and the Miraculous
135	Introducing the Kingdom of Heaven
136	Choosing the Final Six Apostles
138	Fishers of Men
139	First Work of the Twelve
142	Five Months of Testing
142	The Twelve Apostles
144	Organization of the Apostles
151	The Ordination of the Twelve
155	The Sermon on the Mount and the Beatitudes

[CHAPTER VI]

157 Beginning the Public Work

158	Leaving Galilee
160	The Passover at Jerusalem
163	Nicodemus and the Sanhedrin
163	Nalda, the Woman at Jacob's Well
168	What Prayer Meant to Jesus
169	The Lord's Prayer
170	Conference with John's Apostles

[CHAPTER VII]

173 The Year of Signs and Wonders

174	The Healing at Sundown
178	The Leper at Iron
180	At the Pool of Bethesda
181	The Penitent Woman
183	The Six Jerusalem Spies
184	The Kingdom's First Hospital
184	The Dependable David Zebedee
187	The Man with the Withered Hand
188	Healing the Paralytic
190	The Women's Evangelistic Corps
191	How Jesus Emancipated Women
194	The Ten Women Evangelists
194	The Nazareth Rejection
197	Jairus and His Daughter
201	Feeding the Five Thousand
203	The King-Making Episode

[CHAPTER VIII]

207 The Sifting of the Kingdom

208	The Epochal Sermon
212	Last Days at Capernaum
214	The Hasty Flight
217	Teaching at Tyre
220	Peter's Confession
223	Son of Man, Son of God
225	The Transfiguration
226	Meaning of the Transfiguration
228	The Epileptic Boy
231	Peter's Protest

[CHAPTER IX]

235 "Before Abraham Was, I Am"

236	Public Announcement of Divinity
239	The Woman Taken in Adultery
240	"I Am the Light of the World"
242	The Truth Will Set You Free
243	The Seventy Evangelists
244	The Rich Young Man
247	The Good Samaritan
249	An Open Challenge to the Sanhedrin
251	The Good Shepherd
254	The Ten Lepers

255	The Sermon at Gerasa		**[CHAPTER XI]**
257	The Message from Bethany	**327**	**"It Is Finished!"**
260	The Talk About Angels	328	The Betrayal and Arrest of Jesus
261	The Resurrection of Lazarus	332	Before the Sanhedrin Court
265	What Became of Lazarus	334	Simon Peter's Tears of Agony
266	Meeting of the Sanhedrin	336	The Trial Before Pilate
268	The Prodigal Son	339	Before Herod and the Return to Pilate
271	"Make Haste Zaccheus"	345	The Crucifixion
274	"As Jesus Passed By"	347	The End of Judas Iscariot
		352	Meaning of the Death on the Cross

	[CHAPTER X]		**[CHAPTER XII]**
277	**The Final Days**	**355**	**"I Am the Resurrection and the Life"**
278	Judas Turns Traitor	356	The Resurrection
280	Your King Comes As the Lowly One	360	The Walk with Two Brothers
285	Cleansing the Temple	363	Appearances to the Apostles
288	Purging the Den of Robbers	367	Appearance by the Lake
288	Challenging the Master's Authority	371	Visiting with the Apostles
290	Tuesday Morning in the Temple	372	Resurrection Appearances
292	The Inquiring Greeks	374	Chart of the Nineteen Appearances
295	The Last Temple Discourse	377	The Master's Ascension
298	Status of Individual Jews	379	Bestowal of the Spirit of Truth
299	Foretelling the End of Jerusalem	382	The Significance of Pentecost
305	One Day Alone with God		
308	The Last Supper	386	Conclusion
316	Love One Another As I Have Loved You	390	Timeline of the Life of Jesus
318	The Last Group Prayer	392	Bible and Urantia Book References
321	I Am the Way, the Truth, and the Life	394	Glossary of Urantia Book Terms
322	Alone in Gethsemane	395	Index

Maps

74	Jesus Tours the Mediterranean World
159	Palestine in the Times of Christ
375	The Nine Localities (of resurrection appearances)

2	C. Michael Dudash — *Light of the World*
388	C. Michael Dudash — *Follow Me*

ARTWORK

HARRY ANDERSON
115 John the Baptist Baptizing Jesus;
259 Suffer Little Children to Come to Me;
290 The Tribute Coin; 338 Pilate Confronts Christ

TADDEO DI BARTOLO
143 The Twelve Apostles

ALEXANDRE BIDA
214 The Priests Take Counsel with the Herodians

CARL BLOCH
15 The Annunciation; 227 Transfiguration of Christ;
287 Jesus Clears the Temple; 335 Peter's Denial

ANTONIO CISERI
342 Ecce Homo

HAROLD COPPING
181 The Pool of Bethesda; 230 Jesus Heals the Epileptic Boy;
272 The Healing of Blind Bartimeus; 378 Come unto Me

RUSS DOCKEN
50 The Burial of Joseph; 61 Rebecca's Marriage
Proposal; 66 The Master Boatbuilder; 81 The Young
Man Who Was Afraid; 112 My Hour Has Come;
129 Leave No Writings Behind; 186 The Kingdom's
First Hospital; 326 Father Forgive Them

C. MICHAEL DUDASH
2 & 241 Light of the World; 18 On the Way to Bethlehem;
108 Not By Bread Alone; 140 Fishers of Men; 164 Living
Water; 220 Peter's Confession; 302 The Master Teacher;
319 He Lifted His Eyes Toward Heaven; 381 The Comforter;
388 Follow Me

ANDON FONTAINNE
69 Serendipity; 282 The Son of Peace Enters Jerusalem

DANIEL GERHARTZ
172 Forgiven

EUGENE GIRARDET
24 The Flight into Egypt

FRANCESCO HAYEZ
301 The Destruction of the Temple of Jerusalem

HEINRICH HOFMANN
44 Jesus in the Temple;
245 Christ and the Rich Young Ruler

WILLIAM HOLE
28 Jesus as a Boy in Nazareth; 131 The Wedding at Cana

YONGSUNG KIM
239 Forgiven; 250 Healing the Blind Man; 252 Beside Quiet
Waters; 276 Washing of the Feet; 324 Gethsemane Prayer

AKIANE KRAMARIK
275 Jesus

MICHAEL MALM
32 In Joseph's Woodshop; 37 Sabbath Walks with Joseph;
56 The Family Garden; 361 Two Brothers from Emmaus

GERRY METZ
102 The Caravan Conductor

PREM MUKHERJEE
348 No Greater Love

EDWARD OKUŃ
347 Judas

GREG OLSEN
10 O Jerusalem; 22 A Light to the Gentiles;
106 In the World, Not of the World;
122 Worlds Without End; 156 Joy of the Lord;
206 Jesus in the Synagogue; 385 Peace on Earth

DEL PARSON
87 The Intervention; 120 Facing Eternity;
306 One Day Alone with God; 368 Peter Do You Love Me?

VASILY POLENOV
125 Follow Me; 168 Dreams (On the Hill);
208 At the Genisaret Lake

SLAWA RADZISZEWSKA
31 Mother's Love; 35 Forbidden Art; 70 The Library of
Alexandria; 77 Playing with the Shepherd Dog;
78 The Great Lighthouse of Pharos; 83 Appearance
Before Tiberius; 84 The Thoughtless Pagan;
90 The Two Courtesans; 93 Chang, the Chinese Merchant;
96 Tender Loving Care; 98 Trek Across the Desert Sands

WALTER RANE
200 Feeding the Five Thousand;
262 Lazarus, Come Forth!; 314 In Remembrance of Me;
330 I Am He; 358 He Is Not Here

REMBRANDT VAN RIJN
204 The Storm on the Sea of Galilee

J. KIRK RICHARDS
100 Baptism II; 162 Nicodemus; 176 The Healing at
Sundown; 179 Christ among the Lepers;
192 Commissioning the Women's Corps;
234 I Stand at the Door and Knock; 261 Small Angel
in White; 354 Garden Tomb; 366 Jesus Resurrected

DAVID ROBERTS
218 General View of Tyre

STEPHEN SAWYER & SLAWA RADZISZEWSKA
279 The Turning Point

LIZ LEMON SWINDLE
270 The Prodigal Son

LOUIS TIFFANY
119 John the Baptist

JAMES TISSOT
148 The Exhortation to the Apostles; 153 The Sermon on the
Mount; 232 The Protestations of Saint Peter; 266 The Chief
Priests Take Counsel Together; 294 Jerusalem, Jerusalem

VINCENT WILLEM VAN GOGH
248 The Good Samaritan (after Delacroix)

JEREMY WINBORG
12 The Babe of Bethlehem; 48 O Jerusalem, Jerusalem;
199 Jairus's Daughter

But there are also many other things which Jesus did; were every one of them to be written, I suppose that the world itself could not contain the books that would be written.

—JOHN 21:25 RSV

How fitting that the last words of John's gospel should be the first words of this book. *The Untold Story of Jesus* highlights his life and teachings in a biography excerpted from *The Urantia Book*. Many of these historical stories are familiar to readers of the New Testament but dozens are new, including the missing years not found in the Bible. Here you discover Jesus presented as never before, both as divine Son and human hero whose matchless life inspires, comforts, and transforms you.

This new book provides relevant and empowering spiritual insights, helping you navigate the challenging yet promising conditions of the twenty-first century. We live in an exciting era of unprecedented improvements in our material lives brought about by scientific, industrial, and social achievements. Yet in spite of all this progress, many souls feel lonely and displaced. We need God and have an innate thirst for spiritual answers because of that "still, small voice" that lives within us. Finding God by living the personal religion of Jesus satisfies that thirst.

The religion of Jesus is based on faith, love, and selfless service. His pure and original message of unending life through faith in our heavenly Father is the spiritual birthright of every man, woman, and child of every nation, race, religion, and economic status. The teachings of Jesus stand apart from any religious, political, or social institution. The religion *of* Jesus, distinct from the theological religion *about* Jesus, holds the key to happiness and productive living. His spirit invigorates the inner life and provides power from above to transform people who then go out to transform society. The brotherhood of men is founded on the fatherhood of God. The family of God is derived from the love of God—God is love. God the Father divinely loves his children, all of them.

THE ART IN THIS BOOK

The one hundred and eight paintings in this book run the gamut of fine art celebrating the life of Christ. Here you will find both classic and modern paintings by many renowned Christian artists. You will also see forty-two newly commissioned paintings for the first time. Thirty-four artists poured their souls into these portraits of higher spiritual reality. Our deep appreciation and humble gratitude go out to each one of them.

These paintings illustrate Jesus' life journey from his humble birth and childhood to adolescence and manhood; from private to public ministry and on to his death, resurrection, and ascension. The artwork celebrates his diverse life as son, father-brother, carpenter, boat designer and builder, tutor, translator, caravan conductor, teacher, healer, minister, and friend. No one knows what Jesus looked like, but these artists painted their soulful interpretations to spark our imagination of these scenes from the Master's life. Our intent is to give you a visual communion with Jesus that complements the enthralling narrative.

ABOUT THE URANTIA BOOK

The Urantia Book was first published in 1955 and contains four parts. The first three parts present an expansive new revelation of God, the cosmos, the afterlife, angels and the heavenly hosts, world history, and much more. The fourth part is a restatement of the life and teachings of Jesus. This narrative sometimes uses unfamiliar names or terms, which are defined in the glossary on page 394.

The search for the genuine Jesus continues to intrigue humanity. Since the Bible only records an estimated fifty days in his life, it follows that there is more to his story. You will find it here in this detailed history of the Master's entire life, including the public ministry recorded in the Gospels. It is beautifully written in modern, page-turning prose. It provides a coherent and seamless biography of this magnificent personality who continues to shape spiritual progress in our world.

While we have captured many fascinating stories and noble teachings, our highlights represent less than a third of Part IV of *The Urantia Book*. Condensing the life and teachings of Jesus into these pages is like trying to illuminate the sun by lighting a candle. We encourage you to read the original source.

The story of Jesus is one of the most enthralling chapters in human history. The closing passage of John's gospel speaks to a life larger than even the world itself. In John's day the Word was made flesh. In these days the Word is made book.

A Final Thought

We pray that these stories, teachings, and paintings provide you with a new sense of faith, comfort, and purpose. And to you who may not believe in Jesus, we invite you to look again. Read the stories, enjoy the art, and get to know the man through new eyes.

What the world needs now is unconditional love, unfailing compassion and matchless good will. Even after two thousand years, Jesus' teachings have not been practiced on a global scale. When that day surely comes, his inspired life will transform, transfigure, and rule this world. His message of personal faith in a loving heavenly Father coupled with unselfish service to one another is a clear and direct pathway to peace in this life and passage to the next.

May you be blessed, and your life enriched by the supreme adventure that follows! ∎

Of all human knowledge, that which is of greatest value is to know the religious life of Jesus and how he lived it.

—THE URANTIA BOOK (196:1.3)

[GREG OLSEN — *O Jerusalem*]

THE EARLY YEARS

*And the child grew, and waxed strong in spirit,
filled with wisdom: and the grace of God was upon him.*

—LUKE 2:40 KJV

THE BABE OF BETHLEHEM WAS BORN IN JUST THE SAME MANNER AS ALL BABIES BEFORE that day and since have come into the world. He grew up as a child of the realm and wrestled with the vicissitudes of his environment just as do other people. Jesus lived among us for almost thirty-six years. His matchless life was a personal experience of man, mortal man, seeking God and finding him to the fullness during one short life in the flesh.

At the time of his birth, the world was experiencing such a revival of spiritual thinking and religious living as it had never known or has experienced since. When Jesus incarnated on earth, the world presented the most favorable condition for the bestowal that had ever previously prevailed or has since obtained. The entire Mediterranean world was a unified empire with good roads, trade, travel, and widespread domestic peace and prosperity.

Galilee was regarded as an unsophisticated backwater by the religious leaders in Jerusalem, and Nazareth was in especially low regard with its liberal interpretation of both Jewish traditional law and the social restrictions against mingling with gentiles. "Can any good thing come out of Nazareth?" was a common saying in those days. But these tolerant conditions plus its position as a caravan crossroads of trade and travel made it favorable for exposure to life as it was led across the Levant and beyond.

Of all couples living in Palestine at about the time of the bestowal, Joseph and Mary possessed the most ideal combination of widespread racial connections and superior average of personality endowments. Jesus (Joshua ben Joseph) was to appear on earth as an *average* man, that the common people might understand him and receive him. Though they often talked about the future of their eldest child, had you been there, you would only have observed the growing up of a normal, healthy, carefree, but exceedingly inquisitive child of that time and place.

Jesus of Nazareth attained the full realization of the potential of spirit personality in human experience; therefore his life of achieving the Father's will becomes man's most real and ideal revelation of the personality of God. This new biography is both the familiar and the untold story of that life.

———

THE URANTIA BOOK: PAPERS 122–125
NOVEMBER, 8 B.C.–APRIL A.D. 7

[JEREMY WINBORG — *The Babe of Bethlehem*]

NOVEMBER, 8 B.C.

GABRIEL'S ANANOUNCEMENT TO MARY

One evening about sundown, before Joseph had returned home, Gabriel appeared to Mary by the side of a low stone table and, after she had recovered her composure, said: "I come at the bidding of one who is my Master and whom you shall love and nurture. To you, Mary, I bring glad tidings when I announce that the conception within you is ordained by heaven, and that in due time you will become the mother of a son; you shall call him Joshua, and he shall inaugurate the kingdom of heaven on earth and among men. Speak not of this matter save to Joseph and to Elizabeth, your kinswoman, to whom I have also appeared, and who shall presently also bear a son, whose name shall be John, and who will prepare the way for the message of deliverance which your son shall proclaim to men with great power and deep conviction. And doubt not my word, Mary, for this home has been chosen as the mortal habitat of the child of destiny. My benediction rests upon you, the power of the Most Highs will strengthen you, and the Lord of all the earth shall overshadow you."

Mary pondered this visitation secretly in her heart for many weeks until of a certainty she knew she was with child, before she dared to disclose these unusual events to her husband. When Joseph heard all about this, although he had great confidence in Mary, he was much troubled and could not sleep for many nights. At first Joseph had doubts about the Gabriel visitation. Then when he became well-nigh persuaded that Mary had really heard the voice and beheld the form of the divine messenger, he was torn in mind as he pondered how such things could be. How could the offspring of human beings be a child of divine destiny? Never could Joseph reconcile these conflicting ideas until, after several weeks of thought, both he and Mary reached the conclusion that they had been chosen to become the parents of the Messiah, though it had hardly been the Jewish concept that the expected deliverer was to be of divine nature.

Mary persuaded Joseph to let her journey to the City of Judah, four miles west of Jerusalem, in the hills, to visit Elizabeth. Gabriel had informed each of these mothers-to-be of his appearance to the other. Naturally they were anxious to get together, compare experiences, and talk over the probable futures of their sons. Mary remained with her distant cousin for three weeks. Elizabeth did much to strengthen Mary's faith in the vision of Gabriel, so that she returned home more fully dedicated to the call to mother the child of destiny whom she was so soon to present to the world as a helpless babe, an average and normal infant of the realm.

Gabriel's announcement to Mary was made the day following the conception of Jesus and was the only event of supernatural occurrence connected

> "YOU WILL BECOME THE MOTHER OF A SON; YOU SHALL CALL HIM JOSHUA, AND HE SHALL INAUGURATE THE KINGDOM OF HEAVEN ON EARTH AND AMONG MEN."

[CARL BLOCH — *The Annunciation* (detail)]

with her entire experience of carrying and bearing the child of promise. ■

JOSEPH'S DREAM

Joseph did not become reconciled to the idea that Mary was to become the mother of an extraordinary child until after he had experienced a very impressive dream. In this dream a brilliant celestial messenger appeared to him and, among other things, said: "Joseph, I appear by command of Him who now reigns on high, and I am directed to instruct you concerning the son whom Mary shall bear, and who shall become a great light in the world. In him will be life, and his life shall become the light of mankind. He shall first come to his own people, but they will hardly receive him; but to as many as shall receive him to them will he reveal that they are the children of God." After this experience Joseph never again wholly doubted Mary's story of Gabriel's visit and of the promise that the unborn child was to become a divine messenger to the world.

JOSEPH

Had Joseph lived, he undoubtedly would have become a firm believer in the divine mission of his eldest son. Mary alternated between believing and doubting, being greatly influenced by the position taken by her other children and by her friends and relatives, but always was she steadied in her final attitude by the memory of Gabriel's appearance to her immediately after the child was conceived.

In all these visitations nothing was said about the house of David. Nothing was ever intimated about Jesus' becoming a "deliverer of the Jews," not even that he was to be the long-expected Messiah. Jesus was not such a Messiah as the Jews had anticipated, but he was the *world's deliverer*. His mission was to all races and peoples, not to any one group.

Joseph was not of the line of King David. Mary had more of the Davidic ancestry than Joseph. True, Joseph did go to the City of David, Bethlehem, to be registered for the Roman census, but that was because, six generations previously, Joseph's paternal ancestor of that generation, being an orphan, was adopted by one Zadoc, who was a direct descendant of David; hence was Joseph also accounted as of the "house of David."

Most of the so-called Messianic prophecies of the Old Testament were made to apply to Jesus long after his life had been lived on earth. For centuries the Hebrew prophets had proclaimed the coming of a deliverer, and these promises had been construed by successive generations as referring to a new Jewish ruler who would sit upon the throne of David and, by the reputed miraculous methods of Moses, proceed to establish the Jews in Palestine as a powerful nation, free from all foreign domination. Again, many figurative passages found throughout the Hebrew scriptures were subsequently misapplied to the life mission of Jesus. Many Old Testament sayings were so distorted as to appear to fit some episode of the Master's earth life. Jesus himself onetime publicly denied any connection with the royal house of David. Even the passage, "a maiden shall bear a son," was made to read, "a virgin shall bear a son." ■

JOSEPH AND MARY

Joseph was a mild-mannered man, extremely conscientious, and in every way faithful to the religious conventions and practices of his people. He talked little but thought much. The sorry plight of the Jewish people caused Joseph much sadness. As a youth, among his eight brothers and sisters, he had been more cheerful, but in the earlier years of married life (during Jesus' childhood) he was subject to periods of mild spiritual discouragement. These temperamental manifestations were greatly improved just before his untimely death and after the economic condition of his family had been enhanced by his advancement from the rank of carpenter to the role of a prosperous contractor.

Mary's temperament was quite opposite to that of her husband. She was usually cheerful, was very rarely downcast, and possessed an ever-sunny disposition. Mary indulged in free and frequent expression of her emotional feelings and was never observed to be sorrowful until after the sudden death of Joseph. And she had hardly recovered from this shock when she had thrust upon her the anxieties and questionings aroused by the extraordinary career of her eldest son, which was so rapidly unfolding before her astonished gaze. But throughout all this unusual experience Mary was composed, courageous, and fairly wise in her relationship with her strange and little-understood first-born son and his surviving brothers and sisters.

Jesus derived much of his unusual gentleness and marvelous sympathetic understanding of human nature from his father; he inherited his gift as a great teacher and his tremendous capacity for righteous indignation from his mother. In emotional reactions to his adult-life environment, Jesus was at one time like his father, meditative and worshipful, sometimes characterized by apparent sadness; but more often he drove forward in the manner of his mother's optimistic and determined disposition. All in all, Mary's temperament tended to dominate the career of the divine Son as he grew up and swung into the momentous strides of his adult life. In some particulars Jesus was a blending of his parents' traits; in other respects he exhibited the traits of one in contrast with those of the other.

From Joseph Jesus secured his strict training in the usages of the Jewish ceremonials and his unusual acquaintance with the Hebrew scriptures; from Mary he derived a broader viewpoint of religious life and a more liberal concept of personal spiritual freedom.

The families of both Joseph and Mary were well educated for their time. Joseph and Mary were educated far above the average for their day and station in life. He was a thinker; she was a planner, expert in adaptation and practical in immediate execution. Joseph was a black-eyed brunet; Mary, a brown-eyed well-nigh blond type.

Mary was an expert weaver and more than averagely skilled in most of the household arts of that day; she was a good housekeeper and a superior homemaker. Both Joseph and Mary were good teachers, and they saw to it that their children were well versed in the learning of that day.

When Joseph was a young man, he was employed by Mary's father in the work of building an addition to his house, and it was when Mary brought Joseph a cup of water, during a noontime meal, that the courtship of the pair who were destined to become the parents of Jesus really began.

Joseph and Mary were married, in accordance with Jewish custom, at Mary's home in the environs of Nazareth when Joseph was twenty-one years old. This marriage concluded a normal courtship of almost two years' duration. Shortly thereafter they moved into their new home in Nazareth, which had been built by Joseph with the assistance of two of his brothers. The house was located near the foot of the near-by elevated land which so charmingly overlooked the surrounding countryside. In this home, especially prepared, these young and expectant parents had thought to welcome the child of promise, little realizing that this momentous event of a universe was to transpire while they would be absent from home in Bethlehem of Judea.

The larger part of Joseph's family became believers in the teachings of Jesus, but very few of Mary's people ever believed in him until after he departed from this world. Joseph leaned more toward the spiritual concept of the expected Messiah, but Mary and her family, especially her father, held to the idea of the Messiah as a temporal deliverer and political ruler. Mary's ancestors had been prominently identified with the Maccabean activities of the then but recent times.

Joseph held vigorously to the Eastern, or Babylonian, views of the Jewish religion; Mary leaned strongly toward the more liberal and broader Western, or Hellenistic, interpretation of the law and the prophets. ∎

AUGUST 18, 7 B.C.

THE TRIP TO BETHLEHEM FOR THE CENSUS

In the month of March, 8 B.C. (the month Joseph and Mary were married), Caesar Augustus decreed that all inhabitants of the Roman Empire should be numbered, that a census should be made which could be used for effecting better taxation. The Jews had always been greatly prejudiced against any attempt to "number the people," and this, in connection with the serious domestic difficulties of Herod, King of Judea, had conspired to cause the postponement of the taking of this census in the Jewish kingdom for one year. Throughout all the Roman Empire this census was registered in the year 8 B.C., except in the Palestinian kingdom of Herod, where it was taken in 7 B.C., one year later.

Joseph and Mary were poor, and since they had only one beast of burden, Mary, being large with

[C. MICHAEL DUDASH — *On the Way to Bethlehem*]

child, rode on the animal with the provisions while Joseph walked, leading the beast. The building and furnishing of a home had been a great drain on Joseph since he had also to contribute to the support of his parents, as his father had been recently disabled. And so this Jewish couple went forth from their humble home early on the morning of August 18, 7 B.C., on their journey to Bethlehem.

Their first day of travel carried them around the foothills of Mount Gilboa, where they camped for the night by the river Jordan and engaged in many speculations as to what sort of a son would be born to them, Joseph adhering to the concept of a spiritual teacher and Mary holding to the idea of a Jewish Messiah, a deliverer of the Hebrew nation.

Bright and early the morning of August 19, Joseph and Mary were again on their way. They partook of their noontide meal at the foot of Mount Sartaba, overlooking the Jordan valley, and journeyed on, making Jericho for the night, where they stopped at an inn on the highway in the outskirts of the city. Following the evening meal and after much discussion concerning the oppressiveness of Roman rule, Herod, the census enrollment, and the comparative influence of Jerusalem and Alexandria as centers of Jewish learning and culture, the Nazareth travelers retired for the night's rest. Early in the morning of August 20 they resumed their journey, reaching Jerusalem before noon, visiting the temple, and going on to their destination, arriving at Bethlehem in midafternoon.

The inn was overcrowded, and Joseph accordingly sought lodgings with distant relatives, but every room in Bethlehem was filled to overflowing. On returning to the courtyard of the inn, he was informed that the caravan stables, hewn out of the side of the rock and situated just below the inn, had been cleared of animals and cleaned up for the reception of lodgers. Leaving the donkey in the courtyard, Joseph shouldered their bags of clothing and provisions and with Mary descended the stone steps to their lodgings below. They found themselves located in what had been a grain storage room to the front of the stalls and mangers. Tent curtains had been hung, and they counted themselves fortunate to have such comfortable quarters.

Joseph had thought to go out at once and enroll, but Mary was weary; she was considerably distressed and besought him to remain by her side, which he did. ∎

AUGUST 21, 7 B.C.

THE BIRTH OF JESUS

All that night Mary was restless so that neither of them slept much. By the break of day the pangs of childbirth were well in evidence, and at noon, August 21, 7 B.C., with the help and kind ministrations of women fellow travelers, Mary was delivered of a male child. Jesus of Nazareth was born into the world, was wrapped in the clothes which Mary had brought along for such a possible contingency, and laid in a near-by manger.

In just the same manner as all babies before

that day and since have come into the world, the promised child was born; and on the eighth day, according to the Jewish practice, he was circumcised and formally named Joshua (Jesus).

The next day after the birth of Jesus, Joseph made his enrollment. Meeting a man they had talked with two nights previously at Jericho, Joseph was taken by him to a well-to-do friend who had a room at the inn, and who said he would gladly exchange quarters with the Nazareth couple. That afternoon they moved up to the inn, where they lived for almost three weeks until they found lodgings in the home of a distant relative of Joseph.

The second day after the birth of Jesus, Mary sent word to Elizabeth that her child had come and received word in return inviting Joseph up to Jerusalem to talk over all their affairs with Zacharias. The following week Joseph went to Jerusalem to confer with Zacharias. Both Zacharias and Elizabeth had become possessed with the sincere conviction that Jesus was indeed to become the Jewish deliverer, the Messiah, and that their son John was to be his chief of aides, his right-hand man of destiny. And since Mary held these same ideas, it was not difficult to prevail upon Joseph to remain in Bethlehem, the City of David, so that Jesus might grow up to become the successor of David on the throne of all Israel. Accordingly, they remained in Bethlehem more than a year, Joseph meantime working some at his carpenter's trade.

At the noontide birth of Jesus the seraphim of Urantia, assembled under their directors, did sing anthems of glory over the Bethlehem manger, but these utterances of praise were not heard by human ears. No shepherds nor any other mortal creatures came to pay homage to the babe of Bethlehem until the day of the arrival of certain priests from Ur, who were sent down from Jerusalem by Zacharias.

These priests from Mesopotamia had been told sometime before by a strange religious teacher of their country that he had had a dream in which he was informed that "the light of life" was about to appear on earth as a babe and among the Jews. And thither went these three teachers looking for this "light of life." After many weeks of futile search in Jerusalem, they were about to return to Ur when Zacharias met them and disclosed his belief that Jesus was the object of their quest and sent them on to Bethlehem, where they found the babe and left their gifts with Mary, his earth mother. The babe was almost three weeks old at the time of their visit. ∎

AUGUST, 7 B.C.

THE PRESENTATION IN THE TEMPLE

Moses had taught the Jews that every first-born son belonged to the Lord, and that, in lieu of his sacrifice as was the custom among the heathen nations, such a son might live provided his parents would redeem him by the payment of five shekels to any authorized priest. There was also a Mosaic ordinance which directed that a mother, after the passing of a certain period of time, should present herself (or have someone make the proper sacrifice for her) at the temple for purification. It was customary to perform both of these ceremonies at the same time. Accordingly, Joseph and Mary went up to the temple at Jerusalem in person to present Jesus to the priests and effect his redemption and also to make the proper sacrifice to insure Mary's ceremonial purification from the alleged uncleanness of childbirth.

There lingered constantly about the courts of the temple two remarkable characters, Simeon a singer and Anna a poetess. Simeon was a Judean, but Anna was a Galilean. This couple

were frequently in each other's company, and both were intimates of the priest Zacharias, who had confided the secret of John and Jesus to them. Both Simeon and Anna longed for the coming of the Messiah, and their confidence in Zacharias led them to believe that Jesus was the expected deliverer of the Jewish people.

Zacharias knew the day Joseph and Mary were expected to appear at the temple with Jesus, and he had prearranged with Simeon and Anna to indicate, by the salute of his upraised hand, which one in the procession of first-born children was Jesus.

For this occasion Anna had written a poem which Simeon proceeded to sing, much to the astonishment of Joseph, Mary, and all who were assembled in the temple courts. And this was their hymn of the redemption of the first-born son:

Blessed be the Lord, the God of Israel,
For he has visited us and wrought
redemption for his people;
He has raised up a horn of
salvation for all of us
In the house of his servant David.
Even as he spoke by the mouth
of his holy prophets—
Salvation from our enemies and from
the hand of all who hate us;
To show mercy to our fathers, and
remember his holy covenant—
The oath which he swore to
Abraham our father,
To grant us that we, being delivered out
of the hand of our enemies,
Should serve him without fear,
In holiness and righteousness before
him all our days.
Yes, and you, child of promise, shall be
called the prophet of the Most High;

For you shall go before the face of the
Lord to establish his kingdom;
To give knowledge of salvation
to his people
In the remission of their sins.
Rejoice in the tender mercy of our God
because the dayspring from on
high has now visited us
To shine upon those who sit in
darkness and the shadow of death;
To guide our feet into ways of peace.
And now let your servant depart in
peace, O Lord, according to your word,
For my eyes have seen your salvation,
Which you have prepared before
the face of all peoples;
A light for even the unveiling
of the gentiles
And the glory of your people Israel.

On the way back to Bethlehem, Joseph and Mary were silent—confused and overawed. Mary was much disturbed by the farewell salutation of Anna, the aged poetess, and Joseph was not in harmony with this premature effort to make Jesus out to be the expected Messiah of the Jewish people. ∎

OCTOBER, 6 B.C.

THE ESCAPE FROM HEROD

But the watchers for Herod were not inactive. When they reported to him the visit of the priests of Ur to Bethlehem, Herod summoned these Chaldeans to appear before him. He inquired diligently of these wise men about the new "king of the Jews," but they gave him little satisfaction, explaining that the babe had been

[GREG OLSEN — *A Light to the Gentiles*]

[EUGENE GIRARDET — *The Flight into Egypt*]

born of a woman who had come down to Bethlehem with her husband for the census enrollment. Herod, not being satisfied with this answer, sent them forth with a purse and directed that they should find the child so that he too might come and worship him, since they had declared that his kingdom was to be spiritual, not temporal. But when the wise men did not return, Herod grew suspicious. As he turned these things over in his mind, his informers returned and made full report of the recent occurrences in the temple, bringing him a copy of parts of the Simeon song which had been sung at the redemption ceremonies of Jesus. But they had failed to follow Joseph and Mary, and Herod was very angry with them when they could not tell him whither the pair had taken the babe. He then dispatched searchers to locate Joseph

and Mary. Knowing Herod pursued the Nazareth family, Zacharias and Elizabeth remained away from Bethlehem. The boy baby was secreted with Joseph's relatives.

Joseph was afraid to seek work, and their small savings were rapidly disappearing. Even at the time of the purification ceremonies at the temple, Joseph deemed himself sufficiently poor to warrant his offering for Mary two young pigeons as Moses had directed for the purification of mothers among the poor.

When, after more than a year of searching, Herod's spies had not located Jesus, and because of the suspicion that the babe was still concealed in Bethlehem, he prepared an order directing that a systematic search be made of every house in Bethlehem, and that all boy babies under two years of age should be killed. In this manner Herod hoped to make sure that this child who was to become "king of the Jews" would be destroyed. And thus perished in one day sixteen boy babies in Bethlehem of Judea. But intrigue and murder, even in his own immediate family, were common occurrences at the court of Herod.

The massacre of these infants took place about the middle of October, 6 B.C., when Jesus was a little over one year of age. But there were believers in the coming Messiah even among Herod's court attachés, and one of these, learning of the order to slaughter the Bethlehem boy babies, communicated with Zacharias, who in turn dispatched a messenger to Joseph; and the night before the massacre Joseph and Mary departed from Bethlehem with the babe for Alexandria in Egypt. In order to avoid attracting attention, they journeyed alone to Egypt with Jesus. They went to Alexandria on funds provided by Zacharias, and there Joseph worked at his trade while Mary and Jesus lodged with well-to-do relatives of Joseph's family. They sojourned in Alexandria two full years, not returning to Bethlehem until after the death of Herod. ∎

6 B.C.–4 B.C.

SOJOURN IN ALEXANDRIA

Owing to the uncertainties and anxieties of their sojourn in Bethlehem, Mary did not wean the babe until they had arrived safely in Alexandria, where the family was able to settle down to a normal life. They lived with kinsfolk, and Joseph was well able to support his family as he secured work shortly after their arrival. He was employed as a carpenter for several months and then elevated to the position of foreman of a large group of workmen employed on one of the public buildings then in process of construction. This new experience gave him the idea of becoming a contractor and builder after their return to Nazareth.

Throughout the two years of their sojourn at Alexandria, Jesus enjoyed good health and continued to grow normally. Aside from a few friends and relatives no one was told about Jesus' being a "child of promise." One of Joseph's relatives revealed this to a few friends in Memphis, descendants of the distant Ikhnaton, and they, with a small group of Alexandrian believers, assembled at the palatial home of Joseph's relative-benefactor a short time before the return to Palestine to wish the Nazareth family well and to pay their respects to the child. On this occasion the assembled friends presented Jesus with a complete copy of the Greek translation of the Hebrew scriptures. But this copy of the Jewish sacred writings was not placed in Joseph's hands until both he and Mary had finally declined the invitation of their Memphis and Alexandrian friends to remain in Egypt. These believers insisted that the child of destiny would be able to exert a far greater world influence as a resident of Alexandria than of any designated place in Palestine. These persuasions delayed their departure for Palestine for some time after they received the news of Herod's death.

Joseph and Mary finally took leave of Alexandria on a boat belonging to their friend Ezraeon, bound for Joppa, arriving at that port late in August of the year 4 B.C. They went directly to Bethlehem, where they spent the entire month of September in counsel with their friends and relatives concerning whether they should remain there or return to Nazareth.

Mary had never fully given up the idea that Jesus ought to grow up in Bethlehem, the City of David. Joseph did not really believe that their son was to become a kingly deliverer of Israel. Besides, he knew that he himself was not really a descendant of David; that his being reckoned among the offspring of David was due to the adoption of one of his ancestors into the Davidic line of descent. Mary, of course, thought the City of David the most appropriate place in which the new candidate for David's throne could be reared, but Joseph preferred to take chances with Herod Antipas rather than with his brother Archelaus. He entertained great fears for the child's safety in Bethlehem or in any other city in Judea, and surmised that Archelaus would be more likely to pursue the menacing policies of his father, Herod, than would Antipas in Galilee. And besides all these reasons, Joseph was outspoken in his preference for Galilee as a better place in which to rear and educate the child, but it required three weeks to overcome Mary's objections. ∎

OCTOBER, 4 B.C.

BACK IN NAZARETH

By the first of October Joseph had convinced Mary and all their friends that it was best for them to return to Nazareth. Accordingly, early in October, 4 B.C., they departed from Bethlehem for Nazareth, going by way of Lydda and Scythopolis. They started out early one Sunday morning, Mary and the child riding on their newly acquired beast of burden, while Joseph and five accompanying kinsmen proceeded on foot; Joseph's relatives refused to permit them to make the trip to Nazareth alone. They feared to go to Galilee by Jerusalem and the Jordan valley, and the western routes were not altogether safe for two lone travelers with a child of tender years.

On the fourth day of the journey the party reached its destination in safety. They arrived unannounced at the Nazareth home, which had been occupied for more than three years by one of Joseph's married brothers, who was indeed surprised to see them; so quietly had they gone about their business that neither the family of Joseph nor that of Mary knew they had even left Alexandria. The next day Joseph's brother moved his family, and Mary, for the first time since Jesus' birth, settled down with her little family to enjoy life in their own home. In less than a week Joseph secured work as a carpenter, and they were supremely happy.

The home of Jesus was not far from the high hill in the northerly part of Nazareth, some distance from the village spring, which was in the eastern section of the town. Jesus' family dwelt in the outskirts of the city, and this made it all the easier for him subsequently to enjoy frequent strolls in the country and to make trips up to the top of this near-by highland, the highest of all the hills of southern Galilee save the Mount Tabor range to the east and the hill of Nain, which was about the same height. Their home was located a little to the south and east of the southern promontory of this hill and about midway between the base of this elevation and the road leading out of Nazareth toward Cana. Aside from climbing the hill, Jesus' favorite stroll was to follow a narrow trail winding about the base of the hill in a northeasterly direction to a point where it joined the road to Sepphoris.

The home was a one-room stone structure with a flat roof and an adjoining building for housing the animals. The furniture consisted of a low stone table, earthenware and stone dishes and pots, a loom, a lampstand, several small stools, and mats for sleeping on the stone floor. In the back yard, near the animal annex, was the shelter which covered the oven and the mill for grinding grain. It required two persons to operate this type of mill, one to grind and another to feed the grain. As a small boy Jesus often fed grain to this mill while his mother turned the grinder.

In later years, as the family grew in size, they would all squat about the enlarged stone table to enjoy their meals, helping themselves from a common dish, or pot, of food. During the winter, at the evening meal the table would be lighted by a small, flat clay lamp, which was filled with olive oil. After the birth of Martha, Joseph built an addition to this house, a large room, which was used as a carpenter shop during the day and as a sleeping room at night.

Jesus was about three years and two months old at the time of their return to Nazareth. He had stood all these travels very well and was in excellent health and full of childish glee and excitement at having premises of his own to run about in and to enjoy. But he greatly missed the association of his Alexandrian playmates.

On the way to Nazareth Joseph had persuaded Mary that it would be unwise to spread the word among their Galilean friends and relatives that Jesus was a child of promise. They agreed to refrain from all mention of these matters to anyone. And they were both very faithful in keeping this promise. ■

MARY

All through these early years of Jesus' helpless infancy, Mary maintained one long and constant vigil lest anything befall her child which might jeopardize his welfare or in any way interfere with his future mission on earth; no mother was ever more devoted to her child. Only an affectionate mother can know the burden that Mary carried in her heart for the safety of her son during these years of his infancy and early childhood.

LIFE IN NAZARETH, AGES FOUR TO FIVE

Jesus' entire fourth year was a period of normal physical development and of unusual mental activity. Meantime he had formed a very close attachment for a neighbor boy about his own age named Jacob. Jesus and Jacob were always happy in their play, and they grew up to be great friends and loyal companions.

It was midsummer of this same year that Joseph built a small workshop close to the village spring and near the caravan tarrying lot. After this he did very little carpenter work by the day. He had as associates two of his brothers and several other mechanics, whom he sent out to work while he remained at the shop making yokes and plows and doing other woodwork. He also did some work in leather and with rope and canvas. And Jesus, as he grew up, when not at school, spent his time about equally between helping his mother with home duties and watching his father work at the shop, meanwhile listening to the conversation and gossip of the caravan conductors and passengers from the four corners of the earth.

In July of this year, one month before Jesus was four years old, an outbreak of malignant intestinal trouble spread over all Nazareth from contact with the caravan travelers. Mary became so alarmed by the danger of Jesus being exposed to this epidemic of disease that she bundled up both her children and fled to the country home of her brother, several miles south of Nazareth on the Megiddo road near Sarid. They did not return to Nazareth for more than two months; Jesus greatly enjoyed this, his first experience on a farm.

In something more than a year after the return to Nazareth the boy Jesus arrived at the age of his first personal and wholehearted moral decision; and there came to abide with him a Thought Adjuster, a divine gift of the Paradise Father. This event occurred on February 11, 2 B.C. Jesus was no more aware of the coming of the divine Monitor than are the millions upon millions of other children who, before and since that day, have likewise received these Thought Adjusters to indwell their minds and work for the ultimate spiritualization of these minds and the eternal survival of their evolving immortal souls.

From this day in February throughout the human unfolding of the incarnation, the

[WILLIAM HOLE — *Jesus as a Boy in Nazareth* (detail)]

guardianship of Jesus was destined to rest in the keeping of this indwelling Adjuster and the associated seraphic guardians.

The most valuable part of Jesus' early education was secured from his parents in answer to his thoughtful and searching inquiries. Joseph never failed to do his full duty in taking pains and spending time answering the boy's numerous questions. From the time Jesus was five years old until he was ten, he was one continuous question mark. While Joseph and Mary could not always answer his questions, they never failed fully to discuss his inquiries and in every other possible way to assist him in his efforts to reach a satisfactory solution of the problem which his alert mind had suggested.

Already, with his mother's help, Jesus had mastered the Galilean dialect of the Aramaic tongue; and now his father began teaching him Greek. Mary spoke little Greek, but Joseph was a fluent speaker of both Aramaic and Greek. The textbook for the study of the Greek language was the copy of the Hebrew scriptures—a complete version of the law and the prophets, including the Psalms—which had been presented to them on leaving Egypt. There were only two complete copies of the Scriptures in Greek in all Nazareth, and the possession of one of them by the carpenter's family made Joseph's home a much-sought place and enabled Jesus, as he grew up, to meet an almost endless procession of earnest students and sincere truth seekers. Before this year ended, Jesus had assumed custody of this priceless manuscript, having been told on his sixth birthday that the sacred book had been presented to him by Alexandrian

friends and relatives. And in a very short time he could read it readily.

The first great shock of Jesus' young life occurred when he was not quite six years old. It had seemed to the lad that his father—at least his father and mother together—knew everything. Imagine, therefore, the surprise of this inquiring child, when he asked his father the cause of a mild earthquake which had just occurred, to hear Joseph say, "My son, I really do not know." Thus began that long and disconcerting disillusionment in the course of which Jesus found out that his earthly parents were not all-wise and all-knowing.

Joseph's first thought was to tell Jesus that the earthquake had been caused by God, but a moment's reflection admonished him that such an answer would immediately be provocative of further and still more embarrassing inquiries. Even at an early age it was very difficult to answer Jesus' questions about physical or social phenomena by thoughtlessly telling him that either God or the devil was responsible. In harmony with the prevailing belief of the Jewish people, Jesus was long willing to accept the doctrine of good spirits and evil spirits as the possible explanation of mental and spiritual phenomena, but he very early became doubtful that such unseen influences were responsible for the physical happenings of the natural world.

Before Jesus was six years of age, in the early summer of 1 B.C., Zacharias and Elizabeth and their son John came to visit the Nazareth family. Jesus and John had a happy time during this, their first visit within their memories. Although the visitors could remain only a few days, the parents talked over many things, including the future plans for their sons. While they were thus engaged, the lads played with blocks in the sand on top of the house and in many other ways enjoyed themselves in true boyish fashion. ∎

LIFE IN NAZARETH, AGES SIX TO SEVEN

D uring this year Joseph and Mary had trouble with Jesus about his prayers. He insisted on talking to his heavenly Father much as he would talk to Joseph, his earthly father. This departure from the more solemn and reverent modes of communication with Deity was a bit disconcerting to his parents, especially to his mother, but there was no persuading him to change; he would say his prayers just as he had been taught, after which he insisted on having "just a little talk with my Father in heaven."

This year Jesus made great progress in adjusting his strong feelings and vigorous impulses to the demands of family co-operation and home discipline. Mary was a loving mother but a fairly strict disciplinarian. In many ways, however, Joseph exerted the greater control over Jesus as it was his practice to sit down with the boy and fully explain the real and underlying reasons for the necessity of disciplinary curtailment of personal desires in deference to the welfare and tranquillity of the entire family. When the situation had been explained to Jesus, he was always intelligently and willingly co-operative with parental wishes and family regulations.

Much of his spare time—when his mother did not require his help about the house—was spent studying the flowers and plants by day and the stars by night. He evinced a troublesome penchant for lying on his back and gazing wonderingly up into the starry heavens long after his usual bedtime in this well-ordered Nazareth household.

Jesus, in company with a neighbor boy and later his brother James, delighted to play in the far corner of the family carpenter shop, where they had great fun with the shavings and the blocks of wood. It was always difficult for Jesus to comprehend the harm of certain sorts of play which were forbidden on the Sabbath, but he never failed to conform to his parents' wishes. He had a capacity for humor and play which was afforded little opportunity for expression in the environment of his day and generation, but up to the age of fourteen he was cheerful and lighthearted most of the time.

Mary maintained a dovecote on top of the animal house adjoining the home, and they used the profits from the sale of doves as a special charity fund, which Jesus administered after he deducted the tithe and turned it over to the officer of the synagogue.

The only real accident Jesus had up to this time was a fall down the back-yard stone stairs which led up to the canvas-roofed bedroom. It happened during an unexpected July sandstorm from the east. The hot winds, carrying blasts of fine sand, usually blew during the rainy season, especially in March and April. It was extraordinary to have such a storm in July. When the storm came up, Jesus was on the housetop playing, as was his habit, for during much of the dry season this was his accustomed playroom. He was blinded by the sand when descending the stairs and fell. After this accident Joseph built a balustrade up both sides of the stairway.

And this was but one of a number of such minor accidents which subsequently befell this inquisitive and adventurous youth. If you envisage the average childhood and youth of an aggressive

[SLAWA RADZISZEWSKA — *Mother's Love*]

boy, you will have a fairly good idea of the youthful career of Jesus, and you will be able to imagine just about how much anxiety he caused his parents, particularly his mother. ∎

AUGUST, A.D. 1

SCHOOL DAYS

Jesus was now seven years old, the age when Jewish children were supposed to begin their formal education in the synagogue schools. Accordingly, in August of this year he entered upon his eventful school life at Nazareth. Already this lad was a fluent reader, writer, and speaker of two languages, Aramaic and Greek. He was now to acquaint himself with the task of learning to read, write, and speak the Hebrew language. And

he was truly eager for the new school life which was ahead of him.

Jesus early became a master of Hebrew, and as a young man, when no visitor of prominence happened to be sojourning in Nazareth, he would often be asked to read the Hebrew scriptures to the faithful assembled in the synagogue at the regular Sabbath services.

Next, in addition to his more formal schooling, Jesus began to make contact with human nature from the four quarters of the earth as men from many lands passed in and out of his father's repair shop. When he grew older, he mingled freely with the caravans as they tarried near the spring for rest and nourishment. Being a fluent speaker of Greek, he had little trouble in conversing with the majority of the caravan travelers and conductors.

Nazareth was a caravan way station and crossroads of travel and largely gentile in population; at the same time it was widely known as a center of liberal interpretation of Jewish traditional law. In Galilee the Jews mingled more freely with the gentiles than was their practice in Judea. And of all the cities of Galilee, the Jews of Nazareth were most liberal in their interpretation of the social restrictions based on the fears of contamination as a result of contact with the gentiles. And these conditions gave rise to the common saying in Jerusalem, "Can any good thing come out of Nazareth?"

Jesus received his moral training and spiritual culture chiefly in his own home. He secured much of his intellectual and theological education from the chazan. But his real education—that equipment of mind and heart for the actual test of grappling with the difficult problems of life—he obtained by mingling with his fellow men. It was this close association with his fellow men, young and old, Jew and gentile, that afforded him the opportunity to know the human race. Jesus was highly educated in that he thoroughly understood men and devotedly loved them.

Throughout his years at the synagogue he was a brilliant student, possessing a great advantage since he was conversant with three languages. The Nazareth chazan, on the occasion of Jesus' finishing the course in his school, remarked to Joseph that he feared he "had learned more from Jesus' searching questions" than he had "been able to teach the lad."

When entering school at seven years (at this time the Jews had just inaugurated a compulsory education law), it was customary for the pupils to choose their "birthday text," a sort of golden rule to guide them throughout their studies, one upon which they often expatiated at their graduation when thirteen years old. The text which Jesus chose was from the Prophet Isaiah: "The spirit of the Lord God is upon me, for the Lord has anointed me; he has sent me to bring good news to the meek, to bind up the brokenhearted, to proclaim liberty to the captives, and to set the spiritual prisoners free."

Before he was eight years of age, he was known to all the mothers and young women of Nazareth, who had met him and talked with him at the spring, which was not far from his home, and which was one of the social centers of contact and gossip for the entire town. This year Jesus learned to milk the family cow and care for the other animals. During this and the following year he also learned to make cheese and to weave. When he was ten years of age, he was an expert loom operator. It was about this time that Jesus and the neighbor boy Jacob became great friends of the potter who worked near the flowing spring; and as they watched Nathan's deft fingers mold the clay on the potter's wheel, many times both of them determined to be potters when they grew up. Nathan was very fond of the lads and often gave

[MICHAEL MALM — *In Joseph's Woodshop*]

them clay to play with, seeking to stimulate their creative imaginations by suggesting competitive efforts in modeling various objects and animals. ▪

THE INVITATION TO JERUSALEM

This was an interesting year at school. Although Jesus was not an unusual student, he was a diligent pupil and belonged to the more progressive third of the class, doing his work so well that he was excused from attendance one week out of each month. This week he usually spent either with his fisherman uncle on the shores of the Sea of Galilee near Magdala or on the farm of another uncle (his mother's brother) five miles south of Nazareth.

About this time Jesus met a teacher of mathematics from Damascus, and learning some new techniques of numbers, he spent much time on mathematics for several years. He developed a keen sense of numbers, distances, and proportions.

Jesus began to enjoy his brother James very much and by the end of this year had begun to teach him the alphabet.

This year Jesus made arrangements to exchange dairy products for lessons on the harp. He had an unusual liking for everything musical. Later on he did much to promote an interest in vocal music among his youthful associates. By the time he was eleven years of age, he was a skillful harpist and greatly enjoyed entertaining both family and friends with his extraordinary interpretations and able improvisations.

In February, Nahor, one of the teachers in a Jerusalem academy of the rabbis, came to Nazareth to observe Jesus, having been on a similar mission to Zacharias's home near Jerusalem. He came to Nazareth at the instigation of John's father. While at first he was somewhat shocked by Jesus' frankness and unconventional manner of relating himself to things religious, he attributed it to the remoteness of Galilee from the centers of Hebrew learning and culture and advised Joseph and Mary to allow him to take Jesus back with him to Jerusalem, where he could have the advantages of education and training at the center of Jewish culture. Mary was half persuaded to consent; she was convinced her eldest son was to become the Messiah, the Jewish deliverer; Joseph hesitated; he was equally persuaded that Jesus was to grow up to become a man of destiny, but what that destiny would prove to be he was profoundly uncertain. But he never really doubted that his son was to fulfill some great mission on earth. The more he thought about Nahor's advice, the more he questioned the wisdom of the proposed sojourn in Jerusalem.

Because of this difference of opinion between Joseph and Mary, Nahor requested permission to lay the whole matter before Jesus. Jesus listened attentively, talked with Joseph, Mary, and a neighbor, Jacob the stone mason, whose son was his favorite playmate, and then, two days later, reported that since there was such a difference of opinion among his parents and advisers, and since he did not feel competent to assume the responsibility for such a decision, not feeling strongly one way or the other, in view of the whole situation, he had finally decided to "talk with my Father who is in heaven"; and while he was not perfectly sure about the answer, he rather felt he should remain at home "with my father and mother," adding, "they who love me so much should be able to do more for me and guide me more safely than strangers who can only view my body and observe my mind but can hardly truly know me." They all marveled, and Nahor went his way, back to Jerusalem. And it was many years before the subject of Jesus' going away from home again came up for consideration. ▪

[SLAWA RADZISZEWSKA — *Forbidden Art*]

A.D. 3

TROUBLE AT SCHOOL

Although Jesus might have enjoyed a better opportunity for schooling at Alexandria than in Galilee, he could not have had such a splendid environment for working out his own life problems with a minimum of educational guidance, at the same time enjoying the great advantage of constantly contacting with such a large number of all classes of men and women hailing from every part of the civilized world. Had he remained at Alexandria, his education would have been directed by Jews and along exclusively Jewish lines. At Nazareth he secured an education and received a training which more acceptably prepared him to understand the gentiles, and which gave him a better and more balanced idea of the relative merits of the Eastern, or Babylonian, and the Western, or Hellenic, views of Hebrew theology.

The most serious trouble as yet to come up at school occurred in late winter when Jesus dared to challenge the chazan regarding the teaching that all images, pictures, and drawings were idolatrous in nature. Jesus delighted in drawing landscapes as well as in modeling a great variety of objects in potter's clay. Everything of that sort was strictly forbidden by Jewish law, but up to this time he had managed to disarm his parents' objection to such an extent that they had permitted him to continue in these activities.

But trouble was again stirred up at school when one of the more backward pupils discovered Jesus drawing a charcoal picture of the teacher on the floor of the schoolroom. There it was, plain as day, and many of the elders had viewed it before the committee went to call on Joseph to demand that something be done to suppress the lawlessness of his eldest son. And though this was not the first time complaints had come to Joseph and Mary about the doings of their versatile and aggressive child, this was the most serious of all the accusations which had thus far been lodged against him. Jesus listened to the indictment of his artistic efforts for some time, being seated on a large stone just outside the back door. He resented their blaming his father for his alleged misdeeds; so in he marched, fearlessly confronting his accusers. The elders were thrown into confusion. Some were inclined to view the episode humorously, while one or two seemed to think the boy was sacrilegious if not blasphemous. Joseph was nonplused, Mary indignant, but Jesus insisted on being heard. He had his say, courageously defended his viewpoint, and with consummate self-control announced that

he would abide by the decision of his father in this as in all other matters controversial. And the committee of elders departed in silence.

Mary endeavored to influence Joseph to permit Jesus to model in clay at home, provided he promised not to carry on any of these questionable activities at school, but Joseph felt impelled to rule that the rabbinical interpretation of the second commandment should prevail. And so Jesus no more drew or modeled the likeness of anything from that day as long as he lived in his father's house. But he was unconvinced of the wrong of what he had done, and to give up such a favorite pastime constituted one of the great trials of his young life.

In the latter part of June, Jesus, in company with his father, first climbed to the summit of Mount Tabor. It was a clear day and the view was superb. It seemed to this nine-year-old lad that he had really gazed upon the entire world excepting India, Africa, and Rome. ∎

A.D. 4

SABBATH WALKS WITH JOSEPH

Nazareth was one of the twenty-four priest centers of the Hebrew nation. But the Galilean priesthood was more liberal

[MICHAEL MALM — *Sabbath Walks with Joseph* (detail)]

in the interpretation of the traditional laws than were the Judean scribes and rabbis. And at Nazareth they were also more liberal regarding the observance of the Sabbath. It was therefore the custom for Joseph to take Jesus out for walks on Sabbath afternoons, one of their favorite jaunts being to climb the high hill near their home, from which they could obtain a panoramic view of all Galilee. To the northwest, on clear days, they could see the long ridge of Mount Carmel running down to the sea; and many times Jesus heard his father relate the story of Elijah, one of the first of that long line of Hebrew prophets, who reproved Ahab and exposed the priests of Baal. To the north Mount Hermon raised its snowy peak in majestic splendor and monopolized the skyline, almost 3,000 feet of the upper slopes glistening white with perpetual snow. Far to the east they could discern the Jordan valley and, far beyond, the rocky hills of Moab. Also to the south and the east, when the sun shone upon their marble walls, they could see the Greco-Roman cities of the Decapolis, with their amphitheaters and pretentious temples. And when they lingered toward the going down of the sun, to the west they could make out the sailing vessels on the distant Mediterranean.

From four directions Jesus could observe the caravan trains as they wended their way in and out of Nazareth, and to the south he could overlook the broad and fertile plain country of Esdraelon, stretching off toward Mount Gilboa and Samaria.

When they did not climb the heights to view the distant landscape, they strolled through the countryside and studied nature in her various

SCYTHOPOLIS

On a trip to Scythopolis, Joseph recounted to Jesus much of the olden history of King Saul, the Philistines, and the subsequent events of Israel's turbulent history. Jesus was tremendously impressed with the clean appearance and well-ordered arrangement of this so-called heathen city. He marveled at the open-air theater and admired the beautiful marble temple dedicated to the worship of the "heathen" gods.

moods in accordance with the seasons. Jesus' earliest training, aside from that of the home hearth, had to do with a reverent and sympathetic contact with nature.

When work and caravan travel were slack, Jesus made many trips with his father on pleasure or business to near-by Cana, Endor, and Nain. Even as a lad he frequently visited Sepphoris, only a little over three miles from Nazareth to the northwest, and from 4 B.C. to about A.D. 25 the capital of Galilee and one of the residences of Herod Antipas.

Jesus continued to grow physically, intellectually, socially, and spiritually. His trips away from home did much to give him a better and more generous understanding of his own family, and by this time even his parents were beginning to learn from him as well as to teach him. Jesus was an original thinker and a skillful teacher, even in his youth. He was in constant collision with the so-called "oral law," but he always sought to adapt himself to the practices of his family. He got along fairly well with the children of his age, but he often grew discouraged with their slow-acting minds. Before he was ten years old, he had become the leader of a group of seven lads who formed themselves into a society for promoting the acquirements of manhood—physical, intellectual, and religious. Among these boys Jesus succeeded in introducing many new games and various improved methods of physical recreation.

Perhaps his most unusual and outstanding trait was his unwillingness to fight for his rights. Since he was such a well-developed lad for his age, it seemed strange to his playfellows that he was disinclined to defend himself even from injustice or when subjected to personal abuse. As it happened, he did not suffer much on account of this trait because of the friendship of Jacob, a neighbor boy, who was one year older. He was the son of the stone mason, a business associate of Joseph. Jacob was a great admirer of Jesus and made it his business to see that no one was permitted to impose upon Jesus because of his aversion to physical combat. Several times older and uncouth youths attacked Jesus, relying upon his reputed docility, but they always suffered swift and certain retribution at the hands of his self-appointed champion and ever-ready defender, Jacob the stone mason's son. ■

THE TRIP WITH JOSEPH TO SCYTHOPOLIS

J oseph early began to instruct Jesus in the diverse means of gaining a livelihood, explaining the advantages of agriculture over industry and trade. Galilee was a more beautiful and prosperous district than Judea, and it cost only about one fourth as much to live there as in Jerusalem and Judea. It was a province of agricultural villages and thriving industrial cities, containing more than two hundred towns of over five thousand population and thirty of over fifteen thousand.

When on his first trip with his father to observe the fishing industry on the lake of Galilee, Jesus had just about made up his mind to become a fisherman; but close association with his father's vocation later on influenced him to become a carpenter, while still later a combination of influences led him to the final choice of becoming a religious teacher of a new order.

About the middle of May the lad accompanied his father on a business trip to Scythopolis, the chief Greek city of the Decapolis, the ancient Hebrew city of Beth-shean. Expanding on Beth-shean, the Greeks and Romans had built a city that was magnificent in young Jesus' eyes. Joseph was much perturbed by the lad's enthusiasm and sought to counteract these favorable impressions by extolling the beauty and grandeur of the Jewish temple at Jerusalem. Jesus had often gazed curiously upon this magnificent Greek city from the hill of Nazareth and had many times inquired about its extensive public works and ornate buildings, but his father had always sought to avoid answering these questions. Now they were face to face with the beauties of this gentile city, and Joseph could not gracefully ignore Jesus' inquiries.

It so happened that just at this time the annual competitive games and public demonstrations of physical prowess between the Greek cities of the Decapolis were in progress at the Scythopolis amphitheater, and Jesus was insistent that his father take him to see the games, and he was so insistent that Joseph hesitated to deny him. The boy was thrilled with the games and entered most heartily into the spirit of the demonstrations of physical development and athletic skill. Joseph was inexpressibly shocked to observe his son's enthusiasm as he beheld these exhibitions of "heathen" vaingloriousness. After the games were finished, Joseph received the surprise of his life when he heard Jesus express his approval of them and suggest that it would be good for the young men of Nazareth if they could be thus benefited by wholesome outdoor physical activities. Joseph talked earnestly and long with Jesus concerning the evil nature of such practices, but he well knew that the lad was unconvinced.

The only time Jesus ever saw his father angry with him was that night in their room at the inn when, in the course of their discussions, the boy so far forgot the trends of Jewish thought as to suggest that they go back home and work for the building of an amphitheater at Nazareth.

When Joseph heard his first-born son express such un-Jewish sentiments, he forgot his usual calm demeanor and, seizing Jesus by the shoulder, angrily exclaimed, "My son, never again let me hear you give utterance to such an evil thought as long as you live." Jesus was startled by his father's display of emotion; he had never before been made to feel the personal sting of his father's indignation and was astonished and shocked beyond expression. He only replied, "Very well, my father, it shall be so." And never again did the boy even in the slightest manner allude to the games and other athletic activities of the Greeks as long as his father lived.

Later on, Jesus saw the Greek amphitheater at Jerusalem and learned how hateful such things were from the Jewish point of view. Nevertheless, throughout his life he endeavored to introduce the idea of wholesome recreation into his personal plans and, as far as Jewish practice would permit, into the later program of regular activities for his twelve apostles.

At the end of this eleventh year Jesus was a vigorous, well-developed, moderately humorous, and fairly lighthearted youth, but from this year on he was more and more given to peculiar seasons of profound meditation and serious contemplation. He was much given to thinking about how he was to carry out his obligations to his family and at the same time be obedient to the call of his mission to the world; already he had conceived that his ministry was not to be limited to the betterment of the Jewish people. ∎

A.D. 6

The Twelfth Year

This was an eventful year in Jesus' life. He continued to make progress at school and was indefatigable in his study of nature, while increasingly he prosecuted his study of the methods whereby men make a living. He began doing regular work in the home carpenter shop and was permitted to manage his own earnings, a very unusual arrangement to obtain in a Jewish family. This year he also learned the wisdom of keeping such matters a secret in the family. He was becoming conscious of the way in which he had caused trouble in the village, and henceforth he became increasingly discreet in concealing everything which might cause him to be regarded as different from his fellows.

Throughout this year he experienced many seasons of uncertainty, if not actual doubt, regarding the nature of his mission. His naturally developing human mind did not yet fully grasp the reality of his dual nature. The fact that he had a single personality rendered it difficult for his consciousness to recognize the double origin of those factors which composed the nature associated with that selfsame personality.

It was a trying experience for Joseph and Mary to undertake the rearing of this unprecedented combination of divinity and humanity, and they deserve great credit for so faithfully and successfully discharging their parental responsibilities. Increasingly Jesus' parents realized that there was something superhuman resident within this eldest son, but they never even faintly dreamed that this son of promise was indeed and in truth the actual creator of this local universe of things and beings. Joseph and Mary lived and died without ever learning that their son Jesus really was the Universe Creator incarnate in mortal flesh.

It was at about this time that the lad became keenly conscious of the difference between the viewpoints of Joseph and Mary regarding the nature of his mission. He pondered much over his parents' differing opinions, often hearing their discussions when they thought he was sound asleep. More and more he inclined to the view of his father, so that his mother was destined to be hurt by the realization that her son was gradually rejecting her guidance in matters having to do with his life career. And, as the years passed, this breach of understanding widened. Less and less did Mary comprehend the significance of Jesus' mission, and increasingly was this good mother hurt by the failure of her favorite son to fulfill her fond expectations.

Joseph entertained a growing belief in the spiritual nature of Jesus' mission. And but for other and more important reasons it does seem unfortunate that he could not have lived to see the fulfillment of his concept of Jesus' bestowal on earth.

Throughout this and the two following years Jesus suffered great mental distress as the result of his constant effort to adjust his personal views of religious practices and social amenities to the established beliefs of his parents. He was distraught by the conflict between the urge to be loyal to his own convictions and the conscientious admonition of dutiful submission to his parents; his supreme conflict was between two great commands which were uppermost in his youthful mind. The one was: "Be loyal to the dictates of your highest convictions of truth and righteousness." The other was: "Honor your father and mother, for they have given you life and the nurture thereof." However, he never shirked the responsibility of making the necessary daily adjustments between these realms of loyalty to one's personal convictions and duty toward one's family, and he achieved the satisfaction of effecting an increasingly harmonious blending of personal convictions and family obligations into a masterful

concept of group solidarity based upon loyalty, fairness, tolerance, and love. ∎

THE TRIP TO JERUSALEM

I n this year the lad of Nazareth passed from boyhood to the beginning of young manhood; his voice began to change, and other features of mind and body gave evidence of the oncoming status of manhood.

THE HOLY CITY

Jesus' first glimpse of Jerusalem was of pretentious palaces and the inspiring temple of his Father. At no time in his life did Jesus ever experience such a purely human thrill as that which at this time so completely enthralled him as he stood there on this April afternoon on the Mount of Olives, drinking in his first view of Jerusalem. And in after years, on this same spot he stood and wept over the city which was about to reject another prophet, the last and the greatest of her heavenly teachers.

It was about the middle of February that Jesus became humanly assured that he was destined to perform a mission on earth for the enlightenment of man and the revelation of God. Momentous decisions, coupled with far-reaching plans, were formulating in the mind of this youth, who was, to outward appearances, an average Jewish lad of Nazareth. The intelligent life of all the universe looked on with fascination and amazement as all this began to unfold in the thinking and acting of the now adolescent carpenter's son.

On the first day of the week, March 20, A.D. 7, Jesus graduated from the course of training in the local school connected with the Nazareth synagogue. This was a great day in the life of any ambitious Jewish family, the day when the first-born son was pronounced a "son of the commandment" and the ransomed first-born of the Lord God of Israel, a "child of the Most High" and servant of the Lord of all the earth.

Jesus, having now reached the threshold of young manhood and having been formally graduated from the synagogue schools, was qualified to proceed to Jerusalem with his parents to participate with them in the celebration of his first Passover. The Passover feast of this year fell on Saturday, April 9, A.D. 7. A considerable company (103) made ready to depart from Nazareth early Monday morning, April 4, for Jerusalem.

Women seldom went to the Passover feast at Jerusalem; they were not required to be present. Jesus, however, virtually refused to go unless his mother would accompany them. And when his mother decided to go, many other Nazareth women were led to make the journey, so that the Passover company contained the largest number of women, in proportion to men, ever to go up to the Passover from Nazareth. Ever and anon, on the way to Jerusalem, they chanted the one hundred and thirtieth Psalm.

The much-dreaded Archelaus had been deposed, and they had little to fear in taking Jesus to Jerusalem. Twelve years had passed since the first Herod had sought to destroy the babe of Bethlehem, and no one would now think of associating that affair with this obscure lad of Nazareth.

By the fourth and last day's journey the road was a continuous procession of pilgrims. They now began to climb the hills leading up to Jerusalem. As they neared the top, they could look across the Jordan to the mountains beyond and south over the sluggish waters of the Dead Sea. About halfway up to Jerusalem, Jesus gained his first view of the Mount of Olives (the region to be so much a part of his subsequent life), and Joseph pointed out to him that the Holy City lay just beyond this ridge, and the lad's heart beat fast with joyous anticipation of soon beholding the city and house of his heavenly Father.

On the eastern slopes of Olivet they paused for rest in the borders of a little village called Bethany. The hospitable villagers poured forth to minister to the pilgrims, and it happened that Joseph and his family had stopped near the house of one Simon, who had three children about the same age as Jesus—Mary, Martha, and Lazarus. They invited the Nazareth family in for refreshment, and a lifelong friendship sprang up between the two families. Many times afterward, in his eventful life, Jesus stopped in this home.

They pressed on, soon standing on the brink of Olivet, and Jesus saw for the first time (in his memory) the Holy City. No incident in all Jesus' eventful earth career was more engaging, more humanly thrilling, than this, his first remembered visit to Jerusalem.

Jesus was profoundly impressed by the temple and all the associated services and other activities. For the first time since he was four years old, he was too much preoccupied with his own meditations to ask many questions. He did, however, ask his father several embarrassing questions (as he had on previous occasions) as to why the heavenly Father required the slaughter of so many innocent and helpless animals. And his father well knew from the expression on the lad's face that his answers and attempts at explanation were unsatisfactory to his deep-thinking and keen-reasoning son.

From the time they left Nazareth until they reached the summit of the Mount of Olives, Jesus experienced one long stress of expectant anticipation. All through a joyful childhood he had reverently heard of Jerusalem and its temple; now he was soon to behold them in reality; but when he once entered its sacred portals, the great disillusionment began.

Though many of the temple rituals very touchingly impressed his sense of the beautiful and the symbolic, he was always disappointed by the explanation of the real meanings of these ceremonies which his parents would offer in answer to his many searching inquiries. Jesus simply would not accept explanations of worship and religious devotion which involved belief in the wrath of

God or the anger of the Almighty. In further discussion of these questions, after the conclusion of the temple visit, when his father became mildly insistent that he acknowledge acceptance of the orthodox Jewish beliefs, Jesus turned suddenly upon his parents and, looking appealingly into the eyes of his father, said: "My father, it cannot be true—the Father in heaven cannot so regard his erring children on earth. The heavenly Father cannot love his children less than you love me. And I well know, no matter what unwise thing I might do, you would never pour out wrath upon me nor vent anger against me. If you, my earthly father, possess such human reflections of the Divine, how much more must the heavenly Father be filled with goodness and overflowing with mercy. I refuse to believe that my Father in heaven loves me less than my father on earth."

When Joseph and Mary heard these words of their first-born son, they held their peace. And never again did they seek to change his mind about the love of God and the mercifulness of the Father in heaven.

The Heavenly Messenger

On the day before the Passover Sabbath, flood tides of spiritual illumination swept through the mortal mind of Jesus and filled his human heart to overflowing with affectionate pity for the spiritually blind and morally ignorant multitudes assembled for the celebration of the ancient Passover commemoration. This was one of the most extraordinary days that the Son of God spent in the flesh; and during the night, for the first time in his earth career, there appeared to him an assigned messenger from Salvington, commissioned by Immanuel, who said: "The hour has come. It is time that you began to be about your Father's business."

And so, even ere the heavy responsibilities of the Nazareth family descended upon his youthful shoulders, there now arrived the celestial messenger to remind this lad, not quite thirteen years of age, that the hour had come to begin the resumption of the responsibilities of a universe. This was the first act of a long succession of events which finally culminated in the completion of the Son's bestowal on Urantia and the replacing of "the government of a universe on his human-divine shoulders."

Thus ends the career of the Nazareth lad, and begins the narrative of that adolescent youth—the increasingly self-conscious divine human—who now begins the contemplation of his world career as he strives to integrate his expanding life purpose with the desires of his parents and his obligations to his family and the society of his day and age. ∎

APRIL 17, A.D. 7

YOUNG JESUS TEACHING IN THE TEMPLE

It had been arranged that the Nazareth party should gather in the region of the temple at midforenoon on the first day of the week after the Passover festival had ended. This they did and started out on the return journey to Nazareth. Jesus had gone into the temple to listen to the

discussions while his parents awaited the assembly of their fellow travelers. Presently the company prepared to depart, the men going in one group and the women in another as was their custom in journeying to and from the Jerusalem festivals. Jesus had gone up to Jerusalem in company with his mother and the women. Being now a young man of the consecration, he was supposed to journey back to Nazareth in company with his father and the men. But as the Nazareth party moved on toward Bethany, Jesus was completely absorbed in the discussion of angels, in the temple, being wholly unmindful of the passing of the time for the departure of his parents. And he did not realize that he had been left behind until the noontime adjournment of the temple conferences.

The Nazareth travelers did not miss Jesus because Mary surmised he journeyed with the men, while Joseph thought he traveled with the women since he had gone up to Jerusalem with the women, leading Mary's donkey. They did not discover his absence until they reached Jericho and prepared to tarry for the night. After making inquiry of the last of the party to reach Jericho and learning that none of them had seen their son, they spent a sleepless night, turning over in their minds what might have happened to him, recounting many of his unusual reactions to the events of Passover week, and mildly chiding each other for not seeing to it that he was in the group before they left Jerusalem.

In the meantime, Jesus had remained in the temple throughout the afternoon, listening to the discussions and enjoying the more quiet and decorous atmosphere, the great crowds of Passover week having about disappeared. At the conclusion of the afternoon discussions, in none of which Jesus participated, he betook himself to Bethany, arriving just as Simon's family made ready to

[HEINRICH HOFMANN — *Jesus in the Temple*]

partake of their evening meal. The three youngsters were overjoyed to greet Jesus, and he remained in Simon's house for the night. He visited very little during the evening, spending much of the time alone in the garden meditating.

Early next day Jesus was up and on his way to the temple. On the brow of Olivet he paused and wept over the sight his eyes beheld—a spiritually impoverished people, tradition bound and living under the surveillance of the Roman legions. Early forenoon found him in the temple with his mind made up to take part in the discussions. Meanwhile, Joseph and Mary also had arisen with the early dawn with the intention of retracing their steps to Jerusalem. First, they hastened to the house of their relatives, where they had lodged as a family during the Passover week, but inquiry elicited the fact that no one had seen Jesus. After searching all day and finding no trace of him, they returned to their relatives for the night.

The Second Day

At the second conference Jesus had made bold to ask questions, and in a very amazing way he participated in the temple discussions but always in a manner consistent with his youth. Sometimes his pointed questions were somewhat embarrassing to the learned teachers of the Jewish law, but he evinced such a spirit of candid fairness, coupled with an evident hunger for knowledge, that the majority of the temple teachers were disposed to treat him with every consideration. But when he presumed to question the justice of putting to death a drunken gentile who had wandered outside the court of the gentiles and unwittingly entered the forbidden and reputedly sacred precincts of the temple, one of the more intolerant teachers grew impatient with the lad's implied criticisms and, glowering down upon him, asked how old he was. Jesus replied, "thirteen years lacking a trifle more than four months." "Then," rejoined the now irate teacher, "why are you here, since you are not of age as a son of the law?" And when Jesus explained that he had received consecration during the Passover, and that he was a finished student of the Nazareth schools, the teachers with one accord derisively replied, "We might have known; he is from Nazareth." But the leader insisted that Jesus was not to be blamed if the rulers of the synagogue at Nazareth had graduated him, technically, when he was twelve instead of thirteen; and notwithstanding that several of his detractors got up and left, it was ruled that the lad might continue undisturbed as a pupil of the temple discussions.

When this, his second day in the temple, was finished, again he went to Bethany for the night. And again he went out in the garden to meditate and pray. It was apparent that his mind was concerned with the contemplation of weighty problems.

The Third Day

Jesus' third day with the scribes and teachers in the temple witnessed the gathering of many spectators who, having heard of this youth from Galilee, came to enjoy the experience of seeing a lad confuse the wise men of the law. Simon also came down from Bethany to see what the boy was up to. Throughout this day Joseph and Mary continued their anxious search for Jesus, even going

> JESUS HAD MADE BOLD TO ASK QUESTIONS, AND IN A VERY AMAZING WAY HE PARTICIPATED IN THE TEMPLE DISCUSSIONS BUT ALWAYS IN A MANNER CONSISTENT WITH HIS YOUTH.

several times into the temple but never thinking to scrutinize the several discussion groups, although they once came almost within hearing distance of his fascinating voice.

When the day was over, Simon and Jesus wended their way back to Bethany. For most of the distance both the man and the boy were silent. Again Jesus paused on the brow of Olivet, but as he viewed the city and its temple, he did not weep; he only bowed his head in silent devotion.

After the evening meal at Bethany he again declined to join the merry circle but instead went to the garden, where he lingered long into the night, vainly endeavoring to think out some definite plan of approach to the problem of his life-work and to decide how best he might labor to reveal to his spiritually blinded countrymen a more beautiful concept of the heavenly Father and so set them free from their terrible bondage to law, ritual, ceremonial, and musty tradition. But the clear light did not come to the truth-seeking lad. ■

MARY AND JOSEPH FIND JESUS

Jesus was strangely unmindful of his earthly parents; even at breakfast, when Lazarus's mother remarked that his parents must be about home by that time, Jesus did not seem to comprehend that they would be somewhat worried about his having lingered behind.

Again he journeyed to the temple, but he did not pause to meditate at the brow of Olivet. In the course of the morning's discussions much time was devoted to the law and the prophets, and the teachers were astonished that Jesus was so familiar with the Scriptures, in Hebrew as well as Greek. But they were amazed not so much by his knowledge of truth as by his youth.

At the afternoon conference they had hardly begun to answer his question relating to the purpose of prayer when the leader invited the lad to come forward and, sitting beside him, bade him state his own views regarding prayer and worship.

The evening before, Jesus' parents had heard about this strange youth who so deftly sparred with the expounders of the law, but it had not occurred to them that this lad was their son. They had about decided to journey out to the home of Zacharias as they thought Jesus might have gone thither to see Elizabeth and John. Thinking Zacharias might perhaps be at the temple, they stopped there on their way to the City of Judah. As they strolled through the courts of the temple, imagine their surprise and amazement when they recognized the voice of the missing lad and beheld him seated among the temple teachers.

Joseph was speechless, but Mary gave vent to her long-pent-up fear and anxiety when, rushing up to the lad, now standing to greet his astonished parents, she said: "My child, why have you treated us like this? It is now more than three days that your father and I have searched for you sorrowing. Whatever possessed you to desert us?" It was a tense moment. All eyes were turned on Jesus to hear what he would say. His father looked reprovingly at him but said nothing.

It should be remembered that Jesus was supposed to be a young man. He had finished the regular schooling of a child, had been recognized as a son of the law, and had received consecration as a citizen of Israel. And yet his mother more than mildly upbraided him before all the people assembled, right in the midst of the most serious and sublime effort of his young life, thus bringing to an inglorious termination one of the greatest opportunities ever to be granted him to function as a teacher of truth, a preacher of righteousness, a revealer of the loving character of his Father in heaven.

But the lad was equal to the occasion. When

"O JERUSALEM, JERUSALEM, AND THE PEOPLE THEREOF, WHAT SLAVES YOU ARE, BUT I WILL RETURN TO CLEANSE YONDER TEMPLE AND DELIVER MY PEOPLE FROM THIS BONDAGE!"

you take into fair consideration all the factors which combined to make up this situation, you will be better prepared to fathom the wisdom of the boy's reply to his mother's unintended rebuke. After a moment's thought, Jesus answered his mother, saying: "Why is it that you have so long sought me? Would you not expect to find me in my Father's house since the time has come when I should be about my Father's business?"

Everyone was astonished at the lad's manner of speaking. Silently they all withdrew and left him standing alone with his parents. Presently the young man relieved the embarrassment of all three when he quietly said: "Come, my parents, none has done aught but that which he thought best. Our Father in heaven has ordained these things; let us depart for home."

In silence they started out, arriving at Jericho for the night. Only once did they pause, and that on the brow of Olivet, when the lad raised his staff aloft and, quivering from head to foot under the surging of intense emotion, said: "O Jerusalem, Jerusalem, and the people thereof, what slaves you are—subservient to the Roman yoke and victims of your own traditions—but I will return to cleanse yonder temple and deliver my people from this bondage!"

On the three days' journey to Nazareth Jesus said little; neither did his parents say much in his presence. They were truly at a loss to understand the conduct of their first-born son, but they did treasure in their hearts his sayings, even though they could not fully comprehend their meanings.

Upon reaching home, Jesus made a brief statement to his parents, assuring them of his affection and implying that they need not fear he would again give any occasion for their suffering anxiety because of his conduct. He concluded this momentous statement by saying: "While I must do the will of my Father in heaven, I will also be obedient to my father on earth. I will await my hour."

Though Jesus, in his mind, would many times refuse to *consent* to the well-intentioned but misguided efforts of his parents to dictate the course of his thinking or to establish the plan of his work on earth, still, in every manner consistent with his dedication to the doing of his Paradise Father's will, he did most gracefully *conform* to the desires of his earthly father and to the usages of his family in the flesh.

Joseph was puzzled, but Mary, as she reflected on these experiences, gained comfort, eventually viewing his utterance on Olivet as prophetic of the Messianic mission of her son as Israel's deliverer. She set to work with renewed energy to mold his thoughts into patriotic and nationalistic channels and enlisted the efforts of her brother, Jesus' favorite uncle; and in every other way did the mother of Jesus address herself to the task of preparing her first-born son to assume the leadership of those who would restore the throne of David and forever cast off the gentile yoke of political bondage.   ✶

[JEREMY WINBORG — *O Jerusalem, Jerusalem*]

CHAPTER II

THE MISSING YEARS: FAMILY LIFE

Train up a child in the way he should go:
and when he is old, he will not depart from it.

—PROVERBS 22:6 KJV

THE NEXT THREE CHAPTERS COMPRISE THE SO-CALLED MISSING YEARS OF JESUS. THE BIBLE is silent on the sayings and doings of the Son of Man from a boy of nearly thirteen teaching in the temple, to his baptism in the river Jordan eighteen years and nine months later. Conjecture surrounding this mysterious gap has abounded, but the lost years have remained an untold story until these days of the Word made book.

These years began as the tragic death of Joseph thrust the responsibilities of caring for his widowed and pregnant mother and seven brothers and sisters upon this fourteen-year-old lad of Nazareth. To the best of his ability Jesus endeavored to take the place of his father in comforting and ministering to his mother during this trying and especially sad ordeal. Over the next twelve years that he lived under the same roof with his family, no father could have loved and nurtured his children any more affectionately and faithfully than Jesus cared for his siblings. And he was equally faithful in preparing the family for his departure to begin his public ministry.

As the years passed, this young carpenter of Nazareth increasingly measured every institution of society and every usage of religion by the unvarying test: What does it do for the human soul? does it bring God to man? does it bring man to God? While this youth did not wholly neglect the recreational and social aspects of life, more and more he devoted his time and energies to just two purposes: the care of his family and the preparation to do his Father's heavenly will on earth.

Having thus tasted the actual experience of living these adolescent years on a world beset by evil and distraught by sin, the Son of Man became possessed of full knowledge about the life experience of the youth of all realms, and thus forever he became the understanding refuge for the distressed and perplexed adolescents of all ages and on all worlds throughout his creation.

How well he understood life in the home, field, and workshop is shown by his subsequent teachings, which so repletely reveal his intimate contact with all phases of human experience.

THE URANTIA BOOK: PAPERS 126–129
SEPTEMBER, A.D. 8–MARCH, A.D. 22

[RUSS DOCKEN — *The Burial of Joseph* (detail)]

THE DEATH OF JOSEPH

All did go well until that fateful day of Tuesday, September 25, when a runner from Sepphoris brought to this Nazareth home the tragic news that Joseph had been severely injured by the falling of a derrick while at work on the governor's residence. The messenger from Sepphoris had stopped at the shop on the way to Joseph's home, informing Jesus of his father's accident, and they went together to the house to break the sad news to Mary. Jesus desired to go immediately to his father, but Mary would hear to nothing but that she must hasten to her husband's side. She directed that James, then ten years of age, should accompany her to Sepphoris while Jesus remained home with the younger children until she should return, as she did not know how seriously Joseph had been injured. But Joseph died of his injuries before Mary arrived. They brought him to Nazareth, and on the following day he was laid to rest with his fathers.

Just at the time when prospects were good and the future looked bright, an apparently cruel hand struck down the head of this Nazareth household, the affairs of this home were disrupted, and every plan for Jesus and his future education was demolished. This carpenter lad, now just past fourteen years of age, awakened to the realization that he had not only to fulfill the commission of his heavenly Father to reveal the divine nature on earth and in the flesh, but that his young human nature must also shoulder the responsibility of caring for his widowed mother and seven brothers and sisters—and another yet to be born. This lad of Nazareth now became the sole support and comfort of this so suddenly bereaved family. Thus were permitted those occurrences of the natural order of events on Urantia which would force this young man of destiny so early to assume these heavy but highly educational and disciplinary responsibilities attendant upon becoming the head of a human family, of becoming father to his own brothers and sisters, of supporting and protecting his mother, of functioning as guardian of his father's home, the only home he was to know while on this world.

Jesus cheerfully accepted the responsibilities so suddenly thrust upon him, and he carried them faithfully to the end. At least one great problem and anticipated difficulty in his life had been tragically solved—he would not now be expected to go to Jerusalem to study under the rabbis. It remained always true that Jesus "sat at no man's feet." He was ever willing to learn from even the humblest of little children, but he never derived authority to teach truth from human sources.

Still he knew nothing of the Gabriel visit to his mother before his birth; he only learned of this from John on the day of his baptism, at the beginning of his public ministry.

The economic affairs of the family continued to run fairly smoothly as there was quite a sum of money on hand at the time of Joseph's death.

ALL DID GO WELL UNTIL THAT FATEFUL DAY OF SEPTEMBER 25, WHEN JOSEPH WAS SEVERELY INJURED BY THE FALLING OF A DERRICK WHILE AT WORK ON THE GOVERNOR'S RESIDENCE.

Jesus early demonstrated the possession of keen business judgment and financial sagacity. He was liberal but frugal; he was saving but generous. He proved to be a wise and efficient administrator of his father's estate.

But in spite of all that Jesus and the Nazareth neighbors could do to bring cheer into the home, Mary, and even the children, were overcast with sadness. Joseph was gone. Joseph was an unusual husband and father, and they all missed him. And it seemed all the more tragic to think that he died ere they could speak to him or hear his farewell blessing. ∎

A.D. 9

THE SON OF MAN

In the course of this year Jesus found a passage in the so-called Book of Enoch which influenced him in the later adoption of the term "Son of Man" as a designation for his bestowal mission on Urantia. He had thoroughly considered the idea of the Jewish Messiah and was firmly convinced that he was not to be that Messiah. He longed to help his father's people, but he never expected to lead Jewish armies in overthrowing the foreign domination of Palestine. He knew he would never sit on the throne of David at Jerusalem. Neither did he believe that his mission was that of a spiritual deliverer or moral teacher solely to the Jewish people. In no sense, therefore, could his life mission be the fulfillment of the intense longings and supposed Messianic prophecies of the Hebrew scriptures; at least, not as the Jews understood these predictions of the prophets. Likewise he was certain he was never to appear as the Son of Man depicted by the Prophet Daniel.

But when the time came for him to go forth as a world teacher, what would he call himself? What claim should he make concerning his mission? By what name would he be called by the people who would become believers in his teachings?

While turning all these problems over in his mind, he found in the synagogue library at Nazareth, among the apocalyptic books which he had been studying, this manuscript called "The Book of Enoch"; and though he was certain that it had not been written by Enoch of old, it proved very intriguing to him, and he read and reread it many times. There was one passage which particularly impressed him, a passage in which this term "Son of Man" appeared. The writer of this so-called Book of Enoch went on to tell about this Son of Man, describing the work he would do on earth and explaining that this Son of Man, before coming down on this earth to bring salvation to mankind, had walked through the courts of heavenly glory with his Father, the Father of all; and that he had turned his back upon all this grandeur and glory to come down on earth to proclaim salvation to needy mortals. As Jesus would read these passages (well understanding that much of the Eastern mysticism which had become admixed with these teachings was erroneous), he responded in his heart and recognized in his mind that of all the Messianic predictions of the Hebrew scriptures and of all the theories about the Jewish deliverer, none was so near the truth as this story tucked away in this only partially accredited Book of Enoch; and he then and there decided to adopt as his inaugural title "the Son of Man." And this he did when he subsequently began his public work. Jesus had an unerring ability for the recognition of truth, and truth he never hesitated to embrace, no matter from what source it appeared to emanate.

By this time he had quite thoroughly settled many things about his forthcoming work for the world, but he said nothing of these matters to his mother, who still held stoutly to the idea of his being the Jewish Messiah.

With the coming of his fifteenth birthday, Jesus could officially occupy the synagogue pulpit on the Sabbath day. Many times before, in the absence of speakers, Jesus had been asked to read the Scriptures, but now the day had come when, according to law, he could conduct the service. Therefore on the first Sabbath after his fifteenth birthday the chazan arranged for Jesus to conduct the morning service of the synagogue. And when all the faithful in Nazareth had assembled, the young man, having made his selection of Scriptures, stood up and began to read:

"The spirit of the Lord God is upon me, for the Lord has anointed me; he has sent me to bring good news to the meek, to bind up the brokenhearted, to proclaim liberty to the captives, and to set the spiritual prisoners free; to proclaim the year of God's favor and the day of our God's reckoning; to comfort all mourners, to give them beauty for ashes, the oil of joy in the place of mourning, a song of praise instead of the spirit of sorrow, that they may be called trees of righteousness, the planting of the Lord, wherewith he may be glorified."

And when he had read the rest of this selected passage from Isaiah in full, he sat down, and the people went to their homes, pondering over the words which he had so graciously read to them. Never had his townspeople seen him so magnificently solemn; never had they heard his voice so earnest and so sincere; never had they observed him so manly and decisive, so authoritative. ▪

A.D. 9

THE FINANCIAL STRUGGLE

Before the end of this year Mary saw the family funds diminishing. She turned the sale of doves over to James. Presently they bought a second cow, and with the aid of Miriam they began the sale of milk to their Nazareth neighbors.

Gradually Jesus and his family returned to the simple life of their earlier years. Their clothes and even their food became simpler. They had plenty of milk, butter, and cheese. In season they enjoyed the produce of their garden, but each passing month necessitated the practice of greater frugality. Their breakfasts were very plain; they saved their best food for the evening meal. However, among these Jews lack of wealth did not imply social inferiority.

Apparently all Jesus' plans for a career were thwarted. The future did not look bright as matters now developed. But he did not falter; he was not discouraged. He lived on, day by day, doing well the present duty and faithfully discharging the *immediate* responsibilities of his station in life. Jesus' life is the everlasting comfort of all disappointed idealists.

The pay of a common day-laboring carpenter was slowly diminishing. By the end of this year Jesus could earn, by working early and late, only the equivalent of about twenty-five cents a day. By the next year they found it difficult to pay the civil taxes, not to mention the synagogue assessments and the temple tax of one-half shekel. During this year the tax collector tried to squeeze extra revenue out of Jesus, even threatening to take his harp.

Fearing that the copy of the Greek scriptures might be discovered and confiscated by the tax collectors, Jesus, on his fifteenth birthday, presented it to the Nazareth synagogue library as his maturity offering to the Lord.

The great shock of his fifteenth year came when Jesus went over to Sepphoris to receive the decision of Herod regarding the appeal taken to him in the dispute about the amount of money due Joseph at the time of his accidental death. Jesus and Mary had hoped for the receipt of a considerable sum of money when the treasurer at Sepphoris had offered them a paltry amount. Joseph's brothers had taken an appeal to Herod himself, and now Jesus stood in the palace and heard Herod decree that his father had nothing due him at the time of his death. And for such an unjust decision Jesus never again trusted Herod Antipas. It is not surprising that he once alluded to Herod as "that fox."

The close work at the carpenter's bench during this and subsequent years deprived Jesus of the opportunity of mingling with the caravan passengers. The family supply shop had already been taken over by his uncle, and Jesus worked altogether in the home shop, where he was near to help Mary with the family. About this time he began sending James up to the camel lot to gather information about world events, and thus he sought to keep in touch with the news of the day.

As he grew up to manhood, he passed through all those conflicts and confusions which the average young persons of previous and subsequent ages have undergone. And the rigorous experience of supporting his family was a sure safeguard against his having overmuch time for idle meditation or the indulgence of mystic tendencies.

This was the year that Jesus rented a considerable piece of land just to the north of their home, which was divided up as a family garden plot. Each of the older children had an individual garden, and they entered into keen competition in their agricultural efforts. Their eldest brother spent some time with them in the garden each day during the season of vegetable cultivation. As Jesus worked with his younger brothers and sisters in the garden, he many times entertained the wish that they were all located on a farm out in the country where they could enjoy the liberty and freedom of an unhampered life. But they did not find themselves growing up in the country; and Jesus, being a thoroughly practical youth as well as an idealist, intelligently and vigorously attacked his problem just as he found it, and did everything within his power to adjust himself and his family to the realities of their situation and to adapt their condition to the highest possible satisfaction of their individual and collective longings. ∎

HEAD OF HOUSEHOLD

As Jesus entered upon his adolescent years, he found himself the head and sole support of a large family. Within a few years after his father's death all their property was gone. As time passed, he became increasingly conscious of his pre-existence; at the same time he began more fully to realize that he was present on earth and in the flesh for the express purpose of revealing his Paradise Father to the children of men.

This physically strong and robust youth also acquired the full growth of his human intellect, not the full experience of human thinking but the fullness of capacity for such intellectual development. He possessed a healthy and well-proportioned body, a keen and analytical mind, a kind and sympathetic disposition, a somewhat fluctuating but aggressive temperament, all of which were becoming organized into a strong, striking, and attractive personality.

TRYING TIMES

No adolescent youth who has lived or ever will live on this world or any other world has had or ever will have more weighty problems to resolve or more intricate difficulties to untangle. No youth of Urantia will ever be called upon to pass through more testing conflicts or more trying situations than Jesus himself endured during those strenuous years from fifteen to twenty.

[Michael Malm — *The Family Garden*]

He was a real though youthful father to the family; he spent every possible hour with the youngsters, and they truly loved him. His mother grieved to see him work so hard; she sorrowed that he was day by day toiling at the carpenter's bench earning a living for the family instead of being, as they had so fondly planned, at Jerusalem studying with the rabbis. While there was much about her son that Mary could not understand, she did love him, and she most thoroughly appreciated the willing manner in which he shouldered the responsibility of the home.

At about this time there was considerable agitation, especially at Jerusalem and in Judea, in favor of rebellion against the payment of taxes to Rome. There was coming into existence a strong nationalist party, presently to be called the Zealots. The Zealots, unlike the Pharisees, were not willing to await the coming of the Messiah. They proposed to bring things to a head through political revolt.

A group of organizers from Jerusalem arrived in Galilee and were making good headway until they reached Nazareth. When they came to see Jesus, he listened carefully to them and asked many questions but refused to join the party. He declined fully to disclose his reasons for not enlisting, and his refusal had the effect of keeping out many of his youthful fellows in Nazareth.

Mary did her best to induce him to enlist, but she could not budge him. She went so far as to intimate that his refusal to espouse the nationalist cause at her behest was insubordination, a violation of his pledge made upon their return from Jerusalem that he would be subject to his parents; but in answer to this insinuation he only laid a kindly hand on her shoulder and, looking into her face, said: "My mother, how could you?" And Mary withdrew her statement.

But trouble began to brew in Nazareth. Jesus' attitude in these matters had resulted in creating a division among the Jewish youths of the city. About half had joined the nationalist organization, and the other half began the formation of an opposing group of more moderate patriots, expecting Jesus to assume the leadership. They were amazed when he refused the honor offered him, pleading as an excuse his heavy family responsibilities, which they all allowed. But the situation was still further complicated when, presently, a wealthy Jew, Isaac, a moneylender to the gentiles, came forward agreeing to support Jesus' family if he would lay down his tools and assume leadership of these Nazareth patriots.

Jesus, then scarcely seventeen years of age, was confronted with one of the most delicate and difficult situations of his early life. His position was made more difficult because his mother and uncle, and even his younger brother James, all urged him to join the nationalist cause. All the better Jews of Nazareth had enlisted, and those young men who had not joined the movement would all enlist the moment Jesus changed his mind. He had but one wise counselor in all Nazareth, his old teacher, the chazan, who counseled him about his reply to the citizens' committee of Nazareth when they came to ask for his answer to the public appeal which had been made. His family was in a turmoil, his youthful friends in division, and the entire Jewish contingent of the town in a hubbub. And to think that he was to blame for it all!

Something had to be done. He must state his position, and this he did bravely and diplomatically to the satisfaction of many, but not all. He adhered to the terms of his original plea, maintaining that his first duty was to his family, that a widowed mother and eight brothers and sisters needed something more than mere money could buy—the physical necessities of life—that they were entitled to a father's watchcare and guidance, and that he could not in clear conscience release himself from the obligation which a cruel accident had thrust upon him. He paid compliment to his mother and eldest brother for being willing to release him but reiterated that loyalty to a dead father forbade his leaving the family no matter how much money was forthcoming for their material support, making his never-to-be-forgotten statement that "money cannot love." Everyone in Nazareth well knew he was a good father to his family, and this was a matter so near the heart of every noble Jew that Jesus' plea found an appreciative response in the hearts of many of his hearers; and some of those who were not thus minded were disarmed by a speech made by James, which, while not on the program, was delivered at this time. That very day the chazan had rehearsed James in his speech, but that was their secret.

The crisis for the time being was over, but never was this incident forgotten in Nazareth. The agitation persisted; not again was Jesus in universal favor; the division of sentiment was never fully overcome.

In September, A.D. 12, Elizabeth and John came to visit the Nazareth family. John, having lost his father, intended to return to the Judean hills to engage in agriculture and sheep raising unless Jesus advised him to remain in Nazareth to take up carpentry or some other line of work. They did not know that the Nazareth family was practically penniless. The more Mary and Elizabeth talked about their sons, the more they became convinced that it would be good for the two young men to work together and see more of each other.

Jesus and John had many talks together; and they talked over some very intimate and personal matters. When they had finished this visit, they decided not again to see each other until they should meet in their public service after "the heavenly Father should call" them to their work. John was tremendously impressed by what he saw at Nazareth that he should return home and labor for the support of his mother. He became convinced that he was to be a part of Jesus' life mission, but he saw that Jesus was to occupy many years with the rearing of his family; so he was much more content to return to his home and settle down to the care of their little farm and to minister to the needs of his mother. And never again did John and Jesus see each other until that day by the Jordan some thirteen years later when the Son of Man presented himself for baptism.

Jesus' Parenting Style

By the time Jesus was nineteen years old, he and Mary were getting along much better. She regarded him less as a son; he had become to her more a father to her children. Each day's life swarmed with practical and immediate difficulties. For four years their standard of living had steadily declined, and they felt the pinch of increasing poverty. Less frequently they spoke of his lifework, for, as time passed, all their thought was mutually devoted to the support and upbringing of their family of four boys and three girls.

By the beginning of this year Jesus had fully won his mother to the acceptance of his methods of child training—the positive injunction to do good in the place of the older Jewish method of forbidding to do evil. In his home and throughout his public-teaching career Jesus invariably employed the *positive* form of exhortation. Always and everywhere did he say, "You shall do this—you ought to do that." Never did he employ the negative mode of teaching derived from the ancient taboos. He refrained from placing emphasis on evil by forbidding it, while he exalted the good by commanding its performance. Prayer time in this household was the occasion for discussing anything and everything relating to the welfare of the family.

Jesus began wise discipline upon his brothers and sisters at such an early age that little or no punishment was ever required to secure their prompt and wholehearted obedience. The only exception was Jude, upon whom on sundry occasions Jesus found it necessary to impose penalties for his infractions of the rules of the home. On three occasions when it was deemed wise to punish Jude for self-confessed and deliberate violations of the family rules of conduct, his punishment was fixed by the unanimous decree of the older children and was assented to by Jude himself before it was inflicted.

While Jesus was most methodical and systematic in everything he did, there was also in all his administrative rulings a refreshing elasticity of interpretation and an individuality of adaptation that greatly impressed all the children with the spirit of justice which actuated their father-brother. He never arbitrarily disciplined

JESUS' EIGHT SIBLINGS

JAMES: Born in the early morning hours of April 2, 3 B.C. Jesus was thrilled by the thought of having a baby brother, and he would stand around by the hour just to observe the baby's early activities. James was a well-balanced and even-tempered youth, but he was not so spiritually inclined as Jesus. He was a much better student than Joseph, who, while a faithful worker, was even less spiritually minded. After James was married, Jesus formally and solemnly abdicated as head of Joseph's house, and most touchingly established his brother as "head and protector of my father's house," and he proved equal to the trust.

James always inclined to believe in his eldest brother's mission on earth, but he lost contact with Jesus' work and drifted into grave doubting regarding claims that Jesus was the Messiah. Later on when he became connected with the early Christian movement, he suffered immeasurably as a result of his failure to enjoy an earlier association with Jesus and his disciples.

MIRIAM: Born on the night of July 11, 2 B.C. Miriam was a well-balanced and level-headed daughter with a keen appreciation of things noble and spiritual. She was the belle of the family, if not of the city.

JOSEPH: Born Wednesday morning, March 16, A.D. 1. Joseph was a plodder and not up to the intellectual level of the other children.

SIMON: Born on Friday evening, April 14, A.D. 2. Simon was a well-meaning boy but too much of a dreamer. He was slow in getting settled down in life and was the cause of considerable anxiety to Jesus

and Mary. But he was always a well-intentioned lad.

MARTHA: Born on Thursday night, September 13, A.D. 3. Martha was slow in thought and action but a very dependable and efficient child.

JUDE: Born Wednesday evening, June 24, A.D. 5. Complications attended the birth of this, the seventh child. Jude was a firebrand. He had the highest of ideals, but he was unstable in temperament. He had all and more of his mother's determination and aggressiveness, but he lacked much of her sense of proportion and discretion. When Jesus took him to Jerusalem for his first Passover, he was arrested and jailed after a violently verbal outburst directed at a Roman legionnaire. Jude made considerable trouble for Jesus, and always was the trouble of this same nature—clashes with the civil authorities because of his thoughtless and unwise patriotic outbursts. But Jude came to his sober senses after his marriage.

AMOS: Born Sunday night, January 9, A.D. 7. Five years later, on Saturday afternoon, December 3, A.D. 12, little Amos, their baby brother died after a week's illness with a high fever.

RUTH: The baby of the family was born on Wednesday evening, April 17, A.D. 9, the only child Joseph did not welcome into the world. Baby Ruth was the sunshine of the home, but they did not spoil her. Though thoughtless of speech, she was most sincere of heart and a beautiful child. She just about worshiped her big brother and father.

Of all the Master's family in the flesh, only Ruth believed wholeheartedly and continuously in the divinity of his mission on earth.

his brothers and sisters, and such uniform fairness and personal consideration greatly endeared Jesus to all his family.

James and Simon grew up trying to follow Jesus' plan of placating their bellicose and sometimes irate playmates by persuasion and nonresistance, and they were fairly successful; but Joseph and Jude, while assenting to such teachings at home, made haste to defend themselves when assailed by their comrades; in particular was Jude guilty of violating the spirit of these teachings. But nonresistance was not a *rule* of the family. No penalty was attached to the violation of personal teachings.

In general, all of the children, particularly the girls, would consult Jesus about their childhood troubles and confide in him just as they would have in an affectionate father.

As time passed, Jesus did much to liberalize and modify the family teachings and practices related to Sabbath observance and many other phases of religion, and to all these changes Mary gave hearty assent. By this time Jesus had become the unquestioned head of the house.

This year Jude started to school, and it was necessary for Jesus to sell his harp in order to defray these expenses. Thus disappeared the last of his recreational pleasures. He loved to play the harp when tired in mind and weary in body, but he comforted himself with the thought that at least the harp was safe from seizure by the tax collector. ■

A.D. 13

REBECCA'S UNDYING LOVE

Although Jesus was poor, his social standing in Nazareth was in no way impaired. He was one of the foremost young men of the city and very highly regarded by most of the young women. Since Jesus was such a splendid specimen of robust and intellectual manhood, and considering his reputation as a spiritual leader, it was not strange that Rebecca, the eldest daughter of Ezra, a wealthy merchant and trader of Nazareth, should discover that she was slowly falling in love with this son of Joseph. She first confided her affection to Miriam, Jesus' sister, and Miriam in turn talked all this over with her mother. Mary was intensely aroused. Was she about to lose her son, now become the indispensable head of the family? Would troubles never cease? What next could happen? And then she paused to contemplate what effect marriage would have upon Jesus' future career; not often, but at least sometimes, did she recall the fact that Jesus was a "child of promise." After she and Miriam had talked this matter over, they decided to make an effort to stop it before Jesus learned about it, by going direct to Rebecca, laying the whole story before her, and honestly telling her about their belief that Jesus was a son of destiny; that he was to become a great religious leader, perhaps the Messiah.

Rebecca listened intently; she was thrilled with the recital and more than ever determined to cast her lot with this man of her choice and to share his career of leadership. She argued (to herself) that such a man would all the more need a faithful and efficient wife. She interpreted Mary's efforts to dissuade her as a natural reaction to the dread of losing the head and sole support of her family; but knowing that her father approved of her attraction for the carpenter's son, she rightly reckoned that he would gladly supply the family with sufficient income fully to compensate for the loss of Jesus' earnings. When her father agreed to such a plan, Rebecca had further conferences with Mary and Miriam, and when she failed to win their support, she made bold to go directly to Jesus. This she did with the co-operation of her father, who invited Jesus to their home for the celebration of Rebecca's seventeenth birthday.

Jesus listened attentively and sympathetically to the recital of these things, first by the father, then by

Rebecca herself. He made kindly reply to the effect that no amount of money could take the place of his obligation personally to rear his father's family, to "fulfill the most sacred of all human trusts—loyalty to one's own flesh and blood." Rebecca's father was deeply touched by Jesus' words of family devotion and retired from the conference. His only remark to Mary, his wife, was: "We can't have him for a son; he is too noble for us."

Then began that eventful talk with Rebecca. Thus far in his life, Jesus had made little distinction in his association with boys and girls, with young men and young women. His mind had been altogether too much occupied with the pressing problems of practical earthly affairs and the intriguing contemplation of his eventual career "about his Father's business" ever to have given serious consideration to the consummation of personal love in human marriage. But now he was face to face with another of those problems which every average human being must confront and decide. Indeed was he "tested in all points like as you are."

After listening attentively, he sincerely thanked Rebecca for her expressed admiration, adding,

[RUSS DOCKEN — *Rebecca's Marriage Proposal*]

"it shall cheer and comfort me all the days of my life." He explained that he was not free to enter into relations with any woman other than those of simple brotherly regard and pure friendship. He made it clear that his first and paramount duty was

JESUS AND ROMANTIC LOVE

Jesus lived the normal and average social life of a youth, adolescent, and adult Jewish male of first-century Palestine. The great cultural stability of the Jewish people was in the strength of their family groups along with a highly evolved institution of marriage. Although he never did, it would have been wholly honorable and consistent with Jesus' earth mission to enter the marriage relation.

The Jews had a strong sense of romantic love as one sees in the impassioned poetry found in the Song of Solomon. But for Jesus, love was unselfish, unconditional, and divine.

The story of Rebecca's love for Jesus was whispered about Nazareth and later on at Capernaum, so that, while in the years to follow many women loved Jesus even as men loved him, not again did he have to reject the personal proffer of another good woman's devotion. From this time on human affection for Jesus partook more of the nature of worshipful and adoring regard. Both men and women loved him devotedly and for what he was, not with any tinge of self-satisfaction or desire for affectionate possession. But for many years, whenever the story of Jesus' human personality was recited, the devotion of Rebecca was recounted.

Miriam, knowing fully about the affair of Rebecca and knowing how her brother had forsaken even the love of a beautiful maiden (not realizing the factor of his future career of destiny), came to idealize Jesus and to love him with a touching and profound affection as for a father as well as for a brother.

the rearing of his father's family, that he could not consider marriage until that was accomplished; and then he added: "If I am a son of destiny, I must not assume obligations of lifelong duration until such a time as my destiny shall be made manifest."

Rebecca was heartbroken. She refused to be comforted and importuned her father to leave Nazareth until he finally consented to move to Sepphoris. In after years, to the many men who sought her hand in marriage, Rebecca had but one answer. She lived for only one purpose—to await the hour when this, to her, the greatest man who ever lived would begin his career as a teacher of living truth. And she followed him devotedly through his eventful years of public labor, being present (unobserved by Jesus) that day when he rode triumphantly into Jerusalem; and she stood "among the other women" by the side of Mary on that fateful and tragic afternoon when the Son of Man hung upon the cross, to her, as well as to countless worlds on high, "the one altogether lovely and the greatest among ten thousand." ∎

A.D. 14

THE VISIT WITH LAZARUS, MARTHA, AND MARY

Although they could hardly afford it, Jesus had a strange longing to go up to Jerusalem for the Passover. His mother, knowing of his recent experience with Rebecca, wisely urged him to make the journey. He was not markedly conscious of it, but what he most wanted was an opportunity to talk with Lazarus and to visit with Martha and Mary. Next to his own family he loved these three most of all.

In making this four-day trip to Jerusalem, he went by way of Megiddo, Antipatris, and Lydda, in part covering the same route traversed when he was brought back to Nazareth from Egypt.

Jesus passed on through Jerusalem, only pausing to look upon the temple and the gathering throngs of visitors. He had a strange and increasing aversion to this Herod-built temple with its politically appointed priesthood. He wanted most of all to see Lazarus, Martha, and Mary. Lazarus was the same age as Jesus and now head of the house; by the time of this visit Lazarus's mother had also been laid to rest. Martha was a little over one year older than Jesus, while Mary was two years younger. And Jesus was the idolized ideal of all three of them.

On this visit occurred one of those periodic outbreaks of rebellion against tradition—the expression of resentment for those ceremonial practices which Jesus deemed misrepresentative of his Father in heaven. Not knowing Jesus was coming, Lazarus had arranged to celebrate the Passover with friends in an adjoining village down the Jericho road. Jesus now proposed that they celebrate the feast where they were, at Lazarus's house. "But," said Lazarus, "we have no paschal lamb." And then Jesus entered upon a prolonged and convincing dissertation to the effect that the Father in heaven was not truly concerned with such childlike and meaningless rituals. After solemn and fervent prayer they rose, and Jesus said: "Let the childlike and darkened minds of my people serve their God as Moses directed; it is better that they do, but let us who have seen the light of life no longer approach our Father by the darkness of death. Let us be free in the knowledge of the truth of our Father's eternal love."

That evening about twilight these four sat down and partook of the first Passover feast ever to be celebrated by devout Jews without the paschal lamb. The unleavened bread and the wine had been made ready for this Passover, and these emblems, which Jesus termed "the bread of life" and "the water of life," he served to his companions, and they ate in solemn conformity with the teachings just imparted. It was his custom to engage in this sacramental ritual whenever he paid subsequent visits to Bethany. When he returned home, he told all this to his mother. She was shocked at first but came gradually to see his viewpoint; nevertheless, she was greatly relieved when Jesus assured her that he did not intend to introduce this new idea of the Passover in their family. At home with the children he continued, year by year, to eat the Passover "according to the law of Moses."

It was during this year that Mary had a long talk with Jesus about marriage. She frankly asked him if he would get married if he were free from his family responsibilities. Jesus explained to her that, since immediate duty forbade his marriage, he had given the subject little thought. He expressed himself as doubting that he would ever enter the marriage state; he said that all such things must await "my hour," the time when "my Father's work must begin." Having settled already in his mind that he was not to become the father of children in the flesh, he gave very little thought to the subject of human marriage.

This year he began anew the task of further weaving his mortal and divine natures into a simple and effective *human individuality*. And he continued to grow in moral status and spiritual understanding. ∎

A.D. 20

JAMES INSTALLED AS HEAD OF THE FAMILY

As this year began, Jesus of Nazareth became strongly conscious that he possessed a wide range of potential power. But he was likewise fully persuaded that this power was not to be employed by his personality as the Son of Man, at least not until his hour should come.

At this time he thought much but said little

Summary of Ages Twenty-one to Twenty-five

AGE 21:   As Jesus of Nazareth entered upon the early years of his adult life, he continued to live a normal and average human life on earth. He labored, grew weary, rested, and slept. He hungered and satisfied such cravings with food; he thirsted and quenched his thirst with water. He experienced the full gamut of human feelings and emotions; he was "in all things tested, even as you are." Of his human nature he was never in doubt. But of his divine nature there was always room for doubt and conjecture, at least this was true right up to the event of his baptism. While he understood his dual nature, his self-realization of divinity was a slow and progressive experience during this year.

AGE 22:   Jesus was now the father–brother to seven siblings that ranged in age from 7 to 18. This year was marked by adolescent trials and tribulations and Jesus was kept busy helping these youngsters adjust to their emotional and intellectual lives as they grew up. For six months of this year Jesus took work in Sepphoris where he learned metal arts; during this time he placed James in charge of family affairs and the repair shop, while Joseph was given responsibility for the home bench. Jesus' motive in taking this long leave was to prepare the older boys for full family responsibility by slowly weaning them from his day-to-day care. During his six-month absence, he returned to Nazareth regularly to check up on the family, but in Sepphoris, Jesus lived with gentiles, studying not only their ways of living but the workings of their minds.

AGE 23:   The financial pressures were eased during this year, as four family members were now employed. Jesus took Simon to Jerusalem for Passover this year, allowing himself a three-week vacation, the longest time away from daily toil since the death of his father. While in Jerusalem, Jesus was offered a position with an Oriental import business based in Damascus but he declined, citing family responsibilities. It was during this Jerusalem trip that Jesus met Stephen, a young Hellenist. Fifteen years later, Stephen became the first martyr to the new Christian religion; his death was witnessed by Saul of Tarsus, who was mightily inspired by Stephen's devotion and courage. And it was this Saul who later became the aggressive and indomitable Paul, the philosopher, if not the sole founder, of the Christian religion.

AGE 24:   This year Jesus was offered a position as chief chazan in the Alexandrian synagogue, a position that would later be expanded to chief teacher and religious leader in that city. But Jesus declined saying, "My hour has not come." The last six months of this year, Jesus enjoyed a very uneventful season, allowing him to commune frequently with the Father. He made great progress during this time in the mastery of his mind. James and Miriam approached Jesus with plans for their upcoming marriages. And these plans were approved by Jesus for a time two years hence.

AGE 25:   Jesus was now a robust and refined specimen of manhood with superb physical development, a keen, penetrating, active mind, and a divine spirit. The repair shop was finally paid off and the family even managed to start saving for times ahead. Jesus continued to work in the shop but always made time for his baby sister, Ruth, and bevies of youngsters who made the repair shop their favorite playground and "Uncle Joshua" their favorite storyteller. It was difficult for his friends to comprehend the range of his intellectual activities, how he could so suddenly and so completely swing from the profound discussion of politics, philosophy, or religion to the lighthearted and joyous playfulness of these tots of from five to ten years of age. As his own brothers and sisters grew up, as he gained more leisure, and before the grandchildren arrived, he paid a great deal of attention to these little ones. But he did not live on earth long enough to enjoy the grandchildren very much.

about the relation of himself to his Father in heaven. And the conclusion of all this thinking was expressed once in his prayer on the hilltop, when he said: "Regardless of who I am and what power I may or may not wield, I always have been, and always will be, subject to the will of my Paradise Father." And yet, as this man walked about Nazareth to and from his work, it was literally true—as concerned a vast universe—that "in him were hidden all the treasures of wisdom and knowledge."

This year Jesus enjoyed more than usual leisure, and he devoted much time to training James in the management of the repair shop and Joseph in the direction of home affairs. Mary sensed that he was making ready to leave them. Leave them to go where? To do what? She had about given up the thought that Jesus was the Messiah. She could not understand him; she simply could not fathom her first-born son.

At last the day had come when all Jesus' brothers had chosen, and were established in, their lifework. The stage was being set for Jesus' departure from home.

In November a double wedding occurred. James and Esta, and Miriam and Jacob were married. It was truly a joyous occasion. Even Mary was once more happy except every now and then when she realized that Jesus was preparing to go away.

James and his bride, Esta, moved into a neat little home on the west side of town, the gift of her father. While James continued his support of his mother's home, his quota was cut in half because of his marriage, and Joseph was formally installed by Jesus as head of the family.

The day after this double wedding Jesus held an important conference with James. He told James, confidentially, that he was preparing to leave home. He presented full title to the repair shop to James, formally and solemnly abdicated as head of Joseph's house, and most touchingly established his brother James as "head and protector of my father's house." He drew up, and they both signed, a secret compact in which it was stipulated that, in return for the gift of the repair shop, James would henceforth assume full financial responsibility for the family, thus releasing Jesus from all further obligations in these matters. After the contract was signed, after the budget was so arranged that the actual expenses of the family would be met without any contribution from Jesus, Jesus said to James: "But, my son, I will continue to send you something each month until my hour shall have come, but what I send shall be used by you as the occasion demands. Apply my funds to the family necessities or pleasures as you see fit. Use them in case of sickness or apply them to meet the unexpected emergencies which may befall any individual member of the family."

And thus did Jesus make ready to enter upon the second and home-detached phase of his adult life before the public entrance upon his Father's business. ∎

A.D. 21

Jesus Leaves His Family

In January of this year, A.D. 21, on a rainy Sunday morning, Jesus took unceremonious leave of his family, only explaining that he was going over to Tiberias and then on a visit to other cities about the Sea of Galilee. And thus he left them, never again to be a regular member of that household.

He spent one week at Tiberias, the new city which was soon to succeed Sepphoris as the capital of Galilee; and finding little to interest him, he passed on successively through Magdala and Bethsaida to Capernaum, where he stopped to pay a visit to his father's friend Zebedee. Zebedee's sons were fishermen; he himself was a boatbuilder. Jesus

of Nazareth was an expert in both designing and building; he was a master at working with wood; and Zebedee had long known of the skill of the Nazareth craftsman. For a long time Zebedee had contemplated making improved boats; he now laid his plans before Jesus and invited the visiting carpenter to join him in the enterprise, and Jesus readily consented.

Jesus worked with Zebedee only a little more than one year, but during that time he created a new style of boat and established entirely new methods of boatmaking. By superior technique and greatly improved methods of steaming the boards, Jesus and Zebedee began to build boats of a very superior type, craft which were far more safe for sailing the lake than were the older types. For several years Zebedee had more work, turning out these new-style boats, than his small establishment could handle; in less than five years practically all the craft on the lake had been built in the shop of Zebedee at Capernaum. Jesus became well known to the Galilean fisherfolk as the designer of the new boats.

Zebedee was a moderately well-to-do man; his boatbuilding shops were on the lake to the south of Capernaum, and his home was situated down the lake shore near the fishing headquarters of Bethsaida. Jesus lived in the home of Zebedee during the year and more he remained at Capernaum. He had long worked alone in the world, that is, without a father, and greatly enjoyed this period of working with a father-partner.

Zebedee's wife, Salome, was a relative of Annas, onetime high priest at Jerusalem and still the most influential of the Sadducean group, having been deposed only eight years previously. Salome became a great admirer of Jesus. She loved him as she loved her own sons, James, John, and David, while her four daughters looked upon Jesus as

their elder brother. Jesus often went out fishing with James, John, and David, and they learned that he was an experienced fisherman as well as an expert boatbuilder.

Throughout this year Jesus built boats and continued to observe how men lived on earth. Frequently he would go down to visit at the caravan station, Capernaum being on the direct travel route from Damascus to the south. Capernaum was a strong Roman military post, and the garrison's commanding officer was a gentile believer in Yahweh, "a devout man," as the Jews were wont to designate such proselytes. This officer belonged to a wealthy Roman family, and he took it upon himself to build a beautiful synagogue in Capernaum, which had been presented to the Jews a short time before Jesus came to live with Zebedee. Jesus conducted the services in this new synagogue more than half the time this year, and some of the caravan people who chanced to attend remembered him as the carpenter from Nazareth.

Once a week Jesus held a meeting with the entire household, shop, and shore helpers, for Zebedee had many employees. And it was among these workers that Jesus was first called "the Master." They all loved him. He enjoyed his labors with Zebedee in Capernaum, but he missed the children playing out by the side of the Nazareth carpenter shop.

This was the last year of his settled life. Never again did Jesus spend a whole year in one place or at one undertaking. The days of his earth pilgrimages were rapidly approaching. Periods of intense activity were not far in the future, but there were now about to intervene between his simple but intensely active life of the past and his still more intense and strenuous public ministry, a few years of extensive travel and highly diversified personal

[RUSS DOCKEN — *The Master Boatbuilder*]

activity. His training as a man of the realm had to be completed before he could enter upon his career of teaching and preaching. ∎

A.D. 22

THE WEALTHY TRAVELERS FROM INDIA

In March, A.D. 22, Jesus took leave of Zebedee and of Capernaum. He asked for a small sum of money to defray his expenses to Jerusalem. While working with Zebedee he had drawn only small sums of money, which each month he would send to the family at Nazareth. One month Joseph would come down to Capernaum for the money; the next month Jude would come over to Capernaum, get the money from Jesus, and take it up to Nazareth. Jude's fishing headquarters was only a few miles south of Capernaum.

When Jesus took leave of Zebedee's family, he agreed to remain in Jerusalem until Passover time, and they all promised to be present for that event. They even arranged to celebrate the Passover supper together. They all sorrowed when Jesus left them, especially the daughters of Zebedee.

Presently the time of the Passover drew near, and along with the throngs from every quarter there arrived at Jerusalem from Capernaum, Zebedee and his entire family. They all stopped at the spacious home of Annas, where they celebrated the Passover as one happy family.

By apparent chance, Jesus met a wealthy traveler and his son, a young man about seventeen years of age. These travelers hailed from India, and being on their way to visit Rome and various other points on the Mediterranean, they had arranged to arrive in Jerusalem during the Passover, hoping to find someone whom they could engage as interpreter for both and tutor for the son. The father was insistent that Jesus consent to travel with them. Jesus told him about his family and that it was hardly fair to go away for almost two years, during which time they might find themselves in need. Whereupon, this traveler from the Orient proposed to advance to Jesus the wages of one year so that he could intrust such funds to his friends for the safeguarding of his family against want. And Jesus agreed to make the trip.

Throughout this tour of the Roman world, for many reasons, Jesus was known as the *Damascus scribe*. At Corinth and other stops on the return trip he was, however, known as the *Jewish tutor*.

This was an eventful period in Jesus' life. While on this journey he made many contacts with his fellow men, but this experience is a phase of his life which he never revealed to any member of his family nor to any of the apostles. Jesus lived out his life in the flesh and departed from this world without anyone knowing that he had made this extensive trip. Some of his friends thought he had returned to Damascus; others thought he had gone to India. His own family inclined to the belief that he was in Alexandria, as they knew that he had once been invited to go there for the purpose of becoming an assistant chazan.

[ANDON FONTAINNE — *Serendipity*]

When Jesus returned to Palestine, he did nothing to change the opinion of his family that he had gone from Jerusalem to Alexandria; he permitted them to continue in the belief that all the time he had been absent from Palestine had been spent in that city of learning and culture. Only Zebedee the boatbuilder of Bethsaida knew the facts about these matters, and Zebedee told no one.

In all your efforts to decipher the meaning of Jesus' life on Urantia, you must be mindful of the motivation of the bestowal. If you would comprehend the meaning of many of his apparently strange doings, you must discern the purpose of his sojourn on your world. He was consistently careful not to build up an overattractive and attention-consuming personal career. He wanted to make no unusual or overpowering appeals to his fellow men. He was dedicated to the work of revealing the heavenly Father to his fellow mortals and at the same time was consecrated to the sublime task of living his mortal earth life all the while subject to the will of the same Paradise Father.

It will also always be helpful in understanding Jesus' life on earth if all mortal students of this divine bestowal will remember that, while he lived this life of incarnation *on* Urantia, he lived it *for* his entire universe. There was something special and inspiring associated with the life he lived in the flesh of mortal nature for every single inhabited sphere throughout all the universe. The same is also true of all those worlds which have become habitable since the eventful times of his sojourn on Urantia. And it will likewise be equally true of all worlds which may become inhabited by will creatures in all the future history of this universe. ✳

THE MISSING YEARS: TRAVEL AND MINISTRY

For this reason he had to be made like them, fully human in every way, in order that he might become a merciful and faithful high priest in service to God...

—HEBREWS 2:17 NIV

JESUS KNOWS ABOUT THE THOUGHTS AND FEELINGS, THE URGES AND IMPULSES, OF THE HUMAN life from birth to death. He did not come down to live his life on earth as the perfect and detailed example for all people to copy. But as he lived his mortal life in his day and *as he was,* so did he thereby set the example for all of us thus to live our lives in our day and *as we are.* Jesus had now made every preparation for detaching himself permanently from the Nazareth home; and this was not easy for him to do. Since he had given himself so fully to his family, he loved them with a great and fervent affection. But as the times of his settled family life ended, those of his earth pilgrimages began. The Son of Man, during the time and through the experiences of this upcoming tour of the Roman world, practically completed his educational contact-training with the diversified peoples of the world of his day and generation. By the time of his return to Nazareth, through the medium of this travel-training he had just about learned how man lived and wrought out his existence on earth.

The real purpose of his trip around the Mediterranean basin was to *know men.* He came very close to hundreds of humankind on this journey. He met and loved all manner of men, rich and poor, high and low, black and white, educated and uneducated, cultured and uncultured, animalistic and spiritual, religious and irreligious, moral and immoral.

To the onlooking celestial intelligences, this Mediterranean trip was the most enthralling of all Jesus' earth experiences, at least of all his career right up to the event of his crucifixion and mortal death. This was the fascinating period of his *personal ministry* in contrast with the soon-following epoch of public ministry. This unique episode was all the more engrossing because he was at this time still the carpenter of Nazareth, the boatbuilder of Capernaum, the scribe of Damascus; he was still the Son of Man. He was still a man among men.

THE URANTIA BOOK: PAPERS 130–133
APRIL, A.D. 22–DECEMBER, A.D. 23

[SLAWA RADZISZEWSKA — *The Library of Alexandria*]

EMBARKING FROM CAESAREA

The tour of the Roman world consumed most of the twenty-eighth and the entire twenty-ninth year of Jesus' life on earth. Jesus and the two natives from India—Gonod and his son Ganid—left Jerusalem on a Sunday morning, April 26, A.D. 22. They made their journey according to schedule, and Jesus said good-bye to the father and son in the city of Charax on the Persian Gulf on the tenth day of December the following year.

From Jerusalem they went to Caesarea by way of Joppa. At Caesarea they took a boat for Alexandria. From Alexandria they sailed for Lasea in Crete. From Crete they sailed for Carthage, touching at Cyrene. At Carthage they took a boat for Naples, stopping at Malta, Syracuse, and Messina. From Naples they went to Capua, whence they traveled by the Appian Way to Rome.

It was while working four months at Damascus that Jesus had picked up the rudiments of the language spoken by Gonod and Ganid. While there he had labored on translations from Greek into one of the languages of India, being assisted by a native of Gonod's home district.

On this Mediterranean tour Jesus spent about half of each day teaching Ganid and acting as interpreter during Gonod's business conferences and social contacts. The remainder of each day, which was at his disposal, he devoted to making those close personal contacts with his fellow men,

those intimate associations with the mortals of the realm, which so characterized his activities during these years that just preceded his public ministry.

From firsthand observation and actual contact Jesus acquainted himself with the higher material and intellectual civilization of the Occident and the Levant; from Gonod and his brilliant son he learned a great deal about the civilization and culture of India and China, for Gonod, himself a citizen of India, had made three extensive trips to the empire of the yellow race.

Ganid, the young man, learned much from Jesus during this long and intimate association. They developed a great affection for each other, and the lad's father many times tried to persuade Jesus to return with them to India, but Jesus always declined, pleading the necessity for returning to his family in Palestine.

Jesus and his friends tarried in Caesarea beyond the time expected because one of the huge steering paddles of the vessel on which they intended to embark was discovered to be in danger of cleaving. The captain decided to remain in port while a new one was being made. There was a shortage of skilled woodworkers for this task, so Jesus volunteered to assist. During the evenings Jesus and his friends strolled about on the beautiful wall which served as a promenade around the port. Ganid greatly enjoyed Jesus' explanation of the water system of the city and the technique whereby the tides were utilized to flush the city's streets and sewers. This youth of India was much impressed with the temple of Augustus, situated upon an elevation and surmounted by a

EASTERN MISSIONARIES

It was regrettable that there was no one like Peter to go into China, or like Paul to enter India, where the spiritual soil was then so favorable for planting the seed of the new gospel of the kingdom. The teachings of Jesus would have made just such an immediate and effective appeal to the minds of the spiritually hungry Asiatic peoples as did the preaching of Peter and Paul in the West.

From Gonod and his brilliant son Ganid, Jesus learned a great deal about the civilization and culture of India and China.

colossal statue of the Roman emperor. The second afternoon of their stay the three of them attended a performance in the enormous amphitheater which could seat twenty thousand persons, and that night they went to a Greek play at the theater. These were the first exhibitions of this sort Ganid had ever witnessed, and he asked Jesus many questions about them. On the morning of the third day they paid a formal visit to the governor's palace, for Caesarea was the capital of Palestine and the residence of the Roman procurator.

At their inn there also lodged a merchant from Mongolia, and since this Far-Easterner talked Greek fairly well, Jesus had several long visits with him. This man was much impressed with Jesus' philosophy of life and never forgot his words of wisdom regarding "the living of the heavenly life while on earth by means of daily submission to the will of the heavenly Father." This merchant was a Taoist, and he had thereby become a strong believer in the doctrine of a universal Deity. When he returned to Mongolia, he began to teach these advanced truths to his neighbors and to his business associates, and as a direct result of such activities, his eldest son decided to become a Taoist priest. This young man exerted a great influence in behalf of advanced truth throughout his lifetime and was devotedly loyal to the doctrine of the One God—the Supreme Ruler of Heaven.

One of the young men who worked with Jesus one day on the steering paddle became much interested in the words which he dropped from hour to hour as they toiled in the shipyard. When Jesus intimated that the Father in heaven was interested in the welfare of his children on earth, this young Greek, Anaxand, said: "If the Gods are interested in me, then why do they not remove the cruel and unjust foreman of this workshop?" He was startled when Jesus replied, "Since you know the ways of kindness and value justice, perhaps the Gods have brought this erring man near that you may lead him into this better way. Maybe you are the salt which is to make this brother more agreeable to all other men; that is, if you have not lost your savor. As it is, this man is your master in that his evil ways unfavorably influence you. Why not assert your mastery of evil by virtue of the power of goodness and thus become the master of all relations between the two of you? I predict that the good in you could overcome the evil in him if you gave it a fair and living chance. There is no adventure in the course of mortal existence more enthralling than to enjoy the exhilaration of becoming the material life partner with spiritual energy and divine truth in one of their triumphant struggles with error and evil. It is a marvelous and transforming experience to become the living channel of spiritual light to the mortal who sits in spiritual darkness. If you are more blessed with truth than is this man, his need should challenge you. Surely you are not the coward who could stand by on the seashore and watch a fellow man who could not swim perish! How much more of value is this man's soul floundering in darkness compared to his body drowning in water!"

Anaxand was mightily moved by Jesus' words. Presently he told his superior what Jesus had said, and that night they both sought Jesus' advice as

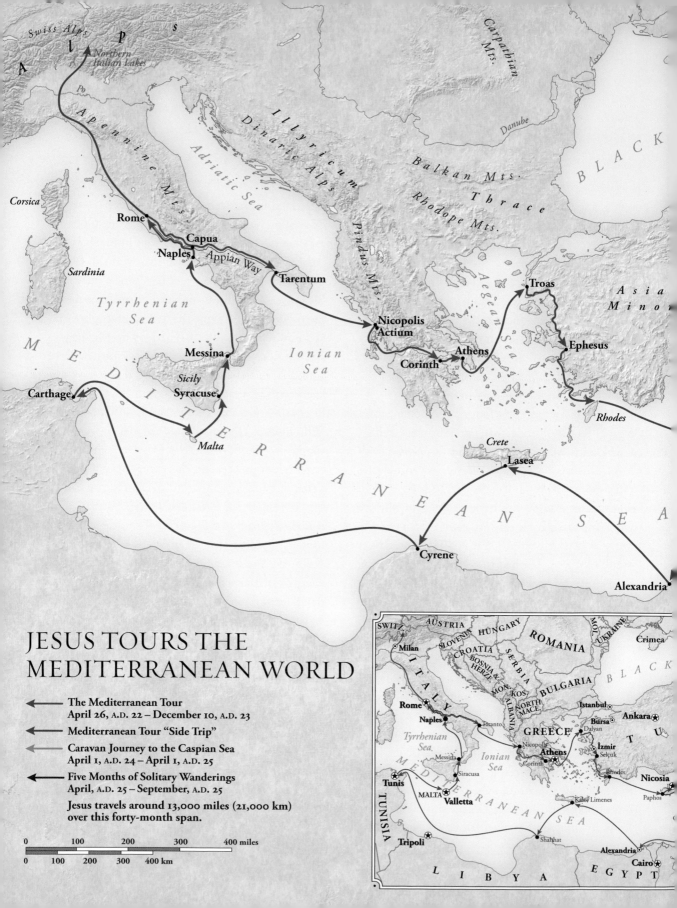

Swiss Alps
Northern
Italian Lakes
A L P s
Po
Apennine Mts.
Dinaric Alps
Illyricum
Carpathian Mts.
Danube
Adriatic Sea
Balkan Mts.
Thrace
Rhodope Mts.
BLACK
Corsica
Rome
Capua
Naples
Appian Way
Tarentum
Pindus Mts.
Troas
Asia Minor
Sardinia
Tyrrhenian Sea
Nicopolis
Actium
Athens
Ephesus
Corinth
Aegean Sea
Messina
Ionian Sea
MEDITERRANEAN
Sicily
Syracuse
Carthage
Malta
Rhodes
Crete
Lasea
EAN SEA
Cyrene
Alexandria

JESUS TOURS THE MEDITERRANEAN WORLD

← The Mediterranean Tour
April 26, A.D. 22 – December 10, A.D. 23

← Mediterranean Tour "Side Trip"

← Caravan Journey to the Caspian Sea
April 1, A.D. 24 – April 1, A.D. 25

← Five Months of Solitary Wanderings
April, A.D. 25 – September, A.D. 25

Jesus travels around 13,000 miles (21,000 km)
over this forty-month span.

0   100   200   300   400 miles

0   100   200   300   400 km

SWITZ.
AUSTRIA
HUNGARY
ROMANIA
Milan
ITALY
SLOVENIA
CROATIA
BOSNIA & HERZE.
SERBIA
MON.
BULGARIA
UKRAINE
MOL.
Crimea
BLACK
Rome
Naples
Taranto
NORTH MACE.
ALBANIA
Nicopolis
GREECE
Athens
Corinth
Istanbul
Bursa
Dalyan
Ankara
İzmir
Selçuk
T U
Tyrrhenian Sea
Messina
Siracusa
Ionian Sea
Rhodes
Nicosia
Paphos
TUNIS
MEDITERRANEAN SEA
MALTA
Valletta
Kaloi Limenes
Tripoli
TUNISIA
Shahhat
Alexandria
Cairo
L I B Y A
E G Y P T

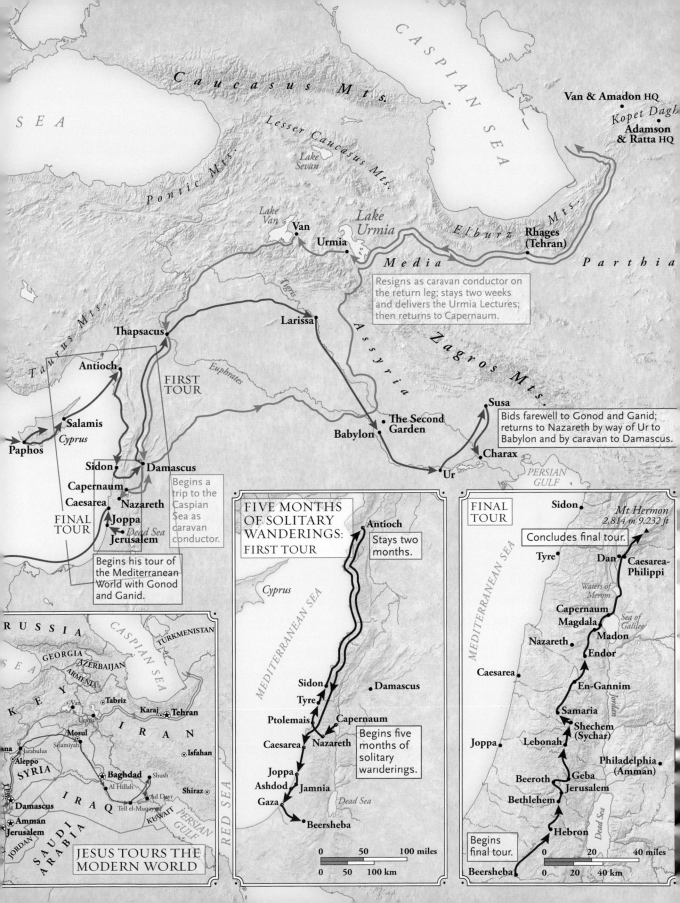

CASPIAN SEA

SEA

Caucasus Mts.

Lesser Caucasus Mts.

Lake
Sevan

Van & Amadon HQ

Kopet Dagh

Adamson & Ratta HQ

Pontic Mts.

Lake Van

Van

Urmia

Lake Urmia

Elburz Mts.

Rhages (Tehran)

Media

Parthia

Larissa

Tigris

Resigns as caravan conductor on the return leg; stays two weeks and delivers the Urmia Lectures; then returns to Capernaum.

Taurus Mts.

Thapsacus

Euphrates

Assyria

Zagros Mts.

Antioch

FIRST TOUR

Susa

Bids farewell to Gonod and Ganid; returns to Nazareth by way of Ur to Babylon and by caravan to Damascus.

Salamis

Cyprus

Sidon

Damascus

The Second Garden

Babylon

Charax

PERSIAN GULF

Paphos

Capernaum

Caesarea

Nazareth

Ur

Begins a trip to the Caspian Sea as caravan conductor.

FINAL TOUR

Joppa

Dead Sea

Jerusalem

Begins his tour of the Mediterranean World with Gonod and Ganid.

FIVE MONTHS OF SOLITARY WANDERINGS: FIRST TOUR

Antioch

Stays two months.

FINAL TOUR

Sidon

Mt Hermon 2,814 m 9,232 ft

Cyprus

Concludes final tour.

Tyre

Dan

Caesarea-Philippi

MEDITERRANEAN SEA

Waters of Merom

Capernaum

Sea of Galilee

Magdala

Sidon

Damascus

Nazareth

Madon

Tyre

Endor

Ptolemais

Capernaum

Caesarea

En-Gannim

Caesarea

Nazareth

Samaria

Begins five months of solitary wanderings.

Shechem (Sychar)

Joppa

Lebonah

Jordan

Joppa

Philadelphia (Amman)

Ashdod

Jamnia

Geba

Beeroth

Gaza

Dead Sea

Jerusalem

Bethlehem

Dead Sea

Beersheba

Hebron

0   50   100 miles

0   50   100 km

Begins final tour.

Beersheba

0   20   40 miles

0   20   40 km

RUSSIA

CASPIAN SEA

GEORGIA

TURKMENISTAN

AZERBAIJAN

SEA

ARMENIA

KEY

Tabriz

Van

Urmia

Karaj

Tehran

IRAN

Selamiyah

Mosul

Isfahan

Aleppo

Baghdad

Shush

SYRIA

Al Hillah

Shiraz

IRAQ

Ad Dayr

Tell el-Muqayyar

Damascus

KUWAIT

PERSIAN GULF

Amman

Jerusalem

JORDAN

SAUDI ARABIA

RED SEA

JESUS TOURS THE MODERN WORLD

Jarabulus

to the welfare of their souls. And later on, after the Christian message had been proclaimed in Caesarea, both of these men, one a Greek and the other a Roman, believed Philip's preaching and became prominent members of the church which he founded. Later this young Greek was appointed the steward of a Roman centurion, Cornelius, who became a believer through Peter's ministry. Anaxand continued to minister light to those who sat in darkness until the days of Paul's imprisonment at Caesarea, when he perished, by accident, in the great slaughter of twenty thousand Jews while he ministered to the suffering and dying.

Ganid was, by this time, beginning to learn how his tutor spent his leisure in this unusual personal ministry to his fellow men, and the young Indian set about to find out the motive for these incessant activities. He asked, "Why do you occupy yourself so continuously with these visits with strangers?" And Jesus answered: "Ganid, no man is a stranger to one who knows God. In the experience of finding the Father in heaven you discover that all men are your brothers, and does it seem strange that one should enjoy the exhilaration of meeting a newly discovered brother? To become acquainted with one's brothers and sisters, to know their problems and to learn to love them, is the supreme experience of living."

This was a conference which lasted well into the night, in the course of which the young man requested Jesus to tell him the difference between the will of God and that human mind act of choosing which is also called will. In substance Jesus said: The will of God is the way of God, partnership with the choice of God in the face of any potential alternative. To do the will of God, therefore, is the progressive experience of becoming more and more like God, and God is the source and destiny of all that is good and beautiful and true. The will of man is the way of man, the sum and substance of that which the mortal chooses to be and do. Will is the deliberate choice of a self-conscious being which leads to decision-conduct based on intelligent reflection.

That afternoon Jesus and Ganid had both enjoyed playing with a very intelligent shepherd dog, and Ganid wanted to know whether the dog had a soul, whether it had a will, and in response to his questions Jesus said: "The dog has a mind which can know material man, his master, but cannot know God, who is spirit; therefore the dog does not possess a spiritual nature and cannot enjoy a spiritual experience. The dog may have a will derived from nature and augmented by training, but such a power of mind is not a spiritual force, neither is it comparable to the human will, inasmuch as it is not *reflective*—it is not the result of discriminating higher and moral meanings or choosing spiritual and eternal values. It is the possession of such powers of spiritual discrimination and truth choosing that makes mortal man a moral being, a creature endowed with the attributes of spiritual responsibility and the potential of eternal survival." Jesus went on to explain that it is the absence of such mental powers in the animal which makes it forever impossible for the animal world to develop language in time or to experience anything equivalent to personality survival in eternity. As a result of this day's

> "TO BECOME ACQUAINTED WITH ONE'S BROTHERS AND SISTERS, TO KNOW THEIR PROBLEMS AND TO LEARN TO LOVE THEM, IS THE SUPREME EXPERIENCE OF LIVING."

[SLAWA RADZISZEWSKA — *Playing with the Shepherd Dog*]

instruction Ganid never again entertained belief in the transmigration of the souls of men into the bodies of animals. ∎

THE LIGHTHOUSE AT ALEXANDRIA

It had been an eventful visit at Caesarea, and when the boat was ready, Jesus and his two friends departed at noon one day for Alexandria in Egypt.

The three enjoyed a most pleasant passage to Alexandria. Ganid was delighted with the voyage and kept Jesus busy answering questions. As they approached the city's harbor, the young man was thrilled by the great lighthouse of Pharos, located on the island which Alexander had joined by a mole to the mainland, thus creating two magnificent harbors and thereby making Alexandria the maritime commercial crossroads of Africa, Asia, and Europe. This great lighthouse was one of the seven wonders of the world and was the forerunner of all subsequent lighthouses. They arose early in the morning to view this splendid lifesaving device of man, and amidst the exclamations of Ganid Jesus said: "And you, my son, will be like this lighthouse when you return to India, even after

[SLAWA RADZISZEWSKA — *The Great Lighthouse of Pharos*]

your father is laid to rest; you will become like the light of life to those who sit about you in darkness, showing all who so desire the way to reach the harbor of salvation in safety." And as Ganid squeezed Jesus' hand, he said, "I will." ∎

THE ALEXANDRIAN LIBRARY

By the fourth hour after landing they were settled near the eastern end of the long and broad avenue, one hundred feet wide and five miles long, which stretched on out to the western limits of this city of one million people. After the first survey of the city's chief attractions—university (museum), library, the royal mausoleum of Alexander, the palace, temple of Neptune, theater, and gymnasium—Gonod addressed himself to business while Jesus and Ganid went to the library, the greatest in the world. Here were assembled nearly a million manuscripts from all the civilized world: Greece, Rome, Palestine, Parthia, India, China, and even Japan. In this library Ganid saw the largest collection of Indian literature in all the world; and they spent some time here each day throughout their stay in Alexandria. Jesus told Ganid about the translation of the Hebrew scriptures into Greek at this place. And they discussed again and again all the religions of the world, Jesus endeavoring to point out to this young mind the truth in each, always adding: "But Yahweh is the God developed from the revelations of Melchizedek and the covenant of Abraham. The Jews were the offspring of Abraham and subsequently occupied the very land wherein Melchizedek had lived and taught, and from which he sent teachers to all the world; and their religion eventually portrayed a clearer recognition of the Lord God of Israel as the Universal Father in heaven than any other world religion."

Under Jesus' direction Ganid made a collection of the teachings of all those religions of the world which recognized a Universal Deity, even though they might also give more or less recognition to subordinate deities. During the Alexandrian sojourn, the young man spent much of his time and no small sum of his father's money in the making of this abstract about God and his relations with mortal man and employed more than threescore learned translators. After much discussion Jesus and Ganid decided that the Romans had no real God in their religion, that their religion was hardly more than emperor worship. The Greeks, they concluded, had a philosophy but hardly a religion with a personal God. The mystery cults they discarded because of the confusion of their multiplicity, and because their varied concepts of Deity seemed to be derived from other and older religions.

Ganid was much surprised to discover that the best of the authors of the world's sacred literature all more or less clearly recognized the existence of an eternal God and were much in agreement with regard to his character and his relationship with mortal man. ∎

THE YOUNG MAN WHO WAS AFRAID

While they were up in the mountains at Crete, Jesus had a long talk with a young man who was fearful and downcast. Failing to derive comfort and courage from association with his fellows, this youth had sought the solitude of the hills; he had grown up with a feeling of helplessness and inferiority. These natural tendencies had been augmented by numerous difficult circumstances which the lad had encountered as he grew up, notably, the loss of his father when he was twelve years of age. As they met, Jesus said: "Greetings, my friend! why so downcast on such a beautiful day? If something has happened to distress you, perhaps I can in some manner assist you. At any rate it affords me real pleasure to proffer my services."

The young man was disinclined to talk, and so Jesus made a second approach to his soul, saying: "I understand you come up in these hills to get away from folks; so, of course, you do not want to talk with me, but I would like to know whether you are familiar with these hills; do you know the direction of the trails? and, perchance, could you inform me as to the best route to Phenix?" Now this youth was very familiar with these mountains, and he really became much interested in telling Jesus the way to Phenix, so much so that he marked out all the trails on the ground and fully explained every detail. But he was startled and made curious when Jesus, after saying good-bye and making as if he were taking leave, suddenly turned to him, saying: "I well know you wish to be left alone with your disconsolation; but it would be neither kind nor fair for me to receive such generous help from you as to how best to find my way to Phenix and then unthinkingly to go away from you without making the least effort to answer your appealing request for help and guidance regarding the best route to the goal of destiny which you seek in your heart while you tarry here on the mountainside. As you so well know the trails to Phenix, having traversed them many times, so do I well know the way to the city of your disappointed hopes and thwarted ambitions. And since you have asked me for help, I will not disappoint you." The youth was almost overcome, but he managed to stammer out, "But—I did not ask you for anything—" And Jesus, laying a gentle hand on his shoulder, said: "No, son, not with words but with longing looks did you appeal to my heart. My boy, to one who loves his fellows there is an eloquent appeal for help in your countenance of discouragement and despair. Sit down with me while I tell you of the service trails and happiness highways which lead from the sorrows of self to the joys of loving activities in the brotherhood of men and in the service of the God of heaven."

By this time the young man very much desired to talk with Jesus, and he knelt at his feet imploring Jesus to help him, to show him the way of escape from his world of personal sorrow and defeat. Said Jesus: "My friend, arise! Stand up like a man! You may be surrounded with small enemies and be retarded by many obstacles, but the big things and the real things of this world and the universe are on your side. The sun rises every morning to salute you just as it does the most powerful and prosperous man on earth. Look—you have a strong body and powerful muscles—your physical equipment is better than the average. Of course, it is just about useless while you sit out here on the mountainside and grieve over your misfortunes, real and fancied. But you could do great things with your body if you would hasten off to where great things are waiting to be done. You are trying to run away from your unhappy self, but it cannot be done. You and your problems of living are real; you cannot escape them as long as you live. But look again, your mind is clear and capable. Your strong body has an intelligent mind to direct it. Set your mind at work to solve its problems; teach your intellect to work for you; refuse longer to be dominated by fear like an unthinking animal. Your mind should be your courageous ally in the solution of your life problems rather than your

being, as you have been, its abject fear-slave and the bond servant of depression and defeat. But most valuable of all, your potential of real achievement is the spirit which lives within you, and which will stimulate and inspire your mind to control itself and activate the body if you will release it from the fetters of fear and thus enable your spiritual nature to begin your deliverance from the evils of inaction by the power-presence of living faith. And then, forthwith, will this faith vanquish fear of men by the compelling presence of that new and all-dominating *love of your fellows* which will so soon fill your soul to overflowing because of the consciousness which has been born in your heart that you are a child of God.

"This day, my son, you are to be reborn, re-established as a man of faith, courage, and devoted service to man, for God's sake. And when you become so readjusted to life within yourself, you become likewise readjusted to the universe; you have been born again—born of the spirit—and henceforth will your whole life become one of victorious accomplishment. Trouble will invigorate you; disappointment will spur you on; difficulties will challenge you; and obstacles will stimulate you. Arise, young man! Say farewell to the life of cringing fear and fleeing cowardice. Hasten back to duty and live your life in the flesh as a son of God, a mortal dedicated to the ennobling service of man on earth and destined to the superb and eternal service of God in eternity."

And this youth, Fortune, subsequently became the leader of the Christians in Crete and the close associate of Titus in his labors for the uplift of the Cretan believers.

The travelers were truly rested and refreshed when they made ready about noon one day to sail for Carthage in northern Africa, stopping for two

---

[RUSS DOCKEN — *The Young Man Who Was Afraid*]

days at Cyrene. It was here that Jesus and Ganid gave first aid to a lad named Rufus, who had been injured by the breakdown of a loaded oxcart. They carried him home to his mother, and his father, Simon, little dreamed that the man whose cross he subsequently bore by orders of a Roman soldier was the stranger who once befriended his son. ∎

THE SOJOURN AT ROME

Since Gonod carried greetings from the princes of India to Tiberius, the Roman ruler, on the third day after their arrival in Rome the two Indians and Jesus appeared before him. The morose emperor was unusually cheerful on this day and chatted long with the trio. And when they had gone from his presence, the emperor, referring to Jesus, remarked to the aide standing on his right, "If I had that fellow's kingly bearing and gracious manner, I would be a real emperor, eh?"

Jesus learned much about men while in Rome, but the most valuable of all the manifold experiences of his six months' sojourn in that city was his contact with, and influence upon, the religious leaders of the empire's capital.

PREPARING THE WAY

Through his method of instruction, Jesus prepared Rome's religious leaders for the subsequent recognition of additional and similar truths in the teachings of the early Christian missionaries. It was this early acceptance of the teachings of the gospel preachers which gave that powerful impetus to the rapid spread of Christianity in Rome and from there throughout the empire.

Before the end of the first week in Rome Jesus had sought out, and had made the acquaintance of, the worth-while leaders of the Cynics, the Stoics, and the mystery cults, in particular the Mithraic group. Whether or not it was apparent to Jesus that the Jews were going to reject his mission, he most certainly foresaw that his messengers were presently coming to Rome to proclaim the kingdom of heaven; and he therefore set about, in the most amazing manner, to prepare the way for the better and more certain reception of their message. He selected five of the leading Stoics, eleven of the Cynics, and sixteen of the mystery-cult leaders and spent much of his spare time for almost six months in intimate association with these religious teachers. And this was his method of instruction: Never once did he attack their errors or even mention the flaws in their teachings. In each case he would select the truth in what they taught and then proceed so to embellish and illuminate this truth in their minds that in a very short time this enhancement of the truth effectively crowded out the associated error.

The significance of this remarkable doing can the better be understood when we record the fact that, out of this group of thirty-two Jesus-taught religious leaders in Rome, only two were

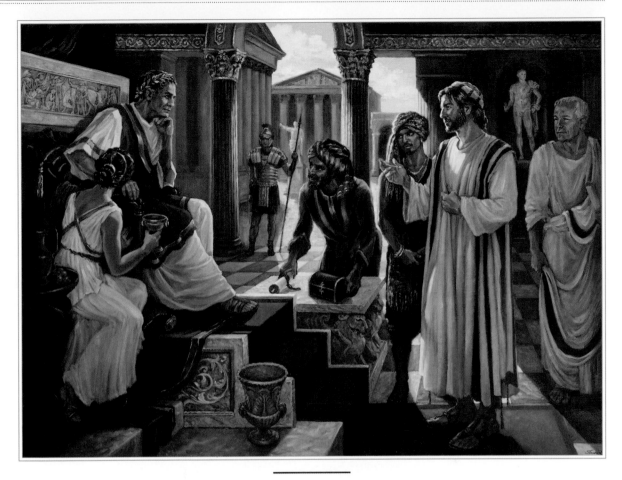

[SLAWA RADZISZEWSKA — *Appearance Before Tiberius*]

unfruitful; the thirty became pivotal individuals in the establishment of Christianity in Rome, and certain of them also aided in turning the chief Mithraic temple into the first Christian church of that city.

Through all their experiences, none of the thirty chosen ones ever realized that they had once talked with the man whose name became the subject of their religious teaching. Jesus' work in behalf of the original thirty-two was entirely personal. In his labors for these individuals the scribe of Damascus never met more than three of them at one time, seldom more than two, while most often he taught them singly. And he could do this great work of religious training because these men and women were not tradition bound; they were not victims of a settled preconception as to all future religious developments.

Many were the times in the years so soon to follow that Peter, Paul, and the other Christian teachers in Rome heard about this scribe of Damascus who had preceded them, and who had so obviously (and as they supposed unwittingly) prepared the way for their coming with the new gospel. Though Paul never really surmised the identity of this scribe of Damascus, he did, a short time before his death, because of the similarity of personal descriptions, reach the conclusion that the "tentmaker of Antioch" was also the "scribe of Damascus." On one occasion, while preaching in

Rome, Simon Peter, on listening to a description of the Damascus scribe, surmised that this individual might have been Jesus but quickly dismissed the idea, knowing full well (so he thought) that the Master had never been in Rome.

Here in Rome also occurred that touching incident in which the Creator of a universe spent several hours restoring a lost child to his anxious mother. This little boy had wandered away from his home, and Jesus found him crying in distress. He and Ganid were on their way to the libraries, but they devoted themselves to getting the child back home. Ganid never forgot Jesus' comment: "You know, Ganid, most human beings are like the lost child. They spend much of their time

[SLAWA RADZISZEWSKA — *The Thoughtless Pagan*]

crying in fear and suffering in sorrow when, in very truth, they are but a short distance from safety and security, even as this child was only a little way from home. And all those who know the way of truth and enjoy the assurance of knowing God should esteem it a privilege, not a duty, to offer guidance to their fellows in their efforts to find the satisfactions of living. Did we not supremely enjoy this ministry of restoring the child to his mother? So do those who lead men to God experience the supreme satisfaction of human service." And from that day forward, for the remainder of his natural life, Ganid was continually on the lookout for lost children whom he might restore to their homes.

The world is filled with hungry souls who famish in the very presence of the bread of life; men die searching for the very God who lives within them. Men seek for the treasures of the kingdom with yearning hearts and weary feet when they are all within the immediate grasp of living faith. Faith is to religion what sails are to a ship; it is an addition of power, not an added burden of life. There is but one struggle for those who enter the kingdom, and that is to fight the good fight of faith. The believer has only one battle, and that is against doubt—unbelief. ■

THE THOUGHTLESS PAGAN

Jesus, Gonod, and Ganid made five trips away from Rome to points of interest in the surrounding territory. On their visit to the northern Italian lakes Jesus had the long talk with Ganid concerning the impossibility of teaching a man about God if the man does not desire to know God. They had casually met a thoughtless pagan while on their journey up to the lakes, and Ganid was surprised that Jesus did not follow out his usual practice of enlisting the man in conversation which would naturally lead up to the discussion of spiritual questions. When Ganid asked his teacher why he evinced so little interest in this pagan, Jesus answered:

"Ganid, the man was not hungry for truth. He was not dissatisfied with himself. He was not ready to ask for help, and the eyes of his mind were not open to receive light for the soul. That man was not ripe for the harvest of salvation; he must be allowed more time for the trials and difficulties of life to prepare him for the reception of wisdom and higher learning. Or, if we could have him live with us, we might by our lives show him the Father in heaven, and thus would he become so attracted by our lives as sons of God that he would be constrained to inquire about our Father. You cannot reveal God to those who do not seek for him; you cannot lead unwilling souls into the joys of salvation. Man must become hungry for truth as a result of the experiences of living, or he must desire to know God as the result of contact with the lives of those who are acquainted with the divine Father before another human being can act as the means of leading such a fellow mortal to the Father in heaven. If we know God, our real business on earth is so to live as to permit the Father to reveal himself in our lives, and thus will all God-seeking persons see the Father and ask for our help in finding out more about the God who in this manner finds expression in our lives." ■

THE RETURN FROM ROME

When preparing to leave Rome, Jesus said good-bye to none of his friends. The scribe of Damascus appeared in Rome without announcement and disappeared in like manner. It was a full year before those who knew and loved him gave up hope of seeing him again. Before the end of the second year small groups of those who had known him found themselves drawn together by their common interest in his teachings and through mutual memory of their good times with him. And these small groups of Stoics, Cynics, and mystery cultists continued to hold these irregular and informal meetings right up to the time of the appearance in Rome of the first preachers of the Christian religion.

Gonod and Ganid had purchased so many things in Alexandria and Rome that they sent all their belongings on ahead by pack train to Tarentum, while the three travelers walked leisurely across Italy over the great Appian Way. On this journey they encountered all sorts of human beings. Many noble Roman citizens and Greek colonists lived along this road, but already the progeny of great numbers of slaves were beginning to make their appearance.

While tarrying at the ship landing at Tarentum, waiting for the boat to unload cargo, the travelers observed a man mistreating his wife. As was his custom, Jesus intervened in behalf of the person subjected to attack. He stepped up behind the irate husband and, tapping him gently on the shoulder, said: "My friend, may I speak with you in private for a moment?" The angry man was nonplused by such an approach and, after a moment of embarrassing hesitation, stammered out—"er—why—yes, what do you want with me?" When Jesus had led him to one side, he said: "My friend, I perceive that something terrible must have happened to you; I very much desire that you tell me what could happen to such a strong man to lead him to attack his wife, the mother of his children, and that right out here before all eyes. I am sure you must feel that you have some good reason for this assault. What did the woman do to deserve such treatment from her husband? As I look upon you, I think I discern in your face the love of justice if not the desire to show mercy. I venture to say that, if you found me out by the wayside, attacked by robbers, you would unhesitatingly rush to my rescue. I dare say you have done many such brave things in the course of your life. Now, my friend, tell me what is the matter? Did the woman do something wrong, or did you foolishly lose your head and thoughtlessly assault her?" It was not so much what he said that touched this man's heart as the kindly look and the sympathetic smile which Jesus bestowed upon him at the conclusion of his remarks. Said the man: "I perceive you are a priest of the Cynics, and I am thankful you restrained me. My wife has done no great wrong; she is a good woman, but she irritates me by the manner in which she picks on me in public, and I lose my temper. I am sorry for my lack of self-control, and I promise to try to live up to my former pledge to one of your brothers who taught me the better way many years ago. I promise you."

And then, in bidding him farewell, Jesus said: "My brother, always remember that man has no rightful authority over woman unless the woman has willingly and voluntarily given him such authority. Your wife has engaged to go through life with you, to help you fight its battles, and to assume the far greater share of the burden of bearing and rearing your children; and in return for this special service it is only fair that she receive from you that special protection which man can give to woman as the partner who must carry, bear, and nurture the children. The loving care and consideration which a man is willing to bestow upon his wife and their children are the measure of that man's attainment of the higher levels of creative and spiritual self-consciousness. Do you not know that men and women are partners with God in that they co-operate to create beings who grow up to possess themselves of the potential of immortal souls? The Father in heaven treats the Spirit Mother of the children of the universe as one equal to himself. It is Godlike to share your life and all that relates thereto on equal terms with the mother partner who so fully shares with you that divine experience of reproducing yourselves

"THE LOVING CARE AND CONSIDERATION WHICH A MAN IS WILLING TO BESTOW UPON HIS WIFE AND THEIR CHILDREN ARE THE MEASURE OF THAT MAN'S ATTAINMENT OF THE HIGHER LEVELS OF CREATIVE AND SPIRITUAL SELF-CONSCIOUSNESS."

[DEL PARSON — *The Intervention*]

in the lives of your children. If you can only love your children as God loves you, you will love and cherish your wife as the Father in heaven honors and exalts the Infinite Spirit, the mother of all the spirit children of a vast universe."

As they went on board the boat, they looked back upon the scene of the teary-eyed couple standing in silent embrace. Having heard the latter half of Jesus' message to the man, Gonod was all day occupied with meditations thereon, and he resolved to reorganize his home when he returned to India.

At Corinth

By the time they reached Corinth, Ganid was becoming very much interested in the Jewish religion, and so it was not strange that, one day as they passed the synagogue and saw the people going in, he requested Jesus to take him to the service. That day they heard a learned rabbi discourse on the "Destiny of Israel," and after the service they met one Crispus, the chief ruler of this synagogue. Many times they went back to the synagogue services, but chiefly to meet Crispus. Ganid grew to be very fond of Crispus, his wife, and their family of five children. He much enjoyed observing how a Jew conducted his family life.

While Ganid studied family life, Jesus was teaching Crispus the better ways of religious living. Jesus held more than twenty sessions with this forward-looking Jew; and it is not surprising, years afterward, when Paul was preaching in this very synagogue, and when the Jews had rejected his message and had voted to forbid his further preaching in the synagogue, and when he then went to

the gentiles, that Crispus with his entire family embraced the new religion, and that he became one of the chief supports of the Christian church which Paul subsequently organized at Corinth.

During the eighteen months Paul preached in Corinth, being later joined by Silas and Timothy, he met many others who had been taught by the "Jewish tutor of the son of an Indian merchant."

Jesus and Ganid were often guests in another Jewish home, that of Justus, a devout merchant, who lived alongside the synagogue. And many times, subsequently, when the Apostle Paul sojourned in this home, did he listen to the recounting of these visits with the Indian lad and his Jewish tutor, while both Paul and Justus wondered whatever became of such a wise and brilliant Hebrew teacher.

Several times in the home of Crispus, Jesus met one Gaius, who subsequently became a loyal supporter of Paul. During these two months in Corinth they held intimate conversations with scores of worth-while individuals, and as a result of all these apparently casual contacts more than half of the individuals so affected became members of the subsequent Christian community. ∎

A.D. 23 CONTINUUM

The Two Courtesans

When in Rome, Ganid observed that Jesus refused to accompany them to the public baths. Several times afterward the young man sought to induce Jesus further to express himself in regard to the relations of the sexes. Though he would answer the lad's questions, he never seemed disposed to discuss these subjects at great length. One evening as they strolled about Corinth out near where the wall of the citadel ran down to the sea, they were accosted by two public women. Ganid had imbibed the idea, and rightly, that Jesus was a man of high ideals, and that he abhorred everything which partook of uncleanness or savored of evil; accordingly he spoke sharply to these women and rudely motioned them away. When Jesus saw this, he said to Ganid: "You mean well, but you should not presume thus to speak to the children of God, even though they chance to be his erring children. Who are we that we should sit in judgment on these women? Do you happen to know all of the circumstances which led them to resort to such methods of obtaining a livelihood? Stop here with me while we talk about these matters." The courtesans were astonished at what he said even more than was Ganid.

As they stood there in the moonlight, Jesus went on to say: "There lives within every human mind a divine spirit, the gift of the Father in heaven. This good spirit ever strives to lead us to God, to help us to find God and to know God; but also within mortals there are many natural physical tendencies which the Creator put there to serve the well-being of the individual and the race. Now, oftentimes, men and women become confused in their efforts to understand themselves and to grapple with the manifold difficulties of making a living in a world so largely dominated by selfishness and sin. I perceive, Ganid, that neither of these women

is willfully wicked. I can tell by their faces that they have experienced much sorrow; they have suffered much at the hands of an apparently cruel fate; they have not intentionally chosen this sort of life; they have, in discouragement bordering on despair, surrendered to the pressure of the hour and accepted this distasteful means of obtaining a livelihood as the best way out of a situation that to them appeared hopeless. Ganid, some people are really wicked at heart; they deliberately choose to do mean things, but, tell me, as you look into these now tear-stained faces, do you see anything bad or wicked?" And as Jesus paused for his reply, Ganid's voice choked up as he stammered out his answer: "No, Teacher, I do not. And I apologize for my rudeness to them—I crave their forgiveness." Then said Jesus: "And I bespeak for them that they have forgiven you as I speak for my Father in heaven that he has forgiven them. Now all of you come with me to a friend's house where we will seek refreshment and plan for the new and better life ahead." Up to this time the amazed women had not uttered a word; they looked at each other and silently followed as the men led the way.

Imagine the surprise of Justus' wife when, at this late hour, Jesus appeared with Ganid and these two strangers, saying: "You will forgive us for coming at this hour, but Ganid and I desire a bite to eat, and we would share it with these our new-found friends, who are also in need of nourishment; and besides all this, we come to you with the thought that you will be interested in counseling with us as to the best way to help these women get a new start in life. They can tell you their story, but I surmise they have

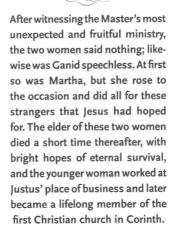

THE COURTESANS

After witnessing the Master's most unexpected and fruitful ministry, the two women said nothing; likewise was Ganid speechless. At first so was Martha, but she rose to the occasion and did all for these strangers that Jesus had hoped for. The elder of these two women died a short time thereafter, with bright hopes of eternal survival, and the younger woman worked at Justus' place of business and later became a lifelong member of the first Christian church in Corinth.

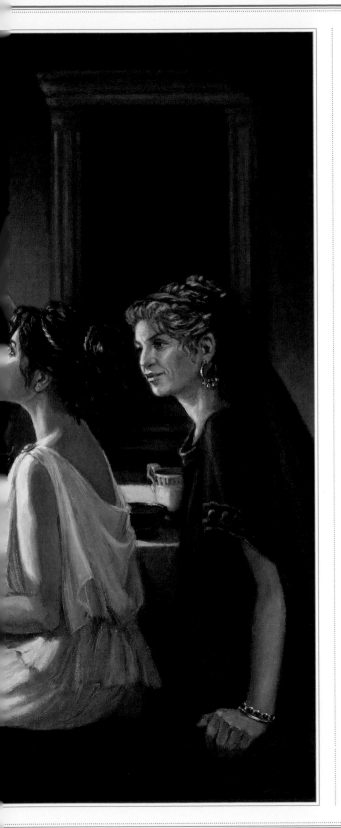

had much trouble, and their very presence here in your house testifies how earnestly they crave to know good people, and how willingly they will embrace the opportunity to show all the world— and even the angels of heaven—what brave and noble women they can become."

When Martha, Justus' wife, had spread the food on the table, Jesus, taking unexpected leave of them, said: "As it is getting late, and since the young man's father will be awaiting us, we pray to be excused while we leave you here together— three women—the beloved children of the Most High. And I will pray for your spiritual guidance while you make plans for a new and better life on earth and eternal life in the great beyond."

Thus did Jesus and Ganid take leave of the women.

PERSONAL WORK
IN CORINTH

Jesus and Ganid had many more interesting experiences in Corinth. They had close converse with a great number of persons who greatly profited by the instruction they received from Jesus.

The miller he taught about grinding up the grains of truth in the mill of living experience so as to render the difficult things of divine life readily receivable by even the weak and feeble among one's fellow mortals. Said Jesus: "Give the milk of truth to those who are babes in spiritual perception. In your living and loving ministry serve spiritual food in attractive form and suited to the capacity of receptivity of each of your inquirers."

To the Roman centurion he said: "Render unto Caesar the things which are Caesar's and unto God the things which are God's. The sincere service of

[SLAWA RADZISZEWSKA — *The Two Courtesans*]

God and the loyal service of Caesar do not conflict unless Caesar should presume to arrogate to himself that homage which alone can be claimed by Deity. Loyalty to God, if you should come to know him, would render you all the more loyal and faithful in your devotion to a worthy emperor."

To the earnest leader of the Mithraic cult he said: "You do well to seek for a religion of eternal salvation, but you err to go in quest of such a glorious truth among man-made mysteries and human philosophies. Know you not that the mystery of eternal salvation dwells within your own soul? Do you not know that the God of heaven has sent his spirit to live within you, and that this spirit will lead all truth-loving and God-serving mortals out of this life and through the portals of death up to the eternal heights of light where God waits to receive his children? And never forget: You who know God are the sons of God if you truly yearn to be like him."

To the Epicurean teacher he said: "You do well to choose the best and esteem the good, but are you wise when you fail to discern the greater things of mortal life which are embodied in the spirit realms derived from the realization of the presence of God in the human heart? The great thing in all human experience is the realization of knowing the God whose spirit lives within you and seeks to lead you forth on that long and almost endless journey of attaining the personal presence of our common Father, the God of all creation, the Lord of universes."

To the Greek contractor and builder he said: "My friend, as you build the material structures of men, grow a spiritual character in the similitude of the divine spirit within your soul. Do not let your achievement as a temporal builder outrun your attainment as a spiritual son of the kingdom of heaven. While you build the mansions of time for another, neglect not to secure your title to the mansions of eternity for yourself. Ever remember, there is a city whose foundations are righteousness and truth, and whose builder and maker is God."

To the Roman judge he said: "As you judge men, remember that you yourself will also some day come to judgment before the bar of the Rulers of a universe. Judge justly, even mercifully, even as you shall some day thus crave merciful consideration at the hands of the Supreme Arbiter. Judge as you would be judged under similar circumstances, thus being guided by the spirit of the law as well as by its letter. And even as you accord justice dominated by fairness in the light of the need of those who are brought before you, so shall you have the right to expect justice tempered by mercy when you sometime stand before the Judge of all the earth."

To the mistress of the Greek inn he said: "Minister your hospitality as one who entertains the children of the Most High. Elevate the drudgery of your daily toil to the high levels of a fine art through the increasing realization that you minister to God in the persons whom he indwells by his spirit which has descended to live within the hearts of men, thereby seeking to transform their minds and lead their souls to the knowledge of the Paradise Father of all these bestowed gifts of the divine spirit." ∎

MINISTRY TO HUNGRY SOULS

Jesus had many visits with a Chinese merchant. In saying good-bye, he admonished him: "Worship only God, who is your true spirit ancestor. Remember that the Father's spirit ever lives within you and always points your soul-direction heavenward. If you follow the unconscious leadings of this immortal spirit, you are certain to continue on in the uplifted way of finding God. And when you do attain the Father in heaven, it will be because by seeking him you have become more and more like him. And so farewell, Chang,

[SLAWA RADZISZEWSKA — *Chang, the Chinese Merchant*]

"Farewell, Chang, but we shall meet again in the worlds of light where the Father of spirit souls has provided many delightful stopping-places."

but only for a season, for we shall meet again in the worlds of light where the Father of spirit souls has provided many delightful stopping-places for those who are Paradise-bound."

To the traveler from Britain he said: "My brother, I perceive you are seeking for truth, and I suggest that the spirit of the Father of all truth may chance to dwell within you. Did you ever sincerely endeavor to talk with the spirit of your own soul? Such a thing is indeed difficult and seldom yields consciousness of success; but every honest attempt of the material mind to communicate with its indwelling spirit meets with certain success, notwithstanding that the majority of all such magnificent human experiences must long remain as superconscious registrations in the souls of such God-knowing mortals."

To the runaway lad Jesus said: "Remember, there are two things you cannot run away from— God and yourself. Wherever you may go, you take with you yourself and the spirit of the heavenly Father which lives within your heart. My son, stop trying to deceive yourself; settle down to the courageous practice of facing the facts of life; lay firm hold on the assurances of sonship with God and the certainty of eternal life, as I have instructed you. From this day on purpose to be a real man, a man determined to face life bravely and intelligently."

To the condemned criminal he said at the last hour: "My brother, you have fallen on evil times. You lost your way; you became entangled in the meshes of crime. From talking to you, I well know you did not plan to do the thing which is about to cost you your temporal life. But you did do this evil, and your fellows have adjudged you guilty; they have determined that you shall die. You or I may not deny the state this right of self-defense in the manner of its own choosing. There seems to be no way of humanly escaping the penalty of your wrongdoing. Your fellows must judge you by what you did, but there is a Judge to whom you may appeal for forgiveness, and who will judge you by your real motives and better intentions. You need not fear to meet the judgment of God if your repentance is genuine and your faith sincere. The fact that your error carries with it the death penalty imposed by man does not prejudice the chance of your soul to obtain justice and enjoy mercy before the heavenly courts."

Jesus enjoyed many intimate talks with a large number of hungry souls, too many to find a place in this record. The three travelers enjoyed their sojourn in Corinth. Excepting Athens, which was more renowned as an educational center, Corinth was the most important city in Greece during these Roman times, and their two months' stay in this thriving commercial center afforded opportunity for all three of them to gain much valuable experience. Their sojourn in this city was one of the most interesting of all their stops on the way back from Rome.

Gonod had many interests in Corinth, but finally his business was finished, and they prepared to sail for Athens. They traveled on a small boat which could be carried overland on a land track from one of Corinth's harbors to the other, a distance of ten miles. ∎

THE CONCLUSION OF THE TOUR

They shortly arrived at the olden center of Greek science and learning, and Ganid was thrilled with the thought of being in Athens, of being in Greece, the cultural center of the onetime Alexandrian empire, which had extended its borders even to his own land of India. There was little business to transact; so Gonod spent most of his time with Jesus and Ganid, visiting the many points of interest and listening to the interesting discussions of the lad and his versatile teacher.

A great university still thrived in Athens, and the trio made frequent visits to its halls of learning. Jesus and Ganid had thoroughly discussed the teachings of Plato when they attended the lectures in the museum at Alexandria. They all enjoyed the art of Greece, examples of which were still to be found here and there about the city.

On leaving Athens, the travelers went by way of Troas to Ephesus, the capital of the Roman province of Asia. They made many trips out to the famous temple of Artemis of the Ephesians, about two miles from the city. Artemis was the most famous goddess of all Asia Minor and a perpetuation of the still earlier mother goddess of ancient Anatolian times. The crude idol exhibited in the enormous temple dedicated to her worship was reputed to have fallen from heaven. Not all of Ganid's early training to respect images as symbols of divinity had been eradicated, and he thought it best to purchase a little silver shrine in honor of this fertility goddess of Asia Minor. That night they talked at great length about the worship of things made with human hands.

Of all the large cities they visited on this tour of the Mediterranean, they here accomplished the least of value to the subsequent work of the Christian missionaries. Christianity secured its start in Ephesus largely through the efforts of Paul, who resided here more than two years, making tents for a living and conducting lectures on religion and philosophy each night in the main audience chamber of the school of Tyrannus.

Shortly the travelers set sail for Cyprus, stopping at Rhodes. They enjoyed the long water voyage and arrived at their island destination much rested in body and refreshed in spirit.

It was their plan to enjoy a period of real rest and play on this visit to Cyprus as their tour of the Mediterranean was drawing to a close. They landed at Paphos and at once began the assembly of supplies for their sojourn of several weeks in the near-by mountains. On the third day after their arrival they started for the hills with their well-loaded pack animals.

For two weeks the trio greatly enjoyed themselves, and then, without warning, young Ganid was suddenly taken grievously ill. For two weeks he suffered from a raging fever, oftentimes becoming delirious; both Jesus and Gonod were kept busy attending the sick boy. Jesus skillfully and tenderly cared for the lad, and the father was amazed by both the gentleness and adeptness manifested in all his ministry to the afflicted youth. They were far from human habitations, and the boy was too ill to be moved; so they prepared as best they could to nurse him back to health right there in the mountains.

During Ganid's convalescence of three weeks Jesus told him many interesting things about nature and her various moods. And what fun they had as they wandered over the mountains, the boy asking questions, Jesus answering them, and the father marveling at the whole performance.

Antioch was the capital of the Roman province of Syria, and here the imperial governor had his residence. Antioch had half a million inhabitants;

it was the third city of the empire in size and the first in wickedness and flagrant immorality. Gonod had considerable business to transact; so Jesus and Ganid were much by themselves. They visited everything about this polyglot city except the grove of Daphne. Gonod and Ganid visited this notorious shrine of shame, but Jesus declined to accompany them. Such scenes were not so shocking to Indians, but they were repellent to an idealistic Hebrew.

Jesus became sober and reflective as he drew nearer Palestine and the end of their journey. He visited with few people in Antioch; he seldom went about in the city. After much questioning as to why his teacher manifested so little interest in Antioch, Ganid finally induced Jesus to say: "This city is not far from Palestine; maybe I shall come back here sometime."

After preparing their luggage for the camel caravan, they passed on down to Sidon and thence over to Damascus, and after three days they made ready for the long trek across the desert sands.

The caravan trip across the desert was not a new experience for these much-traveled men. After Ganid had watched his teacher help with the loading of their twenty camels and observed him volunteer to drive their own animal, he exclaimed, "Teacher, is there anything that you cannot do?" Jesus only smiled, saying, "The teacher surely is not without honor in the eyes of a diligent pupil." And so they set forth for the ancient city of Ur.

Jesus was much interested in the early history of Ur, the birthplace of Abraham, and he was equally fascinated with the ruins and traditions of Susa, so much so that Gonod and Ganid extended their stay in these parts three weeks in order to afford Jesus more time to conduct his investigations and also to provide the better opportunity to persuade him to go back to India with them. ∎

[Slawa Radziszewska — *Tender Loving Care*]

THE THREE FRIENDS PART

At last the day came for the separation. They were all brave, especially the lad, but it was a trying ordeal. They were tearful of eye but courageous of heart. In bidding his teacher farewell, Ganid said: "Farewell, Teacher, but not forever. When I come again to Damascus, I will look for you. I love you, for I think the Father in heaven must be something like you; at least I know you are much like what you have told me about him. I will remember your teaching, but most of all, I will never forget you." Said the father, "Farewell to a great teacher, one who has made us better and helped us to know God." And Jesus replied, "Peace be upon you, and may the blessing of the Father in heaven ever abide with you." And Jesus stood on the shore and watched as the small boat carried them out to their anchored ship. Thus the Master left his friends from India at Charax, never to see them again in this world; nor were they, in this world, ever to know that the man who later appeared as Jesus of Nazareth was this same friend they had just taken leave of—Joshua their teacher.

In India, Ganid grew up to become an influential man, a worthy successor of his eminent father, and he spread abroad many of the noble truths which he had learned from Jesus, his beloved teacher. Later on in life, when Ganid heard of the strange teacher in Palestine who terminated his career on a cross, though he recognized the similarity between the gospel of this Son of Man and the teachings of his Jewish tutor, it never occurred to him that these two were actually the same person.

Thus ended that chapter in the life of the Son of Man which might be termed:

The mission of Joshua the teacher. ✳

[SLAWA RADZISZEWSKA — *Trek Across Desert Sands*]

CHAPTER IV

THE MISSING YEARS: THE TRANSITION

The heavens were opened unto him, and he saw the Spirit of God descending as a dove, and coming upon him; and lo, a voice out of the heavens, saying, This is my beloved Son, in whom I am well pleased.

—MATTHEW 3:16–17 ERV

THE TWO YEARS OF TRANSITION BEGAN WITH AN ADVENTURE OF EXPLORATION AND MINISTRY as the conductor of a large caravan to the Caspian Sea. Jesus returned to Palestine, and after five months of solitary wanderings, he lived alone with God for six weeks wet with the dews of Mount Hermon. It was here near the end of his sojourn and as the Son of Man, as Joshua ben Joseph, that he confronted his archenemies and defeated them in power. A much-changed man came down from the mountain, and after a time of waiting for "my hour to come," he presented himself to John the Baptist for baptism in the Jordan at thirty-one and a half years old.

During the Mediterranean journey Jesus had carefully studied the people he met and the countries through which he passed, and at about this time he reached his final decision as to the remainder of his life on earth. He had fully considered and now finally approved the plan which provided that he be born of Jewish parents in Palestine, and he therefore deliberately returned to Galilee to await the beginning of his lifework as a public teacher of truth; he began to lay plans for a public career in the land of his father Joseph's people, and he did this of his own free will.

Jesus had found out through personal and human experience that Palestine was the best place in all the Roman world wherein to set forth the closing chapters, and to enact the final scenes, of his life on earth. For the first time he became fully satisfied with the program of openly manifesting his true nature and of revealing his divine identity among the Jews and gentiles of his native Palestine. He definitely decided to finish his life on earth and to complete his career of mortal existence in the same land in which he entered the human experience as a helpless babe. His bestowal career began among the Jews in Palestine, and he chose to terminate his life in Palestine and among the Jews.

THE URANTIA BOOK: PAPERS 134–135
APRIL, A.D. 24–JANUARY, A.D. 26

[J. KIRK RICHARDS — *Baptism II*]

MANAGING A CARAVAN TO THE CASPIAN SEA

After taking leave of Gonod and Ganid at Charax (in December of A.D. 23), Jesus returned by way of Ur to Babylon, where he joined a desert caravan that was on its way to Damascus. From Damascus he went to Nazareth, stopping only a few hours at Capernaum, where he paused to call on Zebedee's family. There he met his brother James, who had sometime previously come over to work in his place in Zebedee's boatshop. After talking with James and Jude (who also chanced to be in Capernaum) and after turning over to his brother James the little house which John Zebedee had managed to buy, Jesus went on to Nazareth.

At the end of his Mediterranean journey Jesus had received sufficient money to meet his living expenses almost up to the time of the beginning of his public ministry. But aside from Zebedee of Capernaum and the people whom he met on this extraordinary trip, the world never knew that he made this journey. His family always believed that he spent this time in study at Alexandria. Jesus never confirmed these beliefs, neither did he make open denial of such misunderstandings.

During his stay of a few weeks at Nazareth, Jesus visited with his family and friends, spent some time at the repair shop with his brother Joseph, but devoted most of his attention to Mary and Ruth. Ruth was then nearly fifteen years old, and this was Jesus' first opportunity to have long talks with her since she had become a young woman.

Both Simon and Jude had for some time wanted to get married, but they had disliked to do this without Jesus' consent; accordingly they had postponed these events, hoping for their eldest brother's return. Though they all regarded James as the head of the family in most matters, when it came to getting married, they wanted the blessing of Jesus. So Simon and Jude were married at a double

[GERRY METZ (1943–2018) — *The Caravan Conductor*]

wedding in early March of this year, A.D. 24. All the older children were now married; only Ruth, the youngest, remained at home with Mary.

Jesus visited with the individual members of his family quite normally and naturally, but when they were all together, he had so little to say that they remarked about it among themselves. Mary especially was disconcerted by this unusually peculiar behavior of her first-born son.

About the time Jesus was preparing to leave Nazareth, the conductor of a large caravan which was passing through the city was taken violently ill, and Jesus, being a linguist, volunteered to take his place. Since this trip would necessitate his absence

for a year, and inasmuch as all his brothers were married and his mother was living at home with Ruth, Jesus called a family conference at which he proposed that his mother and Ruth go to Capernaum to live in the home which he had so recently given to James. Accordingly, a few days after Jesus left with the caravan, Mary and Ruth moved to Capernaum, where they lived for the rest of Mary's life in the home that Jesus had provided. Joseph and his family moved into the old Nazareth home.

This was one of the more unusual years in the inner experience of the Son of Man; great progress was made in effecting working harmony between his human mind and the indwelling Adjuster. The Adjuster had been actively engaged in reorganizing the thinking and in rehearsing the mind for the great events which were in the not then distant future. The personality of Jesus was preparing for his great change in attitude toward the world. These were the in-between times, the transition stage of that being who began life as God appearing as man, and who was now making ready to complete his earth career as man appearing as God.

It was the first of April, A.D. 24, when Jesus left Nazareth on the caravan trip to the Caspian Sea region. The caravan which Jesus joined as its conductor was going from Jerusalem by way of Damascus and Lake Urmia through Assyria, Media, and Parthia to the southeastern Caspian Sea region. It was a full year before he returned from this journey.

For Jesus this caravan trip was another adventure of exploration and personal ministry. He had an interesting experience with his caravan family—passengers, guards, and camel drivers. Scores of men, women, and children residing along the route followed by the caravan lived richer lives as a result of their contact with Jesus, to them, the extraordinary conductor of a commonplace caravan. Not all who enjoyed these occasions of his personal ministry profited thereby, but the vast majority of those who met and talked with him were made better for the remainder of their natural lives.

Of all his world travels this Caspian Sea trip carried Jesus nearest to the Orient and enabled him to gain a better understanding of the Far-Eastern peoples. He made intimate and personal contact with every one of the surviving races of Urantia excepting the red. He equally enjoyed his personal ministry to each of these varied races and blended peoples, and all of them were receptive to the living truth which he brought them. The Europeans from the Far West and the Asiatics from the Far East alike gave attention to his words of hope and eternal life and were equally influenced by the life of loving service and spiritual ministry which he so graciously lived among them.

The caravan trip was successful in every way. This was a most interesting episode in the human life of Jesus, for he functioned during this year in an executive capacity, being responsible for the material intrusted to his charge and for the safe conduct of the travelers making up the caravan party. And he most faithfully, efficiently, and wisely discharged his multiple duties. ▪

A.D. 25

THE URMIA LECTURES

On the return from the Caspian region, Jesus gave up the direction of the caravan at Lake Urmia, where he tarried for slightly over two weeks. He returned as a passenger with a later caravan to Damascus, where the owners of the camels besought him to remain in their service. Declining this offer, he journeyed on with the caravan train to Capernaum, arriving the first of April, A.D. 25. No longer did he regard Nazareth as his home. Capernaum had become the home of Jesus, James, Mary, and Ruth. But Jesus never again lived with his family; when in Capernaum he made his home with the Zebedees.

On the way to the Caspian Sea, Jesus had stopped several days for rest and recuperation at the old Persian city of Urmia on the western shores of Lake Urmia. On the largest of a group of islands situated a short distance offshore near Urmia was located a large building—a lecture amphitheater—dedicated to the "spirit of religion." This structure was really a temple of the philosophy of religions.

This temple of religion had been built by a wealthy merchant citizen of Urmia and his three sons. This man was Cymboyton, and he numbered among his ancestors many diverse peoples.

The lectures and discussions in this school of religion began at ten o'clock every morning in the week. The afternoon sessions started at three o'clock, and the evening debates opened at eight o'clock. Cymboyton or one of his three sons always presided at these sessions of teaching, discussion, and debate. The founder of this unique school of religions lived and died without ever revealing his personal religious beliefs.

On several occasions Jesus participated in these discussions, and before he left Urmia, Cymboyton arranged with Jesus to sojourn with them for two weeks on his return trip and give twenty-four lectures on "The Brotherhood of Men," and to conduct twelve evening sessions of questions, discussions, and debates on his lectures in particular and on the brotherhood of men in general.

In accordance with this arrangement, Jesus stopped off on the return trip and delivered these lectures. This was the most systematic and formal of all the Master's teaching on Urantia. Never before or after did he say so much on one subject as was contained in these lectures and discussions on the brotherhood of men. In reality these lectures were on the "Kingdom of God" and the "Kingdoms of Men."

More than thirty religions and religious cults were represented on the faculty of this temple of religious philosophy. These teachers were chosen, supported, and fully accredited by their respective religious groups. At this time there were about seventy-five teachers on the faculty, and they lived in cottages each accommodating about a dozen persons. Every new moon these groups were changed by the casting of lots. Intolerance, a contentious spirit, or any other disposition to interfere with the smooth running of the community would bring about the prompt and summary dismissal of the offending teacher. He would be unceremoniously dismissed, and his alternate in waiting would be immediately installed in his place.

These teachers of the various religions made a great effort to show how similar their religions were in regard to the fundamental things of this life and the next. There was but one doctrine which had to be accepted in order to gain a seat on this faculty—every teacher must represent a religion which recognized God—some sort of supreme Deity. There were five independent teachers on the faculty who did not represent any organized religion, and it was as such an independent teacher that Jesus appeared before them. ∎

THE YEAR OF
SOLITARY WANDERINGS

When Jesus returned from the journey to the Caspian Sea, he knew that his world travels were about finished. He made only one more trip outside of Palestine, and that was into Syria. After a brief visit to Capernaum, he went to Nazareth, stopping over a few days to visit. In the middle of April he left Nazareth for Tyre. From there he journeyed on north, tarrying for a few days at Sidon, but his destination was Antioch.

This is the year of Jesus' solitary wanderings through Palestine and Syria. Throughout this year of travel he was known by various names in different parts of the country: the carpenter of Nazareth, the boatbuilder of Capernaum, the scribe of Damascus, and the teacher of Alexandria.

At Antioch the Son of Man lived for over two months, working, observing, studying, visiting, ministering, and all the while learning how man lives, how he thinks, feels, and reacts to the environment of human existence. For three weeks of this period he worked as a tentmaker. He remained longer in Antioch than at any other place he visited on this trip. Ten years later, when the Apostle Paul was preaching in Antioch and heard his followers speak of the doctrines of the *Damascus scribe,* he little knew that his pupils had heard the voice, and listened to the teachings, of the Master himself.

Jesus then started on his final tour, as a private individual, through the heart of Palestine, going from Beersheba in the south to Dan in the north. On this journey northward he stopped at Hebron, Bethlehem (where he saw his birthplace),

[GREG OLSEN — *In the World, Not of the World*]

Jerusalem (he did not visit Bethany), Beeroth, Lebonah, Sychar, Shechem, Samaria, Geba, En-Gannim, Endor, Madon; passing through Magdala and Capernaum, he journeyed on north; and passing east of the Waters of Merom, he went by Karahta to Dan, or Caesarea-Philippi. ∎

AUGUST, A.D. 25

THE GREAT TEMPTATION

The indwelling Thought Adjuster now led Jesus to forsake the dwelling places of men and betake himself up to Mount Hermon that he might finish his work of mastering his human mind and complete the task of effecting his full consecration to the remainder of his lifework on earth.

This was one of those unusual and extraordinary epochs in the Master's earth life on Urantia. Another and very similar one was the experience he passed through when alone in the hills near Pella just subsequent to his baptism. This period of isolation on Mount Hermon marked the termination of his purely human career, that is, the technical termination of the mortal bestowal, while the later isolation marked the beginning of the more divine phase of the bestowal. And Jesus lived alone with God for six weeks on the slopes of Mount Hermon.

After spending some time in the vicinity of Caesarea-Philippi, Jesus made ready his supplies, and securing a beast of burden and a lad named Tiglath, he proceeded along the Damascus road to a village sometime known as Beit Jenn in the foothills of Mount Hermon. Here, near the middle of August, A.D. 25, he established his headquarters, and leaving his supplies in the custody of Tiglath, he ascended the lonely slopes of the mountain.

[C. MICHAEL DUDASH — *Not By Bread Alone*]

Tiglath accompanied Jesus this first day up the mountain to a designated point about 6,000 feet above sea level, where they built a stone container in which Tiglath was to deposit food twice a week.

The first day, after he had left Tiglath, Jesus had ascended the mountain only a short way when he paused to pray. Among other things he asked his Father to send back the guardian seraphim to "be with Tiglath." He requested that he be permitted to go up to his last struggle with the realities of mortal existence alone. And his request was granted. He went into the great test with only his indwelling Adjuster to guide and sustain him.

Jesus spent the last three weeks of August and the first three weeks of September on Mount Hermon. During these weeks he finished the mortal task of achieving the circles of mind-understanding and personality-control. Throughout this period of communion with his heavenly Father the indwelling Adjuster also completed the assigned services. The mortal goal of this earth creature was there attained. Only the final phase of mind and Adjuster attunement remained to be consummated.

After more than five weeks of unbroken communion with his Paradise Father, Jesus became absolutely assured of his nature and of the certainty of his triumph over the material levels of time-space personality manifestation. He fully believed in, and did not hesitate to assert, the ascendancy of his divine nature over his human nature.

Near the end of the mountain sojourn Jesus asked his Father if he might be permitted to hold

ARCHENEMIES

Jesus ate frugally while on the mountain; he abstained from all food only a day or two at a time. The superhuman beings who confronted him on this mountain, and with whom he wrestled in spirit, and whom he defeated in power, were *real*; they were his archenemies in the system of Satania; they were not phantasms of the imagination evolved out of the intellectual vagaries of a weakened and starving mortal who could not distinguish reality from the visions of a disordered mind.

conference with his Satania enemies as the Son of Man, as Joshua ben Joseph. This request was granted. During the last week on Mount Hermon the great temptation, the universe trial, occurred. Satan (representing Lucifer) and the rebellious Planetary Prince, Caligastia, were present with Jesus and were made fully visible to him. And this "temptation," this final trial of human loyalty in the face of the misrepresentations of rebel personalities, had not to do with food, temple pinnacles, or presumptuous acts. It had not to do with the kingdoms of this world but with the sovereignty of a mighty and glorious universe. The symbolism of your records was intended for the backward ages of the world's childlike thought. And subsequent generations should understand what a great struggle the Son of Man passed through that eventful day on Mount Hermon.

To the many proposals and counterproposals of the emissaries of Lucifer, Jesus only made reply: "May the will of my Paradise Father prevail, and you, my rebellious son, may the Ancients of Days judge you divinely. I am your Creator-father; I can hardly judge you justly, and my mercy you have already spurned. I commit you to the adjudication of the Judges of a greater universe."

To all the Lucifer-suggested compromises and makeshifts, to all such specious proposals about the incarnation bestowal, Jesus only made reply, "The will of my Father in Paradise be done." And when the trying ordeal was finished, the detached guardian seraphim returned to Jesus' side and ministered to him.

On an afternoon in late summer, amid the trees

and in the silence of nature, Michael of Nebadon won the unquestioned sovereignty of his universe. On that day he completed the task set for Creator Sons to live to the full the incarnated life in the likeness of mortal flesh on the evolutionary worlds of time and space. The universe announcement of this momentous achievement was not made until the day of his baptism, months afterward, but it all really took place that day on the mountain. And when Jesus came down from his sojourn on Mount Hermon, the Lucifer rebellion in Satania and the Caligastia secession on Urantia were virtually settled. Jesus had paid the last price required of him to attain the sovereignty of his universe, which in itself regulates the status of all rebels and determines that all such future upheavals (if they ever occur) may be dealt with summarily and effectively. Accordingly, it may be seen that the so-called "great temptation" of Jesus took place sometime before his baptism and not just after that event.

At the end of this sojourn on the mountain, as Jesus was making his descent, he met Tiglath coming up to the rendezvous with food. Turning him back, he said only: "The period of rest is over; I must return to my Father's business." He was a silent and much changed man as they journeyed back to Dan, where he took leave of the lad, giving him the donkey. He then proceeded south by the same way he had come, to Capernaum. ∎

JANUARY, A.D. 26

THE TIME OF WAITING

It was now near the end of the summer, and Jesus went to the chest containing his personal effects, which had remained in Zebedee's

THE WAR IN HEAVEN

While the infamous names of Lucifer and Satan are well known on earth, Caligastia is not. Lucifer was the sovereign of Satania, a system of one thousand inhabitable worlds, earth included. Satan (a once-respected name), was his first lieutenant.

Caligastia was the Planetary Prince of our world. As such it was his duty to direct its destiny in early development by acting as its administrative head. He was trusted to represent and uphold the Father's purposes and plans on an inhabited sphere such as ours.

Two hundred thousand years ago the nefarious Lucifer led his system into rebellion, prompting the seven years of "war in heaven" of which our record speaks. — Revelation 12:7–9. The traitorous Caligastia cast his lot with Lucifer. As a result of his tragic betrayal of trust, our world was darkened by rebellion and has pursued a stormy course ever since.

During the rebellion, very little was heard of Lucifer in our world owing to the fact that he assigned Satan to advocate his cause here. But the "devil" is none other than Caligastia, our deposed Prince. Since Pentecost he is servile to Michael, and has absolutely no power to enter the minds of men; neither can he draw near to their souls to tempt or corrupt them unless they really desire to be cursed with his wicked presence. After the pouring out of the Spirit of Truth upon all flesh, there never again can be such a thing as demoniacal possession.

At the time Jesus was here in the flesh, Lucifer, Satan, and Caligastia were leagued together to effect the miscarriage of his bestowal mission. But they signally failed. Jesus once said that he "beheld Satan falling as lightning from heaven." — Luke 10:18. And of Caligastia: "The old order is bringing itself to judgment; the Prince of this world I have cast down." — John 12:30–31. (See also p. 294).

workshop, put on his apron, and presented himself for work, saying, "It behooves me to keep busy while I wait for my hour to come." And he worked several months, until January of the following year, in the boatshop, by the side of his brother James. After this period of working with Jesus, no matter what doubts came up to becloud James's understanding of the lifework of the Son of Man, he never again really and wholly gave up his faith in the mission of Jesus.

During this final period of Jesus' work at the boatshop, he spent most of his time on the interior finishing of some of the larger craft. He took great pains with all his handiwork and seemed to experience the satisfaction of human achievement when he had completed a commendable piece of work. Though he wasted little time upon trifles, he was a painstaking workman when it came to the essentials of any given undertaking.

As time passed, rumors came to Capernaum of one John who was preaching while baptizing penitents in the Jordan, and John preached: "The kingdom of heaven is at hand; repent and be baptized." Jesus listened to these reports as John slowly worked his way up the Jordan valley from the ford of the river nearest to Jerusalem. But Jesus worked on, making boats, until John had journeyed up the river to a point near Pella in the month of January of the next year, A.D. 26, when he laid down his tools, declaring, "My hour has come," and presently presented himself to John for baptism.

But a great change had been coming over Jesus. Few of the people who had enjoyed his visits and ministrations as he had gone up and down in the land ever subsequently recognized in the public teacher the same person they had known and loved as a private individual in former years. And there was a reason for this failure of his early

[RUSS DOCKEN — *My Hour Has Come*]

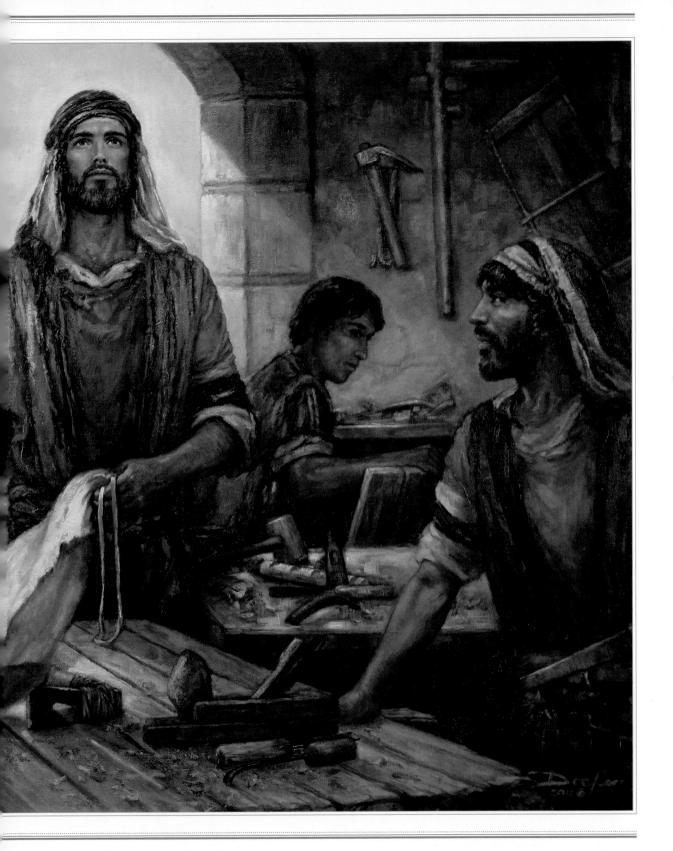

beneficiaries to recognize him in his later role of public and authoritative teacher. For long years this transformation of mind and spirit had been in progress, and it was finished during the eventful sojourn on Mount Hermon. ∎

THE BAPTISM IN THE JORDAN

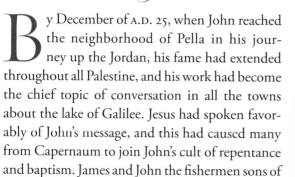

By December of A.D. 25, when John reached the neighborhood of Pella in his journey up the Jordan, his fame had extended throughout all Palestine, and his work had become the chief topic of conversation in all the towns about the lake of Galilee. Jesus had spoken favorably of John's message, and this had caused many from Capernaum to join John's cult of repentance and baptism. James and John the fishermen sons of Zebedee had gone down in December, soon after John took up his preaching position near Pella, and had offered themselves for baptism. They went to see John once a week and brought back to Jesus fresh, firsthand reports of the evangelist's work.

Jesus' brothers James and Jude had talked about going down to John for baptism; and now that Jude had come over to Capernaum for the Sabbath services, both he and James, after listening to Jesus' discourse in the synagogue, decided to take counsel with him concerning their plans. This was on Saturday night, January 12, A.D. 26. Jesus requested that they postpone the discussion until the following day, when he would give them his answer. He slept very little that night, being in close communion with the Father in heaven. He had arranged to have noontime lunch with his brothers and to advise them concerning baptism by John. That Sunday morning Jesus was working as usual in the boatshop. James and Jude had arrived with the lunch and were waiting in the lumber room for him, as it was not yet time for the midday recess, and they knew that Jesus was very regular about such matters.

Just before the noon rest, Jesus laid down his tools, removed his work apron, and merely announced to the three workmen in the room with him, "My hour has come." He went out to his brothers James and Jude, repeating, "My hour has come—let us go to John." And they started immediately for Pella, eating their lunch as they journeyed. This was on Sunday, January 13. They tarried for the night in the Jordan valley and arrived on the scene of John's baptizing about noon of the next day.

John had just begun baptizing the candidates for the day. Scores of repentants were standing in line awaiting their turn when Jesus and his two brothers took up their positions in this line of earnest men and women who had become believers in John's preaching of the coming kingdom. John had been inquiring about Jesus of Zebedee's sons. He had heard of Jesus' remarks concerning his preaching, and he was day by day expecting to see him arrive on the scene, but he had not expected to greet him in the line of baptismal candidates.

Being engrossed with the details of rapidly baptizing such a large number of converts, John did not look up to see Jesus until the Son of Man stood in his immediate presence. When John recognized Jesus, the ceremonies were halted for a moment while he greeted his cousin in the flesh and asked, "But why do you come down into the water to greet me?" And Jesus answered, "To be subject to your baptism." John replied: "But I have need to be baptized by you. Why do you come to me?" And Jesus whispered to John: "Bear with me now, for it becomes us to set this example for my brothers standing here with me, and that the people may know that my hour has come."

There was a tone of finality and authority in Jesus' voice. John was atremble with emotion as he made ready to baptize Jesus of Nazareth in the

Jordan at noon on Monday, January 14, A.D. 26. Thus did John baptize Jesus and his two brothers James and Jude. And when John had baptized these three, he dismissed the others for the day, announcing that he would resume baptisms at noon the next day. As the people were departing, the four men still standing in the water heard a strange sound, and presently there appeared for a moment an apparition immediately over the head of Jesus, and they heard a voice saying, "This is my beloved Son in whom I am well pleased." A great change came over the countenance of Jesus, and coming up out of the water in silence he took leave of them, going toward the hills to the east. And no man saw Jesus again for forty days.

John followed Jesus a sufficient distance to tell

[HARRY ANDERSON — *John the Baptist Baptizing Jesus*]

him the story of Gabriel's visit to his mother ere either had been born, as he had heard it so many times from his mother's lips. He allowed Jesus to continue on his way after he had said, "Now I know of a certainty that you are the Deliverer." But Jesus made no reply.

This day of baptism ended the purely human life of Jesus. The divine Son has found his Father, the Universal Father has found his incarnated Son, and they speak the one to the other.

(Jesus was almost thirty-one and one-half years old when he was baptized. While Luke says that Jesus was baptized in the fifteenth year of the reign of Tiberius Caesar, which would be A.D. 29 since Augustus died in A.D. 14, it should be recalled that Tiberius was coemperor with Augustus for two and one-half years before the death of Augustus, having had coins struck in his honor in October, A.D. 11. The fifteenth year of his actual rule was, therefore, this very year of A.D. 26, that of Jesus' baptism. And this was also the year that Pontius Pilate began his rule as governor of Judea.) ∎

A.D. 26

JOHN THE BAPTIST

After the experience of this day the preaching of John took on new and certain notes of proclamation concerning the coming kingdom and the expected Messiah. It was a tense time, these forty days of tarrying, waiting for the return of Jesus. But John continued to preach with great power, and his disciples began at about this time to preach to the overflowing throngs which gathered around John at the Jordan.

These were strenuous days in John's experience, and he prayed for the return of Jesus. Some of John's disciples organized scouting parties to go in search of Jesus, but John forbade, saying: "Our times are in the hands of the God of heaven; he will direct his chosen Son."

It was early on the morning of Sabbath, February 23, that the company of John, engaged in eating their morning meal, looked up toward the north and beheld Jesus coming to them. As he approached them, John stood upon a large rock and, lifting up his sonorous voice, said: "Behold the Son of God, the deliverer of the world! This is he of whom I have said, 'After me there will come one who is preferred before me because he was before me.' For this cause came I out of the wilderness to preach repentance and to baptize with water, proclaiming that the kingdom of heaven is at hand. And now comes one who shall baptize you with the Holy Spirit. And I beheld the divine spirit descending upon this man, and I heard the voice of God declare, 'This is my beloved Son in whom I am well pleased.'"

Jesus bade them return to their food while he sat down to eat with John, his brothers James and Jude having returned to Capernaum.

Early in the morning of the next day he took leave of John and his disciples, going back to Galilee. He gave them no word as to when they would

The Rugged and Fiery Prophet

John was the greatest of all the prophets as Jesus himself declared some three months before John's execution, when he said: "Verily, verily, I say to you, among those born of women there has not arisen a greater than John the Baptist."

John was born in the City of Judah, March 25, 7 B.C., in accordance with the promise that Gabriel made to Elizabeth in June of the previous year when he announced to her: "You shall call your son John. He will grow up dedicated to the Lord your God, and when he has come to full years, he will gladden your heart because he will turn many souls to God, and he will also proclaim the coming of the soul-healer of your people and the spirit-liberator of all mankind. Your kinswoman Mary shall be the mother of this child of promise, and I will also appear to her."

John grew up to become a Nazarite, and being greatly impressed with Elijah, adopted his style of dress and speech. He lived the simple life of a shepherd in the wilderness of Judea near the Engedi colony at the Dead Sea. At last he settled that he was to become the herald of the Messiah and went forth from Engedi one day in March of A.D. 25 to begin his short but brilliant career as a public preacher, proclaiming: "Repent, for the kingdom of heaven is at hand!"

It was apparent to all who heard John that he was more than a preacher. The great majority of those who listened to this strange man who had come up from the Judean wilderness went away believing that they had heard the voice of a prophet.

There was still another and a *new* feature about his work: He baptized every one of his believers in the Jordan "for the remission of sins." In his short career of only fifteen months, he baptized considerably over one hundred thousand penitents.

After the baptism of Jesus, the character of John's preaching gradually changed into a proclamation of mercy for the common people, while he denounced with renewed vehemence the corrupt political and religious rulers. It was near the village of Adam that he made the memorable attack upon Herod Antipas for divorcing his wife Phasaelis, and unlawfully taking Herodias, the wife of his brother Philip. His fiery denunciation landed this rugged and noble child of nature into Herod's despicable prison in the fortress of Machaerus where he languished for more than a year and a half; in no small part due to the intense and bitter hatred of Herodias.

In celebration of his birthday Herod made a great feast. Herodias had failed to bring about John's death by direct appeal to Herod, so she now set herself to the task of having John put to death by cunning planning.

In the course of the evening's festivities and entertainment, Herodias presented her daughter to dance before the banqueters. Herod was very much pleased with the damsel's performance and being well under the influence of his many wines, called her before him and said: "You are charming. I am much pleased with you. Ask me on this my birthday for whatever you desire, and I will give it to you, even to the half of my kingdom." The young lady drew aside and inquired of her mother what she should ask of Herod. Herodias said, "Go to Herod and ask for the head of John the Baptist." And the young woman, returning to the banquet table, said to Herod, "I request that you forthwith give me the head of John the Baptist on a platter."

Herod was filled with fear and sorrow, but because of his oath and because of all those who sat at meat with him, he would not deny the request. So John was beheaded that night of January 10, A.D. 28. A soldier brought the head of the prophet on a platter and presented it to the damsel who gave the platter to her mother. When John's disciples heard of this, they came to the prison for the body of John, and after laying it in a tomb, they went and told Jesus.

again see him. To John's inquiries about his own preaching and mission Jesus only said, "My Father will guide you now and in the future as he has in the past." And these two great men separated that morning on the banks of the Jordan, never again to greet each other in the flesh.

Since Jesus had gone north into Galilee, John felt led to retrace his steps southward. Accordingly, on Sunday morning, March 3, John and the remainder of his disciples began their journey south. About one quarter of John's immediate followers had meantime departed for Galilee in quest of Jesus. There was a sadness of confusion about John. He never again preached as he had before baptizing Jesus. He somehow felt that the responsibility of the coming kingdom was no longer on his shoulders. He felt that his work was almost finished; he was disconsolate and lonely. But he preached, baptized, and journeyed on southward. Near the village of Adam, John tarried for several weeks, and it was here that he made the memorable attack upon Herod Antipas for unlawfully taking the wife of another man.

John Is Arrested

Herod Antipas, in whose territory John had been preaching, became alarmed lest he and his disciples should start a rebellion. Herod also resented John's public criticisms of his domestic affairs. In view of all this, Herod decided to put John in prison. Accordingly, very early in the morning of June 12, before the multitude arrived to hear the preaching and witness the baptizing, the agents of Herod placed John under arrest. As weeks passed and he was not released, his disciples scattered over all Palestine, many of them going into Galilee to join the followers of Jesus.

After he had been in prison several months, a group of his disciples came to him and, after reporting concerning the public activities of Jesus, said: "So you see, Teacher, that he who was with you at the upper Jordan prospers and receives all who come to him. He even feasts with publicans and sinners. You bore courageous witness to him, and yet he does nothing to effect your deliverance." But John answered his friends: "This man can do nothing unless it has been given him by his Father in heaven. You well remember that I said, 'I am not the Messiah, but I am one sent on before to prepare the way for him.' And that I did. He who has the bride is the bridegroom, but the friend of the bridegroom who stands near by and hears him rejoices greatly because of the bridegroom's voice. This, my joy, therefore is fulfilled. He must increase but I must decrease. I am of this earth and have declared my message. Jesus of Nazareth comes down to the earth from heaven and is above us all. The Son of Man has descended from God, and the words of God he will declare to you. For the Father in heaven gives not the spirit by measure to his own Son. The Father loves his Son and will presently put all things in the hands of this Son. He who believes in the Son has eternal life. And these words which I speak are true and abiding."

These disciples were amazed at John's pronouncement, so much so that they departed in silence. John was also much agitated, for he perceived that he had uttered a prophecy. Never again did he wholly doubt the mission and divinity of Jesus. But it was a sore disappointment to John that Jesus sent him no word, that he came not to see him, and that he exercised none of his great power to deliver him from prison. But Jesus knew all about this. He had great love for John, but being now cognizant of his divine nature and knowing fully the great things in preparation for John when he departed from this world and also knowing that John's work on earth was finished, he constrained himself not to interfere in the natural outworking of the great preacher-prophet's career.

This long suspense in prison was humanly unbearable. Just a few days before his death John again sent trusted messengers to Jesus, inquiring: "Is my work done? Why do I languish in prison?

[LOUIS TIFFANY — *John the Baptist*]

Are you truly the Messiah, or shall we look for another?" And when these two disciples gave this message to Jesus, the Son of Man replied: "Go back to John and tell him that I have not forgotten but to suffer me also this, for it becomes us to fulfill all righteousness. Tell John what you have seen and heard—that the poor have good tidings preached to them—and, finally, tell the beloved herald of my earth mission that he shall be abundantly blessed in the age to come if he finds no occasion to doubt and stumble over me." And this was the last word John received from Jesus. This message greatly comforted him and did much to stabilize his faith and prepare him for the tragic end of his life in the flesh which followed so soon upon the heels of this memorable occasion. ✳

"My Hour Has Come"

And he said to them, "Follow me, and I will make you fishers of men."
—Matthew 4:19 RSV

There is yet one more missing year not found in the gospel records: The Master's public ministry is generally thought to have lasted somewhere around three years, but it was in fact a year longer. Jesus spent this mostly private first year in training his ambassadors of a spiritual kingdom and sending them out two and two in quiet personal ministry. He has warned them that the world will stumble at his words: "Have I not made it plain to you that my kingdom is not of this world? I have told you many times that I have not come to sit on David's throne. Banish from your minds this idea that my kingdom is a rule of power or a reign of glory." Even though they did not fully comprehend his teaching, they all truly *believed in Jesus*.

The teachings and practices of Jesus regarding tolerance and kindness ran counter to the long-standing attitude of the Jews toward other peoples whom they considered heathen. For generations the Jews had nourished an attitude toward the outside world which made it impossible for them to accept the Master's teachings about the spiritual brotherhood of man. They were unwilling to accept as the Son of God one who taught such new and strange doctrines. These circumstances rendered it impossible for the Jews to fulfill their divine destiny as messengers of the new gospel of religious freedom and spiritual liberty. They could not break the fetters of tradition.

Jesus began his public work at the height of the popular interest in John's preaching and at a time when the Jewish people of Palestine were eagerly looking for the appearance of the Messiah. They devoutly believed that, as Moses had delivered their fathers from Egyptian bondage by miraculous wonders, so would the coming Messiah deliver them from Roman domination by even greater miracles of power and marvels of racial triumph. They were looking for a restoration of Jewish national glory—Israel's temporal exaltation—rather than for the salvation of the world. It therefore becomes evident that Jesus of Nazareth could never satisfy this materialistic Messianic concept of the Jewish mind. Many of their reputed Messianic predictions, had they but viewed these prophetic utterances in a different light, would have very naturally prepared their minds for a recognition of Jesus as the terminator of one age and the inaugurator of a new and better dispensation of mercy and salvation for all nations.

THE URANTIA BOOK: PAPERS 136–140
JANUARY, A.D. 26–JANUARY, A.D. 27

[Del Parson — *Facing Eternity*]

FORTY DAYS IN THE PEREAN WILDERNESS

Following his baptism in the Jordan, Jesus was now wholly self-conscious concerning his relation to the universe of his making and also to the universe of universes, supervised by the Paradise Father, his Father in heaven. He now fully recalled all of the events that took place prior to his incarnation on earth.

Jesus had endured the great temptation of his mortal bestowal before his baptism when he had been wet with the dews of Mount Hermon for six weeks. There on Mount Hermon, as an unaided mortal of the realm, he had met and defeated Caligastia, the prince of this world. He now went into forty days of retirement in the hills of Perea to formulate the plans and determine upon the technique of proclaiming the new kingdom of God in the hearts of men.

Jesus did not go into retirement for the purpose of fasting and for the affliction of his soul. He was not an ascetic, and he came forever to destroy all such notions regarding the approach to God. He desired to be away for a season of quiet meditation so that he could think out the plans and decide upon the procedures for the prosecution of his public labors in behalf of this world and for all other worlds in his local universe.

Throughout all of these forty days of isolation James and John the sons of Zebedee were searching for Jesus. Many times they were not far from his abiding place, but never did they find him.

Day by day, up in the hills, Jesus formulated the plans for the remainder of his Urantia bestowal.

[GREG OLSEN — *Worlds Without End*]

He first decided not to teach contemporaneously with John. He planned to remain in comparative retirement until the work of John achieved its purpose, or until John was suddenly stopped by imprisonment. Jesus well knew that John's fearless and tactless preaching would presently arouse the fears and enmity of the civil rulers. In view of John's precarious situation, Jesus began definitely to plan his program of public labors in behalf of his people and the world, in behalf of every inhabited world throughout his vast universe. Michael's mortal bestowal was *on* Urantia but *for* all worlds of his universe.

Jesus did not fast during this forty days' isolation. The longest period he went without food was his first two days in the hills when he was so engrossed with his thinking that he forgot all about eating. But on the third day he went in search of food. Neither was he *tempted* during this time by any evil spirits or rebel personalities of station on this world or from any other world.

These forty days were the occasion of the final conference between the human and the divine minds, or rather the first real functioning of these two minds as now made one. The results of this momentous season of meditation demonstrated conclusively that the divine mind has triumphantly and spiritually dominated the human intellect. The mind of man has become the mind of God from this time on, and though the selfhood of the mind of man is ever present, always does this spiritualized human mind say, "Not my will but yours be done."

The transactions of this eventful time were not the fantastic visions of a starved and weakened mind, neither were they the confused and puerile symbolisms which afterward gained record as the "temptations of Jesus in the wilderness."

The forty days in the mountain wilderness were not a period of great temptation but rather the period of the Master's *great decisions*. During these days of lone communion with himself and his Father's immediate presence—the Personalized Adjuster (he no longer had a personal seraphic guardian)—he arrived, one by one, at the great

THE SIX GREAT DECISIONS

It was clear to Jesus that there were two ways in which he could manifest himself to the world: his own way or his Father's way. He promised himself that in a situation involving any two ways he would always choose the Father's will. And he lived out the remainder of his earth life always true to that resolve. Even to the bitter end he invariably subordinated his sovereign will to that of his heavenly Father. As to the specifics of his imminent public career, Jesus made six great decisions which can be summarized as follows:

1. Of the heavenly hosts that attended Jesus throughout his earth life, he decided that he would *not* utilize a single personality of this vast assemblage unless it should become evident that this was his *Father's will*.

2. Of his own personal necessities, he now deliberately chose to pursue the path of normal earthly existence; he would not "command that these stones become loaves of bread." He might use his superhuman power for others, but never for himself.

3. He chose to refrain from all superhuman intervention when the crisis of his life in the flesh should come, and he remained loyal to this decision when they dared him to come down from the cross at Calvary.

4. He chose to establish the kingdom of heaven in the hearts of mankind by natural and ordinary methods; he refused to become a mere wonder-worker.

5. The Jews envisaged a miraculous deliverer, but Jesus chose not to inaugurate the spiritual kingdom with a brilliant and dazzling display of power. Instead he proposed to finish his work just as he began it: as the Son of Man.

6. In all other matters he pledged to always be subject to the will of his Father.

[Vasily Polenov — *Follow Me*]

decisions which were to control his policies and conduct for the remainder of his earth career. Subsequently the tradition of a great temptation became attached to this period of isolation through confusion with the fragmentary narratives of the Mount Hermon struggles, and further because it was the custom to have all great prophets and human leaders begin their public careers by undergoing these supposed seasons of fasting and prayer. It had always been Jesus' practice, when facing any new or serious decisions, to withdraw for communion with his own spirit that he might seek to know the will of God.

Throughout these eventful days Jesus lived in an ancient rock cavern, a shelter in the side of the hills near a village sometime called Beit Adis. He drank from the small spring which came from the side of the hill near this rock shelter.

If the Son of Man had any doubts about his mission and its nature when he went up in the hills after his baptism, he had none when he came back to his fellows following the forty days of isolation and decisions. As he journeyed down the mountain his face shone with the glory of spiritual victory and moral achievement. ▪

Choosing the First Six Apostles

For nearly one full year following his forty days in the wilderness (A.D. 26–27) Jesus was engaged in the choosing, training, and testing of the apostles. The remainder of this chapter chronicles significant milestones of this carefully orchestrated endeavor of preparing these twelve "messengers of the kingdom" for their work as the earthly representatives of his mission to the world.

Early on Saturday morning, February 23, A.D. 26, Jesus came down from the hills to rejoin John's company encamped at Pella. All that day Jesus mingled with the multitude. He ministered to a lad who had injured himself in a fall and journeyed to the near-by village of Pella to deliver the boy safely into the hands of his parents.

During this Sabbath two of John's leading disciples spent much time with Jesus. Of all John's followers one named Andrew was the most profoundly impressed with Jesus; he accompanied him on the trip to Pella with the injured boy. On the way back to John's rendezvous he asked Jesus many questions, and just before reaching their destination, the two paused for a short talk, during which Andrew said: "I have observed you ever since you came to Capernaum, and I believe you are the new Teacher, and though I do not understand all your teaching, I have fully made up my mind to follow you; I would sit at your feet and learn the whole truth about the new kingdom." And Jesus, with hearty assurance, welcomed Andrew as the first of his apostles, that group of twelve who were to labor with him in the work of establishing the new kingdom of God in the hearts of men.

Andrew was a silent observer of, and sincere believer in, John's work, and he had a very able and enthusiastic brother, named Simon, who was one of John's foremost disciples. It would not be amiss to say that Simon was one of John's chief supporters.

Soon after Jesus and Andrew returned to the camp, Andrew sought out his brother, Simon, and taking him aside, informed him that he had settled in his own mind that Jesus was the great Teacher, and that he had pledged himself as a disciple. He went on to say that Jesus had accepted his proffer of service and suggested that he (Simon) likewise go to Jesus and offer himself for fellowship in the service of the new kingdom. Said Simon: "Ever since this man came to work in Zebedee's shop, I have believed he was sent by God, but what about John? Are we to forsake him? Is this the right thing to do?" Whereupon they agreed to go at once to consult John. John was saddened by the thought of losing two of his able advisers and most promising disciples, but he bravely answered their inquiries, saying: "This is but the beginning; presently will my work end, and we shall all become his disciples." Then Andrew beckoned to Jesus to draw aside while he announced that his brother desired to join himself to the service of the new kingdom. And in welcoming Simon as his second apostle, Jesus said: "Simon, your enthusiasm is commendable, but it is dangerous to the work of the kingdom. I admonish you to become more thoughtful in your speech. I would change your name to Peter."

The parents of the injured lad who lived at Pella had besought Jesus to spend the night with them, to make their house his home, and he had promised. Before leaving Andrew and his brother, Jesus said, "Early on the morrow we go into Galilee."

After Jesus had returned to Pella for the night, and while Andrew and Simon were yet discussing the nature of their service in the establishment of the forthcoming kingdom, James and John the sons of Zebedee arrived upon the scene, having just returned from their long and futile searching in the hills for Jesus. When they heard Simon Peter tell how he and his brother, Andrew, had become the first accepted counselors of the new kingdom, and that they were to leave with their new Master on the morrow for Galilee, both James and John were sad. They had known Jesus for some time, and they loved him. They had searched for him many days in the hills, and now they returned to learn that others had been preferred before them. They inquired where Jesus had gone and made haste to find him.

Jesus was asleep when they reached his abode, but they awakened him, saying: "How is it that, while we who have so long lived with you are searching in the hills for you, you prefer others before us and choose Andrew and Simon as your first associates in the new kingdom?" Jesus answered them, "Be calm in your hearts and ask yourselves, 'who directed that you should search for the Son of Man when he was about his Father's business?'" After they had recited the details of their long search in the hills, Jesus further instructed them: "You should learn to search for the secret of the new kingdom in your hearts and not in the hills. That which you sought was already present in your souls. You are indeed my brethren—you needed not to be received by me—already were you of the kingdom, and you should be of good cheer, making ready also to go with us tomorrow into Galilee." John then made bold to ask, "But, Master, will James and I be associates with you in the new kingdom, even as Andrew and Simon?" And Jesus, laying a hand on the shoulder of each of them, said: "My brethren, you were already with me in the spirit of the kingdom, even before these others made request to be received. You, my brethren, have no need to make request for entrance into the kingdom; you have been with me in the kingdom from the beginning. Before men, others may take precedence over you, but in my heart did I also number you in the councils of the kingdom, even before you thought to make this request of me. And even so might you have been first before men had you not been absent engaged in a well-intentioned but self-appointed task of seeking for one who was not lost. In the coming kingdom, be not mindful of those things which foster your anxiety but rather at all times concern yourselves only with doing the will of the Father who is in heaven."

James and John received the rebuke in good grace; never more were they envious of Andrew and Simon. And they made ready, with their two associate apostles, to depart for Galilee the next morning. From this day on the term apostle was employed to distinguish the chosen family of Jesus' advisers from the vast multitude of believing disciples who subsequently followed him.

Late that evening, James, John, Andrew, and Simon held converse with John the Baptist, and with tearful eye but steady voice the stalwart Judean prophet surrendered two of his leading disciples to become the apostles of the Galilean Prince of the coming kingdom.

Choosing Philip and Nathaniel

Sunday morning, February 24, A.D. 26, Jesus took leave of John the Baptist by the river near Pella, never again to see him in the flesh.

That day, as Jesus and his four disciple-apostles departed for Galilee, there was a great tumult in the camp of John's followers. The first great division was about to take place. The day before, John had made his positive pronouncement to Andrew and Ezra that Jesus was the Deliverer. Andrew decided to follow Jesus, but Ezra rejected the mild-mannered carpenter of Nazareth, proclaiming to his associates: "The Prophet Daniel declares that the Son of Man will come with the clouds of heaven, in power and great glory. This Galilean carpenter, this Capernaum boatbuilder, cannot be the Deliverer. Can such a gift of God come out of Nazareth? This Jesus is a relative of John, and through much kindness of heart has our teacher been deceived. Let us remain aloof from this false Messiah." When John rebuked Ezra for these utterances, he drew away with many disciples and hastened south.

While this trouble was brewing among John's followers, Jesus and his four disciple-apostles were well on their way toward Galilee. Before they crossed the Jordan, to go by way of Nain to Nazareth, Jesus, looking ahead and up the road, saw one Philip of Bethsaida with a friend coming toward them. Jesus had known Philip aforetime, and he was also well known to all four of the new apostles. He was on his way with his friend Nathaniel to visit John at Pella to learn more about the reported coming of the kingdom of God, and he was delighted to greet Jesus. Philip had been an admirer of Jesus ever since he first came to Capernaum. But Nathaniel, who lived at Cana of Galilee, did not know Jesus. Philip went forward to greet his friends while Nathaniel rested under the shade of a tree by the roadside.

Peter took Philip to one side and proceeded to explain that they, referring to himself, Andrew, James, and John, had all become associates of Jesus in the new kingdom and strongly urged Philip to volunteer for service. Philip was in a quandary. What should he do? Here, without a moment's warning—on the roadside near the Jordan—there had come up for immediate decision the most momentous question of a lifetime. By this time he was in earnest converse with Peter,

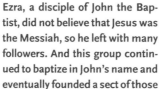

EZRA'S SECT

Ezra, a disciple of John the Baptist, did not believe that Jesus was the Messiah, so he left with many followers. And this group continued to baptize in John's name and eventually founded a sect of those who believed in John but refused to accept Jesus. A remnant of this group, Mandaeans, persists in Mesopotamia even to this day.

Andrew, and John while Jesus was outlining to James the trip through Galilee and on to Capernaum. Finally, Andrew suggested to Philip, "Why not ask the Teacher?"

It suddenly dawned on Philip that Jesus was a really great man, possibly the Messiah, and he decided to abide by Jesus' decision in this matter; and he went straight to him, asking, "Teacher, shall I go down to John or shall I join my friends who follow you?" And Jesus answered, "Follow me." Philip was thrilled with the assurance that he had found the Deliverer.

Philip led Nathaniel to Jesus, who, looking benignly into the face of the sincere doubter, said: "Behold a genuine Israelite, in whom there is no deceit. Follow me." And Nathaniel, turning to Philip, said: "You are right. He is indeed a master of men. I will also follow, if I am worthy." And Jesus nodded to Nathaniel, again saying, "Follow me."

Jesus had now assembled one half of his future corps of intimate associates, five who had for some time known him and one stranger, Nathaniel. Without further delay they crossed the Jordan and, going by the village of Nain, reached Nazareth late that evening.

They all remained overnight with Joseph in Jesus' boyhood home. The associates of Jesus little understood why their new-found teacher was so concerned with completely destroying every vestige of his writing which remained about the home in the form of the ten commandments and other mottoes and sayings. But this proceeding, together with the fact that they never saw him subsequently write—except upon the dust or in the sand—made a deep impression upon their minds.

[RUSS DOCKEN — *Leave No Writings Behind*]

On the next day, Tuesday, they all journeyed over to Cana for the wedding of Naomi, which was to take place on the following day. And in spite of Jesus' repeated warnings that they tell no man about him "until the Father's hour shall come," they insisted on quietly spreading the news abroad that they had found the Deliverer. They each confidently expected that Jesus would inaugurate his assumption of Messianic authority at the forthcoming wedding at Cana, and that he would do so with great power and sublime grandeur. They remembered what had been told them about the phenomena attendant upon his baptism, and they believed that his future course on earth would be marked by increasing manifestations of supernatural wonders and miraculous demonstrations. Accordingly, the entire countryside was preparing to gather together at Cana for the wedding feast of Naomi and Johab the son of Nathan. ▪

FEBRUARY 27, A.D. 26

THE WEDDING AT CANA

By noon on Wednesday almost a thousand guests had arrived in Cana, more than four times the number bidden to the wedding feast. It was a Jewish custom to celebrate weddings on Wednesday, and the invitations had been sent abroad for the wedding one month previously. In the forenoon and early afternoon it appeared more like a public reception for Jesus than a wedding. Everybody wanted to greet this near-famous Galilean, and he was most cordial to all, young and old, Jew and gentile. And everybody rejoiced when Jesus consented to lead the preliminary wedding procession.

Jesus was now thoroughly self-conscious regarding his human existence, his divine pre-existence, and the status of his combined, or fused, human and divine natures. With perfect poise he could at one moment enact the human role or immediately assume the personality prerogatives of the divine nature.

As the day wore on, Jesus became increasingly conscious that the people were expecting him to perform some wonder; more especially he recognized that his family and his six disciple-apostles were looking for him appropriately to announce his forthcoming kingdom by some startling and supernatural manifestation.

Early in the afternoon Mary summoned James, and together they made bold to approach Jesus to inquire if he would admit them to his confidence to the extent of informing them at what hour and at what point in connection with the wedding ceremonies he had planned to manifest himself as the "supernatural one." No sooner had they spoken of these matters to Jesus than they saw they had aroused his characteristic indignation. He said only: "If you love me, then be willing to tarry with me while I wait upon the will of my Father who is in heaven." But the eloquence of his rebuke lay in the expression of his face.

This move of his mother was a great disappointment to the human Jesus, and he was much sobered by his reaction to her suggestive proposal that he permit himself to indulge in some outward demonstration of his divinity. That was one of the very things he had decided not to do when so recently isolated in the hills. For several hours Mary was much depressed. She said to James: "I cannot understand him; what can it all mean? Is there no end to his strange conduct?" James and Jude tried to comfort their mother, while Jesus withdrew for an hour's solitude. But he returned to the gathering and was once more lighthearted and joyous.

The wedding proceeded with a hush of expectancy, but the entire ceremony was finished and not a move, not a word, from the honored guest. Then it was whispered about that the carpenter and boatbuilder, announced by John as "the Deliverer," would show his hand during the evening

[WILLIAM HOLE — *The Wedding at Cana* (detail)]

festivities, perhaps at the wedding supper. But all expectance of such a demonstration was effectually removed from the minds of his six disciple-apostles when he called them together just before the wedding supper and, in great earnestness, said: "Think not that I have come to this place to work some wonder for the gratification of the curious or for the conviction of those who doubt. Rather are we here to wait upon the will of our Father who is in heaven." But when Mary and the others saw him in consultation with his associates, they were fully persuaded in their own minds that something extraordinary was about to happen. And they all sat down to enjoy the wedding supper and the evening of festive good fellowship.

The father of the bridegroom had provided plenty of wine for all the guests bidden to the marriage feast, but how was he to know that the marriage of his son was to become an event so closely associated with the expected manifestation of Jesus as the Messianic deliverer? He was delighted to have the honor of numbering the celebrated Galilean among his guests, but before the wedding supper was over, the servants brought him the disconcerting news that the wine was running short. By the time the formal supper had ended and the guests were strolling about in the garden, the mother of the bridegroom confided to Mary that the supply of wine was exhausted. And Mary confidently said: "Have no worry—I will speak to my son. He will help us."

As Jesus was standing alone in a corner of the garden, his mother approached him, saying, "My son, they have no wine." And Jesus answered, "My good woman, what have I to do with that?" Said

Mary, "But I believe your hour has come; cannot you help us?" Jesus replied: "Again I declare that I have not come to do things in this wise. Why do you trouble me again with these matters?" And then, breaking down in tears, Mary entreated him, "But, my son, I promised them that you would help us; won't you please do something for me?" And then spoke Jesus: "Woman, what have you to do with making such promises? See that you do

THE MASTER AND THE MIRACULOUS

It may seem that this incident rescinded the spirit of the fourth great decision Jesus made in the Perean wilderness (p. 124), when he chose to establish the kingdom of heaven in the hearts of mankind by natural and ordinary methods, refusing to become a mere wonder-worker.

But this was in no sense a miracle. No law of nature was modified, abrogated, or even transcended. Nothing happened but the abrogation of *time* in association with the celestial assembly of the chemical elements requisite for the elaboration of the wine. At Cana on this occasion the agents of the Creator made wine just as they do by the ordinary natural processes *except* that they did it independently of time and with the intervention of superhuman agencies in the matter of the space assembly of the necessary chemical ingredients.

In the scientific sense of the word, "elaborate" means to produce (a substance) from its elements or simpler ingredients. Winemakers do this with every harvest but cannot, of course, abrogate time to age their vintages.

Furthermore it was evident that the enactment of this so-called miracle was not contrary to the will of the Paradise Father, else it would not have transpired, since Jesus had already subjected himself in all things to the Father's will.

Mary and the disciples of Jesus were greatly rejoiced at the supposed miracle which they thought Jesus had intentionally performed, but Jesus withdrew to a sheltered nook of the garden and engaged

in serious thought for a few brief moments. He finally decided that the episode was beyond his personal control under the circumstances and, not being adverse to his Father's will, was inevitable. When he returned to the people, they regarded him with awe; they all believed in him as the Messiah. But Jesus was sorely perplexed, knowing that they believed in him only because of the unusual occurrence which they had just inadvertently beheld. Again Jesus retired for a season to the housetop that he might think it all over. Jesus now fully comprehended that he must constantly be on guard lest his indulgence of sympathy and pity become responsible for repeated episodes of this sort. Nevertheless, many similar events occurred before the Son of Man took final leave of his mortal life in the flesh.

When the Creator himself was on earth, incarnated in the likeness of mortal flesh, it was inevitable that some extraordinary things should happen. But you should never approach Jesus through these so-called miraculous occurrences. Learn to approach the miracle through Jesus, but do not make the mistake of approaching Jesus through the miracle. And this admonition is warranted, notwithstanding that Jesus of Nazareth is the only founder of a religion who performed supermaterial acts on earth.

But religion is never enhanced by an appeal to the so-called miraculous. True religion has nothing to do with alleged miracles, and never does revealed religion point to miracles as proof of authority.

it not again. We must in all things wait upon the will of the Father in heaven."

Mary the mother of Jesus was crushed; she was stunned! As she stood there before him motionless, with the tears streaming down her face, the human heart of Jesus was overcome with compassion for the woman who had borne him in the flesh; and bending forward, he laid his hand tenderly upon her head, saying: "Now, now, Mother Mary, grieve not over my apparently hard sayings, for have I not many times told you that I have come only to do the will of my heavenly Father? Most gladly would I do what you ask of me if it were a part of the Father's will—" and Jesus stopped short, he hesitated. Mary seemed to sense that something was happening. Leaping up, she threw her arms around Jesus' neck, kissed him, and rushed off to the servants' quarters, saying, "Whatever my son says, that do." But Jesus said nothing. He now realized that he had already said—or rather desirefully thought—too much.

Mary was dancing with glee. She did not know how the wine would be produced, but she confidently believed that she had finally persuaded her first-born son to assert his authority, to dare to step forth and claim his position and exhibit his Messianic power. And, because of the presence and association of certain universe powers and personalities, of which all those present were wholly ignorant, she was not to be disappointed. The wine Mary desired and which Jesus, the God-man, humanly and sympathetically wished for, was forthcoming.

Near at hand stood six waterpots of stone, filled with water, holding about twenty gallons apiece. This water was intended for subsequent use in the final purification ceremonies of the wedding celebration. The commotion of the servants about these huge stone vessels, under the busy direction of his mother, attracted Jesus' attention, and going over, he observed that they were drawing wine out of them by the pitcherful.

It was gradually dawning upon Jesus what had happened. Of all persons present at the marriage feast of Cana, Jesus was the most surprised. Others had expected him to work a wonder, but that was just what he had purposed not to do.

When the servants drew this new wine and carried it to the best man, the "ruler of the feast," and when he had tasted it, he called to the bridegroom, saying: "It is the custom to set out first the good wine and, when the guests have well drunk, to bring forth the inferior fruit of the vine; but you have kept the best of the wine until the last of the feast."

AFTER THE WEDDING

Jesus and his apostles departed very early the next morning for Capernaum, going away without taking leave of anyone. On this journey Jesus talked over many things of importance to the coming kingdom with his newly chosen associates and especially warned them to make no mention of the turning of the water into wine. He also advised them to avoid the cities of Sepphoris and Tiberias in their future work.

After supper that evening, in the home of Zebedee and Salome, there was held one of the most important conferences of all Jesus' earthly career. Only the six apostles were present at this meeting; Jude arrived as they were about to separate. These six chosen men had journeyed from Cana to Bethsaida with Jesus, walking, as it were, on air. They were alive with expectancy and thrilled with the thought of having been selected as close associates of the Son of Man. But when Jesus set out to make clear to them who he was and what was to be his mission on earth and how it might possibly end, they were stunned. They could not grasp what he was telling them. They were speechless; even Peter was crushed beyond expression. Only the deep-thinking Andrew dared to make reply to Jesus' words of counsel. When Jesus perceived that they did not comprehend his message, when

JESUS POSSESSED THAT MATCHLESS GRACE OF PERSONALITY WHICH ENABLED HIM SO TO LIVE AMONG THEM THAT THEY WERE NOT DISMAYED BY HIS DIVINITY.

he saw that their ideas of the Jewish Messiah were so completely crystallized, he sent them to their rest while he walked and talked with his brother Jude. And before Jude took leave of Jesus, he said with much feeling: "My father-brother, I never have understood you. I do not know of a certainty whether you are what my mother has taught us, and I do not fully comprehend the coming kingdom, but I do know you are a mighty man of God. I heard the voice at the Jordan, and I am a believer in you, no matter who you are." And when he had spoken, he departed.

That night Jesus did not sleep. Donning his evening wraps, he sat out on the lake shore thinking, thinking until the dawn of the next day. In the long hours of that night of meditation Jesus came clearly to comprehend that he never would be able to make his followers see him in any other light than as the long-expected Messiah. At last he recognized that there was no way to launch his message of the kingdom except as the fulfillment of John's prediction and as the one for whom the Jews were looking. After all, though he was not the Davidic type of Messiah, he was truly the fulfillment of the prophetic utterances of the more spiritually minded of the olden seers. Never again did he wholly deny that he was the Messiah. He decided to leave the final untangling of this complicated situation to the outworking of the Father's will.

The next morning Jesus joined his friends at breakfast, but they were a cheerless group. He visited with them and at the end of the meal gathered them about him, saying: "It is my Father's will that we tarry hereabouts for a season. You have heard John say that he came to prepare the way for the kingdom; therefore it behooves us to await the completion of John's preaching. When the forerunner of the Son of Man shall have finished his work, we will begin the proclamation of the good tidings of the kingdom." He directed his apostles to return to their nets while he made ready to go with Zebedee to the boatshop, promising to see them the next day at the synagogue, where he was to speak, and appointing a conference with them that Sabbath afternoon.

For four long months—March, April, May, and June—this tarrying time continued; Jesus held over one hundred long and earnest, though cheerful and joyous, sessions with these six associates and his own brother James.

Though they called him Rabbi, they were learning not to be afraid of him. Jesus possessed that matchless grace of personality which enabled him so to live among them that they were not dismayed by his divinity. They found it really easy to be "friends with God," God incarnate in the likeness of mortal flesh. This time of waiting severely tested the entire group of believers. Absolutely nothing miraculous happened. Day by day they went about their work, while night after night they sat at Jesus' feet. And they were held together by his matchless personality and by the gracious words which he spoke to them.

Throughout this entire period Jesus spoke in the synagogue but twice. By the end of these many weeks of waiting the reports about his baptism and the wine of Cana had begun to quiet down. And Jesus saw to it that no more apparent miracles happened during this time. But even though they lived so quietly at Bethsaida, reports of the strange doings of Jesus had been carried to Herod Antipas, who in turn sent spies to ascertain what he was about. But Herod was more concerned about the preaching of John. He decided not to molest Jesus, whose work continued along so quietly at Capernaum. ■

JUNE 22, A.D. 26

INTRODUCING THE KINGDOM OF HEAVEN

On Sabbath, June 22, shortly before they went out on their first preaching tour and about ten days after John's imprisonment, Jesus occupied the synagogue pulpit for the second time since bringing his apostles to Capernaum.

A few days before the preaching of this sermon on "The Kingdom," as Jesus was at work in the boatshop, Peter brought him the news of John's arrest. Jesus laid down his tools once more, removed his apron, and said to Peter: "The Father's hour has come. Let us make ready to proclaim the gospel of the kingdom."

Before Jesus preached this memorable sermon on the kingdom of God, the first pretentious effort of his public career, he read from the Scriptures these passages: "You shall be to me a kingdom of priests, a holy people. Yahweh is our judge, Yahweh is our lawgiver, Yahweh is our king; he will save us. Yahweh is my king and my God. He is a great king over all the earth. Loving-kindness is upon Israel in this kingdom. Blessed be the glory of the Lord for he is our King."

When he had finished reading, Jesus said:

"I have come to proclaim the establishment of the Father's kingdom. And this kingdom shall include the worshiping souls of Jew and gentile, rich and poor, free and bond, for my Father is no respecter of persons; his love and his mercy are over all.

"The Father in heaven sends his spirit to indwell the minds of men, and when I shall have finished my work on earth, likewise shall the Spirit of Truth be poured out upon all flesh. And the spirit of my Father and the Spirit of Truth shall establish you in the coming kingdom of spiritual understanding and divine righteousness. My kingdom is not of this world. The Son of Man will not lead forth armies in battle for the establishment of a throne of power or a kingdom of worldly glory. When my kingdom shall have come, you shall know the Son of Man as the Prince of Peace, the revelation of the everlasting Father. The children of this world fight for the establishment and enlargement of the kingdoms of this world, but my disciples shall enter the kingdom of heaven by their moral decisions and by their spirit victories; and when they once enter therein, they shall find joy, righteousness, and eternal life.

"Those who first seek to enter the kingdom, thus beginning to strive for a nobility of character like that of my Father, shall presently possess all else that is needful. But I say to you in all sincerity: Unless you seek entrance into the kingdom with the faith and trusting dependence of a little child, you shall in no wise gain admission.

"Be not deceived by those who come saying here is the kingdom or there is the kingdom, for my Father's kingdom concerns not things visible and material. And this kingdom is even now among you, for where the spirit of God teaches and leads the soul of man, there in reality is the kingdom of heaven. And this kingdom of God is righteousness, peace, and joy in the Holy Spirit.

"John did indeed baptize you in token of repentance and for the remission of your sins, but when you enter the heavenly kingdom, you will be baptized with the Holy Spirit.

"In my Father's kingdom there shall be neither Jew nor gentile, only those who seek perfection through service, for I declare that he who would be great in my Father's kingdom must first become server of all. If you are willing to serve your fellows, you shall sit down with me in my kingdom, even as, by serving in the similitude of the creature, I shall presently sit down with my Father in his kingdom.

"This new kingdom is like a seed growing in the good soil of a field. It does not attain full fruit quickly. There is an interval of time between the establishment of the kingdom in the soul of man and that hour when the kingdom ripens into the full fruit of everlasting righteousness and eternal salvation.

"And this kingdom which I declare to you is not a reign of power and plenty. The kingdom of heaven is not a matter of meat and drink but rather a life of progressive righteousness and increasing joy in the perfecting service of my Father who is in heaven. For has not the Father said of his children of the world, 'It is my will that they should eventually be perfect, even as I am perfect.'

"I have come to preach the glad tidings of the kingdom. I have not come to add to the heavy burdens of those who would enter this kingdom. I proclaim the new and better way, and those who are able to enter the coming kingdom shall enjoy the divine rest. And whatever it shall cost you in the things of the world, no matter what price you may pay to enter the kingdom of heaven, you shall receive manyfold more of joy and spiritual progress in this world, and in the age to come eternal life.

"Entrance into the Father's kingdom waits not upon marching armies, upon overturned kingdoms of this world, nor upon the breaking of captive yokes. The kingdom of heaven is at hand, and all who enter therein shall find abundant liberty and joyous salvation.

"This kingdom is an everlasting dominion.

Those who enter the kingdom shall ascend to my Father; they will certainly attain the right hand of his glory in Paradise. And all who enter the kingdom of heaven shall become the sons of God, and in the age to come so shall they ascend to the Father. And I have not come to call the would-be righteous but sinners and all who hunger and thirst for the righteousness of divine perfection.

"John came preaching repentance to prepare you for the kingdom; now have I come proclaiming faith, the gift of God, as the price of entrance into the kingdom of heaven. If you would but believe that my Father loves you with an infinite love, then you are in the kingdom of God."

When he had thus spoken, he sat down. All who heard him were astonished at his words. His disciples marveled. But the people were not prepared to receive the good news from the lips of this God-man. About one third believed the message even though they could not fully comprehend it; about one third prepared in their hearts to reject such a purely spiritual concept of the expected kingdom, while the remaining one third could not grasp his teaching, many truly believing that he "was beside himself." ∎

JUNE 23, A.D. 26

CHOOSING THE FINAL SIX APOSTLES

The next day, Sunday, June 23, A.D. 26, Jesus imparted his final instructions to the six. He directed them to go forth, two and two, to teach the glad tidings of the kingdom. He forbade them to baptize and advised against public preaching. He went on to explain that later he would permit them to preach in public, but that for a season, and for many reasons, he desired them to acquire practical experience in dealing personally with their fellow men. Jesus purposed to make their first tour entirely one of *personal work.* Although this announcement was something of a disappointment to the apostles, still they saw, at least in part, Jesus' reason for thus beginning the proclamation of the kingdom, and they started out in good heart and with confident enthusiasm. He sent them forth by twos, James and John going to Kheresa, Andrew and Peter to Capernaum, while Philip and Nathaniel went to Tarichea.

Before they began this first two weeks of service, Jesus announced to them that he desired to ordain twelve apostles to continue the work of the kingdom after his departure and authorized each of them to choose one man from among his early converts for membership in the projected corps of apostles. John spoke up, asking: "But, Master, will these six men come into our midst and share all things equally with us who have been with you since the Jordan and have heard all your teaching in preparation for this, our first labor for the kingdom?" And Jesus replied: "Yes, John, the men you choose shall become one with us, and you will teach them all that pertains to the kingdom, even as I have taught you." After thus speaking, Jesus left them.

The six did not separate to go to their work until they had exchanged many words in discussion of Jesus' instruction that each of them should choose a new apostle. Andrew's counsel finally prevailed, and they went forth to their labors. In substance Andrew said: "The Master is right; we are too few to encompass this work. There is need for more teachers, and the Master has manifested great confidence in us inasmuch as he has intrusted us with the choosing of these six new apostles." This morning, as they separated to go to their work, there was a bit of concealed depression in each heart. They knew they were going to miss Jesus, and besides their fear and timidity, this was not the way they had pictured the kingdom of heaven being inaugurated.

This first missionary tour of the six was eminently successful. They all discovered the great value of direct and personal contact with men. They returned to Jesus more fully realizing that, after all, religion is purely and wholly a matter of *personal experience.* They began to sense how hungry were the common people to hear words of religious comfort and spiritual good cheer. When they assembled about Jesus, they all wanted to talk at once, but Andrew assumed charge, and as he called upon them one by one, they made their formal reports to the Master and presented their nominations for the six new apostles.

Jesus, after each man had presented his selection for the new apostleships, asked all the others to vote upon the nomination; thus all six of the new apostles were formally accepted by all of the older six. Then Jesus announced that they would all visit these candidates and give them the call to service.

The newly selected apostles were:

1. **Matthew Levi**, the customs collector of Capernaum, who had his office just to the east of the city, near the borders of Batanea. He was selected by Andrew.

2. **Thomas Didymus**, a fisherman of Tarichea and onetime carpenter and stone mason of Gadara. He was selected by Philip.

3. **James Alpheus**, a fisherman and farmer of Kheresa, was selected by James Zebedee.

4. **Judas Alpheus**, the twin brother of James Alpheus, also a fisherman, was selected by John Zebedee.

5. **Simon Zelotes** was a high officer in the patriotic organization of the Zealots, a position which he gave up to join Jesus' apostles. Before joining the Zealots, Simon had been a merchant. He was selected by Peter.

6. **Judas Iscariot** was an only son of wealthy Jewish parents living in Jericho. He had become attached to John the Baptist, and his Sadducee parents had disowned him. He was looking for employment in these regions when Jesus' apostles found him, and chiefly because of his

experience with finances, Nathaniel invited him to join their ranks. Judas Iscariot was the only Judean among the twelve.

Jesus spent a full day with the six, answering their questions and listening to the details of their reports, for they had many interesting and profitable experiences to relate. They now saw the wisdom of the Master's plan of sending them out to labor in a quiet and personal manner before the launching of their more pretentious public efforts.

The next day Jesus left his twelve apostles quite alone; he wanted them to become acquainted and desired that they be alone to talk over what he had taught them. The Master returned for the evening meal, and during the after-supper hours he talked to them about the ministry of seraphim, and some of the apostles comprehended his teaching. They rested for a night and the next day departed by boat for Capernaum.

Zebedee and Salome had gone to live with their son David so that their large home could be turned over to Jesus and his twelve apostles. Here Jesus spent a quiet Sabbath with his chosen messengers; he carefully outlined the plans for proclaiming the kingdom and fully explained the importance of avoiding any clash with the civil authorities, saying: "If the civil rulers are to be rebuked, leave that task to me. See that you make no denunciations of Caesar or his servants." It was this same evening that Judas Iscariot took Jesus aside to inquire why nothing was done to get John out of prison. And Judas was not wholly satisfied with Jesus' attitude.

The next week was devoted to a program of intense training. Each day the six new apostles were put in the hands of their respective nominators for a thoroughgoing review of all they had learned and experienced in preparation for the work of the kingdom. The older apostles carefully reviewed, for the benefit of the younger six, Jesus' teachings up to that hour. Evenings they all assembled in Zebedee's garden to receive Jesus' instruction.

Jesus endeavored to make clear to his apostles the difference between his teachings and his *life among them* and the teachings which might subsequently spring up *about* him. Said Jesus: "My kingdom and the gospel related thereto shall be the burden of your message. Be not sidetracked into preaching *about* me and *about* my teachings. Proclaim the gospel of the kingdom and portray my revelation of the Father in heaven but do not be misled into the bypaths of creating legends and building up a cult having to do with beliefs and teachings *about* my beliefs and teachings." But again they did not understand why he thus spoke, and no man dared to ask why he so taught them. ∎

FISHERS OF MEN

Jesus had planned for a quiet missionary campaign of five months' personal work. He did not tell the apostles how long this was to last; they worked from week to week. And early on this first day of the week, just as he was about to announce this to his twelve apostles, Simon Peter, James Zebedee, and Judas Iscariot came to have private converse with him. Taking Jesus aside, Peter made bold to say: "Master, we come at the behest of our associates to inquire whether the time is not now ripe to enter into the kingdom. And will you proclaim the kingdom at Capernaum, or are we to move on to Jerusalem? And when shall we learn, each of us, the positions we are to occupy with you in the establishment of the kingdom—" and Peter would have gone on asking further questions, but Jesus raised an admonitory hand and stopped him. And beckoning the other apostles standing near by to join them, Jesus said: "My little children, how long shall I bear with you! Have I not made it plain to you that my kingdom is not of this world? I have told you many times that I have not come to sit on David's throne, and now how is it that you are inquiring which place each of you will occupy in the Father's kingdom? Can you not perceive that I have called you as ambassadors of a spiritual kingdom? Do you not understand that soon, very soon, you are to represent me in the world and in the proclamation of the kingdom, even as I now represent my Father who is in heaven?"

Jesus now asked them how much money they had among them; he also inquired as to what provision had been made for their families. When it developed that they had hardly sufficient funds to maintain themselves for two weeks, he said: "It is not the will of my Father that we begin our work in this way. We will remain here by the sea two weeks and fish or do whatever our hands find to do; and in the meantime, under the guidance of Andrew, the first chosen apostle, you shall so organize yourselves as to provide for everything needful in your future work, both for the present personal ministry and also when I shall subsequently ordain you to preach the gospel and instruct believers." They were all greatly cheered by these words; this was their first clear-cut and positive intimation that Jesus designed later on to enter upon more aggressive and pretentious public efforts.

The apostles spent the remainder of the day perfecting their organization and completing arrangements for boats and nets for embarking on the morrow's fishing as they had all decided to devote themselves to fishing; most of them had been fishermen, even Jesus was an experienced boatman and fisherman. Many of the boats which they used the next few years had been built by Jesus' own hands. And they were good and trustworthy boats.

Jesus enjoined them to devote themselves to fishing for two weeks, adding, "And then will you go forth to become fishers of men." They fished in three groups, Jesus going out with a different group each night. And they all so much enjoyed Jesus! He was a good fisherman, a cheerful companion, and an inspiring friend; the more they worked with him, the more they loved him. Said Matthew one day: "The more you understand some people, the less you admire them, but of this man, even the less I comprehend him, the more I love him."

This plan of fishing two weeks and going out to do personal work in behalf of the kingdom for two weeks was followed for more than five months, even to the end of this year of A.D. 26, until after the cessation of those special persecutions which had been directed against John's disciples subsequent to his imprisonment. ◾

FIRST WORK OF THE TWELVE

After disposing of the fish catches of two weeks, Judas Iscariot, the one chosen to act as treasurer of the twelve, divided the apostolic funds into six equal portions, funds for the care of dependent families having been already provided. And then near the middle of August, in the year A.D. 26, they went forth two and two to the fields of work assigned by Andrew. The first two weeks Jesus went out with Andrew and Peter, the second two weeks with James and John, and so on with the other couples in the order of their choosing. In this way he was able to go out at least once with each couple before he called them together for the beginning of their public ministry.

Jesus taught them to preach the forgiveness of sin through *faith in God* without penance or sacrifice, and that the Father in heaven loves all his children with the same eternal love.

They had wonderful times throughout these five or six months during which they worked as fishermen every alternate two weeks, thereby earning enough money to support themselves in the field for each succeeding two weeks of missionary work for the kingdom.

The common people marveled at the teaching

and ministry of Jesus and his apostles. The rabbis had long taught the Jews that the ignorant could not be pious or righteous. But Jesus' apostles were both pious and righteous; yet they were cheerfully ignorant of much of the learning of the rabbis and the wisdom of the world.

Jesus made plain to his apostles the difference between the repentance of so-called good works as taught by the Jews and the change of mind by faith—the new birth—which he required as the price of admission to the kingdom. He taught his apostles that *faith* was the only requisite to entering the Father's kingdom. John had taught them "repentance—to flee from the wrath to come." Jesus taught, "Faith is the open door for entering into the present, perfect, and eternal love of God." Jesus did not speak like a prophet, one who comes to declare the word of God. He seemed to speak of himself as one having authority. Jesus sought to divert their minds from miracle seeking to the finding of a real and personal experience in the satisfaction and assurance of the indwelling of God's spirit of love and saving grace.

The disciples early learned that the Master had a profound respect and sympathetic regard for *every* human being he met, and they were tremendously impressed by this uniform and unvarying consideration which he so consistently gave to all sorts of men, women, and children. He would pause in the midst of a profound discourse that he might go out in the road to speak good cheer to a passing woman laden with her burden of body and soul. He would interrupt a serious conference with his apostles to fraternize with an intruding child. Nothing ever seemed so important to Jesus as the *individual human* who chanced to be in his immediate presence. He was master and teacher, but he was more—he was also a friend and neighbor, an

[C. MICHAEL DUDASH — *Fishers of Men*]

understanding comrade.

Though Jesus' public teaching mainly consisted in parables and short discourses, he invariably taught his apostles by questions and answers. He would always pause to answer sincere questions during his later public discourses.

The apostles were at first shocked by, but early became accustomed to, Jesus' treatment of women; he made it very clear to them that women were to be accorded equal rights with men in the kingdom. ■

FIVE MONTHS OF TESTING

This somewhat monotonous period of alternate fishing and personal work proved to be a grueling experience for the twelve apostles, but they endured the test. With all of their grumblings, doubts, and transient dissatisfactions they remained true to their vows of devotion and loyalty to the Master. It was their personal association with Jesus during these months of testing that so endeared him to them that they all (save Judas Iscariot) remained loyal and true to him even in the dark hours of the trial and crucifixion. Real men simply could not actually desert a revered teacher who had lived so close to them and had been so devoted to them as had Jesus. Through the dark hours of the Master's death, in the hearts of these apostles all reason, judgment, and logic were set aside in deference to just one extraordinary human emotion—the supreme sentiment of friendship-loyalty. These five months of work with Jesus led these apostles, each one of them, to regard him as the best *friend* he had in all the world. And it was this human sentiment, and not his superb teachings or marvelous doings, that held them together until after the resurrection and the renewal of the proclamation of the gospel of the kingdom.

Not only were these months of quiet work a great test to the apostles, a test which they survived, but this season of public inactivity was a great trial to Jesus' family. By the time Jesus was prepared to launch forth on his public work, his entire family (except Ruth) had practically deserted him. On only a few occasions did they attempt to make subsequent contact with him, and then it was to persuade him to return home with them, for they came near to believing that he was beside himself. They simply could not fathom his philosophy nor grasp his teaching; it was all too much for those of his own flesh and blood.

The apostles carried on their personal work in Capernaum, Bethsaida-Julias, Chorazin, Gerasa, Hippos, Magdala, Cana, Bethlehem of Galilee, Jotapata, Ramah, Safed, Gischala, Gadara, and Abila. Besides these towns they labored in many villages as well as in the countryside. By the end of this period the twelve had worked out fairly satisfactory plans for the care of their respective families. Most of the apostles were married, some had several children, but they had made such arrangements for the support of their home folks that, with some little assistance from the apostolic funds, they could devote their entire energies to the Master's work without having to worry about the financial welfare of their families. ■

THE TWELVE APOSTLES

It is an eloquent testimony to the charm and righteousness of Jesus' earth life that, although he repeatedly dashed to pieces the hopes of his apostles and tore to shreds their every ambition for personal exaltation, only one deserted him.

The apostles learned from Jesus about the kingdom of heaven, and Jesus learned much from them about the kingdom of men, human nature as it lives on Urantia and on the other evolutionary worlds of time and space. These twelve

[TADDEO DI BARTOLO — *The Twelve Apostles* (altarpiece ca. 1400)]

men represented many different types of human temperament, and they had not been made *alike* by schooling. Many of these Galilean fishermen carried heavy strains of gentile blood as a result of the forcible conversion of the gentile population of Galilee one hundred years previously.

Do not make the mistake of regarding the apostles as being altogether ignorant and unlearned. All of them, except the Alpheus twins, were graduates of the synagogue schools, having been thoroughly trained in the Hebrew scriptures and in much of the current knowledge of that day. Seven were graduates of the Capernaum synagogue schools, and there were no better Jewish schools in all Galilee.

When your records refer to these messengers of the kingdom as being "ignorant and unlearned," it was intended to convey the idea that they were laymen, unlearned in the lore of the rabbis and untrained in the methods of rabbinical interpretation of the Scriptures. They were lacking in so-called higher education. In modern times they would certainly be considered uneducated, and in some circles of society even uncultured. One thing is certain: They had not all been put through the same rigid and stereotyped educational curriculum. From adolescence on they had enjoyed separate experiences of learning how to live.

1. ANDREW, THE FIRST CHOSEN

Andrew, chairman of the apostolic corps of the kingdom, was born in Capernaum. He was the oldest child in a family of five—himself, his brother Simon, and three sisters. Andrew was unmarried but made his home with his married brother, Simon Peter. Both were fishermen and partners of James and John the sons of Zebedee.

In A.D. 26, the year he was chosen as an apostle, Andrew was 33, a full year older than Jesus and the oldest of the apostles. He sprang from an excellent line of ancestors and was the ablest man of the twelve. Excepting oratory, he was the peer of his associates in almost every imaginable ability. Jesus never gave Andrew a nickname, a fraternal designation. But even as the apostles soon began to call Jesus Master, so they also designated Andrew by a term the equivalent of Chief.

Every one of the apostles loved Jesus, but it remains true that each of the twelve was drawn toward him because of some certain trait of personality which made a special appeal to the individual apostle. Andrew admired Jesus because of his consistent sincerity, his unaffected dignity. When men once knew Jesus, they were possessed with the urge to share him with their friends; they really wanted all the world to know him.

When the later persecutions finally scattered the apostles from Jerusalem, Andrew journeyed through Armenia, Asia Minor, and Macedonia

ORGANIZATION OF THE APOSTLES

The apostles early organized themselves in the following manner:

1. **ANDREW,** the first chosen apostle, was designated chairman and director general of the twelve.

2. **PETER, JAMES, AND JOHN** were appointed personal companions of Jesus. They were to attend him day and night, to minister to his physical and sundry needs, and to accompany him on those night vigils of prayer and mysterious communion with the Father in heaven.

3. **PHILIP** was made steward of the group. It was his duty to provide food and to see that visitors, and even the multitude of listeners at times, had something to eat.

4. **NATHANIEL** watched over the needs of the families of the twelve. He received regular reports as to the requirements of each apostle's family and, making requisition on Judas, the treasurer, would send funds each week to those in need.

5. **MATTHEW** was the fiscal agent of the apostolic corps. It was his duty to see that the budget was balanced, the treasury replenished. If the funds for mutual support were not forthcoming, if donations sufficient to maintain the party were not received, Matthew was empowered to order the twelve back to their nets for a season. But this was never necessary after they began their public work; he always had sufficient funds in the treasurer's hands to finance their activities.

6. **THOMAS** was manager of the itinerary. It fell upon him to arrange lodgings and in a general way select places for teaching and preaching, thereby insuring a smooth and expeditious travel schedule.

7. **JAMES AND JUDAS** the twin sons of Alpheus were assigned to the management of the multitudes. It was their task to deputize a sufficient number of assistant ushers to enable them to maintain order among the crowds during the preaching.

8. **SIMON ZELOTES** was given charge of recreation and play. He managed the Wednesday programs and also sought to provide for a few hours of relaxation and diversion each day.

9. **JUDAS ISCARIOT** was appointed treasurer. He carried the bag. He paid all expenses and kept the books. He made budget estimates for Matthew from week to week and also made weekly reports to Andrew. Judas paid out funds on Andrew's authorization.

In this way the twelve functioned from their early organization up to the time of the reorganization made necessary by the desertion of Judas, the betrayer. The Master and his disciple-apostles went on in this simple manner until Sunday, January 12, A.D. 27, when he called them together and formally ordained them as ambassadors of the kingdom and preachers of its glad tidings. And soon thereafter they prepared to start for Jerusalem and Judea on their first public preaching tour.

and, after bringing many thousands into the kingdom, was finally apprehended and crucified in Patrae in Achaia. It was two full days before this robust man expired on the cross, and throughout these tragic hours he continued effectively to proclaim the glad tidings of the salvation of the kingdom of heaven.

2. SIMON PETER

When Simon joined the apostles, he was thirty years of age. He was married, had three children, and lived at Bethsaida, near Capernaum. His brother, Andrew, and his wife's mother lived with him. Both Peter and Andrew were fisher partners of the sons of Zebedee.

The Master had known Simon for some time before Andrew presented him as the second of the apostles. When Jesus gave Simon the name Peter, he did it with a smile; it was to be a sort of nickname. Simon was well known to all his friends as an erratic and impulsive fellow. True, later on, Jesus did attach a new and significant import to this lightly bestowed nickname.

The one trait which Peter most admired in Jesus was his supernal tenderness. Peter never grew weary of contemplating Jesus' forbearance. He never forgot the lesson about forgiving the wrongdoer, not only seven times but seventy times and seven. He thought much about these impressions of the Master's forgiving character during those dark and dismal days immediately following his thoughtless and unintended denial of Jesus in the high priest's courtyard.

And so this man Peter, an intimate of Jesus, one of the inner circle, went forth from Jerusalem proclaiming the glad tidings of the kingdom with power and glory until the fullness of his ministry had been accomplished; and he regarded himself as the recipient of high honors when his captors informed him that he must die as his Master had died—on the cross. And thus was Simon Peter crucified in Rome.

3. JAMES ZEBEDEE

James, the older of the two apostle sons of Zebedee, whom Jesus nicknamed "sons of thunder," was thirty years old when he became an apostle. He was married, had four children, and lived near his parents in the outskirts of Capernaum, Bethsaida. He was a fisherman, plying his calling in company with his younger brother John and in association with Andrew and Simon. James and his brother John enjoyed the advantage of having known Jesus longer than any of the other apostles.

That characteristic of Jesus which James most admired was the Master's sympathetic affection. Jesus' understanding interest in the small and the great, the rich and the poor, made a great appeal to him.

When Jesus asked if they were ready to drink the cup, they replied that they were. And as concerns James, it was literally true—he did drink the cup with the Master, seeing that he was the first of the apostles to experience martyrdom, being early put to death with the sword by Herod Agrippa. James was thus the first of the twelve to sacrifice his life upon the new battle line of the kingdom.

James lived his life to the full, and when the end came, he bore himself with such grace and fortitude that even his accuser and informer, who attended his trial and execution, was so touched that he rushed away from the scene of James's death to join himself to the disciples of Jesus.

4. JOHN ZEBEDEE

When he became an apostle, John was twenty-four years old and was the youngest of the twelve. He was unmarried and lived with his parents at Bethsaida; he was a fisherman and worked with his brother James in partnership with Andrew and Peter. Both before and after becoming an apostle, John functioned as the personal agent of Jesus in dealing with the Master's family, and he continued to bear this responsibility as long as Mary the mother of Jesus lived.

Since John was the youngest of the twelve and so closely associated with Jesus in his family affairs, he was very dear to the Master, but it cannot be truthfully said that he was "the disciple whom Jesus loved." You would hardly suspect such a magnanimous personality as Jesus to be guilty of showing favoritism, of loving one of his apostles more than the others. The fact that John was one of the three personal aides of Jesus lent further color to this mistaken idea, not to mention that John, along with his brother James, had known Jesus longer than the others.

Those characteristics of Jesus which John most appreciated were the Master's love and unselfishness; these traits made such an impression on him that his whole subsequent life became dominated by the sentiment of love and brotherly devotion. He talked about love and wrote about love. This "son of thunder" became the "apostle of love"; and at Ephesus, when the aged bishop was no longer able to stand in the pulpit and preach but had to be carried to church in a chair, and when at the close of the service he was asked to say a few words to the believers, for years his only utterance was, "My little children, love one another."

John was in prison several times and was banished to the Isle of Patmos for a period of four years until another emperor came to power in Rome. Had not John been tactful and sagacious, he would undoubtedly have been killed as was his more outspoken brother James.

John traveled much, labored incessantly, and after becoming bishop of the Asia churches, settled down at Ephesus. He directed his associate, Nathan, in the writing of the so-called "Gospel according to John," at Ephesus, when he was ninety-nine years old. Of all the twelve apostles, John Zebedee eventually became the outstanding theologian. He died a natural death at Ephesus in A.D. 103 when he was one hundred and one years of age.

THE BOOK OF REVELATION

When in temporary exile on Patmos, John wrote the Book of Revelation, which we now have in greatly abridged and distorted form. This last book of the Bible contains the surviving fragments of a great revelation, large portions of which were lost, other portions of which were removed, subsequent to John's writing. It is preserved in only fragmentary and adulterated form.

5. PHILIP THE CURIOUS

Philip was twenty-seven years of age when he joined the apostles; he had recently been married, but he had no children at this time. The nickname which the apostles gave him signified "curiosity." Philip was always wanting to be shown. He never seemed to see very far into any proposition. He was not necessarily dull, but he lacked imagination. This lack of imagination was the great weakness of his character. He was a commonplace and matter-of-fact individual.

When the apostles were organized for service, Philip was made steward; it was his duty to see that they were at all times supplied with provisions. And he was a good steward. His strongest characteristic was his methodical thoroughness; he was both mathematical and systematic.

The one quality about Jesus which Philip so continuously admired was the Master's unfailing generosity. Never could Philip find anything in Jesus which was small, niggardly, or stingy, and he worshiped this ever-present and unfailing liberality.

Philip, the onetime steward of the twelve, was a mighty man in the kingdom, winning souls wherever he went; and he was finally crucified and buried at Hierapolis.

6. Honest Nathaniel

Nathaniel, the sixth and last of the apostles to be chosen by the Master himself, was brought to Jesus by his friend Philip. He had been associated in several business enterprises with Philip and, with him, was on the way down to see John the Baptist when they encountered Jesus.

When Nathaniel joined the apostles, he was twenty-five years old and was the next to the youngest of the group. He was the youngest of a family of seven, was unmarried, and the only support of aged and infirm parents, with whom he lived at Cana; his brothers and sister were either married or deceased, and none lived there. Nathaniel and Judas Iscariot were the two best educated men among the twelve. Nathaniel had thought to become a merchant.

Jesus did not himself give Nathaniel a nickname, but the twelve soon began to speak of him in terms that signified honesty, sincerity. He was "without guile." And this was his great virtue; he was both honest and sincere. The weakness of his character was his pride; he was very proud of his family, his city, his reputation, and his nation, all of which is commendable if it is not carried too far. But Nathaniel was inclined to go to extremes with his personal prejudices. He was disposed to prejudge individuals in accordance with his personal opinions. He was not slow to ask the question, even before he had met Jesus, "Can any good thing come out of Nazareth?"

In many respects Nathaniel was the odd genius of the twelve. He was the apostolic philosopher and dreamer, but he was a very practical sort of dreamer. Nathaniel most revered Jesus for his tolerance. He never grew weary of contemplating the broadmindedness and generous sympathy of the Son of Man.

Nathaniel's father (Bartholomew) died shortly after Pentecost, after which this apostle went into Mesopotamia and India proclaiming the glad tidings of the kingdom and baptizing believers. His brethren never knew what became of their onetime philosopher, poet, and humorist. But he also was a great man in the kingdom and did much to spread his Master's teachings, even though he did not participate in the organization of the subsequent Christian church. Nathaniel died in India.

7. Matthew Levi

Matthew, the seventh apostle, was chosen by Andrew. Matthew belonged to a family of tax gatherers, or publicans, but was himself a customs collector in Capernaum, where he lived. He was thirty-one years old and married and had four children. He was a man of moderate wealth, the only one of any means belonging to the apostolic corps. He was a good business man, a good social mixer, and was gifted with the ability to make friends and to get along smoothly with a great variety of people.

It was the Master's forgiving disposition which Matthew most appreciated. He would never cease to recount that faith only was necessary in the business of finding God. He always liked to speak of the kingdom as "this business of finding God."

Though Matthew was a man with a past, he gave an excellent account of himself, and as time went on, his associates became proud of the publican's performances. He was one of the apostles

[JAMES TISSOT — *The Exhortation to the Apostles*]

who made extensive notes on the sayings of Jesus, and these notes were used as the basis of Isador's subsequent narrative of the sayings and doings of Jesus, which has become known as the Gospel according to Matthew.

When persecutions caused the believers to forsake Jerusalem, Matthew journeyed north, preaching the gospel of the kingdom and baptizing believers. He was lost to the knowledge of his former apostolic associates, but on he went, preaching and baptizing, through Syria, Cappadocia, Galatia, Bithynia, and Thrace. And it was in Thrace, at Lysimachia, that certain unbelieving Jews conspired with the Roman soldiers to encompass his death. And this regenerated publican died triumphant in the faith of a salvation he had so

surely learned from the teachings of the Master during his recent sojourn on earth.

8. Thomas Didymus

When Thomas joined the apostles, he was twenty-nine years old, was married, and had four children. Formerly he had been a carpenter and stone mason, but latterly he had become a fisherman and resided at Tarichea, situated on the west bank of the Jordan where it flows out of the Sea of Galilee, and he was regarded as the leading citizen of this little village. He had little education, but he possessed a keen, reasoning mind and was the son of excellent parents, who lived at Tiberias. Thomas had the one truly analytical mind of the twelve; he was the real scientist of the apostolic group.

The early home life of Thomas had been unfortunate; his parents were not altogether happy in their married life, and this was reflected in Thomas's adult experience. He grew up having a very disagreeable and quarrelsome disposition. Even his wife was glad to see him join the apostles; she was relieved by the thought that her pessimistic husband would be away from home most of the time. Thomas also had a streak of suspicion which made it very difficult to get along peaceably with him. Peter was very much upset by Thomas at first, complaining to his brother, Andrew, that Thomas was "mean, ugly, and always suspicious." But the better his associates knew Thomas, the more they liked him. They found he was superbly honest and unflinchingly loyal. He was perfectly sincere and unquestionably truthful, but he was a natural-born faultfinder and had grown up to become a real pessimist. His analytical mind had become cursed with suspicion. He was rapidly losing faith in his fellow men when he became associated with the twelve and thus came in contact with the noble character of Jesus. This association with the Master began at once to transform Thomas's whole disposition and to effect great changes in his mental reactions to his fellow men.

The other apostles held Jesus in reverence because of some special and outstanding trait of his replete personality, but Thomas revered his Master because of his superbly balanced character. It was this matchless symmetry of personality that so charmed Thomas. He probably enjoyed the highest intellectual understanding and personality appreciation of Jesus of any of the twelve.

Thomas had a trying time during the days of the trial and crucifixion. He was for a season in the depths of despair, but he rallied his courage, stuck to the apostles, and was present with them to welcome Jesus on the Sea of Galilee. For a while he succumbed to his doubting depression but eventually rallied his faith and courage. He gave wise counsel to the apostles after Pentecost and,

when persecution scattered the believers, went to Cyprus, Crete, the North African coast, and Sicily, preaching the glad tidings of the kingdom and baptizing believers. And Thomas continued preaching and baptizing until he was apprehended by the agents of the Roman government and was put to death in Malta. Just a few weeks before his death he had begun the writing of the life and teachings of Jesus.

9. AND 10. JAMES AND JUDAS ALPHEUS

James and Judas the sons of Alpheus, the twin fishermen living near Kheresa, were the ninth and tenth apostles and were chosen by James and John Zebedee. They were twenty-six years old and married, James having three children, Judas two.

There is not much to be said about these two commonplace fisherfolk. They loved their Master and Jesus loved them, but they never interrupted his discourses with questions. They understood very little about the philosophical discussions or the theological debates of their fellow apostles, but they rejoiced to find themselves numbered among such a group of mighty men. These two men were almost identical in personal appearance, mental characteristics, and extent of spiritual perception. What may be said of one should be recorded of the other.

James and Judas, who were also called Thaddeus and Lebbeus, had neither strong points nor weak points. The nicknames given them by the disciples were good-natured designations of mediocrity. They were "the least of all the apostles"; they knew it and felt cheerful about it.

James Alpheus especially loved Jesus because of the Master's simplicity. These twins could not comprehend the mind of Jesus, but they did grasp the sympathetic bond between themselves and the heart of their Master. Their minds were not of a high order; they might even reverently be called stupid, but they had a real experience in their spiritual natures. They believed in Jesus; they were sons of God and fellows of the kingdom.

Judas Alpheus was drawn toward Jesus because of the Master's unostentatious humility. Such humility linked with such dignity made a great appeal to Judas. The fact that Jesus would always enjoin silence regarding his unusual acts made a great impression on this simple child of nature.

The twins served faithfully until the end, until the dark days of trial, crucifixion, and despair. They never lost their heart faith in Jesus, and (save John) they were the first to believe in his resurrection. But they could not comprehend the establishment of the kingdom. Soon after their Master was crucified, they returned to their families and nets; their work was done. They had not the ability to go on in the more complex battles of the kingdom. But they lived and died conscious of having been honored and blessed with four years of close and personal association with a Son of God, the sovereign maker of a universe.

11. Simon the Zealot

Simon Zelotes, the eleventh apostle, was chosen by Simon Peter. He was an able man of good ancestry and lived with his family at Capernaum. He was twenty-eight years old when he became attached to the apostles. He was a fiery agitator and was also a man who spoke much without thinking. He had been a merchant in Capernaum before he turned his entire attention to the patriotic organization of the Zealots.

The one thing about Jesus which Simon so much admired was the Master's calmness, his assurance, poise, and inexplicable composure.

After the dispersion because of the Jerusalem persecutions, Simon went into temporary retirement. He was literally crushed. As a nationalist patriot he had surrendered in deference to Jesus' teachings; now all was lost. He was in despair, but in a few years he rallied his hopes and went forth to proclaim the gospel of the kingdom.

He went to Alexandria and, after working up the Nile, penetrated into the heart of Africa, everywhere preaching the gospel of Jesus and baptizing believers. Thus he labored until he was an old man and feeble. And he died and was buried in the heart of Africa.

12. Judas Iscariot

Judas Iscariot, the twelfth apostle, was chosen by Nathaniel. He was born in Kerioth, a small town in southern Judea. When he was a lad, his parents moved to Jericho, where he lived and had been employed in his father's various business enterprises until he became interested in the preaching and work of John the Baptist. Judas's parents were Sadducees, and when their son joined John's disciples, they disowned him.

There was no special trait about Jesus which Judas admired above the generally attractive and exquisitely charming personality of the Master. Judas was never able to rise above his Judean prejudices against his Galilean associates; he would even criticize in his mind many things about Jesus. Him whom eleven of the apostles looked upon as the perfect man, as the "one altogether lovely and the chiefest among ten thousand," this self-satisfied Judean often dared to criticize in his own heart. He really entertained the notion that Jesus was timid and somewhat afraid to assert his own power and authority.

Judas was an only son of unwise parents. When very young, he was pampered and petted; he was a spoiled child. As he grew up, he had exaggerated ideas about his self-importance. He was a poor loser. He had loose and distorted ideas about fairness; he was given to the indulgence of hate and suspicion. He was an expert at misinterpretation of the words and acts of his friends. All through his life Judas had cultivated the habit of getting even with those whom he fancied had mistreated him. His sense of values and loyalties was defective.

Judas became increasingly a brooder over personal disappointment, and finally he became a victim of resentment. His feelings had been many times hurt, and he grew abnormally suspicious of his best friends, even of the Master. Presently he became obsessed with the idea of getting even, anything to avenge himself, yes, even betrayal of his associates and his Master.

Judas then entered into the base and shameful intrigue to betray his Lord and Master and quickly carried the nefarious scheme into effect. During the outworking of his anger-conceived plans of traitorous betrayal, he experienced moments of regret and shame, and in these lucid intervals he faintheartedly conceived, as a defense in his own mind, the idea that Jesus might possibly exert his power and deliver himself at the last moment.

When the sordid and sinful business was all over, this renegade mortal, who thought lightly of selling his friend for thirty pieces of silver to satisfy his long-nursed craving for revenge, rushed out and committed the final act in the drama of fleeing from the realities of mortal existence—suicide.

The eleven apostles were horrified, stunned. Jesus regarded the betrayer only with pity. The worlds have found it difficult to forgive Judas, and his name has become eschewed throughout a far-flung universe. ■

JANUARY 12, A.D. 27

THE ORDINATION
OF THE TWELVE

Just before noon on Sunday, January 12, A.D. 27, Jesus called the apostles together for their ordination as public preachers of the gospel of the kingdom. The twelve were expecting to be called almost any day; so this morning they did not go out far from the shore to fish. Several of them were lingering near the shore repairing their nets and tinkering with their fishing paraphernalia.

As Jesus started down the seashore calling the apostles, he first hailed Andrew and Peter, who were fishing near the shore; next he signaled to James and John, who were in a boat near by, visiting with their father, Zebedee, and mending their nets. Two by two he gathered up the other apostles, and when he had assembled all twelve, he journeyed with them to the highlands north of Capernaum, where he proceeded to instruct them in preparation for their formal ordination.

For once all twelve of the apostles were silent; even Peter was in a reflective mood. At last the long-waited-for hour had come! They were going apart with the Master to participate in some sort of solemn ceremony of personal consecration and collective dedication to the sacred work of representing their Master in the proclamation of the coming of his Father's kingdom.

Jesus now instructed the twelve mortals who had just listened to his declaration concerning the kingdom to kneel in a circle about him. Then the Master placed his hands upon the head of each apostle, beginning with Judas Iscariot and ending with Andrew. When he had blessed them, he extended his hands and prayed:

"My Father, I now bring to you these men, my messengers. From among our children on earth I have chosen these twelve to go forth to represent me as I came forth to represent you. Love them and be with them as you have loved and been with me. And now, my Father, give these men wisdom as I place all the affairs of the coming kingdom in their hands. And I would, if it is your will, tarry on earth a time to help them in their labors for the kingdom. And again, my Father, I thank you for these men, and I commit them to your keeping while I go on to finish the work you have given me to do."

When Jesus had finished praying, the apostles remained each man bowed in his place. And it was many minutes before even Peter dared lift up his eyes to look upon the Master. One by one they embraced Jesus, but no man said aught. A great

The Creator of a universe was placing the affairs of the divine brotheriiood of man under the direction of human minds.

silence pervaded the place while a host of celestial beings looked down upon this solemn and sacred scene—the Creator of a universe placing the affairs of the divine brotherhood of man under the direction of human minds.

The Ordination Sermon

Then Jesus spoke, saying: "Now that you are ambassadors of my Father's kingdom, you have thereby become a class of men separate and distinct from all other men on earth. You are not now as men among men but as the enlightened citizens of another and heavenly country among the ignorant creatures of this dark world. It is not enough that you live as you were before this hour, but henceforth must you live as those who have tasted the glories of a better life and have been sent back to earth as ambassadors of the Sovereign of that new and better world. Of the teacher more is expected than of the pupil; of the master more is exacted than of the servant. Of the citizens of the heavenly kingdom more is required than of the citizens of the earthly rule. Some of the things which I am about to say to you may seem hard, but you have elected to represent me in the world even as I now represent the Father; and as my agents on earth you will be obligated to abide by those teachings and practices which are reflective of my ideals of mortal living on the worlds of space, and which I exemplify in my earth life of revealing the Father who is in heaven.

"I send you forth to proclaim liberty to the spiritual captives, joy to those in the bondage of fear, and to heal the sick in accordance with the will of my Father in heaven. When you find my children in distress, speak encouragingly to them, saying:

- "Happy are the poor in spirit, the humble, for theirs are the treasures of the kingdom of heaven.
- "Happy are they who hunger and thirst for righteousness, for they shall be filled.
- "Happy are the meek, for they shall inherit the earth.
- "Happy are the pure in heart, for they shall see God.

"And even so speak to my children these further words of spiritual comfort and promise:

- "Happy are they who mourn, for they shall be comforted. Happy are they who weep, for they shall receive the spirit of rejoicing.
- "Happy are the merciful, for they shall obtain mercy.
- "Happy are the peacemakers, for they shall be called the sons of God.
- "Happy are they who are persecuted for righteousness' sake, for theirs is the kingdom of heaven. Happy are you when men shall revile you and persecute you and shall say all manner of evil against you falsely. Rejoice and be exceedingly glad, for great is your reward in heaven.

"My brethren, as I send you forth, you are the salt of the earth, salt with a saving savor. But if this

[JAMES TISSOT — *The Sermon on the Mount*]

"I SAY TO YOU: LOVE YOUR ENEMIES, DO GOOD TO THOSE WHO HATE YOU, BLESS THOSE WHO CURSE YOU, AND PRAY FOR THOSE WHO DESPITEFULLY USE YOU."

salt has lost its savor, wherewith shall it be salted? It is henceforth good for nothing but to be cast out and trodden under foot of men.

"You are the light of the world. A city set upon a hill cannot be hid. Neither do men light a candle and put it under a bushel, but on a candlestick; and it gives light to all who are in the house. Let your light so shine before men that they may see your good works and be led to glorify your Father who is in heaven.

"I am sending you out into the world to represent me and to act as ambassadors of my Father's kingdom, and as you go forth to proclaim the glad tidings, put your trust in the Father whose messengers you are. Do not forcibly resist injustice; put not your trust in the arm of the flesh. If your neighbor smites you on the right cheek, turn to him the other also. Be willing to suffer injustice rather than to go to law among yourselves. In kindness and with mercy minister to all who are in distress and in need.

"I say to you: Love your enemies, do good to those who hate you, bless those who curse you, and pray for those who despitefully use you. And whatsoever you believe that I would do to men, do you also to them.

"Your Father in heaven makes the sun to shine on the evil as well as upon the good; likewise he sends rain on the just and the unjust. You are the sons of God; even more, you are now the ambassadors of my Father's kingdom. Be merciful, even as God is merciful, and in the eternal future of the kingdom you shall be perfect, even as your heavenly Father is perfect.

"You are commissioned to save men, not to judge them. At the end of your earth life you will all expect mercy; therefore do I require of you during your mortal life that you show mercy to all of your brethren in the flesh. Make not the mistake of trying to pluck a mote out of your brother's eye when there is a beam in your own eye. Having first cast the beam out of your own eye, you can the better see to cast the mote out of your brother's eye.

"Discern the truth clearly; live the righteous life fearlessly; and so shall you be my apostles and my Father's ambassadors. You have heard it said: 'If the blind lead the blind, they both shall fall into the pit.' If you would guide others into the kingdom, you must yourselves walk in the clear light of living truth. In all the business of the kingdom I exhort you to show just judgment and keen wisdom. Present not that which is holy to dogs, neither cast your pearls before swine, lest they trample your gems under foot and turn to rend you.

"I warn you against false prophets who will come to you in sheep's clothing, while on the inside they are as ravening wolves. By their fruits you shall know them. Do men gather grapes from thorns or figs from thistles? Even so, every good tree brings forth good fruit, but the corrupt tree bears evil fruit. A good tree cannot yield evil fruit, neither can a corrupt tree produce good fruit. Every tree that does not bring forth good fruit is presently hewn down and cast into the fire. In gaining an entrance into the kingdom of heaven, it is the motive that counts. My Father looks into the hearts of men and judges by their inner longings and their sincere intentions.

"In the great day of the kingdom judgment, many will say to me, 'Did we not prophesy in your name and by your name do many wonderful works?' But I will be compelled to say to them, 'I never knew you; depart from me you who are false teachers.' But every one who hears this charge and sincerely executes his commission to represent me before men even as I have represented my Father to you, shall find an abundant entrance into my service and into the kingdom of the heavenly Father."

Never before had the apostles heard Jesus speak in this way, for he had talked to them as one having supreme authority. They came down from the mountain about sundown, but no man asked Jesus a question. ✳

The Sermon on the Mount and the Beatitudes

The "Sermon on the Mount" was Jesus' ordination charge to the twelve apostles. It was the Master's personal commission to those who were to go on preaching the gospel and aspiring to represent him in the world of men even as he was so eloquently and perfectly representative of his Father. Only the twelve heard it.

This is the longest continuous section of Jesus speaking found in the New Testament and includes some of his best-known teachings. It is found in the Gospel of Matthew and is mirrored in Luke's "Sermon on the Plains." The term "beatitudes" comes from the Latin *beatitude*, a state of blessedness, happiness, or fortune, and this momentous sermon started out upon the note of happiness.

From the Sermon on the Mount to the discourse of the Last Supper, Jesus taught his followers to manifest *fatherly* love rather than *brotherly* love. Brotherly love would love your neighbor as you love yourself, and that would be adequate fulfillment of the "golden rule." But fatherly affection would require that you should love your fellow mortals as Jesus loves you.

The Master introduced this discourse by calling attention to four *faith* attitudes as the prelude to the subsequent portrayal of his four transcendent and supreme reactions of fatherly love in contrast to the limitations of mere brotherly love.

He first spoke of those who were poor in spirit, hungered after righteousness, endured meekness, and who were pure in heart. Such spirit-discerning mortals could be expected to attain such levels of divine selflessness as to be able to attempt the amazing exercise of *fatherly* affection; that even as mourners they would be empowered to show mercy, promote peace, and endure persecutions, and throughout all of these trying situations to love even unlovely mankind with a fatherly love. A father's affection can attain levels of devotion that immeasurably transcend a brother's affection.

The faith and the love of these beatitudes strengthen moral character and create happiness. Fear and anger weaken character and destroy happiness. This momentous sermon started out upon the note of happiness.

Without a worthy goal, life becomes aimless and unprofitable, and much unhappiness results. Jesus' discourse at the ordination of the twelve constitutes a master philosophy of life. Jesus exhorted his followers to exercise experiential faith. He admonished them not to depend on mere intellectual assent, credulity, and established authority.

And so it is revealed that the beatitudes of the Sermon on the Mount are based on faith and love and not on law—ethics and duty.

Over three years later (on Saturday, April 22, A.D. 30), the eleven remaining apostles would return to this very place in the highlands north of Capernaum to kneel in a circle about their risen Master and hear him repeat the charges and see him re-enact the ordination scene even as when they were first set apart for the special work of the kingdom.

CHAPTER VI

BEGINNING THE PUBLIC WORK

"And preach as you go, saying, 'The kingdom of heaven is at hand.'"
—MATTHEW 10:7 RSV

JESUS WAS TRULY A MASTER OF MEN; HE EXERCISED GREAT INFLUENCE OVER HIS FELLOW MEN BECAUSE of the combined charm and force of his personality. There was a subtle commanding influence in his rugged, nomadic, and homeless life. There was intellectual attractiveness and spiritual drawing power in his authoritative manner of teaching, in his lucid logic, his strength of reasoning, his sagacious insight, his alertness of mind, his matchless poise, and his sublime tolerance. He was simple, manly, honest, and fearless. With all of this physical and intellectual influence manifest in the Master's presence, there were also all those spiritual charms of being which have become associated with his personality—patience, tenderness, meekness, gentleness, and humility.

Jesus of Nazareth was indeed a strong and forceful personality; he was an intellectual power and a spiritual stronghold. His personality not only appealed to the spiritually minded women among his followers, but also to the educated and intellectual Nicodemus and to the hardy Roman soldier, the captain stationed on guard at the cross, who, when he had finished watching the Master die, said, "Truly, this was a Son of God." And red-blooded, rugged Galilean fishermen called him Master.

His was a dignified manhood; he was good, but natural. Jesus did not pose as a mild, sweet, gentle, and kindly mystic. His teaching was thrillingly dynamic. He not only *meant well*, but he went about actually *doing good*. The Master never said, "Come to me all you who are indolent and all who are dreamers." But he did many times say, "Come to me all you who *labor*, and I will give you rest—spiritual strength." The Master's yoke is, indeed, easy, but even so, he never imposes it; every individual must take this yoke of his own free will.

The materialistic sociologist of today surveys a community, makes a report thereon, and leaves the people as he found them. Two thousand years ago, unlearned Galileans surveyed Jesus giving his life as a spiritual contribution to man's inner experience; and then went out and turned the whole Roman Empire upside down.

THE URANTIA BOOK: PAPERS 141–144
JANUARY, A.D. 27–JANUARY, A.D. 28

[GREG OLSEN — *Joy of the Lord*]

LEAVING GALILEE

On the first day of the week, January 19, A.D. 27, Jesus and the twelve apostles made ready to depart from their headquarters in Bethsaida. The twelve knew nothing of their Master's plans except that they were going up to Jerusalem to attend the Passover feast in April, and that it was the intention to journey by way of the Jordan valley. They did not get away from Zebedee's house until near noon because the families of the apostles and others of the disciples had come to say good-bye and wish them well in the new work they were about to begin.

Just before leaving, the apostles missed the Master, and Andrew went out to find him. After a brief search he found Jesus sitting in a boat down the beach, and he was weeping. The twelve had often seen their Master when he seemed to grieve, and they had beheld his brief seasons of serious preoccupation of mind, but none of them had ever seen him weep. Andrew was somewhat startled to see the Master thus affected on the eve of their departure for Jerusalem, and he ventured to approach Jesus and ask: "On this great day, Master, when we are to depart for Jerusalem to proclaim the Father's kingdom, why is it that you weep? Which of us has offended you?" And Jesus, going back with Andrew to join the twelve, answered him: "No one of you has grieved me. I am saddened only because none of my father Joseph's family have remembered to come over to bid us Godspeed." At this time Ruth was on a visit to her brother Joseph at Nazareth. Other members of his family were kept away by pride, disappointment, misunderstanding, and petty resentment indulged as a result of hurt feelings.

Capernaum was not far from Tiberias, and the fame of Jesus had begun to spread well over all of Galilee and even to parts beyond. Jesus knew that Herod would soon begin to take notice of his work; so he thought best to journey south and into Judea alone with his apostles.

While sojourning at Amathus, Jesus spent much time with the apostles instructing them in the new concept of God; again and again did he impress upon them that *God is a Father*, not a great and supreme bookkeeper who is chiefly engaged in making damaging entries against his erring children on earth, recordings of sin and evil to be used against them when he subsequently sits in judgment upon them as the just Judge of all creation. The Jews had long conceived of God as a king over all, even as a Father of the nation, but never before had large numbers of mortal men held the idea of God as a loving Father of the *individual*.

In answer to Thomas's question, "Who is this God of the kingdom?" Jesus replied: "God is *your* Father, and religion—my gospel—is nothing more nor less than the believing recognition of the truth that you are his son. And I am here among you in the flesh to make clear both of these ideas in my life and teachings."

Jesus also sought to free the minds of his apostles from the idea of offering animal sacrifices as a religious duty. But these men, trained in the religion of the daily sacrifice, were slow to comprehend what he meant. Nevertheless, the Master did not grow weary in his teaching. When he failed to reach the minds of all of the apostles by means of one illustration, he would restate his message and employ another type of parable for purposes of illumination.

On February 26, Jesus, his apostles, and a large group of followers journeyed down the Jordan to the ford near Bethany in Perea, the place where John first made proclamation of the coming kingdom. Jesus with his apostles remained here, teaching and preaching, for four weeks before they went on up to Jerusalem.

The second week of the sojourn at Bethany

PALESTINE IN THE TIMES OF CHRIST

NOTABLE EVENTS

1 Birth of Jesus (Book page no. 20)
Bethlehem: August 21, 7 B.C.

2 Death of Joseph (52)
Sepphoris: September 25, A.D. 8

3 Great Temptation (110)
Mt. Hermon: September, A.D. 25

4 Baptism on the river Jordan (115)
(near Pella): January 14, A.D. 26

5 Elaboration of the Wine (130)
Cana: February 27, A.D. 26

6 Ordination/Sermon on the Mount (151)
Highlands north of Capernaum:
January 12, A.D. 27

7 Samaritan Woman at Jacob's Well (163)
Sychar: June, A.D. 27

8 Kingdom's First Hospital (184)
Bethsaida: May, A.D. 28

9 Ordination of the Women Evangelists (190)
Bethsaida: January 16, A.D. 29

10 Feeding of the Five Thousand (201)
Magadan Park: March 30, A.D. 29

11 Transfiguration (225)
Mt. Hermon: August 15, A.D. 29

12 Resurrection of Lazarus (261)
Bethany: March 2, A.D. 30

◉ Event localities indicated in red

- Ruled by Herod Antipas
- Ruled by Herod Philip
- Roman province of Judea
- Roman province of Syria
- Imperial estate
- Nabatean Kingdom
- .... District or region boundary
- • / ○ City of the Decapolis/location uncertain
- [Paneas] Former name of city

0   10   20   30 miles
0 10 20 30 km

Present-day drainage, coastlines,
and country boundaries
are represented.

Map labels

MEDITERRANEAN SEA

Sidon
Damascus
Tyre
Kanah
Ecdippa [Achzib]
Cadasa
Iron
Asor
Raphana
Merom
GALILEE
Chorazin
Capernaum—6
Ptolemais
Ramah
Bethsaida-Julias
Gennesaret
Magadan Park—10
Bay of Acco (Bay of Haifa)
Jotapata
Bethsaida—8,9
Sycaminium
Magdala
Sea of Galilee (Sea of Kinnereth)
Kheresa
Mt. Carmel 546 m 1,791 ft
Sepphoris—2
Tiberias
Hippos
Ashtaroth
Cana—5
Philoteria
Abila
Bethlehem of Galilee
Nazareth
Dora
Endor
Mt. Tabor 588 m 1,929 ft
Gadara
Legio
Nain
Capitolias
Megiddo (Armageddon)
Jezreel
Caesarea
Scythopolis
Ginae
Pella—4
Gerasa
Narbata
Beit Adis
Dion
West Bank
Mt. Ebal 940 m 3,084 ft
Neapolis
Sebaste
Amathus
Apollonia
Mt. Gerizim 881 m 2,890 ft
Sychar—7
Antipatris
Mt. Sartaba 350 m 1,148 ft
Joppa
Lebonah
Philadelphia (Amman)
Arimathea
Phasaelis
Gadara
Lydda
Bethel
Archelais
Livias
Jamnia
Gazara
Jericho
Esbus
Azotus
Emmaus
Jerusalem
City of Judah
Bethany—12
Mt. Nebo 802 m 2,631 ft
Medeba
Bethlehem—1
Herodium
Ascalon
Dead Sea (Salt Sea)
Marisa
Beth-zur
Machaerus
Lachish
Hebron
Anthedon
Gaza
Eshtemoa
Engedi
Gaza Strip
Kerioth
Masada
Raphia
Beersheba
Malatha
Kir-Moab
EGYPT
Negev
NABATEA
JORDAN

Mt. Hermon—3,11
2,814 m 9,232 ft
Beit Jenn
Luz
Dan
Caesarea-Philippi [Paneas]
ITUREA
SYRIA
GAULANITIS
PHOENICIA
LEBANON
Leontes
Jordan
Kishon
Plain of Sharon
SAMARIA
DECAPOLIS
PEREA
Yarqon
Sorek
Jabbok
Jordan
Arnon
Besor

beyond Jordan, Jesus took Peter, James, and John into the hills across the river and south of Jericho for a three days' rest. The Master taught these three many new and advanced truths about the kingdom of heaven. ∎

THE PASSOVER AT JERUSALEM

The month of April Jesus and the apostles worked in Jerusalem, going out of the city each evening to spend the night at Bethany. Jesus himself spent one or two nights each week in Jerusalem at the home of Flavius, a Greek Jew, where many prominent Jews came in secret to interview him.

The multitudes who came to celebrate the Passover heard the teaching of Jesus, and hundreds of them rejoiced in the good news. But the chief priests and rulers of the Jews became much concerned about Jesus and debated among themselves as to what should be done with him.

The first day in Jerusalem Jesus called upon his friend of former years, Annas, the onetime high priest and relative of Salome, Zebedee's wife. Annas had been hearing about Jesus and his teachings, and when Jesus called at the high priest's home, he was received with much reserve. When Jesus perceived Annas's coldness, he took immediate leave, saying as he departed: "Fear is man's chief enslaver and pride his great weakness; will you betray yourself into bondage to both of these destroyers of joy and liberty?" But Annas made no reply. The Master did

ANDREW'S ROLE

From night to night Andrew carefully instructed his fellow apostles in the delicate and difficult task of getting along smoothly with the followers of John the Baptist. During this first year of Jesus' public ministry more than three fourths of his followers had previously followed John and had received his baptism. This entire year of A.D. 27 was spent in quietly taking over John's work in Perea and Judea.

not again see Annas until the time when he sat with his son-in-law in judgment on the Son of Man.

There was in Jerusalem one Jacob, a wealthy Jewish trader from Crete, and he came to Andrew making request to see Jesus privately. Andrew arranged this secret meeting with Jesus the next evening at the home of one Flavius, a Greek Jew proselyte of the gate. This man could not comprehend the Master's teachings, and he came because he desired to inquire more fully about the kingdom of God. Said Jacob to Jesus: "But, Rabbi, Moses and the olden prophets tell us that Yahweh is a jealous God, a God of great wrath and fierce anger. The prophets say he hates evildoers and takes vengeance on those who obey not his law. You and your disciples teach us that God is a kind and compassionate Father who so loves all men that he would welcome them into this new kingdom of heaven, which you proclaim is so near at hand."

When Jacob finished speaking, Jesus replied: "Jacob, you have well stated the teachings of the olden prophets who taught the children of their generation in accordance with the light of their day. Our Father in Paradise is changeless. But the concept of his nature has enlarged and grown from the days of Moses down through the times of Amos and even to the generation of the prophet Isaiah. And now have I come in the flesh to reveal the Father in new glory and to show forth his love and mercy to all men on all worlds. As the gospel of this kingdom shall spread over the world with its message of good cheer and good will to all men, there will grow up improved and better relations among the families of all nations. As time passes, fathers and their children will love each other more, and thus will be brought about a better understanding of the love of the Father in heaven for his children on earth. Remember, Jacob, that a good and true father not only loves his family as a whole—as a family—but he also truly loves and affectionately cares for each *individual* member.

"You, Jacob, being a father of many, know well the truth of my words." And Jacob said: "But, Master, who told you I was the father of six children? How did you know this about me?" And the Master replied: "Suffice it to say that the Father and the Son know all things, for indeed they see all. Loving your children as a father on earth, you must now accept as a reality the love of the heavenly Father for you—not just for all the children of Abraham, but for *you*, your individual soul."

Then Jesus went on to say: "When your children are very young and immature, and when you must chastise them, they may reflect that their father is angry and filled with resentful wrath. Their immaturity cannot penetrate beyond the punishment to discern the father's farseeing and corrective affection. But when these same children become grown-up men and women, would it not be folly for them to cling to these earlier and misconceived notions regarding their father? As men and women they should now discern their father's love in all these early disciplines. And should not mankind, as the centuries pass, come the better to understand the true nature and loving character of the Father in heaven? What profit have you from successive generations of spiritual illumination

if you persist in viewing God as Moses and the prophets saw him? I say to you, Jacob, under the bright light of this hour you should see the Father as none of those who have gone before ever beheld him. And thus seeing him, you should rejoice to enter the kingdom wherein such a merciful Father rules, and you should seek to have his will of love dominate your life henceforth."

And Jacob answered: "Rabbi, I believe; I desire that you lead me into the Father's kingdom."

The Visit with Nicodemus

One evening at the home of Flavius there came to see Jesus one Nicodemus, a wealthy and elderly member of the Jewish Sanhedrin. He had heard much about the teachings of this Galilean, and so he went one afternoon to hear him as he taught in the temple courts. He would have gone often to hear Jesus teach, but he feared to be seen by the people in attendance upon his teaching, for already were the rulers of the Jews so at variance with Jesus that no member of the Sanhedrin would want to be identified in any open manner with him. Accordingly, Nicodemus had arranged with Andrew to see Jesus privately and after nightfall on this particular evening. Peter, James, and John were in Flavius's garden when the interview began, but later they all went into the house where the discourse continued.

In receiving Nicodemus, Jesus showed no particular deference; in talking with him, there was no compromise or undue persuasiveness. The Master made no attempt to repulse his secretive caller, nor did he employ sarcasm. In all his dealings with the distinguished visitor, Jesus was calm,

"AS THE GOSPEL OF THIS KINGDOM SHALL SPREAD OVER THE WORLD, THERE WILL GROW UP IMPROVED AND BETTER RELATIONS AMONG THE FAMILIES OF ALL NATIONS."

[J. KIRK RICHARDS — *Nicodemus*]

earnest, and dignified. Nicodemus was not an official delegate of the Sanhedrin; he came to see Jesus wholly because of his personal and sincere interest in the Master's teachings.

Upon being presented by Flavius, Nicodemus said: "Rabbi, we know that you are a teacher sent by God, for no mere man could so teach unless God were with him. And I am desirous of knowing more about your teachings regarding the coming kingdom."

Jesus answered Nicodemus: "Verily, verily, I say to you, Nicodemus, except a man be born from above, he cannot see the kingdom of God." Then replied Nicodemus: "But how can a man be born again when he is old? He cannot enter a second time into his mother's womb to be born."

Jesus said: "Nevertheless, I declare to you, except a man be born of the spirit, he cannot enter into the kingdom of God. That which is born of the flesh is flesh, and that which is born of the spirit is spirit. But you should not marvel that I said you must be born from above. When the wind blows, you hear the rustle of the leaves, but you do not see the wind—whence it comes or whither it goes—and so it is with everyone born of the spirit. With the eyes of the flesh you can behold the manifestations of the spirit, but you cannot actually discern the spirit."

Nicodemus replied: "But I do not understand—how can that be?" Said Jesus: "Can it be that you are a teacher in Israel and yet ignorant of all this? It becomes, then, the duty of those who know about the realities of the spirit to reveal these things to those who discern only the manifestations of the material world. But will you believe us if we tell you of the heavenly truths? Do you have the courage, Nicodemus, to believe in one who has descended from heaven, even the Son of Man?"

Nicodemus and the Sanhedrin

Nicodemus was a Pharisee and a member of the Sanhedrin, the highest court of justice and the supreme council in all Jewry. It convened in the Hall of Hewn Stones in the Jerusalem temple. The scribes and rabbis, taken together, were called Pharisees. They referred to themselves as the "associates." The Sadducees also comprised the Sanhedrin and consisted of the priesthood and certain wealthy Jews. These groups were really religious parties, rather than sects.

But Nicodemus did summon faith enough to lay hold of the kingdom. He faintly protested when his colleagues of the Sanhedrin sought to condemn Jesus without a hearing; and with Joseph of Arimathea, he later boldly acknowledged his faith and claimed the body of Jesus by order of Pilate, even when most of the disciples had fled in fear from the scenes of their Master's final suffering and death.

These two former members of the Sanhedrin—along with John Zebedee and the centurion at the cross—bore the body of Jesus to the tomb. They had kept their faith in Jesus more or less a secret, although their fellow Sanhedrists had long suspected them, even before they withdrew from the council. Henceforth they were the most outspoken disciples of Jesus in all Jerusalem.

And Nicodemus said: "But how can I begin to lay hold upon this spirit which is to remake me in preparation for entering into the kingdom?" Jesus answered: "Already does the spirit of the Father in heaven indwell you. If you would be led by this spirit from above, very soon would you begin to see with the eyes of the spirit, and then by the wholehearted choice of spirit guidance would you be born of the spirit since your only purpose in living would be to do the will of your Father who is in heaven. And so finding yourself born of the spirit and happily in the kingdom of God, you would begin to bear in your daily life the abundant fruits of the spirit."

Nicodemus was thoroughly sincere. He was deeply impressed but went away bewildered. Nicodemus was accomplished in self-development, in self-restraint, and even in high moral qualities. He was refined, egoistic, and altruistic; but he did not know how to *submit* his will to the will of the divine Father as a little child is willing to submit to the guidance and leading of a wise and loving earthly father, thereby becoming in reality a son of God, a progressive heir of the eternal kingdom. ■

JUNE, A.D. 27

Nalda, the Woman at Jacob's Well

At the end of June, A.D. 27, because of the increasing opposition of the Jewish religious rulers, Jesus and the twelve departed from Jerusalem, after sending their tents and meager personal effects to be stored at the home of Lazarus at Bethany. Going north into Samaria, they tarried over the Sabbath at Bethel. Here they preached for several days to the people who came from Gophna and Ephraim. A group of citizens from Arimathea and Thamna came over to invite Jesus to visit their villages. The Master and his apostles spent more than two weeks teaching the Jews and Samaritans of this region, many of whom came from as far as Antipatris to hear the good news of the kingdom.

The people of southern Samaria heard Jesus gladly, and the apostles, with the exception of Judas Iscariot, succeeded in overcoming much of

[C. Michael Dudash — *Living Water*] overleaf >

their prejudice against the Samaritans. It was very difficult for Judas to love these Samaritans. The last week of July Jesus and his associates made ready to depart for the new Greek cities of Phasaelis and Archelais near the Jordan.

Not many of the gentiles in the two Greek cities believed in the gospel, but the twelve apostles gained a valuable experience in this their first extensive work with exclusively gentile populations. On a Monday morning, about the middle of the month, Jesus said to Andrew: "We go into Samaria." And they set out at once for the city of Sychar, near Jacob's well.

When the Master and the twelve arrived at Jacob's well, Jesus, being weary from the journey, tarried by the well while Philip took the apostles with him to assist in bringing food and tents from Sychar, for they were disposed to stay in this vicinity for a while. Peter and the Zebedee sons would have remained with Jesus, but he requested that they go with their brethren, saying: "Have no fear for me; these Samaritans will be friendly; only our brethren, the Jews, seek to harm us." And it was almost six o'clock on this summer's evening when Jesus sat down by the well to await the return of the apostles.

The water of Jacob's well was less mineral than that from the wells of Sychar and was therefore much valued for drinking purposes. Jesus was thirsty, but there was no way of getting water from the well. When, therefore, a woman of Sychar came up with her water pitcher and prepared to draw from the well, Jesus said to her, "Give me a drink." This woman of Samaria knew Jesus was a

NALDA'S SALVATION

Jesus' words to Nalda at the well were the first direct, positive, and undisguised pronouncement of his divine nature and sonship which he had made on earth; and it was made to a woman, a Samaritan woman, and a woman of questionable character in the eyes of men up to this moment, but a woman whom the divine eye beheld as having been sinned against more than as sinning of her own desire and as *now* being a human soul who desired salvation, desired it sincerely and wholeheartedly, and that was enough.

Jew by his appearance and dress, and she surmised that he was a Galilean Jew from his accent. Her name was Nalda and she was a comely creature. She was much surprised to have a Jewish man thus speak to her at the well and ask for water, for it was not deemed proper in those days for a self-respecting man to speak to a woman in public, much less for a Jew to converse with a Samaritan. Therefore Nalda asked Jesus, "How is it that you, being a Jew, ask for a drink of me, a Samaritan woman?" Jesus answered: "I have indeed asked you for a drink, but if you could only understand, you would ask me for a draught of the living water." Then said Nalda: "But, Sir, you have nothing to draw with, and the well is deep; whence, then, have you this living water? Are you greater than our father Jacob who gave us this well, and who drank thereof himself and his sons and his cattle also?"

Jesus replied: "Everyone who drinks of this water will thirst again, but whosoever drinks of the water of the living spirit shall never thirst. And this living water shall become in him a well of refreshment springing up even to eternal life." Nalda then said: "Give me this water that I thirst not, neither come all the way hither to draw. Besides, anything which a Samaritan woman could receive from such a commendable Jew would be a pleasure."

Nalda did not know how to take Jesus' willingness to talk with her. She beheld in the Master's face the countenance of an upright and holy man, but she mistook friendliness for commonplace familiarity, and she misinterpreted his figure of speech as a form of making advances to her. And being a woman of lax morals, she was minded openly to become flirtatious, when Jesus, looking straight into her eyes, with a commanding voice said, "Woman, go get your husband and bring him hither." This command brought Nalda to her senses. She saw that she had misjudged the Master's kindness; she perceived that she had misconstrued his manner of speech. She was frightened; she began to realize that she stood in the presence of an unusual person, and groping about in her mind for a suitable reply, in great confusion, she said, "But, Sir, I cannot call my husband, for I have no husband." Then said Jesus: "You have spoken the truth, for, while you may have once had a husband, he with whom you are now living is not your husband. Better it would be if you would cease to trifle with my words and seek for the living water which I have this day offered you."

By this time Nalda was sobered, and her better self was awakened. She was not an immoral woman wholly by choice. She had been ruthlessly and unjustly cast aside by her husband and in dire straits had consented to live with a certain Greek as his wife, but without marriage. Nalda now felt greatly ashamed that she had so unthinkingly spoken to Jesus, and she most penitently addressed the Master, saying: "My Lord, I repent of my manner of speaking to you, for I perceive that you are a holy man or maybe a prophet." And she was just about to seek direct and personal help from the Master when she did what so many have done before and since—dodged the issue of personal salvation by turning to the discussion of theology and philosophy. She quickly turned the conversation from her own needs to a theological controversy. Pointing over to Mount Gerizim, she continued: "Our fathers worshiped on this mountain, and yet *you* would say that in Jerusalem is the place where men ought to worship; which, then, is the right place to worship God?"

Jesus perceived the attempt of the woman's soul to avoid direct and searching contact with its Maker, but he also saw that there was present in her soul a desire to know the better way of life. After all, there was in Nalda's heart a true thirst for the living water; therefore he dealt patiently with her, saying: "Woman, let me say to you that the day is soon coming when neither on this mountain nor in Jerusalem will you worship the Father. But now you worship that which you know not, a mixture of the religion of many pagan gods and gentile philosophies. The Jews at least know whom they worship; they have removed all confusion by concentrating their worship upon one God, Yahweh. But you should believe me when I say that the hour will soon come—even now is—when all sincere worshipers will worship the Father in spirit and in truth, for it is just such worshipers the Father seeks. God is spirit, and they who worship him must worship him in spirit and in truth. Your salvation comes not from knowing how others should worship or where but by receiving into your own heart this living water which I am offering you even now."

But Nalda would make one more effort to avoid the discussion of the embarrassing question of her personal life on earth and the status of her soul before God. Once more she resorted to questions of general religion, saying: "Yes, I know, Sir, that John has preached about the coming of the Converter, he who will be called the Deliverer, and that, when he shall come, he will declare to us all things"—and Jesus, interrupting Nalda, said with startling assurance, "I who speak to you am he."

As Nalda was about to voice her real and personal longing for better things and a more noble

> "I WHO SPEAK TO YOU AM HE."

WHAT PRAYER MEANT TO JESUS

Jesus never prayed as a religious duty. To him prayer was a sincere expression of spiritual attitude, a declaration of soul loyalty, a recital of personal devotion, an expression of thanksgiving, an avoidance of emotional tension, a prevention of conflict, an exaltation of intellection, an ennoblement of desire, a vindication of moral decision, an enrichment of thought, an invigoration of higher inclinations, a consecration of impulse, a clarification of viewpoint, a declaration of faith, a transcendental surrender of will, a sublime assertion of confidence, a revelation of courage, the proclamation of discovery, a confession of supreme devotion, the validation of consecration, a technique for the adjustment of difficulties, and the mighty mobilization of the combined soul powers to withstand all human tendencies toward selfishness, evil, and sin. He lived just such a life of prayerful consecration to the doing of his Father's will and ended his life triumphantly with just such a prayer. The secret of his unparalleled religious life was this consciousness of the presence of God; and he attained it by intelligent prayer and sincere worship—unbroken communion with God—and not by leadings, voices, visions, or extraordinary religious practices.

[VASILY POLENOV — *Dreams (On the Hill)*]

way of living, just as she was ready to speak the real desire of her heart, the twelve apostles returned from Sychar, and coming upon this scene of Jesus' talking so intimately with this woman—this Samaritan woman, and alone—they were more than astonished. They quickly deposited their supplies and drew aside, no man daring to reprove him, while Jesus said to Nalda: "Woman, go your way; God has forgiven you. Henceforth you will live a new life. You have received the living water, and a new joy will spring up within your soul, and you shall become a daughter of the Most High." And the woman, perceiving the disapproval of the apostles, left her waterpot and fled to the city.

As she entered the city, she proclaimed to everyone she met: "Go out to Jacob's well and go quickly, for there you will see a man who told me all I ever did. Can this be the Converter?" And ere the sun went down, a great crowd had assembled at Jacob's well to hear Jesus. And the Master talked to them more about the water of life, the gift of the indwelling spirit.

Jesus and the apostles went into Sychar and preached two days before they established their camp on Mount Gerizim until the end of August. And many of the dwellers in Sychar believed the gospel and made request for baptism, but the apostles of Jesus did not yet baptize. ∎

THE LORD'S PRAYER

September and October were spent in retirement at a secluded camp upon the slopes of Mount Gilboa. The month of September Jesus spent here alone with his apostles, teaching and instructing them in the truths of the kingdom.

Jesus knew that the days of the preliminary work of teaching and preaching were about over, that the next move involved the beginning of the full and final effort of his life on earth, and he did not wish the launching of this undertaking to be in any manner either trying or embarrassing to John the Baptist. Jesus had therefore decided to spend some time in retirement rehearsing his apostles and then to do some quiet work in the cities of the Decapolis until John should be either executed or released to join them in a united effort.

As time passed, the twelve became more devoted to Jesus and increasingly committed to the work of the kingdom. Their devotion was in large part a matter of personal loyalty. They did not grasp his many-sided teaching; they did not fully comprehend the nature of Jesus or the significance of his bestowal on earth.

The central theme of the discussions throughout the entire month of September was prayer and worship. After they had discussed worship for some days, Jesus finally delivered his memorable discourse on prayer in answer to Thomas's request: "Master, teach us how to pray."

John had taught his disciples a prayer, a prayer for salvation in the coming kingdom. Although Jesus never forbade his followers to use John's form of prayer, the apostles very early perceived that their Master did not fully approve of the practice of uttering set and formal prayers. Nevertheless, believers constantly requested to be taught how to pray. The twelve longed to know what form of petition Jesus would approve. And it was chiefly because of this need for some simple petition for the common people that Jesus at this time consented, in answer to Thomas's request, to teach them a suggestive form of prayer.

But the apostles were not yet satisfied; they desired Jesus to give them a model prayer which they could teach the new disciples. After listening to this discourse on prayer, James Zebedee said: "Very good, Master, but we do not desire a form of prayer for ourselves so much as for the newer believers who so frequently beseech us, 'Teach us how acceptably to pray to the Father in heaven.'"

When James had finished speaking, Jesus said: "If, then, you still desire such a prayer, I would present the one which I taught my brothers and sisters in Nazareth:"

Our Father who is in heaven,
    Hallowed be your name.
Your kingdom come; your will be done
    On earth as it is in heaven.
Give us this day our bread for tomorrow;
    Refresh our souls with the water of life.
And forgive us every one our debts
    As we also have forgiven our debtors.
Save us in temptation, deliver us from evil,
    And increasingly make us perfect like yourself.

After Jesus' death and ascension to the Father it became the practice of many believers to finish this so-called Lord's prayer by the addition of—"In the name of the Lord Jesus Christ." Still later on, two lines were lost in copying, and there was added to this prayer an extra clause, reading: "For yours is the kingdom and the power and the glory, forevermore."

Jesus gave the apostles the prayer in collective form as they had prayed it in the Nazareth home. He never taught a formal personal prayer, only group, family, or social petitions. And he never volunteered to do that.

Jesus taught that effective prayer must be:

1. Unselfish—not alone for oneself.
2. Believing—according to faith.
3. Sincere—honest of heart.
4. Intelligent—according to light.
5. Trustful—in submission to the Father's will.

When Jesus spent whole nights on the mountain in prayer, it was mainly for his disciples, particularly for the twelve. The Master prayed very little for himself, although he engaged in much worship of the nature of understanding communion with his Paradise Father. ∎

CONFERENCE WITH JOHN'S APOSTLES

Around the first of October, Philip and some of his fellow apostles were in a near-by village buying food when they met some of the apostles of John the Baptist. As a result of this chance meeting in the market place there came about a three weeks' conference at the Gilboa camp between the apostles of Jesus and the apostles of John, for John had recently appointed twelve of his leaders to be apostles, following the precedent of Jesus. John had done this in response to the urging of Abner, the chief of his loyal supporters. Jesus was present at the Gilboa camp throughout the first week of this joint conference but absented himself the last two weeks.

By the beginning of the second week of this month, Abner had assembled all of his associates at the Gilboa camp and was prepared to go into council with the apostles of Jesus. For three weeks these twenty-four men were in session three times a day and for six days each week. The first week Jesus mingled with them between their forenoon, afternoon, and evening sessions. They wanted the Master to meet with them and preside over their joint deliberations, but he steadfastly refused to participate in their discussions, though he did consent to speak to them on three occasions. These talks by Jesus to the twenty-four were on sympathy, co-operation, and tolerance.

On the afternoon of their final discussion of financial questions, Jesus returned, heard of their deliberations, listened to their decisions, and said: "These, then, are your conclusions, and I shall help you each to carry out the spirit of your united decisions."

Throughout the months of November and December, Jesus and the twenty-four worked quietly in the Greek cities of the Decapolis, chiefly in Scythopolis, Gerasa, Abila, and Gadara. This was really the end of that preliminary period of taking over John's work and organization. Always does the socialized religion of a new revelation pay the price of compromise with the established forms and usages of the preceding religion which it seeks to salvage. Baptism was the price which the followers of Jesus paid in order to carry with them, as a socialized religious group, the followers of John the Baptist. John's followers, in joining Jesus' followers, gave up just about everything except water baptism.

Abner became a devout believer in Jesus and was later on made the head of a group of seventy teachers whom the Master commissioned to preach the gospel.

John had now been in prison a year and a half, and most of this time Jesus had labored very quietly; so it was not strange that John should be led to wonder about the kingdom. John's friends interrupted Jesus' teaching to say to him: "John the Baptist has sent us to ask—are you truly the Deliverer, or shall we look for another?"

Jesus paused to say to John's friends: "Go back and tell John that he is not forgotten. Tell him what you have seen and heard, that the poor have good tidings preached to them." And when Jesus had spoken further to the messengers of John, he turned again to the multitude and said: "Do not think that John doubts the gospel of the kingdom. He makes inquiry only to assure his disciples who are also my disciples. John is no weakling. Let me ask you who heard John preach before Herod put him in prison: What did you behold in John—a reed shaken with the wind? A man of changeable moods and clothed in soft raiment? As a rule they who are gorgeously appareled and who live delicately are in kings' courts and in the mansions of the rich. But what did you see when you beheld John? A prophet? Yes, I say to you, and much more

than a prophet. Of John it was written: 'Behold, I send my messenger before your face; he shall prepare the way before you.'

"Verily, verily, I say to you, among those born of women there has not arisen a greater than John the Baptist; yet he who is but small in the kingdom of heaven is greater because he has been born of the spirit and knows that he has become a son of God."

Many who heard Jesus that day submitted themselves to John's baptism, thereby publicly professing entrance into the kingdom. And the apostles of John were firmly knit to Jesus from that day forward. This occurrence marked the real union of John's and Jesus' followers.

After the messengers had conversed with Abner, they departed for Machaerus to tell all this to John. He was greatly comforted, and his faith was strengthened by the words of Jesus and the message of Abner.

Death of John the Baptist

John the Baptist was executed by order of Herod Antipas on the evening of January 10, A.D. 28. The next day a few of John's disciples who had gone to Machaerus heard of his execution and, going to Herod, made request for his body, which they put in a tomb, later giving it burial at Sebaste, the home of Abner. The following day, January 12, they started north to the camp of John's and Jesus' apostles near Pella, and they told Jesus about the death of John. When Jesus heard their report, he dismissed the multitude and, calling the twenty-four together, said: "John is dead. Herod has beheaded him. Tonight go into joint council and arrange your affairs accordingly. There shall be delay no longer. The hour has come to proclaim the kingdom openly and with power. Tomorrow we go into Galilee."

Accordingly, on the morning of January 13, A.D. 28, Jesus and the apostles, accompanied by some twenty-five disciples, made their way to Capernaum and lodged that night in Zebedee's house. ✳

THE YEAR OF SIGNS AND WONDERS

And they did eat, and were all filled: and there was taken up of fragments that remained to them twelve baskets.

—LUKE 9:17 KJV

NEARLY THREE YEARS INTO HIS PUBLIC MINISTRY, THE FAME OF JESUS, PARTICULARLY AS a healer, had spread to all parts of Palestine and beyond. There began to appear— and continued throughout the remainder of Jesus' life on earth—a peculiar and unexplained series of healing phenomena. Scores of afflicted men, women, and children found restoration of health and happiness as a result of the reconstructive power of the intense faith which impelled them to seek for healing. The beneficiaries of this unconscious healing by Jesus returned to their homes and added to the enlargement of his fame. The Master never explained how these healings were effected, other than that on several occasions he merely said, "I perceive that power has gone forth from me." On one occasion he remarked when touched by an ailing child, "I perceive that life has gone forth from me."

Certain forms of profound human faith were literally and truly *compelling* in the manifestation of healing by certain creative forces and personalities of the universe who were at that time so intimately associated with the Son of Man. It therefore becomes a fact of record that Jesus did frequently suffer people to heal themselves in his presence by their powerful, personal faith.

The healing wonders which every now and then attended Jesus' mission on earth were not a part of his plan of proclaiming the kingdom. They were incidentally inherent in having on earth a divine being of well-nigh unlimited creator prerogatives in association with an unprecedented combination of divine mercy and human sympathy. But such so-called miracles gave Jesus much trouble in that they provided prejudice-raising publicity and afforded much unsought notoriety.

To a wonder-seeking people, these amazing events—beginning with the healing at sundown and culminating in the feeding of the five thousand—could only mean that the wonder-working deliverer of Israel had come. No wonder, then, that the multitude, when it had finished feasting, rose as one man and shouted, "Make him king!" But Jesus refused to be made their worldly king.

THE URANTIA BOOK: PAPERS 145–152
JANUARY, A.D. 28–APRIL, A.D. 29

[DANIEL GERHARTZ — *Forgiven*]

THE HEALING AT SUNDOWN

Jesus and the apostles arrived in Capernaum the evening of Tuesday, January 13. Several days later, on the Sabbath, Jesus delivered a sermon in the synagogue, soon after which a report rapidly spread through the countryside that he had cast out a demon and miraculously healed a man at the conclusion of this afternoon sermon; and many of the people believed it.

In addition, on their way from the synagogue Jesus and his friends stopped by to visit Simon Peter's mother-in-law Amatha, who had for several days been sick with chills and fever. Now it chanced that, at about the time Jesus stood over this sick woman, holding her hand, smoothing her brow, and speaking words of comfort and encouragement, the fever left her. Jesus had not yet had time to explain to his apostles that no miracle had been wrought at the synagogue; and with this incident so fresh and vivid in their minds, and recalling the water and the wine at Cana, they seized upon this coincidence as another miracle, and some of them rushed out to spread the news abroad throughout the city.

Amatha was suffering from malarial fever. She was not miraculously healed by Jesus at this time. Not until several hours later, after sundown, was her cure effected in connection with the extraordinary event which occurred in the front yard of the Zebedee home.

By the time Jesus and his apostles had made ready to partake of their evening meal near the end of this eventful Sabbath day, all Capernaum and its environs were agog over these reputed miracles of healing; and all who were sick or afflicted began preparations to go to Jesus or to have themselves carried there by their friends just as soon as the sun went down. According to Jewish teaching it was not permissible even to go in quest of health during the sacred hours of the Sabbath.

Therefore, as soon as the sun sank beneath the horizon, scores of afflicted men, women, and children began to make their way toward the Zebedee home in Bethsaida. One man started out with his paralyzed daughter just as soon as the sun sank behind his neighbor's house.

The whole day's events had set the stage for this extraordinary sundown scene. Even the text Jesus had used for his afternoon sermon had intimated that sickness should be banished; and he had spoken with such unprecedented power and authority! His message was so compelling! While he made no appeal to human authority, he did speak directly to the consciences and souls of men. Though he did not resort to logic, legal quibbles, or clever sayings, he did make a powerful, direct, clear, and personal appeal to the hearts of his hearers.

That Sabbath was a great day in the earth life of Jesus, yes, in the life of a universe. To all local universe intents and purposes the little Jewish city of Capernaum was the real capital of Nebadon. The handful of Jews in the Capernaum synagogue were not the only beings to hear that momentous closing statement of Jesus' sermon: "Hate is the shadow of fear; revenge the mask of

SYMPATHETIC HEART

Jesus well knew he could never build an enduring spiritual movement upon the foundation of purely material wonders. It had been his consistent policy to refrain from exhibiting his creator prerogatives. Not since Cana had the supernatural or miraculous attended his teaching; still, seeing an afflicted multitude gathered at Zebedee's house touched his sympathetic heart and appealed to his understanding affection.

Six hundred and eight-three men, women, and children were perfectly healed of all their physical diseases and other material disorders.

cowardice." Neither could his hearers forget his blessed words, declaring, "Man is the son of God, not a child of the devil."

Soon after the setting of the sun, as Jesus and the apostles still lingered about the supper table, Peter's wife heard voices in the front yard and, on going to the door, saw a large company of sick folks assembling, and that the road from Capernaum was crowded by those who were on their way to seek healing at Jesus' hands. On seeing this sight, she went at once and informed her husband, who told Jesus.

When the Master stepped out of the front entrance of Zebedee's house, his eyes met an array of stricken and afflicted humanity. He gazed upon almost one thousand sick and ailing human beings; at least that was the number of persons gathered together before him. Not all present were afflicted; some had come assisting their loved ones in this effort to secure healing.

The sight of these afflicted mortals, men, women, and children, suffering in large measure as a result of the mistakes and misdeeds of his own trusted Sons of universe administration, peculiarly touched the human heart of Jesus and challenged the divine mercy of this benevolent Creator Son.

A voice from the front yard exclaimed: "Master, speak the word, restore our health, heal our diseases, and save our souls." No sooner had these words been uttered than a vast retinue of heavenly hosts, such as always attended this incarnated Creator of a universe, made themselves ready to act with creative power should their Sovereign give the signal. This was one of those moments in the earth career of Jesus in which divine wisdom and human compassion were so interlocked in the judgment of the Son of Man that he sought refuge in appeal to his Father's will.

When Peter implored the Master to heed their cry for help, Jesus, looking down upon the afflicted throng, answered: "I have come into the world to reveal the Father and establish his kingdom. For this purpose have I lived my life to this hour. If, therefore, it should be the will of Him who sent me and not inconsistent with my dedication to the proclamation of the gospel of the kingdom of heaven, I would desire to see my children made whole—and—" but the further words of Jesus were lost in the tumult.

Jesus had passed the responsibility of this healing decision to the ruling of his Father. Evidently the Father's will interposed no objection, for the words of the Master had scarcely been uttered when the assembly of celestial personalities serving under the command of Jesus' Personalized Thought Adjuster was mightily astir. The vast retinue descended into the midst of this motley throng of afflicted mortals, and in a moment of time 683 men, women, and children were made whole, were perfectly healed of all their physical diseases and other material disorders. Such a scene was never witnessed on earth before that day, nor since. And for those of us who were present to behold this creative wave of healing, it was indeed a thrilling spectacle.

But of all the beings who were astonished at this sudden and unexpected outbreak of supernatural

healing, Jesus was the most surprised. In a moment when his human interests and sympathies were focused upon the scene of suffering and affliction there spread out before him, he neglected to bear in his human mind the admonitory warnings of his Personalized Adjuster regarding the impossibility of limiting the time element of the creator prerogatives of a Creator Son under certain conditions and in certain circumstances. Jesus desired to see these suffering mortals made whole if his Father's will would not thereby be violated. The Personalized Adjuster of Jesus instantly ruled that such an act of creative energy at that time would not transgress the will of the Paradise Father, and by such a decision—in view of Jesus' preceding expression of healing desire—the creative act *was*. What a *Creator Son* desires and his Father *wills* IS. Not in all of Jesus' subsequent earth life did another such en masse physical healing of mortals take place.

As might have been expected, the fame of this sundown healing at Bethsaida in Capernaum spread throughout all Galilee and Judea and to the regions beyond. Once more were the fears of Herod aroused, and he sent watchers to report on the work and teachings of Jesus and to ascertain if he was the former carpenter of Nazareth or John the Baptist risen from the dead.

Chiefly because of this unintended demonstration of physical healing, henceforth, throughout the remainder of his earth career, Jesus became as much a physician as a preacher. True, he continued his teaching, but his personal work consisted mostly in ministering to the sick and the distressed, while his apostles did the work of public preaching and baptizing believers.

But the majority of those who were recipients of supernatural or creative physical healing at this sundown demonstration of divine energy were not

[J. Kirk Richards — *The Healing at Sundown*]

permanently spiritually benefited by this extraordinary manifestation of mercy. A small number were truly edified by this physical ministry, but the spiritual kingdom was not advanced in the hearts of men by this amazing eruption of timeless creative healing. True religion is never enhanced by an appeal to the miraculous. ∎

THE LEPER AT IRON

The first public preaching tour of Galilee began on January 18 and continued for about two months. On this tour Jesus and the twelve apostles, assisted by the former apostles of John, preached the gospel and baptized believers.

This was the first time Jesus permitted his associates to preach without restraint. It was a source of great satisfaction to the apostles at last to feel they were at liberty to preach without restriction, and they threw themselves into the work of preaching the gospel, ministering to the sick, and baptizing believers, with great earnestness and joy.

At Iron, as in many of even the smaller cities of Galilee and Judea, there was a synagogue, and during the earlier times of Jesus' ministry he would often speak in these synagogues on the Sabbath day. Sometimes he would speak at the morning service, and Peter or one of the other apostles would preach at the afternoon hour. At this time all the synagogues of Galilee and Judea were open to him.

Iron was the site of extensive mineral mines for those days, and since Jesus had never shared the life of the miner, he spent most of his time, while sojourning at Iron, in the mines. While the apostles visited the homes and preached in the public places, Jesus worked in the mines with these underground laborers. The fame of Jesus as a healer had spread even to this remote village, and many sick and afflicted sought help at his hands, and many were greatly benefited by his healing ministry. But in none of these cases did the Master perform a so-called miracle of healing save in that of the leper.

Late on the afternoon of the third day at Iron, as Jesus was returning from the mines, he chanced to pass through a narrow side street on his way to his lodging place. As he drew near the squalid hovel of a certain leprous man, the afflicted one, having heard of his fame as a healer, made bold to accost him as he passed his door, saying as he knelt before him: "Lord, if only you would, you could make me clean. I have heard the message of your teachers, and I would enter the kingdom if I could be made clean." And the leper spoke in this way because among the Jews lepers were forbidden even to attend the synagogue or otherwise engage in public worship. This man really believed that he could not be received into the coming kingdom unless he could find a cure for his leprosy. And when Jesus saw him in his affliction and heard his words of clinging faith, his human heart was touched, and the divine mind was moved with compassion. As Jesus looked upon him, the man fell upon his face and worshiped. Then the Master stretched forth his hand and, touching him,

THIS CLEANSING OF THE LEPER WAS THE FIRST SO-CALLED MIRACLE WHICH JESUS HAD INTENTIONALLY AND DELIBERATELY PERFORMED UP TO THIS TIME.

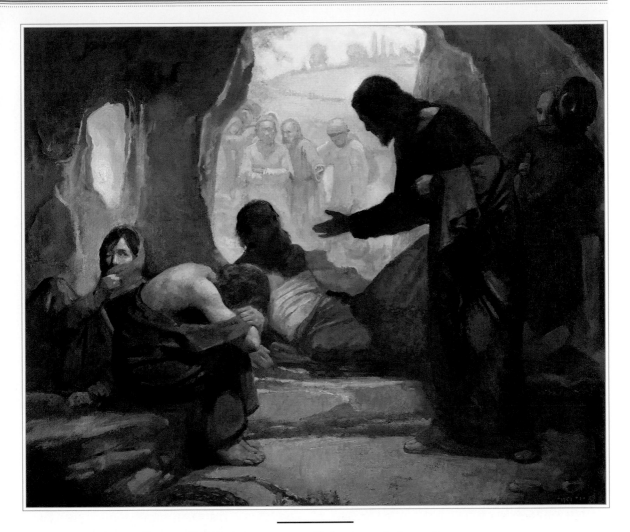

[J. Kirk Richards — *Christ among the Lepers*]

said: "I will—be clean." And immediately he was healed; the leprosy no longer afflicted him.

When Jesus had lifted the man upon his feet, he charged him: "See that you tell no man about your healing but rather go quietly about your business, showing yourself to the priest and offering those sacrifices commanded by Moses in testimony of your cleansing." But this man did not do as Jesus had instructed him. Instead, he began to publish abroad throughout the town that Jesus had cured his leprosy, and since he was known to all the village, the people could plainly see that he had been cleansed of his disease. He did not go to the priests as Jesus had admonished him. As a result of his spreading abroad the news that Jesus had healed him, the Master was so thronged by the sick that he was forced to rise early the next day and leave the village. Although Jesus did not again enter the town, he remained two days in the outskirts near the mines, continuing to instruct the believing miners further regarding the gospel of the kingdom.

This cleansing of the leper was the first so-called miracle which Jesus had intentionally and deliberately performed up to this time. And this was a case of real leprosy. ∎

AT THE POOL OF BETHESDA

Early on the morning of Tuesday, March 30, Jesus and the apostolic party started on their journey to Jerusalem for the Passover, going by the route of the Jordan valley. They arrived on the afternoon of Friday, April 2, and established their headquarters, as usual, at Bethany. Passing through Jericho, they paused to rest while Judas made a deposit of some of their common funds in the bank of a friend of his family. This was the first time Judas had carried a surplus of money, and this deposit was left undisturbed until they passed through Jericho again when on that last and eventful journey to Jerusalem just before the trial and death of Jesus.

The party had an uneventful trip to Jerusalem, but they had hardly got themselves settled at Bethany when from near and far those seeking healing for their bodies, comfort for troubled minds, and salvation for their souls, began to congregate, so much so that Jesus had little time for rest. Therefore they pitched tents at Gethsemane, and the Master would go back and forth from Bethany to Gethsemane to avoid the crowds which so constantly thronged him. The apostolic party spent almost three weeks at Jerusalem, but Jesus enjoined them to do no public preaching, only private teaching and personal work.

The afternoon of the second Sabbath in Jerusalem, as the Master and the apostles were about to participate in the temple services, John said to Jesus, "Come with me, I would show you something." John conducted Jesus out through one of the Jerusalem gates to a pool of water called Bethesda. Surrounding this pool was a structure of five porches under which a large group of sufferers lingered in quest of healing. This was a hot spring whose reddish-tinged water would bubble up at irregular intervals because of gas accumulations in the rock caverns underneath the pool. This periodic disturbance of the warm waters was believed by many to be due to supernatural influences, and it was a popular belief that the first person who entered the water after such a disturbance would be healed of whatever infirmity he had.

The apostles were somewhat restless under the restrictions imposed by Jesus, and John, the youngest of the twelve, was especially restive under this restraint. He had brought Jesus to the pool thinking that the sight of the assembled sufferers would make such an appeal to the Master's compassion that he would be moved to perform a miracle of healing, and thereby would all Jerusalem be astounded and presently be won to believe in the gospel of the kingdom. Said John to Jesus: "Master, see all of these suffering ones; is there nothing we can do for them?" And Jesus replied: "John, why would you tempt me to turn aside from the way I have chosen? Why do you go on desiring to substitute the working of wonders and the healing of the sick for the proclamation of the gospel of eternal truth? My son, I may not do that which you desire, but gather together these sick and afflicted that I may speak words of good cheer and eternal comfort to them."

In speaking to those assembled, Jesus said: "Many of you are here, sick and afflicted, because of your many years of wrong living. Some suffer from the accidents of time, others as a result of the mistakes of their forebears, while some of you struggle under the handicaps of the imperfect conditions of your temporal existence. But my Father works, and I would work, to improve your earthly state but more especially to insure your eternal estate. None of us can do much to change the difficulties of life unless we discover the Father in heaven so wills. After all, we are all beholden to do the will of the Eternal. If you could all be healed of your physical afflictions, you would indeed

And many of those who heard believed the gospel of the kingdom. Some of the afflicted were so inspired and spiritually revivified that they went about proclaiming that they had also been cured of their physical ailments.

One man who had been many years downcast and grievously afflicted by the infirmities of his troubled mind, rejoiced at Jesus' words and, picking up his bed, went forth to his home, even though it was the Sabbath day. This afflicted man had waited all these years for *somebody* to help him; he was such a victim of the feeling of his own helplessness that he had never once entertained the idea of helping himself which proved to be the one thing he had to do in order to effect recovery—take up his bed and walk. ∎

APRIL, A.D. 28

THE PENITENT WOMAN

Though Simon was not a member of the Jewish Sanhedrin, he was an influential Pharisee of Jerusalem. He was a half-hearted believer, and notwithstanding that he might be severely criticized therefor, he dared to invite Jesus and his personal associates, Peter, James, and John, to his home for a social meal. Simon had long observed the Master and was much impressed with his teachings and even more so with his personality.

The wealthy Pharisees were devoted to alms-giving, and they did not shun publicity regarding their philanthropy. Sometimes they would even blow a trumpet as they were about to bestow charity upon some beggar. It was the custom of these Pharisees, when they provided a banquet for distinguished guests, to leave the doors of the house open so that even the street beggars might come in and, standing around the walls of the room behind the couches of the diners, be in position to receive

[HAROLD COPPING — *The Pool of Bethesda*]

marvel, but it is even greater that you should be cleansed of all spiritual disease and find yourselves healed of all moral infirmities. You are all God's children; you are the sons of the heavenly Father. The bonds of time may seem to afflict you, but the God of eternity loves you. And when the time of judgment shall come, fear not, you shall all find, not only justice, but an abundance of mercy. Verily, verily, I say to you: He who hears the gospel of the kingdom and believes in this teaching of sonship with God, has eternal life; already are such believers passing from judgment and death to light and life. And the hour is coming in which even those who are in the tombs shall hear the voice of the resurrection."

portions of food which might be tossed to them by the banqueters.

On this particular occasion at Simon's house, among those who came in off the street was a woman of unsavory reputation who had recently become a believer in the good news of the gospel of the kingdom. This woman was well known throughout all Jerusalem as the former keeper of one of the so-called high-class brothels located hard by the temple court of the gentiles. She had, on accepting the teachings of Jesus, closed up her nefarious place of business and had induced the majority of the women associated with her to accept the gospel and change their mode of living; notwithstanding this, she was still held in great disdain by the Pharisees and was compelled to wear her hair down—the badge of harlotry. This unnamed woman had brought with her a large flask of perfumed anointing lotion and, standing behind Jesus as he reclined at meat, began to anoint his feet while she also wet his feet with her tears of gratitude, wiping them with the hair of her head. And when she had finished this anointing, she continued weeping and kissing his feet.

When Simon saw all this, he said to himself: "This man, if he were a prophet, would have perceived who and what manner of woman this is who thus touches him; that she is a notorious sinner." And Jesus, knowing what was going on in Simon's mind, spoke up, saying: "Simon, I have something which I would like to say to you." Simon answered, "Teacher, say on." Then said Jesus: "A certain wealthy moneylender had two debtors. The one owed him five hundred denarii

and the other fifty. Now, when neither of them had wherewith to pay, he forgave them both. Which of them do you think, Simon, would love him most?" Simon answered, "He, I suppose, whom he forgave the most." And Jesus said, "You have rightly judged," and pointing to the woman, he continued: "Simon, take a good look at this woman. I entered your house as an invited guest, yet you gave me no water for my feet. This grateful woman has washed my feet with tears and wiped them with the hair of her head. You gave me no kiss of friendly greeting, but this woman, ever since she came in, has not ceased to kiss my feet. My head with oil you neglected to anoint, but she has anointed my feet with precious lotions. And what is the meaning of all this? Simply that her many sins have been forgiven, and this has led her to love much. But those who have received but little forgiveness sometimes love but little." And turning around toward the woman, he took her by the hand and, lifting her up, said: "You have indeed repented of your sins, and they are forgiven. Be not discouraged by the thoughtless and unkind attitude of your fellows; go on in the joy and liberty of the kingdom of heaven."

When Simon and his friends who sat at meat with him heard these words, they were the more astonished, and they began to whisper among themselves, "Who is this man that he even dares to forgive sins?" And when Jesus heard them so murmuring, he turned to dismiss the woman, saying, "Woman, go in peace; your faith has saved you."

As Jesus arose with his friends to leave, he turned to Simon and said: "I know your heart, Simon,

A COMMISSION OF SIX SECRET SPIES WAS APPOINTED TO FOLLOW JESUS, TO OBSERVE HIS WORDS AND ACTS, AND AMASS EVIDENCE OF LAWBREAKING AND BLASPHEMY.

how you are torn betwixt faith and doubts, how you are distraught by fear and troubled by pride; but I pray for you that you may yield to the light and may experience in your station in life just such mighty transformations of mind and spirit as may be comparable to the tremendous changes which the gospel of the kingdom has already wrought in the heart of your unbidden and unwelcome guest. And I declare to all of you that the Father has opened the doors of the heavenly kingdom to all who have the faith to enter, and no man or association of men can close those doors even to the most humble soul or supposedly most flagrant sinner on earth if such sincerely seek an entrance." And Jesus, with Peter, James, and John, took leave of their host and went to join the rest of the apostles at the camp in the garden of Gethsemane. ■

THE SIX JERUSALEM SPIES

The chief priests and the religious leaders of the Jews held many secret meetings for the purpose of deciding what to do with Jesus. They were all agreed that something should be done to put a stop to his teaching, but they could not agree on the method. They had hoped that the civil authorities would dispose of him as Herod had put an end to John, but they discovered that Jesus was so conducting his work that the Roman officials were not much alarmed by his preaching. Accordingly, at a meeting which was held the day before Jesus' departure for Capernaum, it was decided that he would have to be apprehended on a religious charge and be tried by the Sanhedrin. Therefore a commission of six secret spies was appointed to follow Jesus, to observe his words and acts, and when they had amassed sufficient evidence of lawbreaking and blasphemy, to return to Jerusalem with their report. These six Jews caught up with the apostolic party, numbering about thirty, at Jericho and, under the pretense of desiring to become disciples, attached themselves to Jesus' family of followers, remaining with the group up to the time of the beginning of the second preaching tour in Galilee; whereupon three of them returned to Jerusalem to submit their report to the chief priests and the Sanhedrin.

But the spies did not have long to wait for their opportunity to accuse Jesus and his associates of Sabbath breaking. As the company passed along the narrow road, the waving wheat, which was just then ripening, was near at hand on either side, and some of the apostles, being hungry, plucked the ripe grain and ate it. It was customary for travelers to help themselves to grain as they passed along the road, and therefore no thought of wrongdoing was attached to such conduct. But the spies seized upon this as a pretext for assailing Jesus. When they saw Andrew rub the grain in his hand, they went up to him and said: "Do you not know that it is unlawful to pluck and rub the grain on the Sabbath day?" And Andrew answered: "But we are hungry and rub only sufficient for our needs; and since when did it become sinful to eat grain on the Sabbath day?" But the Pharisees answered: "You do no wrong in eating, but you do break the law in plucking and rubbing out the grain between your hands; surely your Master would not approve of such acts." Then said Andrew: "But if it is not wrong to eat the grain, surely the rubbing out between our hands is hardly more work than the chewing of the grain, which you allow; wherefore do you quibble over such trifles?" When Andrew intimated that they were quibblers, they were indignant, and rushing back to where Jesus walked along, talking to Matthew, they protested, saying: "Behold, Teacher, your apostles do that which is unlawful on the Sabbath day; they pluck, rub, and eat the grain. We are sure you will command them to cease." And then said Jesus to the accusers: "You are indeed zealous for the law, and you do well to remember the Sabbath day to keep it holy; but did you never read in the Scripture that, one day when David was hungry, he and they who were with him entered the house of God and ate the showbread, which it was not lawful for anyone to eat save the priests? and David also gave this bread to those who were with him. And have you not read in our law that it is lawful to do many needful things on the Sabbath day? And shall I not, before the day is finished, see you eat that which you have brought along for the needs of this day? My good men, you do well to be zealous for the Sabbath, but you would do better to guard the health and well-being of your fellows. I declare that the Sabbath was made for man and not man for the Sabbath. And if you are here present with us to watch my words, then will I openly proclaim that the Son of Man is lord even of the Sabbath."

For several weeks, these spies did their best to ensnare Jesus as a lawbreaker, but the Master consistently left them in confusion and disarray, while comforting the crowds who attended the apostolic party. ∎

THE KINGDOM'S FIRST HOSPITAL

From May 3 to October 3, A.D. 28, Jesus and the apostolic party were in residence at the Zebedee home at Bethsaida. Throughout this five months' period of the dry season an

THE DEPENDABLE DAVID ZEBEDEE

David Zebedee was surely one of the unsung heroes of the early kingdom, and while he labored in the shadows of his more illustrious elder brothers, the apostles James and John, his contributions were nonetheless essential. Of the sons of Zebedee, James was the most interested in Jesus as a teacher, as a philosopher. John cared most for his religious teaching and opinions. David respected him as a mechanic but took little stock in his religious views and philosophic teachings.

David maintained a permanent headquarters for the work of the kingdom in his father's house at Bethsaida. This was the clearinghouse for Jesus' work on earth and the relay station for the messenger service which David carried on between the workers in various parts of Palestine and adjacent regions. He did all of this on his own initiative but with the approval of Andrew. David employed forty to fifty messengers in this intelligence division of the rapidly enlarging and extending work of the kingdom. While thus employed, he partially supported himself by spending some of his time at his old work of fishing.

This efficient and dedicated messenger service kept the scattered kingdom groups fully informed concerning the progress of the others, and the receipt of news from other groups was always a source of encouragement to these scattered and separated workers. An overnight relay messenger service ran over a hundred miles between Jerusalem and Bethsaida. These runners left Jerusalem each evening, relaying at Sychar and Scythopolis, arriving in Bethsaida by breakfast time the next morning.

David's personality and devotion are well illustrated as Jesus prepared to leave Galilee after the crisis at Capernaum. In bidding farewell, David said: "Go forth to your work, Master. Don't let the bigots catch you, and never doubt that the messengers will follow after you. My men will never lose contact with you, and through them you shall know of the enormous camp was maintained by the seaside near the Zebedee residence, which had been greatly enlarged to accommodate the growing family of Jesus. This seaside camp, occupied by an ever-changing population of truth seekers, healing candidates, and curiosity devotees, numbered from five hundred to fifteen hundred. This tented city was under the general supervision of David Zebedee, assisted by the Alpheus twins. The encampment was a model in order and sanitation as well as in its general administration. The sick of different types were segregated and were under the supervision of a believer physician, a Syrian named Elman.

Throughout this period the apostles would go fishing at least one day a week, selling their catch to David for consumption by the seaside encampment. The funds thus received were turned over to the group treasury. The twelve were permitted to spend one week out of each month with their families or friends.

While Andrew continued in general charge of the apostolic activities, Peter was in full charge of the school of the evangelists. The apostles all

kingdom in other parts, and by them we will all know about you. Nothing that might happen to me will interfere with this service, for I have appointed first and second leaders, even a third. I am neither a teacher nor a preacher, but it is in my heart to do this, and none can stop me."

Few of Jesus' followers at this time fully appreciated the great value of the services of the messenger corps. Not only did the messengers keep the believers throughout Palestine in touch with each other and with Jesus and the apostles, but during these dark days they also served as collectors of funds, not only for the sustenance of Jesus and his associates, but also for the support of the families of the twelve apostles and the twelve evangelists..

David also attended to the needs and security of the multitudes which followed after Jesus by establishing encampments in various locations. The largest was an enormous camp maintained by the seaside in Bethsaida, occupied by an ever-changing population of truth seekers, healing candidates, and curiosity devotees, that numbered from five hundred to fifteen hundred. This tented city was operated under his general supervision and was a model in order and sanitation as well as in its general administration. David managed this large tent city so that it became a self-sustaining enterprise, notwithstanding that no one was ever turned away.

His services were particularly valuable during those dark and tragic days of the Master's arrest and crucifixion in April, A.D. 30. This peculiar-minded David Zebedee was the only one of the leading disciples of Jesus who was inclined to take a literal and plain matter-of-fact view of the Master's assertion that he would die and "rise again on the third day."

After the resurrection when the apostles and others refused to believe the report of the five women who represented that they had seen Jesus and talked with him, David assembled his messengers at the home of Nicodemus in Jerusalem and prepared to send them out on their final mission as heralds of the resurrection. The majority of those present endeavored to persuade David not to do this. But they could not influence him. They then sought to dissuade the messengers, but they would not heed the words of doubt. And so, shortly before ten o'clock this Sunday morning, these twenty-six runners went forth as the first heralds of the mighty truth-fact of the resurrected Jesus. And they started out on this mission as they had on so many others, in fulfillment of their oath to David Zebedee and to one another. These men had great confidence in David. They departed on this assignment without even tarrying to talk with those who had seen Jesus; they took David at his word. The majority of them believed what David had told them, and even those who somewhat doubted, carried the message just as certainly and just as swiftly.

That following June in Bethany, David Zebedee was married to Jesus' baby sister Ruth.

did their share in teaching groups of evangelists each forenoon, and both teachers and pupils taught the people during the afternoons. After the evening meal, five nights a week, the apostles conducted question classes for the benefit of the evangelists. Once a week Jesus presided at this question hour, answering the holdover questions from previous sessions.

In five months several thousand came and went at this encampment. Interested persons from every part of the Roman Empire and from the lands east of the Euphrates were in frequent attendance. This was the longest settled and well-organized period of the Master's teaching. Jesus' immediate family spent most of this time at either Nazareth or Cana.

The Bethsaida Hospital

In connection with the seaside encampment, Elman, the Syrian physician, with the assistance of a corps of twenty-five young women and twelve men, organized and conducted for four months what should be regarded as the kingdom's first hospital. At this infirmary, located a short distance to the south of the main tented city, they treated the sick in accordance with all known material methods as well as by the spiritual practices of prayer and faith encouragement. Jesus visited the sick of this encampment not less than three times a week and made personal contact with each sufferer. As far as we know, no so-called miracles of supernatural healing occurred among the one thousand afflicted and ailing persons who went away from this infirmary improved or cured. However, the vast majority of these benefited individuals ceased not to proclaim that Jesus had healed them.

Many of the cures effected by Jesus in connection with his ministry in behalf of Elman's patients did, indeed, appear to resemble the working of miracles, but we were instructed that they were only just such transformations of mind and spirit as may occur in the experience of expectant and faith-dominated persons who are under the immediate and inspirational influence of a strong, positive, and beneficent personality whose ministry banishes fear and destroys anxiety. ■

The Man with the Withered Hand

The second Sabbath before the departure of the apostles and the new corps of evangelists on the second preaching tour of Galilee, Jesus spoke in the Capernaum synagogue on the "Joys of Righteous Living." When Jesus had finished speaking, a large group of those who were maimed, halt, sick, and afflicted crowded up around him, seeking healing. Also in this group were the apostles, many of the new evangelists, and the Pharisaic spies from Jerusalem. Everywhere that Jesus went (except when in the hills about the Father's business) the six Jerusalem spies were sure to follow.

The leader of the spying Pharisees, as Jesus stood talking to the people, induced a man with a withered hand to approach him and ask if it would be lawful to be healed on the Sabbath day or should he seek help on another day. When Jesus saw the man, heard his words, and perceived that he had been sent by the Pharisees, he said: "Come forward while I ask you a question. If you had a sheep and it should fall into a pit on the Sabbath day, would you reach down, lay hold on it, and lift it out? Is it lawful to do such things on the Sabbath day?" And the man answered: "Yes, Master, it would be lawful thus to do well on the

---

[RUSS DOCKEN — *The Kingdom's First Hospital*]

Sabbath day." Then said Jesus, speaking to all of them: "I know wherefore you have sent this man into my presence. You would find cause for offense in me if you could tempt me to show mercy on the Sabbath day. In silence you all agreed that it was lawful to lift the unfortunate sheep out of the pit, even on the Sabbath, and I call you to witness that it is lawful to exhibit loving-kindness on the Sabbath day not only to animals but also to men. How much more valuable is a man than a sheep! I proclaim that it is lawful to do good to men on the Sabbath day." And as they all stood before him in silence, Jesus, addressing the man with the withered hand, said: "Stand up here by my side that all may see you. And now that you may know that it is my Father's will that you do good on the Sabbath day, if you have the faith to be healed, I bid you stretch out your hand."

And as this man stretched forth his withered hand, it was made whole. The people were minded to turn upon the Pharisees, but Jesus bade them be calm, saying: "I have just told you that it is lawful to do good on the Sabbath, to save life, but I did not instruct you to do harm and give way to the desire to kill." The angered Pharisees went away, and notwithstanding it was the Sabbath day, they hastened forthwith to Tiberias and took counsel with Herod, doing everything in their power to arouse his prejudice in order to secure the Herodians as allies against Jesus. But Herod refused to take action against Jesus, advising that they carry their complaints to Jerusalem.

This is the first case of a miracle to be wrought by Jesus in response to the challenge of his enemies.

And the Master performed this so-called miracle, not as a demonstration of his healing power, but as an effective protest against making the Sabbath rest of religion a veritable bondage of meaningless restrictions upon all mankind. This man returned to his work as a stone mason, proving to be one of those whose healing was followed by a life of thanksgiving and righteousness.

The last week of the sojourn at Bethsaida the Jerusalem spies became much divided in their attitude toward Jesus and his teachings. Three of these Pharisees were tremendously impressed by what they had seen and heard. Meanwhile, at Jerusalem, Abraham, a young and influential member of the Sanhedrin, publicly espoused the teachings of Jesus and was baptized in the pool of Siloam by Abner. All Jerusalem was agog over this event, and messengers were immediately dispatched to Bethsaida recalling the six spying Pharisees. ■

OCTOBER, A.D. 28

HEALING THE PARALYTIC

On Friday afternoon, October 1, when Jesus was holding his last meeting with the apostles, evangelists, and other leaders of the disbanding encampment, and with the six Pharisees from Jerusalem seated in the front row of this assembly in the spacious and enlarged front room of the Zebedee home, there occurred one of the strangest and most unique episodes of all Jesus'

THE MASTER PERFORMED THIS MIRACLE AS AN EFFECTIVE
PROTEST AGAINST MAKING THE SABBATH A BONDAGE OF
MEANINGLESS RESTRICTIONS UPON ALL MANKIND.

earth life. The Master was, at this time, speaking as he stood in this large room, which had been built to accommodate these gatherings during the rainy season. The house was entirely surrounded by a vast concourse of people who were straining their ears to catch some part of Jesus' discourse.

While the house was thus thronged with people and entirely surrounded by eager listeners, a man long afflicted with paralysis was carried down from Capernaum on a small couch by his friends. This paralytic had heard that Jesus was about to leave Bethsaida, and having talked with Aaron the stone mason, who had been so recently made whole, he resolved to be carried into Jesus' presence, where he could seek healing. His friends tried to gain entrance to Zebedee's house by both the front and back doors, but too many people were crowded together. But the paralytic refused to accept defeat; he directed his friends to procure ladders by which they ascended to the roof of the room in which Jesus was speaking, and after loosening the tiles, they boldly lowered the sick man on his couch by ropes until the afflicted one rested on the floor immediately in front of the Master. When Jesus saw what they had done, he ceased speaking, while those who were with him in the room marveled at the perseverance of the sick man and his friends. Said the paralytic: "Master, I would not disturb your teaching, but I am determined to be made whole. I am not like those who received healing and immediately forgot your teaching. I would be made whole that I might serve in the kingdom of heaven." Now, notwithstanding that this man's affliction had been brought upon him by his own misspent life, Jesus, seeing his faith, said to the paralytic: "Son, fear not; your sins are forgiven. Your faith shall save you."

When the Pharisees from Jerusalem, together with other scribes and lawyers who sat with them, heard this pronouncement by Jesus, they began to say to themselves: "How dare this man thus speak? Does he not understand that such words are blasphemy? Who can forgive sin but God?" Jesus, perceiving in his spirit that they thus reasoned within their own minds and among themselves, spoke to them, saying: "Why do you so reason in your hearts? Who are you that you sit in judgment over me? What is the difference whether I say to this paralytic, your sins are forgiven, or arise, take up your bed, and walk? But that you who witness all this may finally know that the Son of Man has authority and power on earth to forgive sins, I will say to this afflicted man, Arise, take up your bed, and go to your own house." And when Jesus had thus spoken, the paralytic arose, and as they made way for him, he walked out before them all. And those who saw these things were amazed. Peter dismissed the assemblage, while many prayed and glorified God, confessing that they had never before seen such strange happenings.

And it was about this time that the messengers of the Sanhedrin arrived to bid the six spies return to Jerusalem. When they heard this message, they fell to earnest debate among themselves; and after they had finished their discussions, the leader and two of his associates returned with the messengers to Jerusalem, while three of the spying Pharisees confessed faith in Jesus and, going immediately to the lake, were baptized by Peter and fellowshipped by the apostles as children of the kingdom.

Hardened Hearts

The religious leaders at Jerusalem were becoming well-nigh frantic as a result of the recent conversion of young Abraham and by the desertion of the three spies who had been baptized by Peter, and who were now out with the evangelists on this second preaching tour of Galilee. The Jewish leaders were increasingly blinded by fear and prejudice, while their hearts were hardened by the continued rejection of the appealing truths of the gospel of the kingdom. When men shut off the appeal to the spirit that dwells within them, there is little that can be done to modify their attitude.

When Jesus first met with the evangelists at the Bethsaida camp, in concluding his address, he said: "You should remember that in body and mind—emotionally—men react individually. The only *uniform* thing about men is the indwelling spirit. Though divine spirits may vary somewhat in the nature and extent of their experience, they react uniformly to all spiritual appeals. Only through, and by appeal to, this spirit can mankind ever attain unity and brotherhood." But many of the leaders of the Jews had closed the doors of their hearts to the spiritual appeal of the gospel. From this day on they ceased not to plan and plot for the Master's destruction. They were convinced that Jesus must be apprehended, convicted, and executed as a religious offender, a violator of the cardinal teachings of the Jewish sacred law. ■

JANUARY 16, A.D. 29

THE WOMEN'S EVANGELISTIC CORPS

Of all the daring things which Jesus did in connection with his earth career, the most amazing was his sudden announcement on the evening of January 16: "On the morrow we will set apart ten women for the ministering work of the kingdom." At the beginning of the two weeks' period during which the apostles and the evangelists were to be absent from Bethsaida on their furlough, Jesus requested David to summon his parents back to their home and to dispatch messengers calling to Bethsaida ten devout women who had served in the administration of the former encampment and the tented infirmary. These women had all listened to the instruction given the young evangelists, but it had never occurred to either themselves or their teachers that Jesus would dare to commission women to teach the gospel of the kingdom and minister to the sick.

Jesus authorized these women to effect their own organization and directed Judas to provide funds for their equipment and for pack animals. The ten elected Susanna as their chief and Joanna as their treasurer. From this time on they furnished their own funds; never again did they draw upon Judas for support.

It was most astounding in that day, when women were not even allowed on the main floor of the synagogue (being confined to the women's gallery), to behold them being recognized as authorized teachers of the new gospel of the kingdom. The charge which Jesus gave these ten women as he set them apart for gospel teaching and ministry was the emancipation proclamation which set free all women and for all time; no more was man to look upon woman as his spiritual inferior. This was a decided shock to even the twelve apostles. Notwithstanding they had many times heard the Master say that "in the kingdom of heaven there is neither rich nor poor, free nor bond, male nor female, all are equally the sons and daughters of God," they were literally stunned when he proposed formally to commission these ten women as religious teachers and even to permit their traveling about with them. The whole country

HOW JESUS EMANCIPATED WOMEN

The most astonishing and the most revolutionary feature of Jesus' mission on earth was his attitude toward women. In a day and generation when a man was not supposed to salute even his own wife in a public place, Jesus dared to take women along as teachers of the gospel in connection with his third tour of Galilee. And he had the consummate courage to do this in the face of the rabbinic teaching which declared that it was "better that the words of the law should be burned than delivered to women."

By word and deed, Jesus was unfailingly respectful, understanding, tender, and sympathetic toward women. While in Tarentum, he intervened on behalf of a wife who was being abused by her husband. He counseled the erring man: "My brother, always remember that man has no rightful authority over woman unless the woman has willingly and voluntarily given him such authority. The loving care and consideration which a man is willing to bestow upon his wife and their children are the measure of that man's attainment of the higher levels of creative and spiritual self-consciousness."

Jesus strove to teach his apostles that all women have souls which can choose God as their Father, thereby becoming daughters of God and candidates for life everlasting. But the apostles never ceased to be shocked by Jesus' willingness to talk with women, even women of presumed immoral character.

The first direct and undisguised pronouncement of his divine nature which Jesus made on earth was made to a woman, a Samaritan woman of questionable character in the eyes of men, but a woman whom the divine eye beheld as being a soul who desired salvation sincerely and wholeheartedly, and that was enough. The first five witnesses to the resurrection were women who believed even as the apostles doubted.

Despite her sincere conversion, a former keeper of a Jerusalem brothel was still held in disdain by the Pharisees. But the Master offered her comfort and forgiveness saying, "Be not discouraged by the thoughtless and unkind attitude of your fellows; go on in the joy and liberty of the kingdom of heaven."

In one generation Jesus lifted women out of the disrespectful oblivion and the slavish drudgery of the ages, though many of these gains were gradually lost as the olden customs prevailed in subsequent generations. Nevertheless, the ideal of gender equality has never really died. In many parts of the world women have already earned their rightful place in society. Slowly but surely, the continuing progressive evolution of the diverse global culture is showing positive signs of the Master's lofty ideals of true emancipation for all women.

was stirred up by this proceeding, the enemies of Jesus making great capital out of this move, but everywhere the women believers in the good news stood stanchly behind their chosen sisters and voiced no uncertain approval of this tardy acknowledgment of woman's place in religious work. And this liberation of women, giving them due recognition, was practiced by the apostles immediately after the Master's departure, albeit they fell back to the olden customs in subsequent generations. Throughout the early days of the Christian church women teachers and ministers

[J. KIRK RICHARDS]
[*Commissioning the Women's Corps*] OVERLEAF   >

were called *deaconesses* and were accorded general recognition. But Paul, despite the fact that he conceded all this in theory, never really incorporated it into his own attitude and personally found it difficult to carry out in practice.

It was at Magdala that the women first demonstrated their usefulness and vindicated the wisdom of their choosing. Andrew had imposed rather strict rules upon his associates about doing personal work with women, especially with those of questionable character. When the party entered Magdala, these ten women evangelists were free to enter the evil resorts and preach the glad tidings directly to all their inmates. And when visiting the sick, these women were able to draw very close in their ministry to their afflicted sisters. As the result of the ministry of these ten women (afterward known as the twelve women) at this place, Mary Magdalene was won for the kingdom. Through a succession of misfortunes and in consequence of the attitude of reputable society toward women who commit such errors of judgment, this woman had found herself in one of the nefarious resorts of Magdala. It was Martha and Rachel who made plain to Mary that the doors of the kingdom were open to even such as she. Mary believed the good news and was baptized by Peter the next day.

Mary Magdalene became the most effective teacher of the gospel among this group of twelve women evangelists. She was set apart for such service, together with Rebecca, at Jotapata about four weeks subsequent to her conversion. Mary and Rebecca, with the others of this group, went on through the remainder of Jesus' life on earth, laboring faithfully and effectively for the enlightenment and uplifting of their downtrodden sisters; and when the last and tragic episode in the drama of Jesus' life was being enacted, notwithstanding the apostles all fled but one, these women were all present, and not one either denied or betrayed him.

THE TEN WOMEN EVANGELISTS

SUSANNA, the daughter of the former chazan of the Nazareth synagogue

JOANNA, the wife of Chuza, the steward of Herod Antipas

ELIZABETH, the daughter of a wealthy Jew of Tiberias and Sepphoris

MARTHA, the elder sister of Andrew and Peter

RACHEL, the sister-in-law of Jude, the Master's brother in the flesh

NASANTA, the daughter of Elman, the Syrian physician

MILCHA, a cousin of the Apostle Thomas

RUTH, the eldest daughter of Matthew Levi

CELTA, the daughter of a Roman centurion

AGAMAN, a widow of Damascus.

Subsequently, Jesus added two other women to this group—**MARY MAGDALENE** and **REBECCA,** the daughter of Joseph of Arimathea.

MARCH 4, A.D. 29

THE NAZARETH REJECTION

Before their separation it had been arranged that the twelve apostles, together with the evangelists and the women's corps, should assemble at Nazareth to meet the Master on Friday, March 4. Accordingly, about this time, from all parts of central and southern Galilee these various groups of apostles and evangelists began moving toward Nazareth. By midafternoon, Andrew and Peter, the last to arrive, had reached the encampment prepared by the early arrivals and situated on the highlands to the north of the city. And this was the first time Jesus had visited Nazareth since the beginning of his public ministry.

This Friday afternoon Jesus walked about Nazareth quite unobserved and wholly unrecognized. He passed by the home of his childhood and the carpenter shop and spent a half hour on the hill which he so much enjoyed when a lad. Not since the day of his baptism by John in the Jordan had the Son of Man had such a flood of human emotion stirred up within his soul. While coming down from the mount, he heard the familiar sounds of the trumpet blast announcing the going down of the sun, just as he had so many, many times heard it when a boy growing up in Nazareth. Before returning to the encampment, he walked down by the synagogue where he had gone to school and indulged his mind in many reminiscences of his childhood days. Earlier in the day Jesus had sent Thomas to arrange with the ruler of the synagogue for his preaching at the Sabbath morning service.

The people of Nazareth were never reputed for piety and righteous living. As the years passed, this village became increasingly contaminated by the low moral standards of near-by Sepphoris. Throughout Jesus' youth and young manhood there had been a division of opinion in Nazareth regarding him; there was much resentment when he moved to Capernaum. While the inhabitants of Nazareth had heard much about the doings of their former carpenter, they were offended that he had never included his native village in any of his earlier preaching tours. They had indeed heard of Jesus' fame, but the majority of the citizens were angry because he had done none of his great works in the city of his youth. For months the people

of Nazareth had discussed Jesus much, but their opinions were, on the whole, unfavorable to him.

Thus did the Master find himself in the midst of, not a welcome homecoming, but a decidedly hostile and hypercritical atmosphere. But this was not all. His enemies, knowing that he was to spend this Sabbath day in Nazareth and supposing that he would speak in the synagogue, had hired numerous rough and uncouth men to harass him and in every way possible make trouble.

Most of the older of Jesus' friends, including the doting chazan teacher of his youth, were dead or had left Nazareth, and the younger generation was prone to resent his fame with strong jealousy. They failed to remember his early devotion to his father's family, and they were bitter in their criticism of his neglect to visit his brother and his married sisters living in Nazareth. The attitude of Jesus' family toward him had also tended to increase this unkind feeling of the citizenry. The orthodox among the Jews even presumed to criticize Jesus because he walked too fast on the way to the synagogue this Sabbath morning.

This Sabbath was a beautiful day, and all Nazareth, friends and foes, turned out to hear this former citizen of their town discourse in the synagogue. Many of the apostolic retinue had to remain without the synagogue; there was not room for all who had come to hear him. As a young man Jesus had often spoken in this place of worship, and this morning, when the ruler of the synagogue handed him the roll of sacred writings from which to read the Scripture lesson, none present seemed to recall that this was the very manuscript which he had presented to this synagogue.

It was customary in the synagogue, after the conclusion of the formal service, for the speaker to remain so that those who might be interested could ask him questions. Accordingly, on this Sabbath morning Jesus stepped down into the crowd which pressed forward to ask questions. In this group were many turbulent individuals whose minds were bent on mischief, while about the fringe of this crowd there circulated those debased men who had been hired to make trouble for Jesus. Many of the disciples and evangelists who had remained without now pressed into the synagogue and were not slow to recognize that trouble was brewing. They sought to lead the Master away, but he would not go with them.

Jesus found himself surrounded in the synagogue by a great throng of his enemies and a sprinkling of his own followers, and in reply to their rude questions and sinister banterings he half humorously remarked: "Yes, I am Joseph's son; I am the carpenter, and I am not surprised that you remind me of the proverb, 'Physician heal yourself,' and that you challenge me to do in Nazareth what you have heard I did at Capernaum; but I call you to witness that even the Scriptures declare that 'a prophet is not without honor save in his own country and among his own people.'"

But they jostled him and, pointing accusing fingers at him, said: "You think you are better than the people of Nazareth; you moved away from us, but your brother is a common workman, and your sisters still live among us. We know your mother, Mary. Where are they today? We hear big things about you, but we notice that you do no wonders when you come back." Jesus answered them: "I love the people who dwell in the city where I grew up, and I would rejoice to see you all enter the kingdom of heaven, but the doing of the works of God is not for me to determine. The transformations of grace are wrought in response to the living faith of those who are the beneficiaries."

Jesus would have good-naturedly managed the crowd and effectively disarmed even his violent enemies had it not been for the tactical blunder of one of his own apostles, Simon Zelotes, who, with the help of Nahor, one of the younger evangelists, had meanwhile gathered together a group of Jesus' friends from among the crowd and, assuming a belligerent attitude, had served notice on the enemies of the Master to go hence. Jesus had long taught the apostles that a soft answer turns away wrath, but his followers were not accustomed to seeing their beloved teacher, whom they so willingly called Master, treated with such discourtesy and disdain. It was too much for them, and they found themselves giving expression to passionate and vehement resentment, all of which only tended to arouse the mob spirit in this ungodly and uncouth assembly. And so, under the leadership of hirelings, these ruffians laid hold upon Jesus and rushed him out of the synagogue to the brow of a near-by precipitous hill, where they were minded to shove him over the edge to his death below. But just as they were about to push him over the edge of the cliff, Jesus turned suddenly upon his captors and, facing them, quietly folded his arms. He said nothing, but his friends were more than astonished when, as he started to walk forward, the mob parted and permitted him to pass on unmolested.

Jesus, followed by his disciples, proceeded to their encampment, where all this was recounted. And they made ready that evening to go back to Capernaum early the next day, as Jesus had directed. This turbulent ending of the third public preaching tour had a sobering effect upon all of Jesus' followers. They were beginning to realize the meaning of some of the Master's teachings; they were awaking to the fact that the kingdom would come only through much sorrow and bitter disappointment. They left Nazareth as a sober and serious group of disillusioned preachers of the gospel of truth and not as an enthusiastic and all-conquering band of triumphant crusaders. ∎

Jairus and His Daughter

A great crowd was waiting for Jesus in Bethsaida on Tuesday forenoon. Among this throng were the new observers from the Jerusalem Sanhedrin who had come down to Capernaum to find cause for the Master's apprehension and conviction. As Jesus spoke with those who had assembled to greet him, Jairus, one of the rulers of the synagogue, made his way through the crowd and, falling down at his feet, took him by the hand and besought that he would hasten away with him, saying: "Master, my little daughter, an only child, lies in my home at the point of death. I pray that you will come and heal her." Hearing this, Jesus said: "I will go with you."

As Jesus went along with Jairus, the large crowd which had heard the father's request followed on to see what would happen. Shortly before they reached the ruler's house, as they hastened through a narrow street and as the throng jostled him, Jesus suddenly stopped, exclaiming, "Someone touched me." And when those who were near him denied that they had touched him, Peter spoke up: "Master, you can see that this crowd presses you, threatening to crush us, and yet you say 'someone has touched me.' What do you mean?" Then Jesus said: "I asked who touched me, for I perceived that living energy had gone forth from me." As Jesus looked about him, his eyes fell upon a near-by woman, who, coming forward, knelt at his feet and said: "For years I have been afflicted with a scourging hemorrhage. I have suffered many things from many physicians; I have spent all my substance, but none could cure me. Then I heard of you, and I thought if I may but touch the hem of his garment, I shall certainly be made whole. And so I pressed forward with the crowd as it moved along until, standing near you, Master, I touched

the border of your garment, and I was made whole; I know that I have been healed of my affliction."

When Jesus heard this, he took the woman by the hand and, lifting her up, said: "Daughter, your faith has made you whole; go in peace." It was her *faith* and not her *touch* that made her whole. And this case is a good illustration of many apparently miraculous cures which attended upon Jesus' earth career, but which he in no sense consciously willed. The passing of time demonstrated that this woman was really cured of her malady. Her faith was of the sort that laid direct hold upon the creative power resident in the Master's person. With the faith she had, it was only necessary to approach the Master's person. It was not at all necessary to touch his garment; that was merely the superstitious part of her belief. Jesus called this woman, Veronica of Caesarea-Philippi, into his presence to correct two errors which might have lingered in her mind, or which might have persisted in the minds of those who witnessed this healing: He did not want Veronica to go away thinking that her fear in attempting to steal her cure had been honored, or that her superstition in associating the touch of his garment with her healing had been effective. He desired all to know that it was her pure and living *faith* that had wrought the cure.

At Jairus's House

Jairus was, of course, terribly impatient of this delay in reaching his home; so they now hastened on at quickened pace. Even before they entered the ruler's yard, one of his servants came out, saying: "Trouble not the Master; your daughter is dead." But Jesus seemed not to heed the servant's words, for, taking with him Peter, James, and John, he turned and said to the grief-stricken father: "Fear not; only believe." When he entered the house, he found the flute-players already there with the mourners, who were making an unseemly tumult; already were the relatives engaged in weeping and wailing. And when he had put all the mourners out of the room, he went in with the father and mother and his three apostles. He had told the mourners that the damsel was not dead, but they laughed him to scorn. Jesus now turned to the mother, saying: "Your daughter is not dead; she is only asleep." And when the house had quieted down, Jesus, going up to where the child lay, took her by the hand and said, "Daughter, I say to you, awake and arise!" And when the girl heard these words, she immediately rose up and walked across the room. And presently, after she had recovered from her daze, Jesus directed that they should give her something to eat, for she had been a long time without food.

Since there was much agitation in Capernaum against Jesus, he called the family together and explained that the maiden had been in a state of coma following a long fever, and that he had merely aroused her, that he had not raised her from the dead. He likewise explained all this to his apostles, but it was futile; they all believed he had raised the little girl from the dead. What Jesus said in explanation of many of these apparent miracles had little effect on his followers. They were miracle-minded and lost no opportunity to ascribe another wonder to Jesus. Jesus and the apostles returned to Bethsaida after he had specifically charged all of them that they should tell no man.

When he came out of Jairus's house, two blind men led by a dumb boy followed him and cried out for healing. About this time Jesus' reputation as a healer was at its very height. Everywhere he went the sick and the afflicted were waiting for him. The Master now looked much worn, and all of his friends were becoming concerned lest he continue his work of teaching and healing to the point of actual collapse.

Jesus' apostles, let alone the common people, could not understand the nature and attributes of this God-man. Neither has any subsequent generation been able to evaluate what took place on earth in the person of Jesus of Nazareth. And there can never occur an opportunity for either science or religion to check up on these remarkable events for the simple reason that such an extraordinary situation can never again occur, either on this world or on any other world. Never again, on any world in this entire local universe, will a being appear in the likeness of mortal flesh, at the same time embodying all the attributes of creative energy combined with spiritual endowments which transcend time and most other material limitations.

Never before Jesus was on earth, nor since, has it been possible so directly and graphically to secure the results attendant upon the strong and living faith of mortal men and women. Likewise, today, while his absence prevents such material manifestations, you should refrain from placing any sort of limitation on the possible exhibition of his *spiritual power*. Though the Master is absent as a material being, he is present as a spiritual influence in the hearts of men. ∎

[JEREMY WINBORG — *Jairus's Daughter*]

FEEDING THE FIVE THOUSAND

The multitude was daily increasing in size, so much so that David Zebedee desired to establish a new encampment, but Jesus refused consent. The Master had so little rest over the Sabbath that on Sunday morning, March 27, he sought to get away from the people. Some of the evangelists were left to talk to the multitude while Jesus and the twelve planned to escape, unnoticed, to the opposite shore of the lake, where they proposed to obtain much needed rest in a beautiful park south of Bethsaida-Julias. This region was a favorite resorting place for Capernaum folks; they were all familiar with these parks on the eastern shore.

But the people would not have it so. They saw the direction taken by Jesus' boat, and hiring every craft available, they started out in pursuit. Those who could not obtain boats fared forth on foot to walk around the upper end of the lake.

By Wednesday noon about five thousand men, women, and children were assembled here in this park to the south of Bethsaida-Julias. The weather was pleasant, it being near the end of the rainy season in this locality.

Philip had provided a three days' supply of food for Jesus and the twelve, which was in the custody of the Mark lad, their boy of all chores. By afternoon of this, the third day for almost half of this multitude, the food the people had brought with them was nearly exhausted. David Zebedee had no tented city here to feed and accommodate the crowds. Neither had Philip made food provision

[WALTER RANE — *Feeding the Five Thousand*]

for such a multitude. But the people, even though they were hungry, would not go away. It was being quietly whispered about that Jesus, desiring to avoid trouble with both Herod and the Jerusalem leaders, had chosen this quiet spot outside the jurisdiction of all his enemies as the proper place to be crowned king. The enthusiasm of the people was rising every hour.

This was the stage setting about five o'clock on Wednesday afternoon, when Jesus asked James Alpheus to summon Andrew and Philip. Said Jesus: "What shall we do with the multitude? They have been with us now three days, and many of them are hungry. They have no food." Philip and Andrew exchanged glances, and then Philip answered: "Master, you should send these people away so that they may go to the villages around about and buy themselves food." And Andrew, fearing the materialization of the king plot, quickly joined with Philip, saying: "Yes, Master, I think it best that you dismiss the multitude so that they may go their way and buy food while you secure rest for a season." By this time others of the twelve had joined the conference. Then said Jesus: "But I do not desire to send them away hungry; can you not feed them?" This was too much for Philip, and he spoke right up: "Master, in this country place where can we buy bread for this multitude? Two hundred denarii worth would not be enough for lunch."

Before the apostles had an opportunity to express themselves, Jesus turned to Andrew and Philip, saying: "I do not want to send these people away. Here they are, like sheep without a

SHEEP WITHOUT A SHEPHERD

People flocked to Bethsaida-Julias to see Jesus. By Monday afternoon the multitude had increased to more than three thousand. And still—way into the evening—the people continued to flock in, bringing all manner of sick folks with them. Hundreds of interested persons had made their plans to stop over at Capernaum to see and hear Jesus as they traveled to the Passover, and they simply refused to be disappointed.

shepherd. I would like to feed them. What food have we with us?" While Philip was conversing with Matthew and Judas, Andrew sought out the Mark lad to ascertain how much was left of their store of provisions. He returned to Jesus, saying: "The lad has left only five barley loaves and two dried fishes"—and Peter promptly added, "We have yet to eat this evening."

For a moment Jesus stood in silence. There was a faraway look in his eyes. The apostles said nothing. Jesus turned suddenly to Andrew and said, "Bring me the loaves and fishes." And when Andrew had brought the basket to Jesus, the Master said: "Direct the people to sit down on the grass in companies of one hundred and appoint a leader over each group while you bring all of the evangelists here with us."

Jesus took up the loaves in his hands, and after he had given thanks, he broke the bread and gave to his apostles, who passed it on to their associates, who in turn carried it to the multitude. Jesus in like manner broke and distributed the fishes. And this multitude did eat and were filled. And when they had finished eating, Jesus said to the disciples: "Gather up the broken pieces that remain over so that nothing will be lost." And when they had finished gathering up the fragments, they had twelve basketfuls. They who ate of this extraordinary feast numbered about five thousand men, women, and children.

And this is the first and only nature miracle which Jesus performed as a result of his conscious preplanning. It is true that his disciples were disposed to call many things miracles which were not, but this was a genuine supernatural ministration. In this case, so we were taught, Michael multiplied food elements as he always does except for the elimination of the time factor and the visible life channel.   ■

THE KING-MAKING EPISODE

The feeding of the five thousand by supernatural energy was another of those cases where human pity plus creative power equaled that which happened. Now that the multitude had been fed to the full, and since Jesus' fame was then and there augmented by this stupendous wonder, the project to seize the Master and proclaim him king required no further personal direction. The idea seemed to spread through the crowd like a contagion. The reaction of the multitude to this sudden and spectacular supplying of their physical needs was profound and overwhelming. For a long time the Jews had been taught that the Messiah, the son of David, when he should come, would cause the land again to flow with milk and honey, and that the bread of life would be bestowed upon them as manna from heaven was supposed to have fallen upon their forefathers in the wilderness. And was not all of this expectation now fulfilled right before their eyes? When this hungry, undernourished multitude had finished gorging itself with the wonder-food, there was but one unanimous reaction: "Here is our king." The wonder-working deliverer of Israel had come. In the eyes of these simple-minded people the power to feed carried with it the right to rule. No wonder, then, that the multitude, when it had finished feasting, rose as one man and shouted, "Make him king!"

This mighty shout enthused Peter and those of the apostles who still retained the hope of seeing Jesus assert his right to rule. But these false hopes were not to live for long. This mighty shout of the multitude had hardly ceased to reverberate from the near-by rocks when Jesus stepped upon a huge stone and, lifting up his right hand to command their attention, said: "My children, you mean well, but you are shortsighted and material-minded." There was a brief pause; this stalwart Galilean was there majestically posed in the enchanting glow of that eastern twilight. Every inch he looked a king as he continued to speak to this breathless multitude: "You would make me king, not because your souls have been lighted with a great truth, but because your stomachs have been filled with bread. How many times have I told you that my kingdom is not of this world? This kingdom of heaven which we proclaim is a spiritual brotherhood, and no man rules over it seated upon a material throne. My Father in heaven is the all-wise and the all-powerful Ruler over this spiritual brotherhood of the sons of God on earth. Have I so failed in revealing to you the Father of spirits that you would make a king of his Son in the flesh! Now all of you go hence to your own homes. If you must have a king, let the Father of lights be enthroned in the heart of each of you as the spirit Ruler of all things."

These words of Jesus sent the multitude away stunned and disheartened. Many who had believed in him turned back and followed him no more from that day. The apostles were speechless; they stood in silence gathered about the twelve baskets of the fragments of food; only the chore boy, the Mark lad, spoke, "And he refused to be our king." Jesus, before going off to be alone in the hills, turned to Andrew and said: "Take your brethren back to Zebedee's house and pray with them, especially for your brother, Simon Peter."

SIMON PETER'S NIGHT VISION

The apostles, without their Master—sent off by themselves—entered the boat and in silence began to row toward Bethsaida on the western shore of the lake. None of the twelve was so crushed and downcast as Simon Peter. Hardly a word was spoken; they were all thinking of the Master alone in the hills. Had he forsaken them? He had never before sent them all away and refused to go with them. What could all this mean?

Darkness descended upon them, for there had arisen a strong and contrary wind which made progress almost impossible. As the hours of darkness and hard rowing passed, Peter grew weary and fell into a deep sleep of exhaustion. Andrew and James put him to rest on the cushioned seat in the stern of the boat. While the other apostles toiled against the wind and the waves, Peter dreamed a dream; he saw a vision of Jesus coming to them walking on the sea. When the Master seemed to walk on by the boat, Peter cried out, "Save us, Master, save us." And those who were in the rear of the boat heard him say some of these words. As this apparition of the night season continued in Peter's mind, he dreamed that he heard Jesus say: "Be of good cheer; it is I; be not afraid." This was like the balm of Gilead to Peter's disturbed soul; it soothed his troubled spirit, so that (in his dream) he cried out to the Master: "Lord, if it really is you, bid me come and walk with you on the water." And when Peter started to walk upon the water, the boisterous waves frightened him, and as he was about to sink, he cried out, "Lord, save me!" And many of the twelve heard him utter this cry. Then Peter dreamed that Jesus came to the rescue and, stretching forth his hand, took hold and lifted him up, saying: "O, you of little faith, wherefore did you doubt?"

In connection with the latter part of his dream Peter arose from the seat whereon he slept and actually stepped overboard and into the water. And he awakened from his dream as Andrew, James,

[Rembrandt van Rijn — *The Storm on the Sea of Galilee* (detail)]

and John reached down and pulled him out of the sea.

Thursday morning, before daylight, they anchored their boat offshore near Zebedee's house and sought sleep until about noontime. Andrew was first up and, going for a walk by the sea, found Jesus, who shortly after midnight had started to walk around the lake and across the river, back to Bethsaida. He asked Andrew to assemble the apostles and their associates, including the women, saying, "I desire to speak with them." And when all were ready, Jesus said:

"How long shall I bear with you? Are you all slow of spiritual comprehension and deficient in living faith? All these months have I taught you the truths of the kingdom, and yet are you dominated by material motives instead of spiritual considerations.

"And now do you all see that the working of miracles and the performance of material wonders will not win souls for the spiritual kingdom? We fed the multitude, but it did not lead them to hunger for the bread of life neither to thirst for the waters of spiritual righteousness. When their hunger was satisfied, they sought not entrance into the kingdom of heaven but rather sought to proclaim the Son of Man king after the manner of the kings of this world, only that they might continue to eat bread without having to toil therefor. And all this, in which many of you did more or less participate, does nothing to reveal the heavenly Father or to advance his kingdom on earth. Have we not sufficient enemies among the religious leaders of the land without doing that which is likely to estrange also the civil rulers? I pray that

THE ANALYTICAL LUKE

To Peter, his dream of Jesus walking on the water was always real. He sincerely believed that Jesus came to the apostles in the boat that night. He only partially convinced John Mark, which explains why Mark left a portion of the story out of his narrative. Luke, the physician, who made careful search into these matters, concluded that the episode was a vision of Peter's and therefore refused to give place to this story in the preparation of his narrative.

the Father will anoint your eyes that you may see and open your ears that you may hear, to the end that you may have full faith in the gospel which I have taught you."

Jesus then announced that he wished to withdraw for a few days of rest with his apostles, and he forbade any of the disciples or the multitude to follow him. Jesus was preparing for a great crisis of his life on earth, and he therefore spent much time in communion with the Father in heaven.

The news of the feeding of the five thousand and the attempt to make Jesus king aroused widespread curiosity and stirred up the fears of both the religious leaders and the civil rulers throughout all Galilee and Judea. While this great miracle did nothing to further the gospel of the kingdom in the souls of material-minded and halfhearted believers, it did serve the purpose of bringing to a head the miracle-seeking and king-craving proclivities of Jesus' immediate family of apostles and close disciples. This spectacular episode brought an end to the early era of teaching, training, and healing, thereby preparing the way for the inauguration of this last year of proclaiming the higher and more spiritual phases of the new gospel of the kingdom—divine sonship, spiritual liberty, and eternal salvation.

After a nearly three-week sojourn at Jerusalem for the Passover, Jesus and the apostles returned to Bethsaida on Friday, April 29. Immediately on reaching home, Jesus dispatched Andrew to ask of the ruler of the synagogue permission to speak the next day. And Jesus well knew that that would be the last time he would ever be permitted to speak in the Capernaum synagogue. ✳

THE SIFTING OF THE KINGDOM

*After this many of his disciples turned
back and no longer walked with him.*

—JOHN 6:66 ESV

As JESUS WENT FORTH ON A BEAUTIFUL SABBATH AFTERNOON TO PREACH HIS EPOCH-MAKING sermon in the Capernaum synagogue, he comprehended that he faced the immediate declaration of avowed and open warfare by his increasing enemies, and he elected boldly to assume the offensive. At the feeding of the five thousand he had challenged their ideas of the material Messiah; now he chose again openly to attack their concept of the Jewish deliverer. This crisis, which began with the feeding of the five thousand, and which terminated with this Sabbath afternoon sermon, was the outward turning of the tide of popular fame and acclaim. Henceforth, the work of the kingdom was to be increasingly concerned with the more important task of winning lasting spiritual converts for the truly religious brotherhood of mankind.

Thus did the Master elect to discuss and expose the folly of the whole rabbinic system of rules and regulations which was represented by the oral law—the traditions of the elders, all of which were regarded as more sacred and more binding upon the Jews than even the teachings of the Scriptures. And Jesus spoke out with less reserve because he knew the hour had come when he could do nothing more to prevent an open rupture of relations with these religious leaders.

Jesus had recently engaged in the greatest demonstration of supernatural power to characterize his whole career. The feeding of the five thousand was the one event of his earth life which made the greatest appeal to the Jewish concept of the expected Messiah. But this extraordinary advantage was immediately and unexplainedly offset by his prompt and unequivocal refusal to be made king.

In less than a month the enthusiastic and open followers of Jesus, who numbered more than fifty thousand in Galilee alone, shrank to less than five hundred. The apostles began to realize more fully that Jesus was not going to sit on David's throne and that spiritual truth was not to be advanced by material wonders. They dimly foresaw the approaching times of spiritual sifting and cruel adversity.

THE URANTIA BOOK: PAPERS 153–161
APRIL–AUGUST, A.D. 29

[GREG OLSEN — *Jesus in the Synagogue* (detail)]

THE EPOCHAL SERMON

A distinguished congregation greeted Jesus at three o'clock on this exquisite Sabbath afternoon in the new Capernaum synagogue. Jairus presided and handed Jesus the Scriptures to read. The day before, fifty-three Pharisees and Sadducees had arrived from Jerusalem; more than thirty of the leaders and rulers of the neighboring synagogues were also present. These Jewish religious leaders were acting directly under orders from the Sanhedrin at Jerusalem, and they constituted the orthodox vanguard which had come to inaugurate open warfare on Jesus and his disciples. Sitting by the side of these Jewish leaders, in the synagogue seats of honor, were the official observers of Herod Antipas, who had been directed to ascertain the truth concerning the disturbing reports that an attempt had been made by the populace to proclaim Jesus the king of the Jews, over in the domains of his brother Philip.

As they sat there in the synagogue that afternoon before Jesus began to speak, there was just one great mystery, just one supreme question, in the minds of all. Both his friends and his foes pondered just one thought, and that was: "Why did he himself so deliberately and effectively turn back the tide of popular enthusiasm?" And it was immediately before and immediately after this sermon that the doubts and disappointments of his disgruntled adherents grew into unconscious opposition and eventually turned into actual hatred. It was after this sermon in the synagogue that Judas Iscariot entertained his first conscious thought of deserting. But he did, for the time being, effectively master all such inclinations.

[VASILY POLENOV — *At the Genisaret Lake*]

Jesus introduced this sermon by reading from the law as found in Deuteronomy. And when he had finished this reading, he turned to the Prophets and read from Jeremiah. He then continued:

"The priests and teachers of that day sought to kill Jeremiah, but the judges would not consent, albeit, for his words of warning, they did let him down by cords in a filthy dungeon until he sank in mire up to his armpits. That is what this people did to the Prophet Jeremiah when he obeyed the Lord's command to warn his brethren of their impending political downfall. Today, I desire to

ask you: What will the chief priests and religious leaders of this people do with the man who dares to warn them of the day of their spiritual doom? Will you also seek to put to death the teacher who dares to proclaim the word of the Lord, and who fears not to point out wherein you refuse to walk in the way of light which leads to the entrance to the kingdom of heaven?

"What is it you seek as evidence of my mission on earth? We have left you undisturbed in your positions of influence and power while we preached glad tidings to the poor and the outcast. We have made no hostile attack upon that which you hold in reverence but have rather proclaimed new liberty for man's fear-ridden soul. I came into the world to reveal my Father and to establish on earth the spiritual brotherhood of the sons of God, the kingdom of heaven. And notwithstanding that I have so many times reminded you that my kingdom is not of this world, still has my Father granted you many manifestations of material wonders in addition to more evidential spiritual transformations and regenerations.

"What new sign is it that you seek at my hands? I declare that you already have sufficient evidence to enable you to make your decision. Verily, verily,

"I AM THIS BREAD OF LIFE. HE WHO COMES TO ME SHALL NOT HUNGER, WHILE HE WHO BELIEVES ME SHALL NEVER THIRST."

I say to many who sit before me this day, you are confronted with the necessity of choosing which way you will go; and I say to you, as Joshua said to your forefathers, 'choose you this day whom you will serve.' Today, many of you stand at the parting of the ways.

"Some of you, when you could not find me after the feasting of the multitude on the other side, hired the Tiberias fishing fleet, which a week before had taken shelter near by during a storm, to go in pursuit of me, and what for? Not for truth and righteousness or that you might the better know how to serve and minister to your fellow men! No, but rather that you might have more bread for which you had not labored. It was not to fill your souls with the word of life, but only that you might fill the belly with the bread of ease. And long have you been taught that the Messiah, when he should come, would work those wonders which would make life pleasant and easy for all the chosen people. It is not strange, then, that you who have been thus taught should long for the loaves and the fishes. But I declare to you that such is not the mission of the Son of Man. I have come to proclaim spiritual liberty, teach eternal truth, and foster living faith.

"My brethren, hanker not after the meat which perishes but rather seek for the spiritual food that nourishes even to eternal life; and this is the bread of life which the Son gives to all who will take it and eat, for the Father has given the Son this life without measure. And when you asked me, 'What must we do to perform the works of God?' I plainly told you: 'This is the work of God, that you believe him whom he has sent.'"

And then said Jesus, pointing up to the device of a pot of manna which decorated the lintel of this new synagogue, and which was embellished with grape clusters: "You have thought that your forefathers in the wilderness ate manna—the bread of heaven—but I say to you that this was the bread of earth. While Moses did not give your fathers bread from heaven, my Father now stands ready to give you the true bread of life. The bread of heaven is that which comes down from God and gives eternal life to the men of the world. And when you say to me, Give us this living bread, I will answer: I am this bread of life. He who comes to me shall not hunger, while he who believes me shall never thirst. You have seen me, lived with me, and beheld my works, yet you believe not that I came forth from the Father. But to those who do believe—fear not. All those led of the Father shall come to me, and he who comes to me shall in nowise be cast out.

"And now let me declare to you, once and for all time, that I have come down upon the earth, not to do my own will, but the will of Him who sent me. And this is the final will of Him who sent me, that of all those he has given me I should not lose one. And this is the will of the Father: That every one who beholds the Son and who believes him shall have eternal life. Only yesterday did I feed you with bread for your bodies; today I offer you the bread of life for your hungry souls. Will you now take the bread of the spirit as you then so willingly ate the bread of this world?"

As Jesus paused for a moment to look over the congregation, one of the teachers from Jerusalem (a member of the Sanhedrin) rose up and asked:

"Do I understand you to say that you are the bread which comes down from heaven, and that the manna which Moses gave to our fathers in the wilderness did not?" And Jesus answered the Pharisee, "You understood aright." Then said the Pharisee: "But are you not Jesus of Nazareth, the son of Joseph, the carpenter? Are not your father and mother, as well as your brothers and sisters, well known to many of us? How then is it that you appear here in God's house and declare that you have come down from heaven?"

By this time there was much murmuring in the synagogue, and such a tumult was threatened that Jesus stood up and said: "Let us be patient; the truth never suffers from honest examination. I am all that you say but more. The Father and I are one; the Son does only that which the Father teaches him, while all those who are given to the Son by the Father, the Son will receive to himself. You have read where it is written in the Prophets, 'You shall all be taught by God,' and that 'Those whom the Father teaches will hear also his Son.' Every one who yields to the teaching of the Father's indwelling spirit will eventually come to me. Not that any man has seen the Father, but the Father's spirit does live within man. And the Son who came down from heaven, he has surely seen the Father. And those who truly believe this Son already have eternal life.

"I am this bread of life. Your fathers ate manna in the wilderness and are dead. But this bread which comes down from God, if a man eats thereof, he shall never die in spirit. I repeat, I am this living bread, and every soul who attains the realization of this united nature of God and man shall live forever. And this bread of life which I give to all who will receive is my own living and combined nature. The Father in the Son and the Son one with the Father—that is my life-giving revelation to the world and my saving gift to all nations."

When Jesus had finished speaking, the ruler of the synagogue dismissed the congregation, but they would not depart. They crowded up around Jesus to ask more questions while others murmured and disputed among themselves. And this state of affairs continued for more than three hours. It was well past seven o'clock before the audience finally dispersed.

LAST WORDS IN THE SYNAGOGUE

In the midst of the discussions of this after meeting, one of the Pharisees from Jerusalem brought to Jesus a distraught youth who was possessed of an unruly and rebellious spirit. Leading this demented lad up to Jesus, he said: "What can you do for such affliction as this? Can you cast out devils?" And when the Master looked upon the youth, he was moved with compassion and, beckoning for the lad to come to him, took him by the hand and said: "You know who I am; come out of him; and I charge one of your loyal fellows to see that you do not return." And immediately the lad was normal and in his right mind.

When the people marveled, one of the Pharisees stood up and charged that Jesus could do these things because he was in league with devils; that he admitted in the language which he employed in casting out this devil that they were known to

CASTING OUT EVIL

Jesus' healing a distraught youth was his first case of casting an "evil spirit" out of a human being. All of the previous cases were only supposed possession of the devil; but this was a genuine case of demoniac possession, even such as sometimes occurred in those days and right up to the day of Pentecost, when the Master's spirit was poured out upon all flesh, making it forever impossible for these few celestial rebels to take such advantage of certain unstable types of humans.

each other; and he went on to state that the religious teachers and leaders at Jerusalem had decided that Jesus did all his so-called miracles by the power of Beelzebub, the prince of devils. Said the Pharisee: "Have nothing to do with this man; he is in partnership with Satan."

Then said Jesus: "How can Satan cast out Satan? A kingdom divided against itself cannot stand; if a house be divided against itself, it is soon brought to desolation. Can a city withstand a siege if it is not united? If Satan casts out Satan, he is divided against himself; how then shall his kingdom stand? But you should know that no one can enter into the house of a strong man and despoil his goods except he first overpower and bind that strong man. And so, if I by the power of Beelzebub cast out devils, by whom do your sons cast them out? Therefore shall they be your judges. But if I, by the spirit of God, cast out devils, then has the kingdom of God truly come upon you. If you were not blinded by prejudice and misled by fear and pride, you would easily perceive that one who is greater than devils stands in your midst. You compel me to declare that he who is not with me is against me, while he who gathers not with me scatters abroad. Let me utter a solemn warning to you who would presume, with your eyes open and with premeditated malice, knowingly to ascribe the works of God to the doings of devils! Verily, verily, I say to you, all your sins shall be forgiven, even all of your blasphemies, but whosoever shall blaspheme against God with deliberation and wicked intention shall never obtain forgiveness. Since such persistent workers of iniquity will never seek nor receive forgiveness, they are guilty of the sin of eternally rejecting divine forgiveness.

"Many of you have this day come to the parting of the ways; you have come to a beginning of the making of the inevitable choice between the will of the Father and the self-chosen ways of darkness. And as you now choose, so shall you eventually be. You must either make the tree good and its fruit good, or else will the tree become corrupt and its fruit corrupt. I declare that in my Father's eternal kingdom the tree is known by its fruits. But some of you who are as vipers, how can you, having already chosen evil, bring forth good fruits? After all, out of the abundance of the evil in your hearts your mouths speak."

Then stood up another Pharisee, who said: "Teacher, we would have you give us a predetermined sign which we will agree upon as establishing your authority and right to teach. Will you agree to such an arrangement?" And when Jesus heard this, he said: "This faithless and sign-seeking generation seeks a token, but no sign shall be given you other than that which you already have, and that which you shall see when the Son of Man departs from among you."

And when he had finished speaking, his apostles surrounded him and led him from the synagogue. In silence they journeyed home with him to Bethsaida. They were all amazed and somewhat terror-stricken by the sudden change in the Master's teaching tactics. They were wholly unaccustomed to seeing him perform in such a militant manner. ■

LAST DAYS AT CAPERNAUM

Time and again had Jesus dashed to pieces the hopes of his apostles, repeatedly had he crushed their fondest expectations, but no time of disappointment or season of sorrow had ever equaled that which now overtook them. And, too, there was now admixed with their depression a real fear for their safety. They were all surprisingly startled by the suddenness and completeness of the desertion of the populace. They were also somewhat frightened and disconcerted by the unexpected boldness and assertive determination exhibited by the Pharisees who had come down from Jerusalem. But most of all they were bewildered by Jesus' sudden change of tactics. Under ordinary circumstances they would have welcomed the appearance of this more militant attitude, but coming as it did, along with so much that was unexpected, it startled them.

And now, on top of all of these worries, when they reached home, Jesus refused to eat. For hours he isolated himself in one of the upper rooms. It was almost midnight when Joab, the leader of the evangelists, returned and reported that about one third of his associates had deserted the cause. All through the evening loyal disciples had come and gone, reporting that the revulsion of feeling toward the Master was general in Capernaum. The leaders from Jerusalem were not slow to feed this feeling of disaffection and in every way possible to seek to promote the movement away from Jesus and his teachings. During these trying hours the twelve women were in session over at Peter's house. They were tremendously upset, but none of them deserted.

It was a little after midnight when Jesus came down from the upper chamber and stood among the twelve and their associates, numbering about thirty in all. He said: "I recognize that this sifting of the kingdom distresses you, but it is unavoidable. Still, after all the training you have had, was there any good reason why you should stumble at my words? Why is it that you are filled with fear and consternation when you see the kingdom being divested of these lukewarm multitudes and these halfhearted disciples? Why do you grieve when the new day is dawning for the shining forth in new glory of the spiritual teachings of the kingdom of heaven? If you find it difficult to endure this test, what, then, will you do when the Son of Man must return to the Father? When and how will you prepare yourselves for the time when I ascend to the place whence I came to this world?

"My beloved, you must remember that it is the spirit that quickens; the flesh and all that pertains thereto is of little profit. The words which I have spoken to you are spirit and life. Be of good cheer! I have not deserted you. Many shall be offended by the plain speaking of these days. Already you have heard that many of my disciples have turned back; they walk no more with me. From the beginning I knew that these halfhearted believers would fall out by the way. Did I not choose you twelve men and set you apart as ambassadors of the kingdom? And now at such a time as this would you also desert? Let each of you look to his own faith, for one of you stands in grave danger." And when Jesus had finished speaking, Simon Peter said: "Yes, Lord, we are sad and perplexed, but we will never forsake you. You have taught us the words of eternal life. We have believed in you and followed with you all this time. We will not turn back, for we know that you are sent by God." And as Peter ceased speaking, they all with one accord nodded their approval of his pledge of loyalty.

Then said Jesus: "Go to your rest, for busy times are upon us; active days are just ahead."

A Week of Rest

Sunday, May 8, A.D. 29, at Jerusalem, the Sanhedrin passed a decree closing all the synagogues of Palestine to Jesus and his followers. This was a new and unprecedented usurpation of authority by the Jerusalem Sanhedrin. Theretofore each synagogue had existed and functioned as an independent congregation of worshipers and was under the rule and direction of its own board of governors. Only the synagogues of Jerusalem had been subject to the authority of the Sanhedrin. This summary action of the Sanhedrin was followed by the resignation of five of its members. One hundred messengers were immediately dispatched to convey and enforce this decree. Within the short space of two weeks every synagogue in Palestine had bowed to this manifesto of the Sanhedrin except the synagogue at Hebron. The rulers of the Hebron synagogue refused to acknowledge the right of the Sanhedrin

[ALEXANDRE BIDA — *The Priests Take Counsel with the Herodians*]

to exercise such jurisdiction over their assembly. This refusal to accede to the Jerusalem decree was based on their contention of congregational autonomy rather than on sympathy with Jesus' cause. Shortly thereafter the Hebron synagogue was destroyed by fire.

This same Sunday morning, Jesus declared a week's holiday, urging all of his disciples to return to their homes or friends to rest their troubled souls and speak words of encouragement to their loved ones. He said: "Go to your several places to play or fish while you pray for the extension of the kingdom."

This week of rest enabled Jesus to visit many families and groups about the seaside. He also went fishing with David Zebedee on several occasions, and while he went about alone much of the time, there always lurked near by two or three of David's most trusted messengers, who had no uncertain orders from their chief respecting the safeguarding of Jesus. There was no public teaching of any sort during this week of rest.

On May 21, word reached Tiberias that the civil authorities at Jerusalem had no objection to the agreement between Herod and the Pharisees that Jesus be seized and carried to Jerusalem for trial before the Sanhedrin on charges of flouting the sacred laws of the Jewish nation. Accordingly, just before midnight of this day, Herod signed the decree which authorized the officers of the Sanhedrin to seize Jesus within Herod's domains and forcibly to carry him to Jerusalem for trial. ∎

MAY 22, A.D. 29

THE HASTY FLIGHT

May 22 was an eventful day in the life of Jesus. On this Sunday morning, before daybreak, one of David's messengers arrived in great haste from Tiberias, bringing the word that Herod had authorized, or was about to authorize, the arrest of Jesus by the officers of the

Sanhedrin. The receipt of the news of this impending danger caused David Zebedee to arouse his messengers and send them out to all the local groups of disciples, summoning them for an emergency council at seven o'clock that morning. When the sister-in-law of Jude (Jesus' brother) heard this alarming report, she hastened word to all of Jesus' family who dwelt near by, summoning them forthwith to assemble at Zebedee's house. And in response to this hasty call, presently there were assembled Mary, James, Joseph, Jude, and Ruth.

It was about eight o'clock on this Sunday morning when five members of Jesus' earth family arrived on the scene in response to the urgent summons of Jude's sister-in-law. The Pharisees had been laboring to persuade Mary that Jesus was beside himself, demented. They urged her to go with her sons and seek to dissuade him from further efforts at public teaching. They assured Mary that soon Jesus' health would break, and that only dishonor and disgrace could come upon the entire family as a result of allowing him to go on. And so, when the word came from Jude's sister-in-law, all five of them started at once for Zebedee's house, having been together at Mary's home, where they had met with the Pharisees the evening before. They had talked with the Jerusalem leaders long into the night, and all were more or less convinced that Jesus was acting strangely, that he had acted strangely for some time. While Ruth could not explain all of his conduct, she insisted that he had always treated his family fairly and refused to agree to the program of trying to dissuade him from further work.

A DIVIDED FAMILY

Of all his family in the flesh, only one, Ruth, believed wholeheartedly and continuously in the divinity of his mission on earth. Jude and James, and even Joseph, still retained much of their faith in Jesus, but they had permitted pride to interfere with their better judgment and real spiritual inclinations. Mary was likewise torn between love and fear, between mother love and family pride. Though she was harassed by doubts, she could never quite forget the visit of Gabriel ere Jesus was born.

On the way to Zebedee's house they talked these things over and agreed among themselves to try to persuade Jesus to come home with them, for, said Mary: "I know I could influence my son if he would only come home and listen to me." James and Jude had heard rumors concerning the plans to arrest Jesus and take him to Jerusalem for trial. They also feared for their own safety. As long as Jesus was a popular figure in the public eye, his family allowed matters to drift along, but now that the people of Capernaum and the leaders at Jerusalem had suddenly turned against him, they began keenly to feel the pressure of the supposed disgrace of their embarrassing position.

They had expected to meet Jesus, take him aside, and urge him to go home with them. They had thought to assure him that they would forget his neglect of them—they would forgive and forget—if he would only give up the foolishness of trying to preach a new religion which could bring only trouble to himself and dishonor upon his family. To all of this Ruth would say only: "I will tell my brother that I think he is a man of God, and that I hope he would be willing to die before he would allow these wicked Pharisees to stop his preaching." Joseph promised to keep Ruth quiet while the others labored with Jesus.

When they reached the Zebedee house, Jesus was in the very midst of delivering his parting address to the disciples. They sought to gain entrance to the house, but it was crowded to overflowing. Finally they established themselves on the back porch and had word passed in to Jesus, from person to person, so that it finally was whispered to him by Simon Peter, who interrupted his talking for the purpose, and who said: "Behold, your mother and your brothers are outside, and they are very anxious to speak with you." Now it did not occur to his mother how important was the giving of this parting message to his followers, neither did she know that his address was likely to be terminated any moment by the arrival of his apprehenders. She really thought, after so long an apparent estrangement, in view of the fact that she and his brothers had shown the grace actually to come to him, that Jesus would cease speaking and come to them the moment he received word they were waiting.

It was just another of those instances in which his earth family could not comprehend that he must be about his Father's business. And so Mary and his brothers were deeply hurt when, notwithstanding that he paused in his speaking to receive the message, instead of his rushing out to greet them, they heard his musical voice speak with increased volume: "Say to my mother and my brothers that they should have no fear for me. The Father who sent me into the world will not forsake me; neither shall any harm come upon my family. Bid them be of good courage and put their trust in the Father of the kingdom. But, after all, who is my mother and who are my brothers?" And stretching forth his hands toward all of his disciples assembled in the room, he said: "I have no mother; I have no brothers. Behold my mother and behold my brethren! For whosoever does the will of my Father who is in heaven, the same is my mother, my brother, and my sister."

And when Mary heard these words, she collapsed in Jude's arms. They carried her out in the garden to revive her while Jesus spoke the concluding words of his parting message. He would then have gone out to confer with his mother and his brothers, but a messenger arrived in haste from Tiberias bringing word that the officers of the Sanhedrin were on their way with authority to arrest Jesus and carry him to Jerusalem. Andrew received this message and, interrupting Jesus, told it to him.

Andrew did not recall that David had posted some twenty-five sentinels about the Zebedee house, and that no one could take them by surprise; so he asked Jesus what should be done. The Master stood there in silence while his mother, having heard the words, "I have no mother," was recovering from the shock in the garden. It was at just this time that a woman in the room stood up and exclaimed, "Blessed is the womb that bore you and blessed are the breasts that nursed you." Jesus turned aside a moment from his conversation with Andrew to answer this woman by saying, "No, rather is the one blessed who hears the word of God and dares to obey it."

Mary and Jesus' brothers thought that Jesus did not understand them, that he had lost interest in them, little realizing that it was they who failed to understand Jesus. Jesus fully understood how difficult it is for men to break with their past. He knew how human beings are swayed by the preacher's eloquence, and how the conscience responds to emotional appeal as the mind does to logic and reason, but he also knew how far more difficult it is to persuade men to *disown the past.*

It is forever true that all who may think they are misunderstood or not appreciated have in Jesus a sympathizing friend and an understanding counselor. He had warned his apostles that a man's foes may be they of his own household, but he had hardly realized how near this prediction would come to apply to his own experience. Jesus did not forsake his earth family to do his Father's work—they forsook him. Later on, after the Master's death and resurrection, when James became connected with the early Christian movement, he suffered immeasurably as a result of his failure to enjoy this earlier association with Jesus and his disciples.

In passing through these events, Jesus chose to be guided by the limited knowledge of his human mind. He desired to undergo the experience with his associates as a mere man. And it was in the human mind of Jesus to see his family before he left. He did not wish to stop in the midst of his discourse and thus render their first meeting after so long a separation such a public affair. He had intended to finish his address and then have a visit with them before leaving, but this plan was thwarted by the conspiracy of events which immediately followed.

The haste of their flight was augmented by the arrival of a party of David's messengers at the rear entrance of the Zebedee home. The commotion produced by these men frightened the apostles into thinking that these new arrivals might be their apprehenders, and in fear of immediate arrest, they hastened through the front entrance to the waiting boat. And all of this explains why Jesus did not see his family waiting on the back porch.

But he did say to David Zebedee as he entered the boat in hasty flight: "Tell my mother and my brothers that I appreciate their coming, and that I intended to see them. Admonish them to find no offense in me but rather to seek for a knowledge of the will of God and for grace and courage to do that will."

And so it was on this Sunday morning, the twenty-second of May, in the year A.D. 29, that Jesus, with his twelve apostles and the twelve evangelists, engaged in this hasty flight from the Sanhedrin officers who were on their way to Bethsaida with authority from Herod Antipas to arrest him and take him to Jerusalem for trial on charges of blasphemy and other violations of the sacred laws of the Jews. It was almost half past eight this beautiful morning when this company of twenty-five manned the oars and pulled for the eastern shore of the Sea of Galilee. ∎

TEACHING AT TYRE

From July 11 to July 24 they taught in Tyre. Each of the apostles took with him one of the evangelists, and thus two and two they taught and preached in all parts of Tyre and its environs. The polyglot population of this busy seaport heard them gladly, and many were baptized into the outward fellowship of the kingdom. Jesus maintained his headquarters at the home of a Jew named Joseph, a believer, who lived three or four miles south of Tyre, not far from the tomb of Hiram who had been king of the city-state of Tyre during the times of David and Solomon.

Daily, for this period of two weeks, the apostles and evangelists entered Tyre by way of Alexander's mole to conduct small meetings, and each night most of them would return to the encampment at Joseph's house south of the city.

Long into one of these nights the apostles and evangelists continued to ask questions of Jesus, and from the many answers we would present the following thoughts, restated in modern phraseology:

Forceful ambition, intelligent judgment, and seasoned wisdom are the essentials of material

[DAVID ROBERTS — *General View of Tyre*]

success. Leadership is dependent on natural ability, discretion, will power, and determination. Spiritual destiny is dependent on faith, love, and devotion to truth—hunger and thirst for righteousness—the wholehearted desire to find God and to be like him.

Do not become discouraged by the discovery that you are human. Human nature may tend toward evil, but it is not inherently sinful. Be not downcast by your failure wholly to forget some of your regrettable experiences. The mistakes which you fail to forget in time will be forgotten in eternity. Lighten your burdens of soul by speedily acquiring a long-distance view of your destiny, a universe expansion of your career.

Make not the mistake of estimating the soul's worth by the imperfections of the mind or by the appetites of the body. Judge not the soul nor evaluate its destiny by the standard of a single unfortunate human episode. Your spiritual destiny is conditioned only by your spiritual longings and purposes.

Religion is the exclusively spiritual experience of the evolving immortal soul of the God-knowing man, but moral power and spiritual energy are mighty forces which may be utilized in dealing with difficult social situations and in solving intricate economic problems. These moral and spiritual endowments make all levels of human living richer and more meaningful.

You are destined to live a narrow and mean life if you learn to love only those who love you. Human love may indeed be reciprocal, but divine love is outgoing in all its satisfaction-seeking. The less of love in any creature's nature, the greater the love need, and the more does divine love seek to satisfy such need. Love is never self-seeking, and it cannot be self-bestowed. Divine love cannot be self-contained; it must be unselfishly bestowed.

Kingdom believers should possess an implicit faith, a whole-souled belief, in the certain triumph of righteousness. Kingdom builders must be undoubting of the truth of the gospel of eternal salvation. Believers must increasingly learn how to step aside from the rush of life—escape the harassments of material existence—while they refresh the soul, inspire the mind, and renew the spirit by worshipful communion.

God-knowing individuals are not discouraged by misfortune or downcast by disappointment. Believers are immune to the depression consequent upon purely material upheavals; spirit livers are not perturbed by the episodes of the material world. Candidates for eternal life are practitioners of an invigorating and constructive technique for meeting all of the vicissitudes and harassments of mortal living. Every day a true believer lives, he finds it *easier* to do the right thing.

Spiritual living mightily increases true self-respect. But self-respect is not self-admiration. Self-respect is always co-ordinate with the love and service of one's fellows. It is not possible to respect yourself more than you love your neighbor; the one is the measure of the capacity for the other.

As the days pass, every true believer becomes more skillful in alluring his fellows into the love of eternal truth. Are you more resourceful in revealing goodness to humanity today than you were yesterday? Are you a better righteousness recommender this year than you were last year? Are you becoming increasingly artistic in your technique of leading hungry souls into the spiritual kingdom?

Are your ideals sufficiently high to insure your eternal salvation while your ideas are so practical as to render you a useful citizen to function on earth in association with your mortal fellows? In the spirit, your citizenship is in heaven; in the flesh, you are still citizens of the earth kingdoms. Render to the Caesars the things which are material and to God those which are spiritual.

The measure of the spiritual capacity of the evolving soul is your faith in truth and your love for man, but the measure of your human strength of character is your ability to resist the holding of grudges and your capacity to withstand brooding in the face of deep sorrow. Defeat is the true mirror in which you may honestly view your real self.

As you grow older in years and more experienced in the affairs of the kingdom, are you becoming more tactful in dealing with troublesome mortals and more tolerant in living with stubborn associates? Tact is the fulcrum of social leverage, and tolerance is the earmark of a great soul. If you possess these rare and charming gifts, as the days pass you will become more alert and expert in your worthy efforts to avoid all unnecessary social misunderstandings. Such wise souls are able to avoid much of the trouble which is certain to be the portion of all who suffer from lack of emotional adjustment, those who refuse to grow up, and those who refuse to grow old gracefully.

Avoid dishonesty and unfairness in all your efforts to preach truth and proclaim the gospel. Seek no unearned recognition and crave no

THE MISTAKES WHICH YOU FAIL TO FORGET IN TIME WILL BE FORGOTTEN IN ETERNITY. LIGHTEN YOUR BURDENS OF SOUL BY SPEEDILY ACQUIRING A LONG-DISTANCE VIEW OF YOUR DESTINY.

undeserved sympathy. Love, freely receive from both divine and human sources regardless of your deserts, and love freely in return. But in all other things related to honor and adulation seek only that which honestly belongs to you.

The God-conscious mortal is certain of salvation; he is unafraid of life; he is honest and consistent. He knows how bravely to endure unavoidable suffering; he is uncomplaining when faced by inescapable hardship.

The true believer does not grow weary in well-doing just because he is thwarted. Difficulty whets the ardor of the truth lover, while obstacles only challenge the exertions of the undaunted kingdom builder.

And many other things Jesus taught them before they made ready to depart from Tyre. ◾

AUGUST 9, A.D. 29

PETER'S CONFESSION

J esus had gone to Mount Hermon in his early experience with the affairs of the kingdom, and now that he was entering upon the final epoch of his work, he desired to return to this mount of trial and triumph, where he hoped the apostles might gain a new vision of their responsibilities and acquire new strength for the trying times just ahead. As they journeyed along the way, about the time of passing south of the Waters of Merom, the apostles fell to talking among themselves about their recent experiences in Phœnicia and elsewhere and to recounting how their message had been received, and how the different peoples regarded their Master.

As they paused for lunch, Jesus suddenly confronted the twelve with the first question he had

[C. MICHAEL DUDASH — *Peter's Confession*]

ever addressed to them concerning himself. He asked this surprising question, "Who do men say that I am?"

Jesus had spent long months in training these apostles as to the nature and character of the kingdom of heaven, and he well knew the time had come when he must begin to teach them more about his own nature and his personal relationship to the kingdom. And now, as they were seated under the mulberry trees, the Master made ready to hold one of the most momentous sessions of his long association with the chosen apostles.

More than half the apostles participated in answering Jesus' question. They told him that he was regarded as a prophet or as an extraordinary man by all who knew him; that even his enemies greatly feared him, accounting for his powers by the indictment that he was in league with the prince of devils. They told him that some in Judea and Samaria who had not met him personally believed he was John the Baptist risen from the dead. Peter explained that he had been, at sundry times and by various persons, compared with Moses, Elijah, Isaiah, and Jeremiah. When Jesus had listened to this report, he drew himself upon his feet, and looking down upon the twelve sitting about him in a semicircle, with startling emphasis he pointed to them with a sweeping gesture of his hand and asked, "But who say you that I am?" There was a moment of tense silence. The twelve never took their eyes off the Master, and then Simon Peter, springing to his feet, exclaimed:

"You are the Deliverer, the Son of the living God." And the eleven sitting apostles arose to their feet with one accord, thereby indicating that Peter had spoken for all of them.

When Jesus had beckoned them again to be seated, and while still standing before them, he said: "This has been revealed to you by my Father. The hour has come when you should know the truth about me. But for the time being I charge you that you tell this to no man. Let us go hence."

And so they resumed their journey to Caesarea-Philippi, arriving late that evening and stopping at the home of Celsus, who was expecting them. The apostles slept little that night; they seemed to sense that a great event in their lives and in the work of the kingdom had transpired.

The next day they were all seated in the garden at just about noon when the Master appeared. They wore expressions of dignified solemnity, and all arose to their feet as he approached them. Jesus relieved the tension by that friendly and fraternal smile which was so characteristic of him when his followers took themselves, or some happening related to themselves, too seriously. With a commanding gesture he indicated that they should be seated. Never again did the twelve greet their Master by arising when he came into their presence. They saw that he did not approve of such an outward show of respect.

After they had partaken of their meal and were engaged in discussing plans for the forthcoming tour of the Decapolis, Jesus suddenly looked up into their faces and said: "Now that a full day has passed since you assented to Simon Peter's declaration regarding the identity of the Son of Man, I would ask if you still hold to your decision?" On hearing this, the twelve stood upon their feet, and Simon Peter, stepping a few paces forward toward Jesus, said: "Yes, Master, we do. We believe that you are the Son of the living God." And Peter sat down with his brethren.

Jesus, still standing, then said to the twelve: "You are my chosen ambassadors, but I know that, in the circumstances, you could not entertain this belief as a result of mere human knowledge. This is a revelation of the spirit of my Father to your inmost souls. And when, therefore, you make this confession by the insight of the spirit of my Father which dwells within you, I am led to declare that upon this foundation will I build the brotherhood of the kingdom of heaven. Upon this rock of spiritual reality will I build the living temple of spiritual fellowship in the eternal realities of my Father's kingdom. All the forces of evil and the hosts of sin shall not prevail against this human fraternity of the divine spirit. And while my Father's spirit shall ever be the divine guide and mentor of all who enter the bonds of this spirit fellowship, to you and your successors I now deliver the keys of the outward kingdom—the authority over things temporal—the social and economic features of this association of men and women as fellows of the kingdom." And again he charged them, for the time being, that they should tell no man that he was the Son of God.

THE NEW CONCEPT

The new and vital feature of Peter's confession was the clear-cut recognition that Jesus was the Son of God, of his unquestioned divinity. Ever since his baptism and the wedding at Cana these apostles had variously regarded him as the Messiah, but it was not a part of the Jewish concept of the national deliverer that he should be *divine*. The Jews had not taught that the Messiah would spring from divinity; he was to be the "anointed one," but hardly had they contemplated him as being "the Son of God." In the second confession more emphasis was placed upon the *combined nature*,

SON OF MAN, SON OF GOD

Jesus now entered upon the fourth and last stage of his human life in the flesh. The first stage was that of his childhood, the years when he was only dimly conscious of his origin, nature, and destiny as a human being. The second stage was the increasingly self-conscious years of youth and advancing manhood, during which he came more clearly to comprehend his divine nature and human mission. This second stage ended with the experiences and revelations associated with his baptism. The third stage of the Master's earth experience extended from the baptism through the years of his ministry as teacher and healer and up to this momentous hour of Peter's confession at Caesarea-Philippi. This third period of his earth life embraced the times when his apostles and his immediate followers knew him as the Son of Man and regarded him as the Messiah. The fourth and last period of his earth career began here at Caesarea-Philippi and extended on to the crucifixion. This stage of his ministry was characterized by his acknowledgment of divinity and embraced the labors of his last year in the flesh.

Jesus had sincerely endeavored to lead his followers into the spiritual kingdom as a teacher, then as a teacher-healer, but they would not have it so. He well knew that his earth mission could not possibly fulfill the Messianic expectations of the Jewish people; the olden prophets had portrayed a Messiah which he could never be. He sought to establish the Father's kingdom as the Son of Man, but his followers would not go forward in the adventure. Jesus, seeing this, then elected to meet his believers part way and in so doing prepared openly to assume the role of the bestowal Son of God.

the supernal fact that he was the Son of Man *and* the Son of God, and it was upon this great truth of the union of the human nature with the divine nature that Jesus declared he would build the kingdom of heaven.

Jesus had sought to live his life on earth and complete his bestowal mission as the Son of Man. His followers were disposed to regard him as the expected Messiah. Knowing that he could never fulfill their Messianic expectations, he endeavored to effect such a modification of their concept of the Messiah as would enable him partially to meet their expectations. But he now recognized that such a plan could hardly be carried through successfully. He therefore elected boldly to disclose the third plan—openly to announce his divinity, acknowledge the truthfulness of Peter's confession, and directly proclaim to the twelve that he was a Son of God.

The apostles heard much that was new as Jesus talked to them this day in the garden. And some of these pronouncements sounded strange even to them. Among other startling announcements they listened to such as the following:

• "From this time on, if any man would have fellowship with us, let him assume the obligations of sonship and follow me. And when I am no more with you, think not that the world will treat you better than it did your Master. If you love me, prepare to prove this affection by your willingness to make the supreme sacrifice."

• "And mark well my words: I have not come to call the righteous, but sinners. The Son of Man came not to be ministered to, but to minister and to bestow his life as the gift for all. I declare to you that I have come to seek and to save those who are lost."

• "No man in this world now sees the Father except the Son who came forth from the Father. But if the Son be lifted up, he will draw all men to himself, and whosoever believes this truth of

the combined nature of the Son shall be endowed with life that is more than age-abiding."

• "We may not yet proclaim openly that the Son of Man is the Son of God, but it has been revealed to you; wherefore do I speak boldly to you concerning these mysteries. Though I stand before you in this physical presence, I came forth from God the Father. Before Abraham was, I am. I did come forth from the Father into this world as you have known me, and I declare to you that I must presently leave this world and return to the work of my Father."

• "And now can your faith comprehend the truth of these declarations in the face of my warning you that the Son of Man will not meet the expectations of your fathers as they conceived the Messiah? My kingdom is not of this world. Can you believe the truth about me in the face of the fact that, though the foxes have holes and the birds of heaven have nests, I have not where to lay my head?"

• "Nevertheless, I tell you that the Father and I are one. He who has seen me has seen the Father. My Father is working with me in all these things, and he will never leave me alone in my mission, even as I will never forsake you when you presently go forth to proclaim this gospel throughout the world."

• "And now have I brought you apart with me and by yourselves for a little while that you may comprehend the glory, and grasp the grandeur, of the life to which I have called you: the faith-adventure of the establishment of my Father's kingdom in the hearts of mankind, the building of my fellowship of living association with the souls of all who believe this gospel."

The apostles listened to these bold and startling statements in silence; they were stunned. And they dispersed in small groups to discuss and ponder the Master's words. They had confessed that he was the Son of God, but they could not grasp the full meaning of what they had been led to do.

"LAY IN PROVISIONS AND PREPARE YOURSELVES FOR A JOURNEY TO YONDER MOUNTAIN, WHERE THE SPIRIT BIDS ME GO TO BE ENDOWED FOR THE FINISH OF MY WORK ON EARTH."

And now Jesus would take his apostles along with him to Mount Hermon, where he had appointed to inaugurate his fourth phase of earth ministry as the Son of God. Some of them were present at his baptism in the Jordan and had witnessed the beginning of his career as the Son of Man, and he desired that some of them should also be present to hear his authority for the assumption of the new and public role of a Son of God. Accordingly, on the morning of Friday, August 12, Jesus said to the twelve: "Lay in provisions and prepare yourselves for a journey to yonder mountain, where the spirit bids me go to be endowed for the finish of my work on earth. And I would take my brethren along that they may also be strengthened for the trying times of going with me through this experience." ■

AUGUST 12, A.D. 29

THE TRANSFIGURATION

It was near sundown on Friday afternoon, August 12, A.D. 29, when Jesus and his associates reached the foot of Mount Hermon, near the very place where the lad Tiglath once waited while the Master ascended the mountain alone to settle the spiritual destinies of Urantia and technically to terminate the Lucifer rebellion. And here they sojourned for two days in spiritual preparation for the events so soon to follow.

Since he could not take all of his associates with him, he decided to take only the three who were in the habit of accompanying him on such special vigils. Accordingly, only Peter, James, and John shared even a part of this unique experience with the Master.

Early on the morning of Monday, August 15, Jesus and the three apostles began the ascent of Mount Hermon, and this was six days after the memorable noontide confession of Peter by the roadside under the mulberry trees.

Jesus had been summoned to go up on the mountain, apart by himself, for the transaction of important matters having to do with the progress of his bestowal in the flesh as this experience was related to the universe of his own creation. It is significant that this extraordinary event was timed to occur while Jesus and the apostles were in the lands of the gentiles, and that it actually transpired on a mountain of the gentiles.

When a boy, Jesus used to ascend the hill near his home and dream of the battles which had been fought by the armies of empires on the plain of Esdraelon; now he ascended Mount Hermon to receive the endowment which was to prepare him to descend upon the plains of the Jordan to enact the closing scenes of the drama of his bestowal. On this day in August three of his apostles saw him decline to be invested with full universe authority. They looked on in amazement as the celestial messengers departed, leaving him alone to finish out his earth life as the Son of Man and the Son of God.

It was about three o'clock on this beautiful afternoon that Jesus took leave of the three apostles, saying: "I go apart by myself for a season to commune with the Father and his messengers; I bid you tarry here and, while awaiting my return, pray that the Father's will may be done in all your experience in connection with the further bestowal mission of the Son of Man." And after saying this to them, Jesus withdrew for a long conference with Gabriel and the Father Melchizedek, not returning until about six o'clock. When Jesus saw their anxiety over his prolonged absence, he said: "Why were you afraid? You well know I must be about my Father's business; wherefore do you doubt when I am not with you? I now declare that the Son of Man has chosen to go through his full life in your midst and as one of you. Be of good cheer; I will not leave you until my work is finished."

As they partook of their meager evening meal, Peter asked the Master, "How long do we remain on this mountain away from our brethren?" And Jesus answered: "Until you shall see the glory of the Son of Man and know that whatsoever I have declared to you is true." And they talked over the affairs of the Lucifer rebellion while seated about the glowing embers of their fire until darkness drew on and the apostles' eyes grew heavy, for they had begun their journey very early that morning.

When the three had been fast asleep for about half an hour, they were suddenly awakened by a near-by crackling sound, and much to their amazement and consternation, on looking about them, they beheld Jesus in intimate converse with two brilliant beings clothed in the habiliments of the light of the celestial world. And Jesus' face and form shone with the luminosity of a heavenly light. These three conversed in a strange language, but from certain things said, Peter erroneously conjectured that the beings with Jesus were Moses and Elijah; in reality, they were Gabriel and the Father Melchizedek. The physical controllers had arranged for the apostles to witness this scene because of Jesus' request.

The three apostles were so badly frightened that they were slow in collecting their wits, but

MEANING OF THE TRANSFIGURATION

That which Peter, James, and John witnessed on the mount of transfiguration was a fleeting glimpse of a celestial pageant which transpired that eventful day on Mount Hermon. Because Gabriel and Father Melchizedek function in the highest executive roles of Nebadon, this three-hour private conference out of sight of the apostles may thus be seen as an administrative conference of the highest order. The transfiguration was the occasion of:

1. The acceptance of the fullness of the bestowal of the incarnated life of Michael on Urantia. And Gabriel brought Jesus that assurance.

2. The testimony of the satisfaction of the Infinite Spirit as to the fullness of the Urantia bestowal in the likeness of mortal flesh. The universe representative of the Infinite Spirit on this occasion spoke through the Father Melchizedek.

Jesus welcomed this testimony regarding the success of his earth mission, but he noted that his Father did not indicate that the Urantia bestowal was finished; only did the unseen presence of the Father bear witness through Jesus' Personalized Adjuster, saying, "This is my beloved Son; give heed to him." And this was spoken in words to be heard also by the three apostles.

After this celestial visitation Jesus sought to know his Father's will and decided to pursue the mortal bestowal to its natural end. This was the significance of the transfiguration to Jesus. To the three apostles it was an event marking the entrance of the Master upon the final phase of his earth career as the Son of God and the Son of Man.

[CARL BLOCH — *Transfiguration of Christ*]

Peter, who was first to recover himself, said, as the dazzling vision faded from before them and they observed Jesus standing alone: "Jesus, Master, it is good to have been here. We rejoice to see this glory. We are loath to go back down to the inglorious world. If you are willing, let us abide here, and we will erect three tents, one for you, one for Moses, and one for Elijah." And Peter said this because of his confusion, and because nothing else came into his mind at just that moment.

While Peter was yet speaking, a silvery cloud drew near and overshadowed the four of them. The apostles now became greatly frightened, and as they fell down on their faces to worship, they heard a voice, the same that had spoken on the occasion of Jesus' baptism, say: "This is my beloved Son; give heed to him." And when the cloud vanished, again was Jesus alone with the three, and he reached down and touched them, saying: "Arise and be not afraid; you shall see greater things than this." But the apostles were truly afraid; they were a silent and thoughtful trio as they made ready to descend the mountain shortly before midnight. ∎

THE EPILEPTIC BOY

It was shortly before breakfast time on this Tuesday morning when Jesus and his companions arrived at the apostolic camp. As they drew near, they discerned a considerable crowd gathered around the apostles and soon began to hear the loud words of argument and disputation of this group of about fifty persons, embracing the nine apostles and a gathering equally divided between Jerusalem scribes and believing disciples who had tracked Jesus and his associates in their journey from Magadan.

Although the crowd engaged in numerous arguments, the chief controversy was about a certain citizen of Tiberias who had arrived the preceding day in quest of Jesus. This man, James of Safed, had a son about fourteen years old, an only child, who was severely afflicted with epilepsy. In addition to this nervous malady this lad had become possessed by one of those wandering, mischievous, and rebellious midwayers who were then present on earth and uncontrolled, so that the youth was both epileptic and demon-possessed.

For almost two weeks this anxious father, a minor official of Herod Antipas, had wandered about through the western borders of Philip's domains, seeking Jesus that he might entreat him to cure this afflicted son.

Andrew stepped up to greet this father and his son, saying, "Whom do you seek?" Said James: "My good man, I search for your Master. I seek healing for my afflicted son. I would have Jesus cast out this devil that possesses my child." And then the father proceeded to relate to the apostles how his son was so afflicted that he had many times almost lost his life as a result of these malignant seizures.

As the apostles listened, Simon Zelotes and Judas Iscariot stepped into the presence of the father, saying: "We can heal him; you need not wait for the Master's return. We are ambassadors of the kingdom; no longer do we hold these things in secret. Jesus is the Deliverer, and the keys of the kingdom have been delivered to us." By this time Andrew and Thomas were in consultation at one side. Nathaniel and the others looked on in amazement; they were all aghast at the sudden boldness, if not presumption, of Simon and Judas. Then said the father: "If it has been given you to do these works, I pray that you will speak those words which will deliver my child from this bondage." Then Simon stepped forward and, placing his hand on the head of the child, looked directly into his eyes and commanded: "Come out of him, you unclean spirit; in the name of Jesus obey me." But the lad had only a more violent fit, while the

AND AS THEY TALKED, THE YOUTH WAS SEIZED WITH A VIOLENT ATTACK AND FELL IN THEIR MIDST, GNASHING HIS TEETH AND FOAMING AT THE MOUTH.

scribes mocked the apostles in derision, and the disappointed believers suffered the taunts of these unfriendly critics.

Andrew was deeply chagrined at this ill-advised effort and its dismal failure. He called the apostles aside for conference and prayer. After this season of meditation, feeling keenly the sting of their defeat and sensing the humiliation resting upon all of them, Andrew sought, in a second attempt, to cast out the demon, but only failure crowned his efforts. Andrew frankly confessed defeat and requested the father to remain with them overnight or until Jesus' return, saying: "Perhaps this sort goes not out except by the Master's personal command."

As Jesus drew near, the nine apostles were more than relieved to welcome him, and they were greatly encouraged to behold the good cheer and unusual enthusiasm which marked the countenances of Peter, James, and John. They all rushed forward to greet Jesus and their three brethren. As they exchanged greetings, the crowd came up, and Jesus asked, "What were you disputing about as we drew near?" But before the disconcerted and humiliated apostles could reply to the Master's question, the anxious father of the afflicted lad stepped forward and, kneeling at Jesus' feet, said: "Master, I have a son, an only child, who is possessed by an evil spirit. Not only does he cry out in terror, foam at the mouth, and fall like a dead person at the time of seizure, but oftentimes this evil spirit which possesses him rends him in convulsions and sometimes has cast him into the water and even into the fire. With much grinding of teeth and as a result of many bruises, my child

wastes away. His life is worse than death; his mother and I are of a sad heart and a broken spirit. About noon yesterday, seeking for you, I caught up with your disciples, and while we were waiting, your apostles sought to cast out this demon, but they could not do it. And now, Master, will you do this for us, will you heal my son?"

When Jesus had listened to this recital, he touched the kneeling father and bade him rise while he gave the near-by apostles a searching survey. Then said Jesus to all those who stood before him: "O faithless and perverse generation, how long shall I bear with you? How long shall I be with you? How long ere you learn that the works of faith come not forth at the bidding of doubting unbelief?" And then, pointing to the bewildered father, Jesus said, "Bring hither your son." And when James had brought the lad before Jesus, he asked, "How long has the boy been afflicted in this way?" The father answered, "Since he was a very young child." And as they talked, the youth was seized with a violent attack and fell in their midst, gnashing his teeth and foaming at the mouth. After a succession of violent convulsions he lay there before them as one dead. Now did the father again kneel at Jesus' feet while he implored the Master, saying: "If you can cure him, I beseech you to have compassion on us and deliver us from this affliction." And when Jesus heard these words, he looked down into the father's anxious face, saying: "Question not my Father's power of love, only the sincerity and reach of your faith. All things are possible to him who really believes." And then James of Safed spoke those long-to-be-remembered

AND THEN JAMES OF SAFED SPOKE THOSE LONG-TO-BE-REMEMBERED WORDS OF COMMINGLED FAITH AND DOUBT, "LORD, I BELIEVE. I PRAY YOU HELP MY UNBELIEF."

[HAROLD COPPING — *Jesus Heals the Epileptic Boy* (detail)]

words of commingled faith and doubt, "Lord, I believe. I pray you help my unbelief."

When Jesus heard these words, he stepped forward and, taking the lad by the hand, said: "I will do this in accordance with my Father's will and in honor of living faith. My son, arise! Come out of him, disobedient spirit, and go not back into him." And placing the hand of the lad in the hand of the father, Jesus said: "Go your way. The Father has granted the desire of your soul." And all who were present, even the enemies of Jesus, were astonished at what they saw.

This was a true healing of a double affliction, a physical ailment and a spirit malady. And the lad was permanently cured from that hour.

In Celsus' Garden

They remained overnight with Celsus, and that evening in the garden, after they had eaten and rested, the twelve gathered about Jesus, and Thomas said: "Master, while we who tarried behind still remain ignorant of what transpired up on the mountain, and which so greatly cheered our brethren who were with you, we crave to have you talk with us concerning our defeat and instruct us in these matters, seeing that those things which happened on the mountain cannot be disclosed at this time."

And Jesus answered Thomas, saying: "Everything which your brethren heard on the mountain shall be revealed to you in due season. But I will now show you the cause of your defeat. In what you attempted, in which you so completely failed, your purpose was not pure. Your motive was not divine. Your ideal was not spiritual. Your ambition was not altruistic. Your procedure was not based on love, and your goal of attainment was not the will of the Father in heaven."

When Jesus had thus spoken to the twelve, he added: "And now go to your rest, for on the morrow we return to Magadan and there take counsel concerning our mission to the cities and villages of the Decapolis. And in the conclusion of this day's experience, let me declare to each of you that which I spoke to your brethren on the mountain, and let these words find a deep lodgment in your hearts: The Son of Man now enters upon the last phase of the bestowal. We are about to begin those labors which shall presently lead to the great and final testing of your faith and devotion when I shall be delivered into the hands of the men who seek my destruction. And remember what I am saying to you: The Son of Man will be put to death, but he shall rise again."

They retired for the night, sorrowful. They were bewildered; they could not comprehend these words. And while they were afraid to ask aught concerning what he had said, they did recall all of it subsequent to his resurrection. ∎

PETER'S PROTEST

Early this Wednesday morning Jesus and the twelve departed from Caesarea-Philippi for Magadan Park near Bethsaida-Julias. The apostles had slept very little that night, so they were up early and ready to go. Even the stolid Alpheus twins had been shocked by this talk about the death of Jesus. As they journeyed south, just beyond the Waters of Merom they came to the Damascus road, and desiring to avoid the scribes and others whom Jesus knew would presently be coming along after them, he directed that they go on to Capernaum by the Damascus road which passes through Galilee. And he did this because he knew that those who followed after him would go on down over the east Jordan road since they reckoned that Jesus and the apostles would fear to pass through the territory of Herod Antipas. Jesus sought to elude his critics and the crowd which followed him that he might be alone with his apostles this day.

They traveled on through Galilee until well past the time for their lunch, when they stopped in the shade to refresh themselves. And after they had partaken of food, Andrew, speaking to Jesus, said: "Master, my brethren do not comprehend your deep sayings. We have come fully to believe that you are the Son of God, and now we hear these strange words about leaving us, about dying. We do not understand your teaching. Are you speaking to us in parables? We pray you to speak to us directly and in undisguised form."

In answer to Andrew, Jesus said: "My brethren, it is because you have confessed that I am the Son of God that I am constrained to begin to unfold to you the truth about the end of the bestowal of the Son of Man on earth. You insist on clinging to the belief that I am the Messiah, and you will not abandon the idea that the Messiah must sit upon a throne in Jerusalem; wherefore do I persist in telling you that the Son of Man must presently go to Jerusalem, suffer many things, be rejected by the scribes, the elders, and the chief priests, and after all this be killed and raised from the dead. And I speak not a parable to you; I speak the truth to you that you may be prepared for these events when they suddenly come upon us." And while he was yet speaking, Simon Peter, rushing impetuously toward him, laid his hand upon the Master's shoulder and said: "Master, be it far from us to contend with you, but I declare that these things shall never happen to you."

Peter spoke thus because he loved Jesus; but the Master's human nature recognized in these words of well-meant affection the subtle suggestion of temptation that he change his policy of pursuing to the end his earth bestowal in accordance with

[JAMES TISSOT — *The Protestations of Saint Peter*]

"WHAT DOES IT PROFIT A MAN TO GAIN THE WHOLE WORLD AND LOSE HIS OWN SOUL? WHAT WOULD A MAN GIVE IN EXCHANGE FOR ETERNAL LIFE?"

the will of his Paradise Father. And it was because he detected the danger of permitting the suggestions of even his affectionate and loyal friends to dissuade him, that he turned upon Peter and the other apostles, saying: "Get you behind me. You savor of the spirit of the adversary, the tempter. When you talk in this manner, you are not on my side but rather on the side of our enemy. In this way do you make your love for me a stumbling block to my doing the Father's will. Mind not the ways of men but rather the will of God."

After they had recovered from the first shock of Jesus' stinging rebuke, and before they resumed their journey, the Master spoke further: "If any man would come after me, let him disregard himself, take up his responsibilities daily, and follow me. For whosoever would save his life selfishly, shall lose it, but whosoever loses his life for my sake and the gospel's, shall save it. What does it profit a man to gain the whole world and lose his own soul? What would a man give in exchange for eternal life? Be not ashamed of me and my words in this sinful and hypocritical generation, even as I will not be ashamed to acknowledge you when in glory I appear before my Father in the presence of all the celestial hosts. Nevertheless, many of you now standing before me shall not taste death till you see this kingdom of God come with power."

And thus did Jesus make plain to the twelve the painful and conflicting path which they must tread if they would follow him. What a shock these words were to these Galilean fishermen who persisted in dreaming of an earthly kingdom with positions of honor for themselves! But their loyal hearts were stirred by this courageous appeal, and not one of them was minded to forsake him. Jesus was not sending them alone into the conflict; he was leading them. He asked only that they bravely follow.

Slowly the twelve were grasping the idea that Jesus was telling them something about the possibility of his dying. They only vaguely comprehended what he said about his death, while his statement about rising from the dead utterly failed to register in their minds. As the days passed, Peter, James, and John, recalling their experience upon the mount of the transfiguration, arrived at a fuller understanding of certain of these matters.

In all the association of the twelve with their Master, only a few times did they see that flashing eye and hear such swift words of rebuke as were administered to Peter and the rest of them on this occasion. Jesus had always been patient with their human shortcomings, but not so when faced by an impending threat against the program of implicitly carrying out his Father's will regarding the remainder of his earth career. The apostles were literally stunned; they were amazed and horrified. They could not find words to express their sorrow. Slowly they began to realize what the Master must endure, and that they must go through these experiences with him, but they did not awaken to the reality of these coming events until long after these early hints of the impending tragedy of his latter days.

In silence Jesus and the twelve started for their camp at Magadan Park. As the afternoon wore on, though they did not converse with Jesus, they talked much among themselves. ✳

CHAPTER IX

"Before Abraham Was, I Am"

"Behold, I stand at the door, and knock: if any man hear my voice, and open the door, I will come in to him, and will sup with him, and he with me."

—Revelation 3:20 KJV

The presence of people from all of the known world, from Spain to India, made the feast of tabernacles an ideal occasion for Jesus for the first time publicly to proclaim his full gospel in Jerusalem. The apostles at last beheld their Master making the bold announcement of his mission on earth before all the world, as it were. The vast majority of the pilgrims from afar who had heard of him entertained the hope that they might see him at Jerusalem. And they were not disappointed, for on several occasions he taught in Solomon's Porch and elsewhere in the temple courts. These teachings were really the official or formal announcement of the divinity of Jesus to the Jewish people and to the whole world.

Jesus' bold appearance in Jerusalem more than ever confused his followers. Many of his disciples, and even Judas, had dared to think that Jesus had fled in haste into Phoenicia because he feared the Jewish leaders and Herod Antipas. His presence in Jerusalem at the feast of tabernacles, even in opposition to the advice of his followers, sufficed forever to put an end to all whisperings about fear and cowardice.

The audacious boldness of the Master in publicly appearing in Jerusalem overawed his enemies; they were not prepared for such a daring challenge. His enemies were so taken aback by Jesus' unexpected public appearance that they conjectured he must have been promised protection by the Roman authorities. This was one of the reasons why Jesus could publicly visit Jerusalem and live to go away. One or two months before this he would certainly have been put to death.

Every time Jesus went to Jerusalem, his apostles were filled with terror. They were the more afraid as, from day to day, they listened to his increasingly bold pronouncements regarding the nature of his mission on earth. They were unaccustomed to hearing Jesus make such positive claims and such amazing assertions even when preaching among his friends.

THE URANTIA BOOK: PAPERS 162–171
SEPTEMBER, A.D. 29–FRIDAY, MARCH 31, A.D. 30

[J. Kirk Richards — *I Stand at the Door and Knock*]

PUBLIC ANNOUNCEMENT OF DIVINITY

Long before they fled from Galilee, the followers of Jesus had implored him to go to Jerusalem to proclaim the gospel of the kingdom in order that his message might have the prestige of having been preached at the center of Jewish culture and learning; but now that he had actually come to Jerusalem to teach, they were afraid for his life. Knowing that the Sanhedrin had sought to bring Jesus to Jerusalem for trial and recalling the Master's recently reiterated declarations that he must be subject to death, the apostles had been literally stunned by his sudden decision to attend the feast of tabernacles. To all their previous entreaties that he go to Jerusalem he had replied, "The hour has not yet come." Now, to their protests of fear he answered only, "But the hour has come."

During the feast of tabernacles Jesus went boldly into Jerusalem on several occasions and publicly taught in the temple. This he did in spite of the efforts of his apostles to dissuade him. Though they had long urged him to proclaim his message in Jerusalem, they now feared to see him enter the city at this time, knowing full well that the scribes and Pharisees were bent on bringing about his death.

Thousands of believers from all parts of the Roman Empire saw Jesus, heard him teach, and many even journeyed out to Bethany to confer with him regarding the progress of the kingdom in their home districts.

The multitudes who listened to the Master's teachings were divided in their opinions. Some said he was a good man; some a prophet; some that he was truly the Messiah; others said he was a mischievous meddler, that he was leading the people astray with his strange doctrines. His enemies hesitated to denounce him openly for fear of his friendly believers, while his friends feared to acknowledge him openly for fear of the Jewish leaders, knowing that the Sanhedrin was determined to put him to death. But even his enemies marveled at his teaching, knowing that he had not been instructed in the schools of the rabbis.

DIVISION IN THE RANKS

There were many reasons why Jesus was able publicly to preach in the temple courts throughout the days of the feast, and chief of these was the fear that had come over the officers of the Sanhedrin as a result of the secret division of sentiment in their own ranks. It was a fact that many of the members of the Sanhedrin either secretly believed in Jesus or else were decidedly averse to arresting him during the feast, when such large numbers of people were present in Jerusalem, many of whom either believed in him or were at least friendly to the spiritual movement which he sponsored.

The first afternoon that Jesus taught in the temple, a considerable company sat listening to his words depicting the liberty of the new gospel and the joy of those who believe the good news, when a curious listener interrupted him to ask: "Teacher, how is it you can quote the Scriptures and teach the people so fluently when I am told that you are untaught in the learning of the rabbis?" Jesus replied: "No man has taught me the truths which I declare to you. And this teaching is not mine but His who sent me. If any man really desires to do my Father's will, he shall certainly know about my teaching, whether it be God's or whether I speak for myself. He who speaks for himself seeks his own glory, but when I declare the words of the Father, I thereby seek the glory of him who sent me. But

THEY SEEK TO KILL ME BECAUSE THEY KNOW THAT, IF YOU HONESTLY BELIEVE AND DARE TO ACCEPT MY TEACHING, THEIR SYSTEM OF TRADITIONAL RELIGION WILL BE OVERTHROWN.

before you try to enter into the new light, should you not rather follow the light you already have? Moses gave you the law, yet how many of you honestly seek` to fulfill its demands? Moses in this law enjoins you, saying, 'You shall not kill'; notwithstanding this command some of you seek to kill the Son of Man."

When the crowd heard these words, they fell to wrangling among themselves. Some said he was mad; some that he had a devil. Others said this was indeed the prophet of Galilee whom the scribes and Pharisees had long sought to kill. Some said the religious authorities were afraid to molest him; others thought that they laid not hands upon him because they had become believers in him. After considerable debate one of the crowd stepped forward and asked Jesus, "Why do the rulers seek to kill you?" And he replied: "The rulers seek to kill me because they resent my teaching about the good news of the kingdom, a gospel that sets men free from the burdensome traditions of a formal religion of ceremonies which these teachers are determined to uphold at any cost. They circumcise in accordance with the law on the Sabbath day, but they would kill me because I once on the Sabbath day set free a man held in the bondage of affliction. They follow after me on the Sabbath to spy on me but would kill me because on another occasion I chose to make a grievously stricken man completely whole on the Sabbath day. They seek to kill me because they well know that, if you honestly believe and dare to accept my teaching, their system of traditional religion

will be overthrown, forever destroyed. Thus will they be deprived of authority over that to which they have devoted their lives since they steadfastly refuse to accept this new and more glorious gospel of the kingdom of God. And now do I appeal to every one of you: Judge not according to outward appearances but rather judge by the true spirit of these teachings; judge righteously."

Then said another inquirer: "Yes, Teacher, we do look for the Messiah, but when he comes, we know that his appearance will be in mystery. We know whence you are. You have been among your brethren from the beginning. The deliverer will come in power to restore the throne of David's kingdom. Do you really claim to be the Messiah?" And Jesus replied: "You claim to know me and to know whence I am. I wish your claims were true, for indeed then would you find abundant life in that knowledge. But I declare that I have not come to you for myself; I have been sent by the Father, and he who sent me is true and faithful. By refusing to hear me, you are refusing to receive Him who sends me. You, if you will receive this gospel, shall come to know Him who sent me. I know the Father, for I have come from the Father to declare and reveal him to you."

The agents of the scribes wanted to lay hands upon him, but they feared the multitude, for many believed in him. Jesus' work since his baptism had become well known to all Jewry, and as many of these people recounted these things, they said among themselves: "Even though this teacher is from Galilee, and even though he does not meet all of our expectations of the Messiah, we wonder if the deliverer, when he does come, will really do anything more wonderful than this Jesus of Nazareth has already done."

When the Pharisees and their agents heard the people talking this way, they took counsel with their leaders and decided that something should be done forthwith to put a stop to these public appearances of Jesus in the temple courts. The leaders of the Jews, in general, were disposed to avoid a clash with Jesus, believing that the Roman authorities had promised him immunity. They could not otherwise account for his boldness in coming at this time to Jerusalem; but the officers of the Sanhedrin did not wholly believe this rumor. They reasoned that the Roman rulers would not do such a thing secretly and without the knowledge of the highest governing body of the Jewish nation.

Accordingly, Eber, the proper officer of the Sanhedrin, with two assistants was dispatched to arrest Jesus. As Eber made his way toward Jesus, the Master said: "Fear not to approach me. Draw near while you listen to my teaching. I know you have been sent to apprehend me, but you should understand that nothing will befall the Son of Man until his hour comes. You are not arrayed against me; you come only to do the bidding of your masters, and even these rulers of the Jews verily think they are doing God's service when they secretly seek my destruction.

"I bear none of you ill will. The Father loves you, and therefore do I long for your deliverance from the bondage of prejudice and the darkness of tradition. I offer you the liberty of life and the joy of salvation. I proclaim the new and living way, the deliverance from evil and the breaking of the bondage of sin. I have come that you might have life, and have it eternally. You seek to be rid of me and my disquieting teachings. If you could only realize that I am to be with you only a little while! In just a short time I go to Him who sent me into this world. And then will many of you diligently seek me, but you shall not discover my presence, for where I am about to go you cannot come. But all who truly seek to find me shall sometime attain the life that leads to my Father's presence."

Some of the scoffers said among themselves: "Where will this man go that we cannot find him? Will he go to live among the Greeks? Will he destroy himself? What can he mean when he declares that soon he will depart from us, and that we cannot go where he goes?"

Eber and his assistants refused to arrest Jesus; they returned to their meeting place without him. When, therefore, the chief priests and the Pharisees upbraided Eber and his assistants because they had not brought Jesus with them, Eber only replied: "We feared to arrest him in the midst of the multitude because many believe in him. Besides, we never heard a man speak like this man. There is something out of the ordinary about this teacher. You would all do well to go over to hear him." And when the chief rulers heard these words, they were astonished and spoke tauntingly to Eber: "Are you also led astray? Are you about to believe in this deceiver? Have you heard that any of our learned men or any of the rulers have believed in him? Have any of the scribes or the Pharisees been deceived by his clever teachings? How does it come that you are influenced by the behavior of this ignorant multitude who know not the law or the prophets? Do you not know that such untaught people are accursed?" And then answered Eber: "Even so, my masters, but this man speaks to the multitude words of mercy and hope. He cheers the downhearted, and his words were comforting even to our souls. What can there be wrong in these teachings even though he may not be the Messiah of the Scriptures? And even then does not our law require fairness? Do we condemn a man before we hear him?" And the chief of the Sanhedrin was wroth with Eber and, turning upon him, said: "Have you gone mad? Are you by any chance also from Galilee? Search the Scriptures,

[YONGSUNG KIM — *Forgiven*]

and you will discover that out of Galilee arises no prophet, much less the Messiah."

The Sanhedrin disbanded in confusion, and Jesus withdrew to Bethany for the night. ■

THE WOMAN TAKEN IN ADULTERY

It was during this visit to Jerusalem that Jesus dealt with a certain woman of evil repute who was brought into his presence by her accusers and his enemies. The distorted record you have of this episode would suggest that this woman had been brought before Jesus by the scribes and Pharisees, and that Jesus so dealt with them as to indicate that these religious leaders of the Jews might themselves have been guilty of immorality. Jesus well knew that, while these scribes and Pharisees were spiritually blind and intellectually prejudiced by their loyalty to tradition, they were to be numbered among the most thoroughly moral men of that day and generation.

What really happened was this: Early the third morning of the feast, as Jesus approached the temple, he was met by a group of the hired agents of the Sanhedrin who were dragging a woman along with them. As they came near, the spokesman said: "Master, this woman was taken in adultery—in the very act. Now, the law of Moses commands that we should stone such a woman. What do you say should be done with her?"

It was the plan of Jesus' enemies, if he upheld the law of Moses requiring that the self-confessed transgressor be stoned, to involve him in difficulty with the Roman rulers, who had denied the Jews the right to inflict the death penalty without the approval of a Roman tribunal. If he forbade stoning the woman, they would accuse him before the Sanhedrin of setting himself up above Moses and the Jewish law. If he remained silent, they would accuse him of cowardice. But the Master so managed the situation that the whole plot fell to pieces of its own sordid weight.

This woman, once comely, was the wife of an inferior citizen of Nazareth, a man who had been a troublemaker for Jesus throughout his youthful days. The man, having married this woman, did most shamefully force her to earn their living by making commerce of her body. He had come up to the feast at Jerusalem that his wife might thus prostitute her physical charms for financial gain. He had entered into a bargain with the hirelings of the Jewish rulers thus to betray his own wife in her commercialized vice. And so they came with the woman and her companion in transgression for the purpose of ensnaring Jesus into making some statement which could be used against him in case of his arrest.

Jesus, looking over the crowd, saw her husband standing behind the others. He knew what sort of man he was and perceived that he was a party to the despicable transaction. Jesus first walked around to near where this degenerate husband stood and wrote upon the sand a few words which caused him to depart in haste. Then he came back before the woman and wrote again upon the ground for the benefit of her would-be accusers; and when they read his words, they, too, went away, one by one. And when the Master had written in the sand the third time, the woman's companion in evil took his departure, so that, when the Master raised himself up from this writing, he beheld the woman standing alone before him. Jesus said: "Woman, where are your accusers? did no man remain to stone you?" And the woman, lifting up her eyes, answered, "No man, Lord." And then said Jesus: "I know about you; neither do I condemn you. Go your way in peace." And this woman, Hildana, forsook her wicked husband and joined herself to the disciples of the kingdom. ∎

"I Am the Light of the World"

On the evening of the next to the last day of the feast, when the scene was brilliantly illuminated by the lights of the candelabras and the torches, Jesus stood up in the midst of the assembled throng and said:

"I am the light of the world. He who follows me shall not walk in darkness but shall have the light of life. Presuming to place me on trial and assuming to sit as my judges, you declare that, if

[C. Michael Dudash — *Light of the World*]

I bear witness of myself, my witness cannot be true. But never can the creature sit in judgment on the Creator. Even if I do bear witness about myself, my witness is everlastingly true, for I know whence I came, who I am, and whither I go. You who would kill the Son of Man know not whence I came, who I am, or whither I go. You only judge by the appearances of the flesh; you do not perceive the realities of the spirit. I judge no man, not even my archenemy. But if I should choose to judge, my judgment would be true and righteous, for I would judge not alone but in association with my Father, who sent me into the world, and who is the source of all true judgment. You even allow that the witness of two reliable persons may be accepted—well, then, I bear witness of these truths; so also does my Father in heaven. And when I told you this yesterday, in your darkness you asked me, 'Where is your Father?' Truly, you know neither me nor my Father, for if you had known me, you would also have known the Father.

"I have already told you that I am going away, and that you will seek me and not find me, for where I am going you cannot come. You who would reject this light are from beneath; I am from above. You who prefer to sit in darkness are of this world; I am not of this world, and I live in the eternal light of the Father of lights. You all have had abundant opportunity to learn who I am, but you shall have still other evidence confirming the identity of the Son of Man. I am the light of life, and every one who deliberately and with understanding rejects this saving light shall die in his sins. Much I have to tell you, but you are unable to receive my words. However, he who sent me is true and faithful; my Father loves even his erring children. And all that my Father has spoken I also proclaim to the world.

"When the Son of Man is lifted up, then shall you all know that I am he, and that I have done nothing of myself but only as the Father has taught me. I speak these words to you and to your

children. And he who sent me is even now with me; he has not left me alone, for I do always that which is pleasing in his sight."

As Jesus thus taught the pilgrims in the temple courts, many believed. And no man dared to lay hands upon him. ∎

THE TRUTH WILL SET YOU FREE

On the afternoon of the last day of the feast and after the apostles had failed in their efforts to persuade him to flee from Jerusalem, Jesus again went into the temple to teach. Finding a large company of believers assembled in Solomon's Porch, he spoke to them, saying:

"If my words abide in you and you are minded to do the will of my Father, then are you truly my disciples. You shall know the truth, and the truth shall make you free. I know how you will answer me: We are the children of Abraham, and we are in bondage to none; how then shall we be made free? Even so, I do not speak of outward subjection to another's rule; I refer to the liberties of the soul. Verily, verily, I say to you, everyone who commits sin is the bond servant of sin. And you know that the bond servant is not likely to abide forever in the master's house. You also know that the son does remain in his father's house. If, therefore, the Son shall make you free, shall make you sons, you shall be free indeed.

"I know that you are Abraham's seed, yet your leaders seek to kill me because my word has not been allowed to have its transforming influence in their hearts. Their souls are sealed by prejudice and blinded by the pride of revenge. I declare to you the truth which the eternal Father shows me, while these deluded teachers seek to do the things which they have learned only from their temporal fathers. And when you reply that Abraham is your father, then do I tell you that, if you were the children of Abraham, you would do the works of Abraham. Some of you believe my teaching, but others seek to destroy me because I have told you the truth which I received from God. But Abraham did not so treat the truth of God. I perceive that some among you are determined to do the works of the evil one. If God were your Father, you would know me and love the truth which I reveal. Will you not see that I come forth from the Father, that I am sent by God, that I am not doing this work of myself? Why do you not understand my words? Is it because you have chosen to become the children of evil? If you are the children of darkness, you will hardly walk in the light of the truth which I reveal. The children of evil follow only in the ways of their father, who was a deceiver and stood not for the truth because there came to be no truth in him. But now comes the Son of Man speaking and living the truth, and many of you refuse to believe.

"Which of you convicts me of sin? If I, then, proclaim and live the truth shown me by the Father, why do you not believe? He who is of God hears gladly the words of God; for this cause many of you hear not my words, because you are not of God. Your teachers have even presumed to say that I do my works by the power of the prince of devils. One near by has just said that I have a devil, that I am a child of the devil. But all of you who deal honestly with your own souls know full well that I am not a devil. You know that I honor the Father even while you would dishonor me. I seek not my own glory, only the glory of my Paradise Father. And I do not judge you, for there is one who judges for me.

"Verily, verily, I say to you who believe the gospel that, if a man will keep this word of truth alive in his heart, he shall never taste death. And now just at my side a scribe says this statement proves that I have a devil, seeing that Abraham is dead, also the prophets. And he asks: 'Are you so much greater than Abraham and the prophets that you dare to stand here and say that whoso keeps your word shall not taste death? Who do you claim to be that you dare to utter such blasphemies?' And I say to all such that, if I glorify myself, my glory is as nothing. But it is the Father who shall glorify me, even the same Father whom you call God. But you have failed to know this your God and my Father, and I have come to bring you together; to show you how to become truly the sons of God. Though you know not the Father, I truly know him. Even Abraham rejoiced to see my day, and by faith he saw it and was glad."

When the unbelieving Jews and the agents of the Sanhedrin who had gathered about by this time heard these words, they raised a tumult, shouting: "You are not fifty years of age, and yet you talk about seeing Abraham; you are a child of the devil!" Jesus was unable to continue the discourse. He only said as he departed, "Verily, verily, I say to you, before Abraham was, I am." Many of the unbelievers rushed forth for stones to cast at him, and the agents of the Sanhedrin sought to place him under arrest, but the Master quickly made his way through the temple corridors and escaped to a secret meeting place near Bethany where Martha, Mary, and Lazarus awaited him. ∎

THE SEVENTY EVANGELISTS

A few days after the return of Jesus and the twelve to Magadan from Jerusalem, Abner and a group of some fifty disciples arrived from Bethlehem. At this time there were also assembled at Magadan Camp the evangelistic corps, the women's corps, and about one hundred and fifty other true and tried disciples from all parts of Palestine. After devoting a few days to visiting and the reorganization of the camp, Jesus and the twelve began a course of intensive training for this special group of believers, and from this well-trained and experienced aggregation of disciples the Master subsequently chose the seventy teachers and sent them forth to proclaim the gospel of the kingdom.

The seventy were ordained by Jesus on Sabbath afternoon, November 19, at the Magadan Camp, and Abner was placed at the head of these gospel preachers and teachers. This corps of seventy consisted of Abner and ten of the former apostles of John, fifty-one of the earlier evangelists, and eight other disciples who had distinguished themselves in the service of the kingdom.

About two o'clock on this Sabbath afternoon, between showers of rain, a company of believers, augmented by the arrival of David and the majority of his messenger corps and numbering over four hundred, assembled on the shore of the lake of Galilee to witness the ordination of the seventy.

Before Jesus laid his hands upon the heads of the seventy to set them apart as gospel messengers, addressing them, he said: "The harvest is indeed plenteous, but the laborers are few; therefore I exhort all of you to pray that the Lord of the harvest will send still other laborers into his harvest. I am about to set you apart as messengers of the kingdom; I am about to send you to Jew and gentile as lambs among wolves. As you go your ways, two and two, I instruct you to carry neither purse nor extra clothing, for you go forth on this first mission for only a short season. Salute no man by the way, attend only to your work. Whenever you go to stay at a home, first say: Peace be to this household. If those who love peace live therein, you shall abide there; if not, then shall you depart. And having selected this home, remain there for your stay in that city, eating and drinking whatever is set before you. And you do this because the laborer is worthy of his sustenance. Move not from house to house because a better lodging may be offered. Remember, as you go forth proclaiming peace on earth and good will among men, you

must contend with bitter and self-deceived enemies; therefore be as wise as serpents while you are also as harmless as doves.

"And everywhere you go, preach, saying, 'The kingdom of heaven is at hand,' and minister to all who may be sick in either mind or body. Freely you have received of the good things of the kingdom; freely give. If the people of any city receive you, they shall find an abundant entrance into the Father's kingdom; but if the people of any city refuse to receive this gospel, still shall you proclaim your message as you depart from that unbelieving community, saying, even as you leave, to those who reject your teaching: 'Notwithstanding you reject the truth, it remains that the kingdom of God has come near you.' He who hears you hears me. And he who hears me hears Him who sent me. He who rejects your gospel message rejects me. And he who rejects me rejects Him who sent me."

When Jesus had thus spoken, he began with Abner and, as they knelt in a circle about him, laid his hands upon the head of every man.

Early the next morning Abner sent the seventy messengers into all the cities of Galilee, Samaria, and Judea. And these thirty-five couples went forth preaching and teaching for about six weeks, all of them returning to the new camp near Pella, in Perea, on Friday, December 30. ∎

NOVEMBER, A.D. 29

THE RICH YOUNG MAN

Over fifty disciples who sought ordination and appointment to membership in the seventy were rejected by the committee appointed by Jesus to select these candidates. This committee consisted of Andrew, Abner, and the acting head of the evangelistic corps. In all cases where this committee of three were not unanimous in agreement, they brought the candidate

[HEINRICH HOFMANN — *Christ and the Rich Young Ruler*]

to Jesus, and while the Master never rejected a single person who craved ordination as a gospel messenger, there were more than a dozen who, when they had talked with Jesus, no more desired to become gospel messengers.

Andrew brought to Jesus a certain rich young man who was a devout believer, and who desired to receive ordination. This young man, Matadormus, was a member of the Jerusalem Sanhedrin; he had heard Jesus teach and had been subsequently instructed in the gospel of the kingdom by Peter and the other apostles. Jesus talked with Matadormus concerning the requirements of ordination and requested that he defer decision until after he had thought more fully about the matter. Early the next morning, as Jesus was going for a walk, this young man accosted him and said: "Master, I would know from you the assurances of eternal life. Seeing that I have observed all the commandments from my youth, I would like to know what more I must do to gain eternal life?" In answer to this question Jesus said: "If you keep all the commandments—do not commit adultery, do not kill, do not steal, do not bear false witness, do not defraud, honor your parents—you do well, but salvation is the reward of faith, not merely of works. Do you believe this gospel of the kingdom?" And Matadormus answered: "Yes, Master, I do believe everything you and your apostles have taught me." And Jesus said, "Then are you indeed my disciple and a child of the kingdom."

Then said the young man: "But, Master, I am not content to be your disciple; I would be one of your new messengers." When Jesus heard this, he looked down upon him with a great love and said: "I will have you to be one of my messengers if you are willing to pay the price, if you will supply the one thing which you lack." Matadormus replied: "Master, I will do anything if I may be allowed to follow you." Jesus, kissing the kneeling young man on the forehead, said: "If you would be my messenger, go and sell all that you have and, when you have bestowed the proceeds upon the poor or upon your brethren, come and follow me, and you shall have treasure in the kingdom of heaven."

When Matadormus heard this, his countenance fell. He arose and went away sorrowful, for he had great possessions. This wealthy young Pharisee had been raised to believe that wealth was the token of God's favor. Jesus knew that he was not free from the love of himself and his riches. The Master wanted to deliver him from the *love* of wealth, not necessarily from the wealth. While the disciples of Jesus did not part with all their worldly goods, the apostles and the seventy did. Matadormus desired to be one of the seventy new messengers, and that was the reason for Jesus' requiring him to part with all of his temporal possessions.

Almost every human being has some one thing which is held on to as a pet evil, and which the

---

ALMOST EVERY HUMAN BEING HAS SOME ONE THING WHICH IS HELD ON TO AS A PET EVIL, AND WHICH THE ENTRANCE INTO THE KINGDOM OF HEAVEN REQUIRES AS A PART OF THE PRICE OF ADMISSION.

---

entrance into the kingdom of heaven requires as a part of the price of admission. If Matadormus had parted with his wealth, it probably would have been put right back into his hands for administration as treasurer of the seventy. For later on, after the establishment of the church at Jerusalem, he did obey the Master's injunction, although it was then too late to enjoy membership in the seventy, and he became the treasurer of the Jerusalem church, of which James the Lord's brother in the flesh was the head.

Thus always it was and forever will be: Men must arrive at their own decisions. There is a certain range of the freedom of choice which mortals may exercise. The forces of the spiritual world will not coerce man; they allow him to go the way of his own choosing.

Jesus foresaw that Matadormus, with his riches, could not possibly become an ordained associate of men who had forsaken all for the gospel; at the same time, he saw that, without his riches, he would become the ultimate leader of all of them. But, like Jesus' own brethren, he never became great in the kingdom because he deprived himself of that intimate and personal association with the Master which might have been his experience had he been willing to do at this time the very thing which Jesus asked, and which, several years subsequently, he actually did.

Riches have nothing directly to do with entrance into the kingdom of heaven, but the *love of wealth does*. The spiritual loyalties of the kingdom are incompatible with servility to materialistic mammon. Man may not share his supreme loyalty to a spiritual ideal with a material devotion.

Jesus never taught that it was wrong to have wealth. He required only the twelve and the seventy to dedicate all of their worldly possessions to the common cause. But there was one economic abuse which he many times condemned, and that was the unfair exploitation of the weak, unlearned, and less fortunate of men by their strong, keen, and more intelligent fellows. Jesus declared that such inhuman treatment of men, women, and children was incompatible with the ideals of the brotherhood of the kingdom of heaven. ■

DECEMBER, A.D. 29

THE GOOD SAMARITAN

Jesus, taking with him Nathaniel and Thomas, secretly went up to Jerusalem to attend the feast of the dedication. Not until they passed over the Jordan at the Bethany ford, did the two apostles become aware that their Master was going on to Jerusalem. When they perceived that he really intended to be present at the feast of dedication, they remonstrated with him most earnestly, and using every sort of argument, they sought to dissuade him. But their efforts were of no avail; Jesus was determined to visit Jerusalem. To all their entreaties and to all their warnings emphasizing the folly and danger of placing himself in the hands of the Sanhedrin, he would reply only, "I would give these teachers in Israel another opportunity to see the light, before my hour comes."

On they went toward Jerusalem, the two apostles continuing to express their feelings of fear and to voice their doubts about the wisdom of such an apparently presumptuous undertaking. They reached Jericho about half past four and prepared to lodge there for the night.

That evening a considerable company gathered about Jesus and the two apostles to ask questions, many of which the apostles answered, while others the Master discussed. In the course of the evening a certain lawyer, seeking to entangle Jesus in a compromising disputation, said: "Teacher, I would like to ask you just what I should do to inherit eternal life?" Jesus answered, "What is written in the law and the prophets; how do you read the Scriptures?" The lawyer, knowing the teachings of both Jesus and the Pharisees, answered: "To love the Lord God with all your heart, soul, mind, and strength, and your neighbor as yourself." Then said Jesus: "You have answered right; this, if you really do, will lead to life everlasting."

But the lawyer was not wholly sincere in asking this question, and desiring to justify himself while also hoping to embarrass Jesus, he ventured to ask still another question. Drawing a little closer to the Master, he said, "But, Teacher, I should like you to tell me just who is my neighbor?" The lawyer asked this question hoping to entrap Jesus into making some statement that would contravene the Jewish law which defined one's neighbor as "the children of one's people." The Jews looked upon all others as "gentile dogs." This lawyer was somewhat familiar with Jesus' teachings and therefore well knew that the Master thought differently; thus he hoped to lead him into saying something which could be construed as an attack upon the sacred law.

But Jesus discerned the lawyer's motive, and instead of falling into the trap, he proceeded to tell his hearers a story, a story which would be fully appreciated by any Jericho audience. Said Jesus: "A certain man was going down from Jerusalem to Jericho, and he fell into the hands of cruel brigands, who robbed him, stripped him and beat him, and departing, left him half dead. Very soon, by chance, a certain priest was going down that way, and when he came upon the wounded man, seeing his sorry plight, he passed by on the other side of the road. And in like manner a Levite also, when he came along and saw the man, passed by on the other side. Now, about this time, a certain Samaritan, as he journeyed down to Jericho, came

[VINCENT WILLEM VAN GOGH — *The Good Samaritan* (after Delacroix)]

across this wounded man; and when he saw how he had been robbed and beaten, he was moved with compassion, and going over to him, he bound up his wounds, pouring on oil and wine, and setting the man upon his own beast, brought him here to the inn and took care of him. And on the morrow he took out some money and, giving it to the host, said: 'Take good care of my friend, and if the expense is more, when I come back again, I will repay you.' Now let me ask you: Which of these three turned out to be the neighbor of him who fell among the robbers?" And when the lawyer perceived that he had fallen into his own snare, he answered, "He who showed mercy on him." And Jesus said, "Go and do likewise."

The lawyer answered, "He who showed mercy," that he might refrain from even speaking that odious word, Samaritan. The lawyer was forced to give the very answer to the question, "Who is my neighbor?" which Jesus wished given, and which, if Jesus had so stated, would have directly involved him in the charge of heresy. Jesus not only confounded the dishonest lawyer, but he told his hearers a story which was at the same time a beautiful admonition to all his followers and a stunning rebuke to all Jews regarding their attitude toward the Samaritans. And this story has continued to promote brotherly love among all who have subsequently believed the gospel of Jesus.   ■

AN OPEN CHALLENGE TO THE SANHEDRIN

Jesus had attended the feast of tabernacles that he might proclaim the gospel to the pilgrims from all parts of the empire; he now went up to the feast of the dedication for just one purpose: to give the Sanhedrin and the Jewish leaders another chance to see the light. The principal event of these few days in Jerusalem occurred on Friday night at the home of Nicodemus. Here were gathered together some twenty-five Jewish leaders who believed Jesus' teaching. Among this group were fourteen men who were then, or had recently been, members of the Sanhedrin. This meeting was attended by Eber, Matadormus, and Joseph of Arimathea.

The next morning the three went over to Martha's home at Bethany for breakfast and then went immediately into Jerusalem. This Sabbath morning, as Jesus and his two apostles drew near the temple, they encountered a well-known beggar, a man who had been born blind, sitting at his usual place. Although these mendicants did not solicit or receive alms on the Sabbath day, they were permitted thus to sit in their usual places. Jesus paused and looked upon the beggar. As he gazed upon this man who had been born blind, the idea came into his mind as to how he would once more bring his mission on earth to the notice of the Sanhedrin and the other Jewish leaders and religious teachers.

As the Master stood there before the blind man, engrossed in deep thought, Nathaniel, pondering the possible cause of this man's blindness, asked: "Master, who did sin, this man or his parents, that he should be born blind?"

The rabbis taught that all such cases of blindness from birth were caused by sin. Not only were children conceived and born in sin, but a child could be born blind as a punishment for some specific sin committed by its father. They even taught that a child itself might sin before it was born into the world. They also taught that such defects could be caused by some sin or other indulgence of the mother while carrying the child.

There was, throughout all these regions, a lingering belief in reincarnation. The older Jewish teachers, together with Plato, Philo, and many of the Essenes, tolerated the theory that men may

[YONGSUNG KIM — *Healing the Blind Man*]

reap in one incarnation what they have sown in a previous existence. The Master found it difficult to make men believe that their souls had not had previous existences.

Jesus decided to use this beggar in his plans for that day's work, but before doing anything for the blind man, Josiah by name, he proceeded to answer Nathaniel's question. Said the Master: "Neither did this man sin nor his parents that the works of God might be manifest in him. This blindness has come upon him in the natural course of events, but we must now do the works of Him who sent me, while it is still day, for the night will

certainly come when it will be impossible to do the work we are about to perform. When I am in the world, I am the light of the world, but in only a little while I will not be with you."

When Jesus had spoken, he said to Nathaniel and Thomas: "Let us create the sight of this blind man on this Sabbath day that the scribes and Pharisees may have the full occasion which they seek for accusing the Son of Man." Then, stooping over, he spat on the ground and mixed the clay with the spittle, and speaking of all this so that the blind man could hear, he went up to Josiah and put the clay over his sightless eyes, saying: "Go, my son, wash away this clay in the pool of Siloam, and immediately you shall receive your sight." And when Josiah had so washed in the pool of Siloam, he returned to his friends and family, seeing.

Having always been a beggar, he knew nothing else; so, when the first excitement of the creation of his sight had passed, he returned to his usual place of alms-seeking. His friends, neighbors, and all who had known him aforetime, when they observed that he could see, all said, "Is this not Josiah the blind beggar?" Some said it was he, while others said, "No, it is one like him, but this man can see." But when they asked the man himself, he answered, "I am he."

When they began to inquire of him how he was able to see, he answered them: "A man called Jesus came by this way, and when talking about me with his friends, he made clay with spittle, anointed my eyes, and directed that I should go and wash in the pool of Siloam. I did what this man told me, and immediately I received my sight. And that is only a few hours ago. I do not yet know the meaning of much that I see." And when the people who began to gather about him asked where they could find the strange man who had healed him, Josiah could answer only that he did not know.

This is one of the strangest of all the Master's miracles. This man did not ask for healing. He did not know that the Jesus who had directed him to wash at Siloam, and who had promised him vision, was the prophet of Galilee who had preached in Jerusalem during the feast of tabernacles. This man had little faith that he would receive his sight, but the people of that day had great faith in the efficacy of the spittle of a great or holy man; and from Jesus' conversation with Nathaniel and Thomas, Josiah had concluded that his would-be benefactor was a great man, a learned teacher or a holy prophet; accordingly he did as Jesus directed him.

Jesus gave this man his sight by miraculous working, on this Sabbath morning and in Jerusalem near the temple, for the prime purpose of making this act an open challenge to the Sanhedrin and all the Jewish teachers and religious leaders. This was his way of proclaiming an open break with the Pharisees. He was always positive in everything he did. And it was for the purpose of bringing these matters before the Sanhedrin that Jesus brought his two apostles to this man early in the afternoon of this Sabbath day and deliberately provoked those discussions which compelled the Pharisees to take notice of the miracle.　■

JANUARY, A.D. 30

THE GOOD SHEPHERD

A company of over three hundred Jerusalemites, Pharisees and others, followed Jesus north to Pella when he hastened away from the jurisdiction of the Jewish rulers at the ending of the feast of the dedication; and it was in the presence of these Jewish teachers and leaders, as well as in the hearing of the twelve apostles, that Jesus preached the sermon on the "Good Shepherd." After half an hour of informal discussion, speaking to a group of about one hundred, Jesus said:

"On this night I have much to tell you, and since many of you are my disciples and some of you my bitter enemies, I will present my teaching in a parable, so that you may each take for yourself that which finds a reception in your heart.

"Tonight, here before me are men who would be willing to die for me and for this gospel of the kingdom, and some of them will so offer themselves in the years to come; and here also are some of you, slaves of tradition, who have followed me down from Jerusalem, and who, with your darkened and deluded leaders, seek to kill the Son of Man. The life which I now live in the flesh shall judge both of you, the true shepherds and the

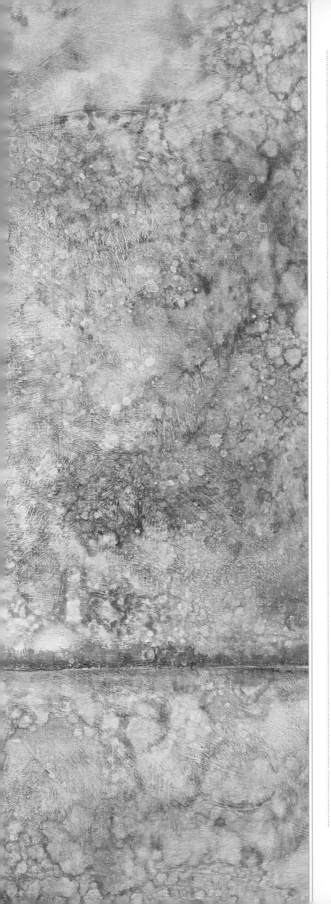

false shepherds. If the false shepherd were blind, he would have no sin, but you claim that you see; you profess to be teachers in Israel; therefore does your sin remain upon you.

"The true shepherd gathers his flock into the fold for the night in times of danger. And when the morning has come, he enters into the fold by the door, and when he calls, the sheep know his voice. Every shepherd who gains entrance to the sheepfold by any other means than by the door is a thief and a robber. The true shepherd enters the fold after the porter has opened the door for him, and his sheep, knowing his voice, come out at his word; and when they that are his are thus brought forth, the true shepherd goes before them; he leads the way and the sheep follow him. His sheep follow him because they know his voice; they will not follow a stranger. They will flee from the stranger because they know not his voice. This multitude which is gathered about us here are like sheep without a shepherd, but when we speak to them, they know the shepherd's voice, and they follow after us; at least, those who hunger for truth and thirst for righteousness do. Some of you are not of my fold; you know not my voice, and you do not follow me. And because you are false shepherds, the sheep know not your voice and will not follow you."

And when Jesus had spoken this parable, no one asked him a question. After a time he began again to speak and went on to discuss the parable:

"You who would be the undershepherds of my Father's flocks must not only be worthy leaders, but you must also *feed* the flock with good food; you are not true shepherds unless you lead your flocks into green pastures and beside still waters.

"And now, lest some of you too easily comprehend this parable, I will declare that I am both

[YONGSUNG KIM — *Beside Quiet Waters*]

the door to the Father's sheepfold and at the same time the true shepherd of my Father's flocks. Every shepherd who seeks to enter the fold without me shall fail, and the sheep will not hear his voice. I, with those who minister with me, am the door. Every soul who enters upon the eternal way by the means I have created and ordained shall be saved and will be able to go on to the attainment of the eternal pastures of Paradise.

"But I also am the true shepherd who is willing even to lay down his life for the sheep. The thief breaks into the fold only to steal, and to kill, and to destroy; but I have come that you all may have life and have it more abundantly. He who is a hireling, when danger arises, will flee and allow the sheep to be scattered and destroyed; but the true shepherd will not flee when the wolf comes; he will protect his flock and, if necessary, lay down his life for his sheep. Verily, verily, I say to you, friends and enemies, I am the true shepherd; I know my own and my own know me. I will not flee in the face of danger. I will finish this service of the completion of my Father's will, and I will not forsake the flock which the Father has intrusted to my keeping.

"But I have many other sheep not of this fold, and these words are true not only of this world. These other sheep also hear and know my voice, and I have promised the Father that they shall all be brought into one fold, one brotherhood of the sons of God. And then shall you all know the voice of one shepherd, the true shepherd, and shall all acknowledge the fatherhood of God.

"And so shall you know why the Father loves me and has put all of his flocks in this domain in my hands for keeping; it is because the Father knows that I will not falter in the safeguarding of the sheepfold, that I will not desert my sheep, and that, if it shall be required, I will not hesitate to lay down my life in the service of his manifold flocks. But, mind you, if I lay down my life, I will take it up again. No man nor any other creature can take away my life. I have the right and the power to lay down my life, and I have the same power and right to take it up again. You cannot understand this, but I received such authority from my Father even before this world was."

When they heard these words, his apostles were confused, his disciples were amazed, while the Pharisees from Jerusalem and around about went out into the night, saying, "He is either mad or has a devil." But even some of the Jerusalem teachers said: "He speaks like one having authority; besides, who ever saw one having a devil open the eyes of a man born blind and do all of the wonderful things which this man has done?"

On the morrow about half of these Jewish teachers professed belief in Jesus, and the other half in dismay returned to Jerusalem and their homes. ∎

FEBRUARY 19, A.D. 30

THE TEN LEPERS

From February 11 to 20, Jesus and the twelve made a tour of all the cities and villages of northern Perea where the associates of Abner and the members of the women's corps were working. They found these messengers of the gospel meeting with success, and Jesus repeatedly called the attention of his apostles to the fact that the gospel of the kingdom could spread without the accompaniment of miracles and wonders.

This entire mission of three months in Perea was successfully carried on with little help from the apostles, and the gospel from this time on reflected, not so much Jesus' personality, as his *teachings*.

One day Jesus went with the twelve over to Amathus, near the border of Samaria, and as they approached the city, they encountered a group of ten lepers who sojourned near this place. Nine of this group were Jews, one a Samaritan. Ordinarily these Jews would have refrained from all association or contact with this Samaritan, but their common affliction was more than enough to overcome all religious prejudice. They had heard much of Jesus and his earlier miracles of healing, and since the seventy made a practice of announcing the time of Jesus' expected arrival when the Master was out with the twelve on these tours, the ten lepers had been made aware that he was expected to appear in this vicinity at about this time; and they were, accordingly, posted here on the outskirts of the city where they hoped to attract his attention and ask for healing. When the lepers saw Jesus drawing near them, not daring to approach him, they stood afar off and cried to him: "Master, have mercy on us; cleanse us from our affliction. Heal us as you have healed others."

Accordingly, when Simon Zelotes observed the Samaritan among the lepers, he sought to induce the Master to pass on into the city without even hesitating to exchange greetings with them. Said Jesus to Simon: "But what if the Samaritan loves God as well as the Jews? Should we sit in judgment on our fellow men? Who can tell? if we make these ten men whole, perhaps the Samaritan will prove more grateful even than the Jews. Do you feel certain about your opinions, Simon?" And Simon quickly replied, "If you cleanse them, you will soon find out." And Jesus replied: "So shall it be, Simon, and you will soon know the truth regarding the gratitude of men and the loving mercy of God."

Jesus, going near the lepers, said: "If you would be made whole, go forthwith and show yourselves to the priests as required by the law of Moses." And as they went, they were made whole. But when the Samaritan saw that he was being healed, he turned back and, going in quest of Jesus, began to glorify God with a loud voice. And when he had found the Master, he fell on his knees at his feet and gave thanks for his cleansing. The nine others, the Jews, had also discovered their healing, and while they also were grateful for their cleansing, they continued on their way to show themselves to the priests.

As the Samaritan remained kneeling at Jesus'

feet, the Master, looking about at the twelve, especially at Simon Zelotes, said: "Were not ten cleansed? Where, then, are the other nine, the Jews? Only one, this alien, has returned to give glory to God." And then he said to the Samaritan, "Arise and go your way; your faith has made you whole."

Jesus looked again at his apostles as the stranger departed. And the apostles all looked at Jesus, save Simon Zelotes, whose eyes were downcast. The twelve said not a word. Neither did Jesus speak; it was not necessary that he should.

Though all ten of these men really believed they had leprosy, only four were thus afflicted. The other six were cured of a skin disease which had been mistaken for leprosy. But the Samaritan really had leprosy.

Jesus enjoined the twelve to say nothing about the cleansing of the lepers, and as they went on into Amathus, he remarked: "You see how it is that the children of the house, even when they are insubordinate to their Father's will, take their blessings for granted. They think it a small matter if they neglect to give thanks when the Father bestows healing upon them, but the strangers, when they receive gifts from the head of the house, are filled with wonder and are constrained to give thanks in recognition of the good things bestowed upon them." And still the apostles said nothing in reply to the Master's words. ∎

FEBRUARY, A.D. 30

THE SERMON AT GERASA

As Jesus and the twelve visited with the messengers of the kingdom at Gerasa, one of the Pharisees who believed in him asked this question: "Lord, will there be few or many really saved?" And Jesus, answering, said:

"Even if the door to the way of life is narrow, it is wide enough to admit all who sincerely seek to enter, for I am that door."

"You have been taught that only the children of Abraham will be saved; that only the gentiles of adoption can hope for salvation. Some of you have reasoned that, since the Scriptures record that only Caleb and Joshua from among all the hosts that went out of Egypt lived to enter the promised land, only a comparatively few of those who seek the kingdom of heaven shall find entrance thereto.

"You also have another saying among you, and one that contains much truth: That the way which leads to eternal life is straight and narrow, that the door which leads thereto is likewise narrow so that, of those who seek salvation, few can find entrance through this door. You also have a teaching that the way which leads to destruction is broad, that the entrance thereto is wide, and that there are many who choose to go this way. And this proverb is not without its meaning. But I declare that salvation is first a matter of your personal choosing. Even if the door to the way of life is narrow, it is wide enough to admit all who sincerely seek to enter, for I am that door. And the Son will never refuse entrance to any child of the universe who, by faith, seeks to find the Father through the Son.

"But herein is the danger to all who would postpone their entrance into the kingdom while they continue to pursue the pleasures of immaturity and indulge the satisfactions of selfishness: Having refused to enter the kingdom as a spiritual experience, they may subsequently seek entrance thereto when the glory of the better way becomes revealed in the age to come. And when, therefore, those who spurned the kingdom when I came in the likeness of humanity seek to find an entrance when it is revealed in the likeness of divinity, then will I say to all such selfish ones: I know not whence you are. You had your chance to prepare for this heavenly citizenship, but you refused all such proffers of mercy; you rejected all invitations to come while the door was open. Now, to you who have refused salvation, the door is shut. This door is not open to those who would enter the kingdom for selfish glory. Salvation is not for those who are unwilling to pay the price of wholehearted dedication to doing my Father's will. When in spirit and soul you have turned your backs upon the Father's kingdom, it is useless in mind and body to stand before this door and knock, saying, 'Lord, open to us; we would also be great in the kingdom.' Then will I declare that you are not of my fold. I will not receive you to be among those who have fought the good fight of faith and won the reward of unselfish service in the kingdom on earth. And when you say, 'Did we not eat and drink with you, and did you not teach in our streets?' then shall I again declare that you are spiritual strangers; that we were not fellow servants in the Father's ministry of mercy on earth; that I do not know you; and then shall the Judge of all the earth say to you: 'Depart from us, all you who have taken delight in the works of iniquity.'

"But fear not; every one who sincerely desires to find eternal life by entrance into the kingdom of God shall certainly find such everlasting salvation. But you who refuse this salvation will some day see the prophets of the seed of Abraham sit down with the believers of the gentile nations in this glorified kingdom to partake of the bread of life and to refresh themselves with the water thereof. And they who shall thus take the kingdom in spiritual power and by the persistent assaults of living faith will come from the north and the south and from the east and the west. And, behold, many who are first will be last, and those who are last will many times be first."

This was indeed a new and strange version of the old and familiar proverb of the straight and narrow way.

Slowly the apostles and many of the disciples were learning the meaning of Jesus' early declaration: "Unless you are born again, born of the spirit, you cannot enter the kingdom of God." Nevertheless, to all who are honest of heart and sincere in faith, it remains eternally true: "Behold, I stand at the doors of men's hearts and knock, and if any man will open to me, I will come in and sup with him and will feed him with the bread of life; we shall be one in spirit and purpose, and so shall we ever be brethren in the long and fruitful service of the search for the Paradise Father." And so, whether few or many are to be saved altogether depends on whether few or many will heed the invitation: "I am the door, I am the new and living way, and whosoever wills may enter to embark upon the endless truth-search for eternal life." ■

The Message from Bethany

Very late on Sunday night, February 26, a runner from Bethany arrived at Philadelphia, bringing a message from Martha and Mary which said, "Lord, he whom you love is very sick." This message reached Jesus at the close of the evening conference and just as he was taking leave of the apostles for the night. At first Jesus made no reply. There occurred one of those strange interludes, a time when he appeared to be in communication with something outside of, and beyond, himself. And then, looking up, he addressed the messenger in the hearing of the apostles, saying: "This sickness is really not to the death. Doubt not that it may be used to glorify God and exalt the Son."

Jesus was very fond of Martha, Mary, and their brother, Lazarus; he loved them with a fervent affection. His first and human thought was to go to their assistance at once, but another idea came into his combined mind. He had almost given up hope that the Jewish leaders at Jerusalem would ever accept the kingdom, but he still loved his people, and there now occurred to him a plan whereby the scribes and Pharisees of Jerusalem might have one more chance to accept his teachings; and he decided, his Father willing, to make this last appeal to Jerusalem the most profound and stupendous outward working of his entire earth career. The Jews clung to the idea of a wonder-working deliverer. And though he refused to stoop to the performance of material wonders or to the enactment of temporal exhibitions of political power, he did now ask the Father's consent for the manifestation of his hitherto unexhibited power over life and death.

The Jews were in the habit of burying their dead on the day of their demise; this was a necessary practice in such a warm climate. It often happened that they put in the tomb one who was merely comatose, so that on the second or even the third day, such a one would come forth from the tomb. But it was the belief of the Jews that, while the spirit or soul might linger near the body for two or three days, it never tarried after the third day; that decay was well advanced by the fourth day, and that no one ever returned from the tomb after the lapse of such a period. And it was for these reasons that Jesus tarried yet two full days in Philadelphia before he made ready to start for Bethany.

Accordingly, early on Wednesday morning he said to his apostles: "Let us prepare at once to go into Judea again." And when the apostles heard their Master say this, they drew off by themselves for a time to take counsel of one another. James assumed the direction of the conference, and they all agreed that it was only folly to allow Jesus to go again into Judea, and they came back as one man and so informed him. Said James: "Master, you were in Jerusalem a few weeks back, and the leaders sought your death, while the people were minded to stone you. At that time you gave these men their chance to receive the truth, and we will not permit you to go again into Judea."

Then said Jesus: "But do you not understand that there are twelve hours of the day in which work may safely be done? If a man walks in the day, he does not stumble inasmuch as he has light. If a man walks in the night, he is liable to stumble since he is without light. As long as my day lasts, I fear not to enter Judea. I would do one more mighty work for these Jews; I would give them one more chance to believe, even on their own terms—conditions of outward glory and the visible manifestation of the power of the Father and the love of the Son. Besides, do you not realize that our friend Lazarus has fallen asleep, and I would go to awake him out of this sleep!"

Then said one of the apostles: "Master, if Lazarus has fallen asleep, then will he the more surely recover." It was the custom of the Jews at that time to speak of death as a form of sleep, but as the apostles did not understand that Jesus meant that Lazarus had departed from this world, he now said plainly: "Lazarus is dead. And I am glad for your sakes, even if the others are not thereby saved, that I was not there, to the end that you shall now have new cause to believe in me; and by that which you will witness, you should all

be strengthened in preparation for that day when I shall take leave of you and go to the Father."

When they could not persuade him to refrain from going into Judea, and when some of the apostles were loath even to accompany him, Thomas addressed his fellows, saying: "We have told the Master our fears, but he is determined to go to Bethany. I am satisfied it means the end; they will surely kill him, but if that is the Master's choice, then let us acquit ourselves like men of courage; let us go also that we may die with him." And it was ever so; in matters requiring deliberate and sustained courage, Thomas was always the mainstay of the twelve apostles.

Blessing the Little Children

That evening Jesus' message regarding marriage and the blessedness of children spread all over Jericho, so that the next morning, long before Jesus and the apostles prepared to leave, even before breakfast time, scores of mothers came to where Jesus lodged, bringing their children in their arms and leading them by their hands, and desired that he bless the little ones. When the apostles went out to view this assemblage of mothers with their children, they endeavored to send them away, but these women refused to depart until the Master laid his hands on their children and blessed them. And when the apostles loudly rebuked these mothers, Jesus, hearing the tumult, came out and indignantly reproved them, saying: "Suffer little children to come to me; forbid them not, for of such is the kingdom of heaven. Verily, verily, I say to you, whosoever receives not the kingdom of God as a little child shall hardly enter therein to grow up to the full stature of spiritual manhood."

And when the Master had spoken to his apostles, he received all of the children, laying his hands on them, while he spoke words of courage and

[HARRY ANDERSON — *Suffer Little Children to Come to Me*]

The Talk About Angels

As they journeyed up the hills from Jericho to Bethany, Nathaniel walked most of the way by the side of Jesus, and their discussion of children in relation to the kingdom of heaven led indirectly to the consideration of the ministry of angels. Nathaniel finally asked the Master this question: "Seeing that the high priest is a Sadducee, and since the Sadducees do not believe in angels, what shall we teach the people regarding the heavenly ministers?" Then, among other things, Jesus said:

"The angelic hosts are a separate order of created beings; they are entirely different from the material order of mortal creatures, and they function as a distinct group of universe intelligences. Angels are not of that group of creatures called 'the Sons of God' in the Scriptures; neither are they the glorified spirits of mortal men who have gone on to progress through the mansions on high. Angels are a direct creation, and they do not reproduce themselves. The angelic hosts have only a spiritual kinship with the human race. As man progresses in the journey to the Father in Paradise, he does traverse a state of being at one time analogous to the state of the angels, but mortal man never becomes an angel.

"The angels never die, as man does. The angels are immortal unless, perchance, they become involved in sin as did some of them with the deceptions of Lucifer. The angels are the spirit servants in heaven, and they are neither all-wise nor all-powerful. But all of the loyal angels are truly pure and holy.

"And do you not remember that I said to you once before that, if you had your spiritual eyes anointed, you would then see the heavens opened and behold the angels of God ascending and descending? It is by the ministry of the angels that one world may be kept in touch with other worlds, for have I not repeatedly told you that I have other sheep not of this fold? And these angels are not the spies of the spirit world who watch upon you and then go forth to tell the Father the thoughts of your heart and to report on the deeds of the flesh. The Father has no need of such service inasmuch as his own spirit lives within you. But these angelic spirits do function to keep one part of the heavenly creation informed concerning the doings of other and remote parts of the universe. And many of the angels, while functioning in the government of the Father and the universes of the Sons, are assigned to the service of the human races. When I taught you that many of these seraphim are ministering spirits, I spoke not in figurative language nor in poetic strains. And all this is true, regardless of your difficulty in comprehending such matters.

"Many of these angels are engaged in the work of saving men, for have I not told you of the seraphic joy when one soul elects to forsake sin and begin the search for God? I did even tell you of the joy in the *presence of the angels* of heaven over one sinner who repents, thereby indicating the existence of other and higher orders of celestial beings who are likewise concerned in the spiritual welfare and with the divine progress of mortal man.

"Also are these angels very much concerned with the means whereby man's spirit is released from the tabernacles of the flesh and his soul escorted to the mansions in heaven. Angels are the sure and heavenly guides of the soul of man during that uncharted and indefinite period of time which intervenes between the death of the flesh and the new life in the spirit abodes."

And he would have spoken further with Nathaniel regarding the ministry of angels, but he was interrupted by the approach of Martha, who had been informed that the Master was drawing near to Bethany by friends who had observed him ascending the hills to the east. And she now hastened to greet him.

[J. Kirk Richards — *Small Angel in White*]

hope to their mothers.

Jesus often talked to his apostles about the celestial mansions saying, "In my Father's house are many mansions." He taught that the advancing children of God must there grow up spiritually as children grow up physically on this world. And so does the sacred oftentimes appear to be the common, as on this day these children and their mothers little realized that the onlooking celestial intelligences beheld the children of Jericho playing with the Creator of a universe.

Woman's status in Palestine was much improved by Jesus' teaching; and so it would have been throughout the world if his followers had not departed so far from that which he painstakingly taught them.

It was also at Jericho, in connection with the discussion of the early religious training of children in habits of divine worship, that Jesus impressed upon his apostles the great value of beauty as an influence leading to the urge to worship, especially with children. The Master by precept and example taught the value of worshiping the Creator in the midst of the natural surroundings of creation. He preferred to commune with the heavenly Father amidst the trees and among the lowly creatures of the natural world. ∎

THE RESURRECTION OF LAZARUS

It was shortly after noon when Martha started out to meet Jesus as he came over the brow of the hill near Bethany. Her brother, Lazarus, had been dead four days and had been laid away in their private tomb at the far end of the garden late on Sunday afternoon. The stone at the entrance of the tomb had been rolled in place on the morning of this day, Thursday.

When Martha and Mary sent word to Jesus concerning Lazarus's illness, they were confident the Master would do something about it. They knew that their brother was desperately sick, and though they hardly dared hope that Jesus would leave his work of teaching and preaching to come to their assistance, they had such confidence in his power to heal disease that they thought he would just speak the curative words, and Lazarus would immediately be made whole. And when Lazarus died a few hours after the messenger left Bethany for Philadelphia, they reasoned that it was because the Master did not learn of their brother's illness until it was too late, until he had already been dead for several hours.

But they, with all of their believing friends, were greatly puzzled by the message which the runner brought back Tuesday forenoon when he reached

Bethany. The messenger insisted that he heard Jesus say, "…this sickness is really not to the death." Neither could they understand why he sent no word to them nor otherwise proffered assistance.

Mary had given up the thought of Jesus' coming and was abandoned to her grief, but Martha clung to the hope that Jesus would come, even up to the time on that very morning when they rolled the stone in front of the tomb and sealed the entrance. Even then she instructed a neighbor lad to keep watch down the Jericho road from the brow of the hill to the east of Bethany; and it was this lad who brought tidings to Martha that Jesus and his friends were approaching.

When Martha met Jesus, she fell at his feet, exclaiming, "Master, if you had been here, my brother would not have died!" Many fears were passing through Martha's mind, but she gave expression to no doubt, nor did she venture to criticize or question the Master's conduct as related to Lazarus's death. When she had spoken, Jesus reached down and, lifting her upon her feet, said, "Only have faith, Martha, and your brother shall rise again." Then answered Martha: "I know that he will rise again in the resurrection of the last day; and even now I believe that whatever you shall ask of God, our Father will give you."

Then said Jesus, looking straight into the eyes of Martha: "I am the resurrection and the life; he who believes in me, though he dies, yet shall he live. In truth, whosoever lives and believes in me shall never really die. Martha, do you believe this?" And Martha answered the Master: "Yes, I have long believed that you are the Deliverer, the Son of the living God, even he who should come to this world."

Martha led Mary to Jesus, and when she saw him, she fell at his feet, exclaiming, "If you had only been here, my brother would not have died!"

[WALTER RANE — *Lazarus, Come Forth!*]

And when Jesus saw how they all grieved over Lazarus, his soul was moved with compassion.

At the Tomb of Lazarus

After Jesus had spent a few moments in comforting Martha and Mary, apart from the mourners, he asked them, "Where have you laid him?" Then Martha said, "Come and see." And as the Master followed on in silence with the two sorrowing sisters, he wept. When the friendly Jews who followed after them saw his tears, one of them said: "Behold how he loved him. Could not he who opened the eyes of the blind have kept this man from dying?" By this time they were standing before the family tomb, a small natural cave, or declivity, in the ledge of rock which rose up some thirty feet at the far end of the garden plot.

Many of Jesus' enemies were inclined to sneer at his manifestations of affection, and they said among themselves: "If he thought so much of this man, why did he tarry so long before coming to Bethany? If he is what they claim, why did he not save his dear friend? What is the good of healing strangers in Galilee if he cannot save those whom he loves?"

And so, on this Thursday afternoon at about half past two o'clock, was the stage all set in this little hamlet of Bethany for the enactment of the greatest of all works connected with the ministry of Jesus, the greatest manifestation of divine power during his incarnation in the flesh, since his own resurrection occurred after he had been liberated from the bonds of mortal habitation.

The small group assembled before Lazarus's tomb little realized the presence near at hand of a vast concourse of celestial beings assembled under the leadership of Gabriel and now in waiting, vibrating with expectancy and ready to execute the bidding of their beloved Sovereign.

When Jesus spoke those words of command, "Take away the stone," the assembled celestial hosts made ready to enact the drama of the resurrection of Lazarus in the likeness of his mortal flesh.

When Martha and Mary heard this command of Jesus directing that the stone in front of the tomb be rolled away, they were filled with conflicting emotions. Mary hoped that Lazarus was to be raised from the dead, but Martha, while to some extent sharing her sister's faith, was more exercised by the fear that Lazarus would not be presentable, in his appearance, to Jesus, the apostles, and their friends. Said Martha: "Must we roll away the stone? My brother has now been dead four days, so that by this time decay of the body has begun." Martha also said this because she was not certain as to why the Master had requested that the stone be removed; she thought maybe Jesus wanted only to take one last look at Lazarus. She was not settled and constant in her attitude. As they hesitated to roll away the stone, Jesus said: "Did I not tell you at the first that this sickness was not to the death? Have I not come to fulfill my promise? And after I came to you, did I not say that, if you would only believe, you should see the glory of God? Wherefore do you doubt? How long before you will believe and obey?"

When Jesus had finished speaking, his apostles, with the assistance of willing neighbors, laid hold upon the stone and rolled it away from the entrance to the tomb.

As this company of some forty-five mortals stood before the tomb, they could dimly see the form of Lazarus, wrapped in linen bandages, resting on the right lower niche of the burial cave. While these earth creatures stood there in almost breathless silence, a vast host of celestial beings had swung into their places preparatory to answering the signal for action when it should be given by Gabriel, their commander.

Jesus lifted up his eyes and said: "Father, I am thankful that you heard and granted my request. I know that you always hear me, but because of those who stand here with me, I thus speak with you, that they may believe that you have sent me into the world, and that they may know that you are working with me in that which we are about to do." And when he had prayed, he cried with a loud voice, "Lazarus, come forth!"

Though these human observers remained motionless, the vast celestial host was all astir in unified action in obedience to the Creator's word. In just twelve seconds of earth time the hitherto lifeless form of Lazarus began to move and presently sat up on the edge of the stone shelf whereon it had rested. His body was bound about with grave cloths, and his face was covered with a napkin. And as he stood up before them—alive—Jesus said, "Loose him and let him go."

All, save the apostles, with Martha and Mary, fled to the house. They were pale with fright and overcome with astonishment. While some tarried, many hastened to their homes.

Lazarus greeted Jesus and the apostles and asked the meaning of the grave cloths and why he had awakened in the garden. Jesus and the apostles drew to one side while Martha told Lazarus of his death, burial, and resurrection. She had to explain to him that he had died on Sunday and was now brought back to life on Thursday, inasmuch as he had had no consciousness of time since falling asleep in death.

Then went Lazarus over to Jesus and, with his sisters, knelt at the Master's feet to give thanks and offer praise to God. Jesus, taking Lazarus by the hand, lifted him up, saying: "My son, what has happened to you will also be experienced by all who believe this gospel except that they shall be resurrected in a more glorious form. You shall be a living witness of the truth which I spoke—I am the resurrection and the life. But let us all now go into the house and partake of nourishment for these physical bodies."

As they walked toward the house, Gabriel dismissed the extra groups of the assembled heavenly host while he made record of the first instance on Urantia, and the last, where a mortal creature had been resurrected in the likeness of the physical body of death.

Lazarus could hardly comprehend what had occurred. He knew he had been very sick, but he could recall only that he had fallen asleep and been awakened. He was never able to tell anything about these four days in the tomb because he was wholly unconscious. Time is nonexistent to those who sleep the sleep of death. ∎

WHAT BECAME OF LAZARUS

Lazarus remained at the Bethany home, being the center of great interest to many sincere believers and to numerous curious individuals, until the days of the crucifixion of Jesus, when he received warning that the Sanhedrin had decreed his death. The rulers of the Jews were determined to put a stop to the further spread of the teachings of Jesus, and they well judged that it would be useless to put Jesus to death if they permitted Lazarus, who represented the very peak of his wonder-working, to live and bear testimony to the fact that Jesus had raised him from the dead. Already had Lazarus suffered bitter persecution from them.

And so Lazarus took hasty leave of his sisters at Bethany, fleeing down through Jericho and across the Jordan, never permitting himself to rest long until he had reached Philadelphia. Lazarus knew Abner well, and here he felt safe from the murderous intrigues of the wicked Sanhedrin.

Soon after this Martha and Mary disposed of their lands at Bethany and joined their brother in Perea. Meantime, Lazarus had become the treasurer of the church at Philadelphia. He became a strong supporter of Abner in his controversy with Paul and the Jerusalem church and ultimately died, when 67 years old, of the same sickness that carried him off when he was a younger man in his thirties at Bethany.

MEETING OF THE SANHEDRIN

Though many believed in Jesus as a result of this mighty work, others only hardened their hearts the more to reject him. By noon the next day this story had spread over all Jerusalem. Scores of inquiring men and women went to Bethany to look upon Lazarus and talk with him, and the alarmed and disconcerted Pharisees hastily called a meeting of the Sanhedrin that they might determine what should be done about these new developments.

Even though the testimony of this man raised from the dead did much to consolidate the faith of the mass of believers in the gospel of the kingdom, it had little or no influence on the attitude of the religious leaders and rulers at Jerusalem except to hasten their decision to destroy Jesus and stop his work.

At one o'clock the next day, Friday, the Sanhedrin met to deliberate further on the question, "What shall we do with Jesus of Nazareth?" After more than two hours of discussion and acrimonious debate, a certain Pharisee presented a resolution calling for Jesus' immediate death, proclaiming that he was a menace to all Israel and formally committing the Sanhedrin to the decision of death, without trial and in defiance of all precedent.

Time and again had this august body of Jewish leaders decreed that Jesus be apprehended and brought to trial on charges of blasphemy and numerous other accusations of flouting the Jewish sacred law. They had once before even gone so far as to declare he should die, but this was the first time the Sanhedrin had gone on record as desiring to decree his death in advance of a trial. But this

[JAMES TISSOT — *The Chief Priests Take Counsel Together*]

resolution did not come to a vote since fourteen members of the Sanhedrin resigned in a body when such an unheard-of action was proposed. While these resignations were not formally acted upon for almost two weeks, this group of fourteen withdrew from the Sanhedrin on that day, never again to sit in the council. When these resignations were subsequently acted upon, five other members were thrown out because their associates believed they entertained friendly feelings toward Jesus. With the ejection of these nineteen men the Sanhedrin was in a position to try and to condemn Jesus with a solidarity bordering on unanimity.

The following week Lazarus and his sisters were summoned to appear before the Sanhedrin. When their testimony had been heard, no doubt could be entertained that Lazarus had been raised from the dead. Though the transactions of the Sanhedrin virtually admitted the resurrection of Lazarus, the record carried a resolution attributing this and all other wonders worked by Jesus to the power of the prince of devils, with whom Jesus was declared to be in league.

No matter what the source of his wonder-working power, these Jewish leaders were persuaded that, if he were not immediately stopped, very soon all the common people would believe in him; and further, that serious complications with the Roman authorities would arise since so many of his believers regarded him as the Messiah, Israel's deliverer.

It was at this same meeting of the Sanhedrin that Caiaphas the high priest first gave expression to that old Jewish adage, which he so many times repeated: "It is better that one man die, than that the community perish."

Although Jesus had received warning of the doings of the Sanhedrin on this dark Friday afternoon, he was not in the least perturbed and continued resting over the Sabbath with friends in Bethpage, a hamlet near Bethany. Early Sunday morning Jesus and the apostles assembled, by prearrangement, at the home of Lazarus, and taking leave of the Bethany family, they started on their journey back to the Pella encampment.

THE ANSWER TO PRAYER

The apostles were much stirred up in their minds and spent considerable time discussing their recent experiences as they were related to prayer and its answering. They all recalled Jesus' statement to the Bethany messenger at Philadelphia, when he said plainly, "This sickness is not really to the death." And yet, in spite of this promise, Lazarus actually died. All that day, again and again, they reverted to the discussion of this question of the answer to prayer.

Jesus' answers to their many questions may be summarized as follows:

• When a prayer is apparently unanswered, the delay often betokens a better answer, although one which is for some good reason greatly delayed.

• The answers to the prayer of the mortal mind are often of such a nature that they can be received and recognized only after that same praying mind has attained the immortal state. The prayer of the material being can many times be answered only when such an individual has progressed to the spirit level.

• All true prayers are addressed to spiritual beings, and all such petitions must be answered in spiritual terms, and all such answers must consist in spiritual realities. Spirit beings cannot bestow material answers to the spirit petitions of even material beings. Material beings can pray effectively only when they "pray in the spirit."

• No prayer can hope for an answer unless it is born of the spirit and nurtured by faith. Your sincere faith implies that you have in advance virtually granted your prayer hearers the full right to answer your petitions in accordance with that supreme wisdom and that divine love which your faith depicts as always actuating those beings to whom you pray.

- Do not hesitate to pray the prayers of spirit longing; doubt not that you shall receive the answer to your petitions. These answers will be on deposit, awaiting your achievement of those future spiritual levels of actual cosmic attainment, on this world or on others, whereon it will become possible for you to recognize and appropriate the long-waiting answers to your earlier petitions.

- All genuine spirit-born petitions are certain of an answer. Ask and you shall receive. ■

MARCH, A.D. 30

THE PRODIGAL SON

On Thursday afternoon Jesus talked to the multitude about the "Grace of Salvation." In the course of this sermon he retold the story of the lost sheep and the lost coin and then added his favorite parable of the prodigal son. Said Jesus:

"You have been admonished by the prophets from Samuel to John that you should seek for God—search for truth. Always have they said, 'Seek the Lord while he may be found.' And all such teaching should be taken to heart. But I have come to show you that, while you are seeking to find God, God is likewise seeking to find you. Many times have I told you the story of the good shepherd who left the ninety and nine sheep in the fold while he went forth searching for the one that was lost, and how, when he had found the straying sheep, he laid it over his shoulder and tenderly carried it back to the fold. And when the lost sheep had been restored to the fold, you remember that the good shepherd called in his friends and bade them rejoice with him over the finding of the sheep that had been lost. Again I say there is more joy in heaven over one sinner who repents than over the ninety and nine just persons who need no repentance. The fact that souls are *lost*

only increases the interest of the heavenly Father. I have come to this world to do my Father's bidding, and it has truly been said of the Son of Man that he is a friend of publicans and sinners.

"You have been taught that divine acceptance comes after your repentance and as a result of all your works of sacrifice and penitence, but I assure you that the Father accepts you even before you have repented and sends the Son and his associates to find you and bring you, with rejoicing, back to the fold, the kingdom of sonship and spiritual progress. You are all like sheep which have gone astray, and I have come to seek and to save those who are lost.

"And you should also remember the story of the woman who, having had ten pieces of silver made into a necklace of adornment, lost one piece, and how she lit the lamp and diligently swept the house and kept up the search until she found the lost piece of silver. And as soon as she found the coin that was lost, she called together her friends and neighbors, saying, 'Rejoice with me, for I have found the piece that was lost.' So again I say, there is always joy in the presence of the angels of heaven over one sinner who repents and returns to the Father's fold. And I tell you this story to impress upon you that the Father and his Son go forth to *search* for those who are lost, and in this search we employ all influences capable of rendering assistance in our diligent efforts to find those who are lost, those who stand in need of salvation. And so, while the Son of Man goes out in the wilderness to seek for the sheep gone astray, he also searches for the coin which is lost in the house. The sheep wanders away, unintentionally; the coin is covered by the dust of time and obscured by the accumulation of the things of men.

"And now I would like to tell you the story of a thoughtless son of a well-to-do farmer who *deliberately* left his father's house and went off into a foreign land, where he fell into much tribulation. You recall that the sheep strayed away without intention, but this youth left his home with premeditation. It was like this:

"A certain man had two sons; one, the younger, was lighthearted and carefree, always seeking for a good time and shirking responsibility, while his older brother was serious, sober, hard-working, and willing to bear responsibility. Now these two brothers did not get along well together; they were always quarreling and bickering. The younger lad was cheerful and vivacious, but indolent and unreliable; the older son was steady and industrious, at the same time self-centered, surly, and conceited. The younger son enjoyed play but shunned work; the older devoted himself to work but seldom played. This association became so disagreeable that the younger son came to his father and said: 'Father, give me the third portion of your possessions which would fall to me and allow me to go out into the world to seek my own fortune.' And when the father heard this request, knowing how unhappy the young man was at home and with his older brother, he divided his property, giving the youth his share.

"Within a few weeks the young man gathered together all his funds and set out upon a journey to a far country, and finding nothing profitable to do which was also pleasurable, he soon wasted all his inheritance in riotous living. And when he had spent all, there arose a prolonged famine in that country, and he found himself in want. And so, when he suffered hunger and his distress was great, he found employment with one of the citizens of that country, who sent him into the fields to feed swine. And the young man would fain have filled himself with the husks which the swine ate, but no one would give him anything.

"One day, when he was very hungry, he came to himself and said: 'How many hired servants of my father have bread enough and to spare while I perish with hunger, feeding swine off here in a foreign country! I will arise and go to my father, and I will say to him: Father, I have sinned against heaven and against you. I am no more worthy to be called your son; only be willing to make me one of your hired servants.' And when the young man had reached this decision, he arose and started out for his father's house.

"Now this father had grieved much for his son; he had missed the cheerful, though thoughtless, lad. This father loved this son and was always on the lookout for his return, so that on the day he approached his home, even while he was yet afar off, the father saw him and, being moved with loving compassion, ran out to meet him, and with affectionate greeting he embraced and kissed him. And after they had thus met, the son looked up into his father's tearful face and said: 'Father, I have sinned against heaven and in your sight; I am no more worthy to be called a son'—but the lad did not find opportunity to complete his confession because the overjoyed father said to the servants who had by this time come running up: 'Bring quickly his best robe, the one I have saved, and put it on him and put the son's ring on his hand and fetch sandals for his feet.'

"And then, after the happy father had led the footsore and weary lad into the house, he called to his servants: 'Bring on the fatted calf and kill it, and let us eat and make merry, for this my son was dead and is alive again; he was lost and is found.' And they all gathered about the father to rejoice with him over the restoration of his son.

"About this time, while they were celebrating, the elder son came in from his day's work in the field, and as he drew near the house, he heard the music and the dancing. And when he came up to the back door, he called out one of the servants and inquired as to the meaning of all this festivity. And then said the servant: 'Your long-lost brother has come home, and your father has killed the fatted calf to rejoice over his son's safe return. Come in that you also may greet your brother and receive him back into your father's house.'

"But when the older brother heard this, he

[LIZ LEMON SWINDLE — *The Prodigal Son*]

was so hurt and angry he would not go into the house. When his father heard of his resentment of the welcome of his younger brother, he went out to entreat him. But the older son would not yield to his father's persuasion. He answered his father, saying: 'Here these many years have I served you, never transgressing the least of your commands, and yet you never gave me even a kid that I might make merry with my friends. I have remained here to care for you all these years, and you never made rejoicing over my faithful service, but when this your son returns, having squandered your substance with harlots, you make haste to kill the fatted calf and make merry over him.'

"Since this father truly loved both of his sons, he tried to reason with this older one: 'But, my son, you have all the while been with me, and all this which I have is yours. You could have had a kid at any time you had made friends to share your merriment. But it is only proper that you should now join with me in being glad and merry because of your brother's return. Think of it, my son, your brother was lost and is found; he has returned alive to us!'"

This was one of the most touching and effective

of all the parables which Jesus ever presented to impress upon his hearers the Father's willingness to receive all who seek entrance into the kingdom of heaven.

Jesus was very partial to telling these three stories at the same time. He presented the story of the lost sheep to show that, when men unintentionally stray away from the path of life, the Father is mindful of such *lost* ones and goes out, with his Sons, the true shepherds of the flock, to seek the lost sheep. He then would recite the story of the coin lost in the house to illustrate how thorough is the divine *searching* for all who are confused, confounded, or otherwise spiritually blinded by the material cares and accumulations of life. And then he would launch forth into the telling of this parable of the lost son, the reception of the returning prodigal, to show how complete is the *restoration* of the lost son into his Father's house and heart.

Many, many times during his years of teaching, Jesus told and retold this story of the prodigal son. This parable and the story of the good Samaritan were his favorite means of teaching the love of the Father and the neighborliness of man. ∎

"MAKE HASTE ZACCHEUS"

Late on the afternoon of Thursday, March 30, Jesus and his apostles, at the head of a band of about two hundred followers, approached the walls of Jericho. As they came near the gate of the city, they encountered a throng of beggars, among them one Bartimeus, an elderly man who had been blind from his youth. This blind beggar had heard much about Jesus and knew all about his healing of the blind Josiah at Jerusalem. He had not known of Jesus' last visit to Jericho until he had gone on to Bethany. Bartimeus had resolved that he would never again allow Jesus to visit Jericho without appealing to him for the restoration of his sight.

News of Jesus' approach had been heralded throughout Jericho, and hundreds of the inhabitants flocked forth to meet him. When this great crowd came back escorting the Master into the city, Bartimeus, hearing the heavy tramping of the multitude, knew that something unusual was happening, and so he asked those standing near him what was going on. And one of the beggars replied, "Jesus of Nazareth is passing by." When Bartimeus heard that Jesus was near, he lifted up his voice and began to cry aloud, "Jesus, Jesus, have mercy upon me!" And as he continued to cry louder and louder, some of those near to Jesus went over and rebuked him, requesting him to hold his peace; but it was of no avail; he cried only the more and the louder.

When Jesus heard the blind man crying out, he stood still. And when he saw him, he said to his friends, "Bring the man to me." And then they went over to Bartimeus, saying: "Be of good cheer; come with us, for the Master calls for you." When Bartimeus heard these words, he threw aside his cloak, springing forward toward the center of the road, while those near by guided him to Jesus.

Addressing Bartimeus, Jesus said: "What do you want me to do for you?" Then answered the blind man, "I would have my sight restored." And when Jesus heard this request and saw his faith, he said: "You shall receive your sight; go your way; your faith has made you whole." Immediately he received his sight, and he remained near Jesus, glorifying God, until the Master started on the next day for Jerusalem, and then he went before the multitude declaring to all how his sight had

[HAROLD COPPING — *The Healing of Blind Bartimeus* (detail)]

been restored in Jericho.

When the Master's procession entered Jericho, it was nearing sundown, and he was minded to abide there for the night. As Jesus passed by the customs house, Zaccheus the chief publican, or tax collector, happened to be present, and he much desired to see Jesus. This chief publican was very rich and had heard much about this prophet of Galilee. He had resolved that he would see what sort of a man Jesus was the next time he chanced to visit Jericho; accordingly, Zaccheus sought to press through the crowd, but it was too great, and being short of stature, he could not see over their heads. And so the chief publican followed on with the crowd until they came near the center of the city and not far from where he lived. When he saw that he would be unable to penetrate the crowd, and thinking that Jesus might be going right on through the city without stopping, he ran on ahead and climbed up into a sycamore tree whose spreading branches overhung the roadway. He knew that in this way he could obtain a good view of the Master as he passed by. And he was not disappointed, for, as Jesus passed by, he stopped and, looking up at Zaccheus, said: "Make haste, Zaccheus, and come down, for tonight I must abide at your house." And when Zaccheus heard these astonishing words, he almost fell out of the tree in his haste to get down, and going up to Jesus, he expressed great joy that the Master should be willing to stop at his house.

They went at once to the home of Zaccheus, and those who lived in Jericho were much surprised that Jesus would consent to abide with the chief publican. Even while the Master and his apostles lingered with Zaccheus before the door of his house, one of the Jericho Pharisees, standing near by, said: "You see how this man has gone to lodge with a sinner, an apostate son of Abraham who is an extortioner and a robber of his own people." And when Jesus heard this, he looked down at Zaccheus and smiled. Then Zaccheus stood upon a stool and said: "Men of Jericho, hear me! I may be a publican and a sinner, but the great Teacher has come to abide in my house; and before he goes in, I tell you that I am going to bestow one half of all my goods upon the poor, and beginning tomorrow, if I have wrongfully exacted aught from any man, I will restore fourfold. I am going to seek salvation with all my heart and learn to do righteousness in the sight of God."

When Zaccheus had ceased speaking, Jesus said: "Today has salvation come to this home, and you have become indeed a son of Abraham." And turning to the crowd assembled about them, Jesus said: "And marvel not at what I say nor take offense at what we do, for I have all along declared that the Son of Man has come to seek and to save that which is lost."

They lodged with Zaccheus for the night. On the morrow they arose and made their way up the "road of robbers" to Bethany on their way to the Passover at Jerusalem.

They did not start from Jericho until near noon since they sat up late the night before while Jesus taught Zaccheus and his family the gospel of the kingdom. About halfway up the ascending road to Bethany the party paused for lunch while the multitude passed on to Jerusalem, not knowing that Jesus and the apostles were going to abide that night on the Mount of Olives.

When they had finished their lunch, and after the multitude of followers had gone on toward Jerusalem, Jesus, standing there before the apostles in the shade of an overhanging rock by the roadside, with cheerful dignity and a gracious majesty pointed his finger westward, saying: "Come, my brethren, let us go on into Jerusalem, there to receive that which awaits us; thus shall we fulfill the will of the heavenly Father in all things."

And so Jesus and his apostles resumed this, the Master's last journey to Jerusalem in the likeness of the flesh of mortal man. ✳

"As Jesus Passed By"

Jesus spread good cheer everywhere he went. He was full of grace and truth. His associates never ceased to wonder at the gracious words that proceeded out of his mouth. You can cultivate gracefulness, but graciousness is the aroma of friendliness which emanates from a love-saturated soul.

Goodness always compels respect, but when it is devoid of grace, it often repels affection. Goodness is universally attractive only when it is gracious. Goodness is effective only when it is attractive.

Jesus really understood men; therefore could he manifest genuine sympathy and show sincere compassion. But he seldom indulged in pity. While his compassion was boundless, his sympathy was practical, personal, and constructive. Never did his familiarity with suffering breed indifference, and he was able to minister to distressed souls without increasing their self-pity.

Jesus could help men so much because he loved them so sincerely. He truly loved each man, each woman, and each child. He could be such a true friend because of his remarkable insight—he knew so fully what was in the heart and in the mind of man. He was an interested and keen observer. He was an expert in the comprehension of human need, clever in detecting human longings.

Jesus was never in a hurry. He had time to comfort his fellow men "as he passed by." And he always made his friends feel at ease. He was a charming listener. He never engaged in the meddlesome probing of the souls of his associates.

As he comforted hungry minds and ministered to thirsty souls, the recipients of his mercy did not so much feel that they were confessing to him as that they were conferring with him. They had unbounded confidence in him because they saw he had so much faith in them.

He never seemed to be curious about people, and he never manifested a desire to direct, manage, or follow them up. He inspired profound self-confidence and robust courage in all who enjoyed his association. When he smiled on a man, that mortal experienced increased capacity for solving his manifold problems.

Jesus loved men so much and so wisely that he never hesitated to be severe with them when the occasion demanded such discipline. He frequently set out to help a person by asking for help. In this way he elicited interest, appealed to the better things in human nature.

The Master could discern saving faith in the gross superstition of the woman who sought healing by touching the hem of his garment. He was always ready and willing to stop a sermon or detain a multitude while he ministered to the needs of a single person, even to a little child. Great things happened not only because people had faith in Jesus, but also because Jesus had so much faith in them.

Most of the really important things which Jesus said or did seemed to happen casually, "as he passed by." There was so little of the professional, the well-planned, or the premeditated in the Master's earthly ministry. He dispensed health and scattered happiness naturally and gracefully as he journeyed through life. It was literally true, "He went about doing good."

And it behooves the Master's followers in all ages to learn to minister as "they pass by"—to do unselfish good as they go about their daily duties.

[AKIANE KRAMARIK — *Jesus*]

CHAPTER X

THE FINAL DAYS

Jesus said to him, "I am the way, and the truth,
and the life; no one comes to the Father, but by me."

—JOHN 14:6 RSV

A S THE CURTAIN RISES ON THE FINAL SCENES OF HIS BESTOWAL CAREER, JESUS IS NEARLY thirty-six years removed from his humble beginnings in Bethlehem. It has been four years since his baptism and three since the apostles were ordained on the highlands north of Capernaum. And now, the events that are soon to transpire will together compose the most dramatic and far-reaching week in human history. On Sunday he made his famous entry into Jerusalem on a carpet of honor made of garments and palm branches. On Monday he awed the multitudes with the spectacular cleansing of the temple.

On Tuesday, in the quiet and orderly temple court, he delivered his farewell discourse. And the people hung on his words. But when this multitude heard Jesus swing from his merciful last appeal to the Jewish leaders into that sudden and scathing rebuke which bordered on ruthless denunciation, they were stunned and bewildered. That night, while the Sanhedrin sat in death judgment upon Jesus, and while the Master sat with his apostles and certain of his disciples out on the Mount of Olives foretelling the death of the Jewish nation, all Jerusalem was given over to the serious and suppressed discussion of just one question: "What will they do with Jesus?" And this was the situation in Jerusalem and among men on this eventful day while a vast concourse of celestial beings hovered over this momentous scene on earth.

On Thursday evening Jesus established the remembrance supper, the only ceremony or sacrament associated with his whole life mission. Jesus took great pains to *suggest* his meanings rather than to commit himself to *precise definitions*. He did not wish to destroy the individual's concept of divine communion by establishing a precise form; neither did he desire to limit the believer's spiritual imagination by formally cramping it. He rather sought to set man's reborn soul free upon the joyous wings of a new and living spiritual liberty. But those who followed after him in the intervening centuries saw to it that his express desire was effectively thwarted in that his simple spiritual symbolism of that last night in the flesh has been reduced to precise interpretations and subjected to the almost mathematical precision of a set formula. Of all Jesus' teachings none have become more tradition-standardized.

═══════════

THE URANTIA BOOK: PAPERS 172–182
FRIDAY, MARCH 31–THURSDAY, APRIL 6, A.D. 30

[YONGSUNG KIM — *Washing of the Feet*]

JUDAS TURNS TRAITOR

Jesus and the apostles arrived at Bethany shortly after four o'clock on Friday afternoon, March 31, A.D. 30. Lazarus, his sisters, and their friends were expecting them; and since so many people came every day to talk with Lazarus about his resurrection, Jesus was informed that arrangements had been made for him to stay with a neighboring believer, one Simon, the leading citizen of the little village since the death of Lazarus's father.

That evening, Jesus received many visitors, and the common folks of Bethany and Bethpage did their best to make him feel welcome. Although many thought Jesus was now going into Jerusalem, in utter defiance of the Sanhedrin's decree of death, to proclaim himself king of the Jews, the Bethany family—Lazarus, Martha, and Mary—more fully realized that the Master was not that kind of a king; they dimly felt that this might be his last visit to Jerusalem and Bethany.

The chief priests were informed that Jesus lodged at Bethany, but they thought best not to attempt to seize him among his friends; they decided to await his coming on into Jerusalem. Jesus knew about all this, but he was majestically calm; his friends had never seen him more composed and congenial; even the apostles were astounded that he should be so unconcerned when the Sanhedrin had called upon all Jewry to deliver him into their hands. While the Master slept that night, the apostles watched over him by twos, and many of them were girded with swords. Early the next morning they were awakened by hundreds of pilgrims who came out from Jerusalem, even on the Sabbath day, to see Jesus and Lazarus, whom he had raised from the dead.

Pilgrims from outside of Judea, as well as the Jewish authorities, had all been asking: "What do you think? will Jesus come up to the feast?" Therefore, when the people heard that Jesus was at Bethany, they were glad, but the chief priests and Pharisees were somewhat perplexed. They were pleased to have him under their jurisdiction, but they were a trifle disconcerted by his boldness; they remembered that on his previous visit to Bethany, Lazarus had been raised from the dead, and Lazarus was becoming a big problem to the enemies of Jesus.

Six days before the Passover, on the evening after the Sabbath, all Bethany and Bethpage joined in celebrating the arrival of Jesus by a public banquet at the home of Simon. This supper was in honor of both Jesus and Lazarus; it was tendered in defiance of the Sanhedrin. Martha directed the serving of the food; her sister Mary was among the women onlookers as it was against the custom of the Jews for a woman to sit at a public banquet. The agents of the Sanhedrin were present, but they feared to apprehend Jesus in the midst of his friends.

Jesus talked with Simon about Joshua of old, whose namesake he was, and recited how Joshua and the Israelites had come up to Jerusalem

> NEAR THE CLOSE OF THE FEASTING MARY STEPPED FORWARD AND OPENED A LARGE ALABASTER CRUSE OF RARE AND COSTLY OINTMENT; AFTER ANOINTING THE MASTER'S HEAD, SHE POURED IT UPON HIS FEET.

[Stephen Sawyer & Slawa Radziszewska — *The Turning Point*]

through Jericho. In commenting on the legend of the walls of Jericho falling down, Jesus said: "I am not concerned with such walls of brick and stone; but I would cause the walls of prejudice, self-righteousness, and hate to crumble before this preaching of the Father's love for all men."

The banquet went along in a very cheerful and normal manner except that all the apostles were unusually sober. Jesus was exceptionally cheerful and had been playing with the children up to the time of coming to the table.

Nothing out of the ordinary happened until near the close of the feasting when Mary the sister of Lazarus stepped forward from among the group of women onlookers and, going up to where Jesus reclined as the guest of honor, proceeded to open a large alabaster cruse of very rare and costly ointment; and after anointing the Master's head, she began to pour it upon his feet as she took down her hair and wiped them with it. The whole house became filled with the odor of the ointment, and everybody present was amazed at what Mary had done. Lazarus said nothing, but when some of the people murmured, showing indignation that so costly an ointment should be thus used, Judas Iscariot stepped over to where Andrew reclined and said: "Why was this ointment not sold and the money bestowed to feed the poor? You should speak to the Master that he rebuke such waste."

Jesus, knowing what they thought and hearing what they said, put his hand upon Mary's head as she knelt by his side and, with a kindly expression upon his face, said: "Let her alone, every one of you. Why do you trouble her about this, seeing that she has done a good thing in her heart? To you who murmur and say that this ointment should have been sold and the money given to the poor, let me say that you have the poor always with you so that you may minister to them at any time it seems good to you; but I shall not always be with you; I go soon to my Father. This woman has long saved this ointment for my body at its burial, and now that it has seemed good to her to make this anointing in anticipation of my death, she shall not be denied such satisfaction. In the doing of this, Mary has reproved all of you in that by this act she evinces faith in what I have said about my death and ascension to my Father in heaven. This woman shall not be reproved for that which she has this night done; rather do I say to you that in the ages to come, wherever this gospel shall be preached throughout the whole world, what she has done will be spoken of in memory of her."

It was because of this rebuke, which he took as a personal reproof, that Judas Iscariot finally made up his mind to seek revenge for his hurt feelings. Many times had he entertained such ideas subconsciously, but now he dared to think such wicked thoughts in his open and conscious mind. And many others encouraged him in this attitude since the cost of this ointment was a sum equal to the earnings of one man for one year—enough to provide bread for five thousand persons. But Mary loved Jesus; she had provided this precious ointment with which to embalm his body in death, for she believed his words when he forewarned them that he must die, and it was not to be denied her if she changed her mind and chose to bestow this offering upon the Master while he yet lived.

Both Lazarus and Martha knew that Mary had long saved the money wherewith to buy this cruse of spikenard, and they heartily approved of her doing as her heart desired in such a matter, for they were well-to-do and could easily afford to make such an offering.

When the chief priests heard of this dinner in Bethany for Jesus and Lazarus, they began to take counsel among themselves as to what should be done with Lazarus. And presently they decided that Lazarus must also die. They rightly concluded that it would be useless to put Jesus to death if they permitted Lazarus, whom he had raised from the dead, to live. ∎

YOUR KING COMES AS THE LOWLY ONE

On this Sunday morning, in Simon's beautiful garden, the Master called his twelve apostles around him and gave them their final instructions preparatory to entering Jerusalem. He told them that he would probably deliver many addresses and teach many lessons before returning to the Father but advised the apostles to refrain from doing any public work during this Passover sojourn in Jerusalem. He instructed them to remain near him and to "watch and pray." Jesus knew that many of his apostles and immediate followers even then carried swords concealed on their persons, but he made no reference to this fact.

This morning's instructions embraced a brief review of their ministry from the day of their ordination near Capernaum down to this day when they were preparing to enter Jerusalem. The apostles listened in silence; they asked no questions.

After the conference with the apostles Jesus held converse with Lazarus and instructed him to avoid the sacrifice of his life to the vengefulness of the Sanhedrin. It was in obedience to this admonition that Lazarus, a few days later, fled to

JESUS DID NOT DECIDE TO MAKE THIS PUBLIC ENTRANCE INTO JERUSALEM AS A LAST BID FOR POPULAR FAVOR NOR AS A FINAL GRASP FOR POWER.

Philadelphia when the officers of the Sanhedrin sent men to arrest him.

In a way, all of Jesus' followers sensed the impending crisis, but they were prevented from fully realizing its seriousness by the unusual cheerfulness and exceptional good humor of the Master.

Bethany was about two miles from the temple, and it was half past one that Sunday afternoon when Jesus made ready to start for Jerusalem. He had feelings of profound affection for Bethany and its simple people. Nazareth, Capernaum, and Jerusalem had rejected him, but Bethany had accepted him, had believed in him. And it was in this small village, where almost every man, woman, and child were believers, that he chose to perform the mightiest work of his earth bestowal, the resurrection of Lazarus. He did not raise Lazarus that the villagers might believe, but rather because they already believed.

All morning Jesus had thought about his entry into Jerusalem. Heretofore he had always endeavored to suppress all public acclaim of him as the Messiah, but it was different now; he was nearing the end of his career in the flesh, his death had been decreed by the Sanhedrin, and no harm could come from allowing his disciples to give free expression to their feelings, just as might occur if he elected to make a formal and public entry into the city.

Jesus did not decide to make this public entrance into Jerusalem as a last bid for popular favor nor as a final grasp for power. Neither did he do it altogether to satisfy the human longings of his disciples and apostles. Jesus entertained none

of the illusions of a fantastic dreamer; he well knew what was to be the outcome of this visit.

Having decided upon making a public entrance into Jerusalem, the Master was confronted with the necessity of choosing a proper method of executing such a resolve. Jesus thought over all of the many more or less contradictory so-called Messianic prophesies, but there seemed to be only one which was at all appropriate for him to follow. Most of these prophetic utterances depicted a king, the son and successor of David, a bold and aggressive temporal deliverer of all Israel from the yoke of foreign domination. But there was one Scripture that had sometimes been associated with the Messiah by those who held more to the spiritual concept of his mission, which Jesus thought might consistently be taken as a guide for his projected entry into Jerusalem. This Scripture was found in Zechariah, and it said: "Rejoice greatly, O daughter of Zion; shout, O daughter of Jerusalem. Behold, your king comes to you. He is just and he brings salvation. He comes as the lowly one, riding upon an ass, upon a colt, the foal of an ass."

Jesus had long tried by direct teaching to impress upon his apostles and his disciples that his kingdom was not of this world, that it was a purely spiritual matter; but he had not succeeded in this effort. Now, what he had failed to do by plain and personal teaching, he would attempt to accomplish by a symbolic appeal. Accordingly, right after the noon lunch, Jesus called Peter and John, and after directing them to go over to Bethpage, a neighboring village a little off the main

[ANDON FONTAINNE — *The Son of Peace Enters Jerusalem*]

road and a short distance northwest of Bethany, he further said: "Go to Bethpage, and when you come to the junction of the roads, you will find the colt of an ass tied there. Loose the colt and bring it back with you. If anyone asks you why you do this, merely say, 'The Master has need of him.'" And when the two apostles had gone into Bethpage as the Master had directed, they found the colt tied near his mother in the open street and close to a house on the corner. As Peter began to untie the colt, the owner came over and asked why they did this, and when Peter answered him as Jesus had directed, the man said: "If your Master is Jesus from Galilee, let him have the colt." And so they returned bringing the colt with them.

By this time several hundred pilgrims had gathered around Jesus and his apostles. Since mid-forenoon the visitors passing by on their way to the Passover had tarried. Meanwhile, David Zebedee and some of his former messenger associates took it upon themselves to hasten on down to Jerusalem, where they effectively spread the report among the throngs of visiting pilgrims about the temple that Jesus of Nazareth was making a triumphal entry into the city. Accordingly, several thousand of these visitors flocked forth to greet this much-talked-of prophet and wonder-worker, whom some believed to be the Messiah. This multitude, coming out from Jerusalem, met Jesus and the crowd going into the city just after they had passed over the brow of Olivet and had begun the descent into the city.

As the procession started out from Bethany,

there was great enthusiasm among the festive crowd of disciples, believers, and visiting pilgrims, many hailing from Galilee and Perea. Just before they started, the twelve women of the original women's corps, accompanied by some of their associates, arrived on the scene and joined this unique procession as it moved on joyously toward the city.

Before they started, the Alpheus twins put their cloaks on the donkey and held him while the Master got on. As the procession moved toward the summit of Olivet, the festive crowd threw their garments on the ground and brought branches from the near-by trees in order to make a carpet of honor for the donkey bearing the royal Son, the promised Messiah. As the merry crowd moved on toward Jerusalem, they began to sing, or rather to shout in unison, the Psalm, "Hosanna to the son of David; blessed is he who comes in the name of the Lord. Hosanna in the highest. Blessed be the kingdom that comes down from heaven."

Jesus was lighthearted and cheerful as they moved along until he came to the brow of Olivet, where the city and the temple towers came into full view; there the Master stopped the procession, and a great silence came upon all as they beheld him weeping. Looking down upon the vast multitude coming forth from the city to greet him, the Master, with much emotion and with tearful voice, said: "O Jerusalem, if you had

only known, even you, at least in this your day, the things which belong to your peace, and which you could so freely have had! But now are these glories about to be hid from your eyes. You are about to reject the Son of Peace and turn your backs upon the gospel of salvation. The days will soon come upon you wherein your enemies will cast a trench around about you and lay siege to you on every side; they shall utterly destroy you, insomuch that not one stone shall be left upon another. And all this shall befall you because you knew not the time of your divine visitation. You are about to reject the gift of God, and all men will reject you."

When he had finished speaking, they began the descent of Olivet and presently were joined by the multitude of visitors who had come from Jerusalem waving palm branches, shouting hosannas, and otherwise expressing gleefulness and good fellowship. The Master had not planned that these crowds should come out from Jerusalem to meet them; that was the work of others. He never premeditated anything which was dramatic.

Along with the multitude which poured out to welcome the Master, there came also many of the Pharisees and his other enemies. They were so much perturbed by this sudden and unexpected outburst of popular acclaim that they feared to arrest him lest such action precipitate an open revolt of the populace. They greatly feared the attitude of the

A KING OF PEACE

A warrior king always entered a city riding upon a horse; a king on a mission of peace and friendship always entered riding upon an ass. Jesus would not enter Jerusalem as a man on horseback, but he was willing to enter peacefully and with good will as the Son of Man on a donkey.

large numbers of visitors, who had heard much of Jesus, and who, many of them, believed in him.

As they neared Jerusalem, the crowd became more demonstrative, so much so that some of the Pharisees made their way up alongside Jesus and said: "Teacher, you should rebuke your disciples and exhort them to behave more seemly." Jesus answered: "It is only fitting that these children should welcome the Son of Peace, whom the chief priests have rejected. It would be useless to stop them lest in their stead these stones by the roadside cry out."

The Pharisees hastened on ahead of the procession to rejoin the Sanhedrin, which was then in session at the temple, and they reported to their associates: "Behold, all that we do is of no avail; we are confounded by this Galilean. The people have gone mad over him; if we do not stop these ignorant ones, all the world will go after him."

There really was no deep significance to be attached to this superficial and spontaneous outburst of popular enthusiasm. This welcome, although it was joyous and sincere, did not betoken any real or deep-seated conviction in the hearts of this festive multitude. These same crowds were equally as willing quickly to reject Jesus later on this week when the Sanhedrin once took a firm and decided stand against him, and when they became disillusioned—when they realized that Jesus was not going to establish the kingdom in accordance with their long-cherished expectations.

But the whole city was mightily stirred up, insomuch that everyone asked, "Who is this man?" And the multitude answered, "This is the prophet of Galilee, Jesus of Nazareth."

While the Alpheus twins returned the donkey to its owner, Jesus and the ten apostles detached themselves from their immediate associates and strolled about the temple, viewing the preparations for the Passover. No attempt was made to molest Jesus as the Sanhedrin greatly feared the people, and that was, after all, one of the reasons Jesus

had for allowing the multitude thus to acclaim him. The apostles little understood that this was the only human procedure which could have been effective in preventing Jesus' immediate arrest upon entering the city. The Master desired to give the inhabitants of Jerusalem, high and low, as well as the tens of thousands of Passover visitors, this one more and last chance to hear the gospel and receive, if they would, the Son of Peace.

And now, as the evening drew on and the crowds went in quest of nourishment, Jesus and his immediate followers were left alone. What a strange day it had been! The apostles were thoughtful, but speechless. Never, in their years of association with Jesus, had they seen such a day. For a moment they sat down by the treasury, watching the people drop in their contributions: the rich putting much in the receiving box and all giving something in accordance with the extent of their possessions. At last there came along a poor widow, scantily attired, and they observed as she cast two mites (small coppers) into the trumpet. And then said Jesus, calling the attention of the apostles to the widow: "Heed well what you have just seen. This poor widow cast in more than all the others, for all these others, from their superfluity, cast in some trifle as a gift, but this poor woman, even though she is in want, gave all that she had, even her living."

As the evening drew on, they walked about the temple courts in silence, and after Jesus had surveyed these familiar scenes once more, recalling his emotions in connection with previous visits, not excepting the earlier ones, he said, "Let us go up to Bethany for our rest."

This Sunday evening as they returned to Bethany, Jesus walked in front of the apostles. Not a word was spoken until they separated after arriving at Simon's house. No twelve human beings ever experienced such diverse and inexplicable emotions as now surged through the minds and souls of these ambassadors of the kingdom. These sturdy Galileans were confused and disconcerted; they did not know what to expect next; they were too surprised to be much afraid. They knew nothing of the Master's plans for the next day, and they asked no questions. They went to their lodgings, though they did not sleep much, save the twins. But they did not keep armed watch over Jesus at Simon's house. ■

CLEANSING THE TEMPLE

Early on this Monday morning, by prearrangement, Jesus and the apostles assembled at the home of Simon in Bethany, and after a brief conference they set out for Jerusalem. The twelve were strangely silent as they journeyed on toward the temple; they had not recovered from the experience of the preceding day. They were expectant, fearful, and profoundly affected by a certain feeling of detachment growing out of the Master's sudden change of tactics, coupled with his instruction that they were to engage in no public teaching throughout this Passover week.

As this group journeyed down Mount Olivet, Jesus led the way, the apostles following closely behind in meditative silence. There was just one thought uppermost in the minds of all save Judas Iscariot, and that was: What will the Master do today? The one absorbing thought of Judas was: What shall I do? Shall I go on with Jesus and my associates, or shall I withdraw?

It was about nine o'clock on this beautiful morning when these men arrived at the temple. They went at once to the large court where Jesus so often taught, and after greeting the believers who were awaiting him, Jesus mounted one of the teaching platforms and began to address the gathering crowd. The apostles withdrew for a short distance and awaited developments.

A huge commercial traffic had grown up in association with the services and ceremonies of the temple worship. There was the business of providing suitable animals for the various sacrifices. It had become the vogue to buy these animals directly from the temple pens. Gradually there had grown up this custom of selling all kinds of sacrificial animals in the temple courts. An extensive business, in which enormous profits were made, had thus been brought into existence. Part of these gains was reserved for the temple treasury, but the larger part went indirectly into the hands of the ruling high-priestly families.

This sale of animals in the temple prospered because, when the worshiper purchased such an animal, although the price might be somewhat high, no more fees had to be paid, and he could be sure the intended sacrifice would not be rejected on the ground of possessing real or technical blemishes. At one time the greedy priests went so far as to demand the equivalent of the value of a week's labor for a pair of doves which should have been sold to the poor for a few pennies. The "sons of Annas" had already begun to establish their bazaars in the temple precincts, those very merchandise marts which persisted to the time of their final overthrow by a mob three years before the destruction of the temple itself.

But traffic in sacrificial animals and sundry merchandise was not the only way in which the courts of the temple were profaned. At this time there was fostered an extensive system of banking and commercial exchange which was carried on right within the temple precincts.

In the midst of this noisy aggregation of money-changers, merchandisers, and cattle sellers, Jesus, on this Monday morning, attempted to teach the gospel of the heavenly kingdom. He was not alone in resenting this profanation of the temple; the common people, especially the Jewish visitors from foreign provinces, also heartily resented this profiteering desecration of their national house of worship. At this time the Sanhedrin itself held its regular meetings in a chamber surrounded by all this babble and confusion of trade and barter.

As Jesus was about to begin his address, two things happened to arrest his attention. At the money table of a near-by exchanger a violent and heated argument had arisen over the alleged overcharging of a Jew from Alexandria, while at the same moment the air was rent by the bellowing of a drove of some one hundred bullocks which was being driven from one section of the animal pens to another. As Jesus paused, silently but thoughtfully contemplating this scene of commerce and confusion, close by he beheld a simple-minded Galilean, a man he had once talked with in Iron, being ridiculed and jostled about by supercilious and would-be superior Judeans; and all of this combined to produce one of those strange and periodic uprisings of indignant emotion in the soul of Jesus.

To the amazement of his apostles, standing near at hand, who refrained from participation in what so soon followed, Jesus stepped down from the teaching platform and, going over to the lad who was driving the cattle through the court, took from him his whip of cords and swiftly drove the animals from the temple. But that was not all; he strode majestically before the wondering gaze of the thousands assembled in the temple court to the farthest cattle pen and proceeded to open the gates of every stall and to drive out the imprisoned animals. By this time the assembled pilgrims were electrified, and with uproarious shouting they moved toward

the bazaars and began to overturn the tables of the money-changers. In less than five minutes all commerce had been swept from the temple. By the time the near-by Roman guards had appeared on the scene, all was quiet, and the crowds had become orderly; Jesus, returning to the speaker's stand, spoke to the multitude: "You have this day witnessed that which is written in the Scriptures: 'My house shall be called a house of prayer for all nations, but you have made it a den of robbers.'"

But before he could utter other words, the great assembly broke out in hosannas of praise, and presently a throng of youths stepped out from the crowd to sing grateful hymns of appreciation that the profane and profiteering merchandisers had been ejected from the sacred temple.

By this time certain of the priests had arrived on the scene, and one of them said to Jesus, "Do you not hear what the children of the Levites say?" And the Master replied, "Have you never read, 'Out of the mouths of babes and sucklings has praise been perfected'?" And all the rest of that day while Jesus taught, guards set by the people stood watch at every archway, and they would not permit anyone to carry even an empty vessel across the temple courts.

When the chief priests and the scribes heard about these happenings, they were dumfounded. All the more they feared the Master, and all the more they determined to destroy him. But they were nonplused. They did not know how to accomplish his death, for they greatly feared the multitudes, who were now so outspoken in their approval of his overthrow of the profane profiteers. And all this day, a day of quiet and

THE MONEY-CHANGERS

The temple money-changers not only conducted a regular banking business for profit in the exchange of more than twenty sorts of money which the visiting pilgrims would periodically bring to Jerusalem, but they also engaged in all other kinds of transactions pertaining to the banking business. Both the temple treasury and the temple rulers profited tremendously from these commercial activities. It was not uncommon for the temple treasury to hold upwards of ten million dollars while the common people languished in poverty and continued to pay these unjust levies.

[CARL BLOCH — *Jesus Clears the Temple*]

PURGING THE DEN OF ROBBERS

What has always been lacking in the many accounts and depictions of the cleansing of the temple can be summed up in one word: *magnitude*. Herod's Temple was stupendous—its precincts could accommodate over two hundred thousand worshipers at one time—and the commercial traffic was likewise immense. Jesus never raised a hand in violence against any man. After he drove out the herd and then freed the animals, the electrified crowd acted with a hive mind to sweep away all the profane commerce. Had the guards arrived during the tumult, there could easily have been bloodshed. For this complete purge to transpire in under five minutes was well-nigh miraculous.

the refusal to employ force to protect the majority of any given human group against the unfair and enslaving practices of unjust minorities who may be able to entrench themselves behind political, financial, or ecclesiastical power. Shrewd, wicked, and designing men are not to be permitted to organize themselves for the exploitation and oppression of those who, because of their idealism, are not disposed to resort to force for self-protection or for the furtherance of their laudable life projects. ∎

CHALLENGING THE MASTER'S AUTHORITY

On Sunday the triumphal entry into Jerusalem so overawed the Jewish leaders that they refrained from placing Jesus under arrest. Today, this spectacular cleansing of the temple likewise effectively postponed the Master's apprehension. Day by day the rulers of the Jews were becoming more and more determined to destroy him, but they were distraught by two fears, which conspired to delay the hour of striking. The chief priests and the scribes were unwilling to arrest Jesus in public for fear the multitude might turn upon them in a fury of resentment; they also dreaded the possibility of the Roman guards being called upon to quell a popular uprising.

At the noon session of the Sanhedrin it was unanimously agreed that Jesus must be speedily destroyed, inasmuch as no friend of the Master attended this meeting. But they could not agree as to when and how he should be taken into custody. Finally they agreed upon appointing five groups to go out among the people and seek to entangle him in his teaching or otherwise to discredit him in the sight of those who listened to his instruction. Accordingly, about two o'clock, when Jesus had just begun his discourse on "The Liberty of

peace in the temple courts, the people heard Jesus' teaching and literally hung on his words.

This surprising act of Jesus was beyond the comprehension of his apostles. They were so taken aback by this sudden and unexpected move of their Master that they remained throughout the whole episode huddled together near the speaker's stand; they never lifted a hand to further this cleansing of the temple.

If this spectacular event had occurred the day before, at the time of Jesus' triumphal arrival at the temple at the termination of his tumultuous procession through the gates of the city, all the while loudly acclaimed by the multitude, they would have been ready for it, but coming as it did, they were wholly unprepared to participate.

This cleansing of the temple discloses the Master's attitude toward commercializing the practices of religion as well as his detestation of all forms of unfairness and profiteering at the expense of the poor and the unlearned. This episode also demonstrates that Jesus did not look with approval upon

Sonship," a group of these elders of Israel made their way up near Jesus and, interrupting him in the customary manner, asked this question: "By what authority do you do these things? Who gave you this authority?"

It was altogether proper that the temple rulers and the officers of the Jewish Sanhedrin should ask this question of anyone who presumed to teach and perform in the extraordinary manner which had been characteristic of Jesus, especially as concerned his recent conduct in clearing the temple of all commerce. These traders and money-changers all operated by direct license from the highest rulers, and a percentage of their gains was supposed to go directly into the temple treasury. Do not forget that *authority* was the watchword of all Jewry.

The rulers of the temple came before Jesus at this afternoon hour challenging not only his teaching but his acts. Jesus well knew that these very men had long publicly taught that his authority for teaching was Satanic, and that all his mighty works had been wrought by the power of the prince of devils. Therefore did the Master begin his answer to their question by asking them a counter-question. Said Jesus: "I would also like to ask you one question which, if you will answer me, I likewise will tell you by what authority I do these works. The baptism of John, whence was it? Did John get his authority from heaven or from men?"

And when his questioners heard this, they withdrew to one side to take counsel among themselves as to what answer they might give. They had thought to embarrass Jesus before the multitude, but now they found themselves much confused before all who were assembled at that time in the temple court. And their discomfiture was all the more apparent when they returned to Jesus, saying: "Concerning the baptism of John, we cannot answer; we do not know." And they so answered the Master because they had reasoned among themselves: If we shall say from heaven, then will he say, Why did you not believe him, and perchance will add that he received his authority from John; and if we shall say from men, then might the multitude turn upon us, for most of them hold that John was a prophet; and so they were compelled to come before Jesus and the people confessing that they, the religious teachers and leaders of Israel, could not (or would not) express an opinion about John's mission. And when they had spoken, Jesus, looking down upon them, said, "Neither will I tell you by what authority I do these things."

Jesus never intended to appeal to John for his authority; John had never been ordained by the Sanhedrin. Jesus' authority was in himself and in his Father's eternal supremacy.

About four o'clock this afternoon Jesus beckoned to his apostles and indicated that he desired to leave the temple and to go to Bethany for their evening meal and a night of rest. On the way up Olivet Jesus instructed Andrew, Philip, and Thomas that, on the morrow, they should establish a camp nearer the city which they could occupy during the remainder of the Passover week. In compliance with this instruction the following morning they pitched their tents in the hillside ravine overlooking the public camping park of Gethsemane, on a plot of ground belonging to Simon of Bethany.

Again it was a silent group of Jews who made their way up the western slope of Olivet on this Monday night. These twelve men, as never before, were beginning to sense that something tragic was about to happen. While the dramatic cleansing of the temple during the early morning had aroused their hopes of seeing the Master assert himself and manifest his mighty powers, the events of the entire afternoon only operated as an anticlimax in that they all pointed to the certain rejection of Jesus' teaching by the Jewish authorities.

The apostles were gripped by suspense and were held in the firm grasp of a terrible uncertainty. They realized that only a few short days could intervene between the events of the day just passed and the crash of an impending doom. They all felt that something tremendous was about to happen, but they knew not what to expect. They went to their various places for rest, but they slept very little. Even the Alpheus twins were at last aroused to the realization that the events of the Master's life were moving swiftly toward their final culmination. ∎

TUESDAY MORNING IN THE TEMPLE

About seven o'clock on this Tuesday morning Jesus met the apostles, the women's corps, and some two dozen other prominent disciples at the home of Simon. At this meeting he said farewell to Lazarus, giving him that instruction which led him so soon to flee to Philadelphia in Perea, where he later became connected with the missionary movement having its headquarters in that city. Jesus also said good-bye to the aged Simon, and gave his parting advice to the women's corps, as he never again formally addressed them.

And when he had concluded these greetings, he departed for Jerusalem with Andrew, Peter, James, and John as the other apostles set about the establishment of the Gethsemane camp, where they were to go that night, and where they made their headquarters for the remainder of the Master's life in the flesh. About halfway down the slope of Olivet Jesus paused and visited more than an hour with the four apostles.

When Jesus arrived in the temple court and began to teach, he had uttered but few words when a group of the younger students from the academies, who had been rehearsed for this purpose, came forward and by their spokesman addressed Jesus: "Master, we know you are a righteous teacher, and we know that you proclaim the ways of truth, and that you serve only God, for you fear no man, and that you are no respecter

[HARRY ANDERSON — *The Tribute Coin*]

of persons. We are only students, and we would know the truth about a matter which troubles us; our difficulty is this: Is it lawful for us to give tribute to Caesar? Shall we give or shall we not give?" Jesus, perceiving their hypocrisy and craftiness, said to them: "Why do you thus come to tempt me? Show me the tribute money, and I will answer you." And when they handed him a denarius, he looked at it and said, "Whose image and superscription does this coin bear?" And when they answered him, "Caesar's," Jesus said, "Render to Caesar the things that are Caesar's and render to God the things that are God's."

THE GREAT COMMANDMENT

Then came forward one of the groups of the Pharisees to ask harassing questions, and the spokesman, signaling to Jesus, said: "Master, I am a lawyer, and I would like to ask you which, in your opinion, is the greatest commandment?" Jesus answered: "There is but one commandment, and that one is the greatest of all, and that commandment is: 'Hear O Israel, the Lord our God, the Lord is one; and you shall love the Lord your God with all your heart and with all your soul, with all your mind and with all your strength.' This is the first and great commandment. And the second commandment is like this first; indeed, it springs directly therefrom, and it is: 'You shall love your neighbor as yourself.' There is no other commandment greater than these; on these two commandments hang all the law and the prophets."

When the lawyer perceived that Jesus had answered not only in accordance with the highest concept of Jewish religion, but that he had also answered wisely in the sight of the assembled multitude, he thought it the better part of valor openly to commend the Master's reply. Accordingly, he said: "Of a truth, Master, you have well said that God is one and there is none beside him; and that to love him with all the heart, understanding, and strength, and also to love one's neighbor as one's self, is the first and great commandment; and we are agreed that this great commandment is much more to be regarded than all the burnt offerings and sacrifices." When the lawyer answered thus discreetly, Jesus looked down upon him and said, "My friend, I perceive that you are not far from the kingdom of God."

Jesus spoke the truth when he referred to this lawyer as being "not far from the kingdom," for that very night he went out to the Master's camp near Gethsemane, professed faith in the gospel of the kingdom, and was baptized by Josiah, one of the disciples of Abner.

Two or three other groups of the scribes and Pharisees were present and had intended to ask questions, but they were either disarmed by Jesus' answer to the lawyer, or they were deterred by the discomfiture of all who had undertaken to ensnare him. After this no man dared to ask him another question in public.

When no more questions were forthcoming, and as the noon hour was near, Jesus did not resume his teaching but was content merely to ask the Pharisees and their associates a question. Said Jesus: "Since you ask no more questions, I would like to ask you one. What do you think of the Deliverer? That is, whose son is he?" After a brief pause one of the scribes answered, "The Messiah is the son of David." And since Jesus knew that there had been much debate, even among his own disciples, as to whether or not he was the son of David, he asked this further question: "If the Deliverer is indeed the son of David, how is it that, in the Psalm which you accredit to David, he himself, speaking in the spirit, says, 'The Lord said to my lord, sit on my right hand until I make your enemies the footstool of your feet.' If David calls him Lord, how then can he be his son?" Although the rulers, the scribes, and the chief priests made no reply to this question, they likewise refrained from asking him any more questions in an effort to entangle him. They never answered this question which Jesus put to them, but after the Master's death they attempted to escape the difficulty by changing the interpretation of this Psalm so as to make it refer to Abraham instead of the Messiah. Others sought to escape the dilemma by disallowing that David was the author of this so-called Messianic Psalm. ∎

THE INQUIRING GREEKS

About noontime, as Philip was purchasing supplies for the new camp which was that day being established near Gethsemane, he was accosted by a delegation of strangers, a group of believing Greeks from Alexandria, Athens, and Rome, whose spokesman said to the apostle: "You have been pointed out to us by those who know you; so we come to you, Sir, with the request to see Jesus, your Master." Philip was taken by surprise thus to meet these prominent and inquiring Greek gentiles in the market place, and, since Jesus had so explicitly charged all of the twelve not to engage in any public teaching during the Passover week, he was a bit perplexed as to the right way to handle this matter. He was also disconcerted because these men were foreign gentiles. If they had been Jews or near-by and familiar gentiles, he would not have hesitated so markedly. What he did was this: He asked these Greeks to remain right where they were. As he hastened away, they supposed that he went in search of Jesus, but in reality he hurried off to the home of Joseph, where he knew Andrew and the other apostles were at lunch; and calling Andrew out, he explained the purpose of his coming, and then, accompanied by Andrew, he returned to the waiting Greeks.

The two apostles returned with the Greeks to the home of Joseph, where Jesus received them; and they sat near while he spoke to his apostles and a number of leading disciples assembled at this luncheon. Said Jesus:

"My Father sent me to this world to reveal his loving-kindness to the children of men, but those to whom I first came have refused to receive me. True, indeed, many of you have believed my gospel for yourselves, but the children of Abraham and their leaders are about to reject me, and in so doing they will reject Him who sent me. I have freely proclaimed the gospel of salvation to this people; I have told them of sonship with joy, liberty, and life more abundant in the spirit. My Father has done many wonderful works among these fear-ridden sons of men. But truly did the Prophet Isaiah refer to this people when he wrote: 'Lord, who has believed our teachings? And to whom has the Lord been revealed?' Truly have the leaders of my people deliberately blinded their eyes that they see not, and hardened their hearts lest they believe and be saved. All these years have I sought to heal them of their unbelief that they might be recipients of the Father's eternal salvation. I know that not all have failed me; some of you have indeed believed my message. In this room now are a full score of men who were once members of the Sanhedrin, or who were high in the councils of the nation, albeit even some of you still shrink from open confession of the truth lest they cast you out of the synagogue. Some of you are tempted to love the glory of men more than the glory of God. But I am constrained to show forbearance since I fear for the safety and loyalty of even some of those who have been so long near me, and who have lived so close by my side.

"In this banquet chamber I perceive there are assembled Jews and gentiles in about equal numbers, and I would address you as the first and last of such a group that I may instruct in the affairs of the kingdom before I go to my Father."

THE MIGHTY SPIRIT OF THE FATHER'S REPRESENTATION SPOKE TO JESUS, SAYING: "I HAVE GLORIFIED MY NAME IN YOUR BESTOWALS MANY TIMES, AND I WILL GLORIFY IT ONCE MORE."

These Greeks had been in faithful attendance upon Jesus' teaching in the temple. On Monday evening they had held a conference at the home of Nicodemus, which lasted until dawn, and thirty of them had elected to enter the kingdom.

As Jesus stood before them at this time, he perceived the end of one dispensation and the beginning of another. Turning his attention to the Greeks, the Master said:

"He who believes this gospel, believes not merely in me but in Him who sent me. When you look upon me, you see not only the Son of Man but also Him who sent me. I am the light of the world, and whosoever will believe my teaching shall no longer abide in darkness. If you gentiles will hear me, you shall receive the words of life and shall enter forthwith into the joyous liberty of the truth of sonship with God. If my fellow countrymen, the Jews, choose to reject me and to refuse my teachings, I will not sit in judgment on them, for I came not to judge the world but to offer it salvation. Nevertheless, they who reject me and refuse to receive my teaching shall be brought to judgment in due season by my Father and those whom he has appointed to sit in judgment on such as reject the gift of mercy and the truths of salvation. Remember, all of you, that I speak not of myself, but that I have faithfully declared to you that which the Father commanded I should reveal to the children of men. And these words which the Father directed me to speak to the world are words of divine truth, everlasting mercy, and eternal life.

"But to both Jew and gentile I declare the hour has about come when the Son of Man will be glorified. You well know that, except a grain of wheat falls into the earth and dies, it abides alone; but if it dies in good soil, it springs up again to life and bears much fruit. He who selfishly loves his life stands in danger of losing it; but he who is willing to lay down his life for my sake and the gospel's shall enjoy a more abundant existence on earth and in heaven, life eternal. If you will truly follow me, even after I have gone to my Father, then shall you become my disciples and the sincere servants of your fellow mortals.

"I know my hour is approaching, and I am troubled. I perceive that my people are determined to spurn the kingdom, but I am rejoiced to receive these truth-seeking gentiles who come here today inquiring for the way of light. Nevertheless, my heart aches for my people, and my soul is distraught by that which lies just before me. What shall I say as I look ahead and discern what is about to befall me? Shall I say, Father save me from this awful hour? No! For this very purpose have I come into the world and even to this hour. Rather will I say, and pray that you will join me: Father, glorify your name; your will be done."

When Jesus had thus spoken, and as he paused noticeably, the mighty spirit of the Father's representation spoke to Jesus of Nazareth, saying: "I have glorified my name in your bestowals many times, and I will glorify it once more."

While the Jews and gentiles here assembled heard no voice, they could not fail to discern that the Master had paused in his speaking while a message came to him from some superhuman source. They all said, every man to the one who was by him, "An angel has spoken to him."

Then Jesus continued to speak: "All this has not happened for my sake but for yours. I know of a certainty that the Father will receive me and accept my mission in your behalf, but it is needful that you be encouraged and be made ready for the fiery trial which is just ahead. Let me assure you that victory shall eventually crown our united efforts to enlighten the world and liberate mankind. The old order is bringing itself to judgment; the Prince of this world I have cast down; and all men shall become free by the light of the spirit which I will pour out upon all flesh after I have ascended to my Father in heaven.

"And now I declare to you that I, if I be lifted up on earth and in your lives, will draw all men to myself and into the fellowship of my Father. You have believed that the Deliverer would abide on earth forever, but I declare that the Son of Man will be rejected by men, and that he will go back to the Father. Only a little while will I be with you; only a little time will the living light be among this darkened generation. Walk while you have this light so that the oncoming darkness and confusion may not overtake you. He who walks in the darkness knows not where he goes; but if you will choose to walk in the light, you shall all indeed become liberated sons of God. And now,

[JAMES TISSOT — *Jerusalem, Jerusalem*]

all of you, come with me while we go back to the temple and I speak farewell words to the chief priests, the scribes, the Pharisees, the Sadducees, the Herodians, and the benighted rulers of Israel."

Having thus spoken, Jesus led the way over the narrow streets of Jerusalem back to the temple. They had just heard the Master say that this was to be his farewell discourse in the temple, and they followed him in silence and in deep meditation. ∎

THE LAST TEMPLE DISCOURSE

Shortly after two o'clock on this Tuesday afternoon, Jesus, accompanied by eleven apostles, Joseph of Arimathea, the thirty Greeks, and certain other disciples, arrived at the temple and began the delivery of his last address in the courts of the sacred edifice. This discourse was intended to be his last appeal to the Jewish people and the final indictment of his vehement enemies and would-be destroyers—the scribes, Pharisees, Sadducees, and the chief rulers of Israel. Throughout the forenoon the various groups had had an opportunity to question Jesus; this afternoon no one asked him a question.

As the Master began to speak, the temple court was quiet and orderly. The money-changers and the merchandisers had not dared again to enter the temple since Jesus and the aroused multitude had driven them out the previous day. Before beginning the discourse, Jesus tenderly looked down upon this audience which was so soon to hear his farewell public address of mercy to mankind coupled with his last denunciation of the false teachers and the bigoted rulers of the Jews.

"This long time have I been with you, going up and down in the land proclaiming the Father's love for the children of men, and many have seen the light and, by faith, have entered into the kingdom of heaven. In connection with this teaching and preaching the Father has done many wonderful works, even to the resurrection of the dead. Many sick and afflicted have been made whole because they believed; but all of this proclamation of truth and healing of disease has not opened the eyes of those who refuse to see light, those who are determined to reject this gospel of the kingdom.

"In every manner consistent with doing my Father's will, I and my apostles have done our utmost to live in peace with our brethren, to conform with the reasonable requirements of the laws of Moses and the traditions of Israel. We have persistently sought peace, but the leaders of Israel will not have it. By rejecting the truth of God and the light of heaven, they are aligning themselves on the side of error and darkness. There cannot be peace between light and darkness, between life and death, between truth and error.

"Many of you have dared to believe my teachings and have already entered into the joy and liberty of the consciousness of sonship with God. And you will bear me witness that I have offered this same sonship with God to all the Jewish nation, even to these very men who now seek my destruction. And even now would my Father receive these blinded teachers and these hypocritical leaders if they would only turn to him and accept his mercy. Even now it is not too late for this people to receive the word of heaven and to welcome the Son of Man.

"My Father has long dealt in mercy with this people. Generation after generation have we sent our prophets to teach and warn them, and generation after generation have they killed these heaven-sent teachers. And now do your willful high priests and stubborn rulers go right on doing this same thing. As Herod brought about the death of John, you likewise now make ready to destroy the Son of Man.

"As long as there is a chance that the Jews will

"WOE UPON YOU, FALSE TEACHERS, BLIND GUIDES! WHAT CAN BE EXPECTED OF A NATION WHEN THE BLIND LEAD THE BLIND? THEY BOTH SHALL STUMBLE INTO THE PIT OF DESTRUCTION."

turn to my Father and seek salvation, the God of Abraham, Isaac, and Jacob will keep his hands of mercy outstretched toward you; but when you have once filled up your cup of impenitence, and when once you have finally rejected my Father's mercy, this nation will be left to its own counsels, and it shall speedily come to an inglorious end. This people was called to become the light of the world, to show forth the spiritual glory of a God-knowing race, but you have so far departed from the fulfillment of your divine privileges that your leaders are about to commit the supreme folly of all the ages in that they are on the verge of finally rejecting the gift of God to all men and for all ages—the revelation of the love of the Father in heaven for all his creatures on earth.

"And when you do once reject this revelation of God to man, the kingdom of heaven shall be given to other peoples, to those who will receive it with joy and gladness. In the name of the Father who sent me, I solemnly warn you that you are about to lose your position in the world as the standard-bearers of eternal truth and the custodians of the divine law. I am just now offering you your last chance to come forward and repent, to signify your intention to seek God with all your hearts and to enter, like little children and by sincere faith, into the security and salvation of the kingdom of heaven.

"My Father has long worked for your salvation, and I came down to live among you and personally show you the way. Many of both the Jews and the Samaritans, and even the gentiles, have believed the gospel of the kingdom, but those who should be first to come forward and accept the light of heaven have steadfastly refused to believe the revelation of the truth of God—God revealed in man and man uplifted to God.

"This afternoon my apostles stand here before you in silence, but you shall soon hear their voices ringing out with the call to salvation and with the urge to unite with the heavenly kingdom as the sons of the living God. And now I call to witness these, my disciples and believers in the gospel of the kingdom, as well as the unseen messengers by their sides, that I have once more offered Israel and her rulers deliverance and salvation. But you all behold how the Father's mercy is slighted and how the messengers of truth are rejected. Nevertheless, I admonish you that these scribes and Pharisees still sit in Moses' seat, and therefore, until the Most Highs who rule in the kingdoms of men shall finally overthrow this nation and destroy the place of these rulers, I bid you co-operate with these elders in Israel. You are not required to unite with them in their plans to destroy the Son of Man, but in everything related to the peace of Israel you are to be subject to them. In all these matters do whatsoever they bid you and observe the essentials of the law but do not pattern after their evil works. Remember, this is the sin of these rulers: They say that which is good, but they do it not. You well know how these leaders bind heavy burdens on your shoulders, burdens grievous to bear, and that they will not lift as much as one finger to help you bear these weighty burdens. They have oppressed you with ceremonies and enslaved you by traditions.

"Furthermore, these self-centered rulers delight in doing their good works so that they will be seen by men. They make broad their phylacteries and enlarge the borders of their official robes. They crave the chief places at the feasts and demand the chief seats in the synagogues. They covet laudatory salutations in the market places and desire to be called rabbi by all men. And even while they seek all this honor from men, they secretly lay hold of widows' houses and take profit from the services of the sacred temple. For a pretense these hypocrites make long prayers in public and give alms to attract the notice of their fellows.

"While you should honor your rulers and reverence your teachers, you should call no man Father in the spiritual sense, for there is one who is your Father, even God. Neither should you seek to lord it over your brethren in the kingdom. Remember, I have taught you that he who would be greatest among you should become the server of all. If you presume to exalt yourselves before God, you will certainly be humbled; but whoso truly humbles himself will surely be exalted. Seek in your daily lives, not self-glorification, but the glory of God. Intelligently subordinate your own wills to the will of the Father in heaven.

"Mistake not my words. I bear no malice toward these chief priests and rulers who even now seek my destruction; I have no ill will for these scribes and Pharisees who reject my teachings. I know that many of you believe in secret, and I know you will openly profess your allegiance to the kingdom when my hour comes. But how will your rabbis justify themselves since they profess to talk with God and then presume to reject and destroy him who comes to reveal the Father to the worlds?

"Woe upon you, scribes and Pharisees, hypocrites! You would shut the doors of the kingdom of heaven against sincere men because they happen to be unlearned in the ways of your teaching. You refuse to enter the kingdom and at the same time do everything within your power to prevent all others from entering. You stand with your backs to the doors of salvation and fight with all who would enter therein.

"Woe upon you, scribes and Pharisees, hypocrites that you are! for you do indeed encompass land and sea to make one proselyte, and when you have succeeded, you are not content until you have made him twofold worse than he was as a child of the heathen.

"Woe upon you, chief priests and rulers who lay hold of the property of the poor and demand heavy dues of those who would serve God as they think Moses ordained! You who refuse to show mercy, can you hope for mercy in the worlds to come?

"Woe upon you, false teachers, blind guides! What can be expected of a nation when the blind lead the blind? They both shall stumble into the pit of destruction.

"Woe upon you who dissimulate when you take an oath! You are tricksters since you teach that a man may swear by the temple and break his oath, but that whoso swears by the gold in the temple must remain bound. You are all fools and blind. You are not even consistent in your dishonesty, for which is the greater, the gold or the temple which has supposedly sanctified the gold? You also teach that, if a man swears by the altar, it is nothing; but that, if one swears by the gift that is upon the altar, then shall he be held as a debtor. Again are you blind to the truth, for which is the greater, the gift or the altar which sanctifies the gift? How can you justify such hypocrisy and dishonesty in the sight of the God of heaven?

"Woe upon you, scribes and Pharisees and all other hypocrites who make sure that they tithe mint, anise, and cumin and at the same time disregard the weightier matters of the law—faith, mercy, and judgment! Within reason, the one you ought to have done but not to have left the other undone. You are truly blind guides and dumb teachers; you strain out the gnat and swallow the camel.

"Woe upon you, scribes, Pharisees, and hypocrites! for you are scrupulous to cleanse the outside of the cup and the platter, but within there remains the filth of extortion, excesses, and deception. You are spiritually blind. Do you not recognize how much better it would be first to cleanse the inside of the cup, and then that which spills over would of itself cleanse the outside? You wicked reprobates! you make the outward performances of your religion to conform with the letter of your interpretation of Moses' law while your souls are steeped in iniquity and filled with murder.

"Woe upon all of you who reject truth and spurn mercy! Many of you are like whited sepulchres, which outwardly appear beautiful but within are full of dead men's bones and all sorts of uncleanness. Even so do you who knowingly reject the counsel of God appear outwardly to men as holy and righteous, but inwardly your hearts are filled with hypocrisy and iniquity.

"Woe upon you, false guides of a nation! Over yonder have you built a monument to the martyred prophets of old, while you plot to destroy Him of whom they spoke. You garnish the tombs

STATUS OF INDIVIDUAL JEWS

The fact that the spiritual leaders and the religious teachers of the Jewish nation onetime rejected the teachings of Jesus and conspired to bring about his cruel death, does not in any manner affect the status of any individual Jew in his standing before God. And it should not cause those who profess to be followers of the Christ to be prejudiced against the Jew as a fellow mortal. The Jews, as a nation, as a sociopolitical group, paid in full the terrible price of rejecting the Prince of Peace. Long since they ceased to be the spiritual torchbearers of divine truth to the races of mankind, but this constitutes no valid reason why the individual descendants of these long-ago Jews should be made to suffer the persecutions which have been visited upon them by intolerant, unworthy, and bigoted professed followers of Jesus of Nazareth, who was, himself, a Jew by natural birth.

Many times has this unreasoning and un-Christlike hatred and persecution of modern Jews terminated in the suffering and death of some innocent and unoffending Jewish individual whose very ancestors, in the times of Jesus, heartily accepted his gospel and presently died unflinchingly for that truth which they so wholeheartedly believed. What a shudder of horror passes over the onlooking celestial beings as they behold the professed followers of Jesus indulge themselves in persecuting, harassing, and even murdering the later-day descendants of Peter, Philip, Matthew, and others of the Palestinian Jews who so gloriously yielded up their lives as the first martyrs of the gospel of the heavenly kingdom!

How cruel and unreasoning to compel innocent children to suffer for the sins of their progenitors, misdeeds of which they are wholly ignorant, and for which they could in no way be responsible! And to do such wicked deeds in the name of one who taught his disciples to love even their enemies! It has become necessary, in this recital of the life of Jesus, to portray the manner in which certain of his fellow Jews rejected him and conspired to bring about his ignominious death; but we would warn all who read this narrative that the presentation of such a historical recital in no way justifies the unjust hatred, nor condones the unfair attitude of mind, which so many professed Christians have maintained toward individual Jews for many centuries. Kingdom believers, those who follow the teachings of Jesus, must cease to mistreat the individual Jew as one who is guilty of the rejection and crucifixion of Jesus. The Father and his Creator Son have never ceased to love the Jews. God is no respecter of persons, and salvation is for the Jew as well as for the gentile.

> "I SAY THAT YOU WILL NO MORE SEE ME TEACHING IN THE TEMPLE.
> MY WORK FOR YOU IS DONE. BEHOLD, I NOW GO FORTH WITH MY
> CHILDREN, AND YOUR HOUSE IS LEFT TO YOU DESOLATE!"

of the righteous and flatter yourselves that, had you lived in the days of your fathers, you would not have killed the prophets; and then in the face of such self-righteous thinking you make ready to slay him of whom the prophets spoke, the Son of Man. Inasmuch as you do these things, are you witness to yourselves that you are the wicked sons of them who slew the prophets. Go on, then, and fill up the cup of your condemnation to the full!

"Woe upon you, children of evil! John did truly call you the offspring of vipers, and I ask how can you escape the judgment that John pronounced upon you?

"But even now I offer you in my Father's name mercy and forgiveness; even now I proffer the loving hand of eternal fellowship. My Father has sent you the wise men and the prophets; some you have persecuted and others you have killed. Then appeared John proclaiming the coming of the Son of Man, and him you destroyed after many had believed his teaching. And now you make ready to shed more innocent blood. Do you not comprehend that a terrible day of reckoning will come when the Judge of all the earth shall require of this people an accounting for the way they have rejected, persecuted, and destroyed these messengers of heaven? Do you not understand that you must account for all of this righteous blood, from the first prophet killed down to the times of Zechariah, who was slain between the sanctuary and the altar? And if you go on in your evil ways, this accounting may be required of this very generation.

"O Jerusalem and the children of Abraham, you who have stoned the prophets and killed the teachers that were sent to you, even now would I gather your children together as a hen gathers her chickens under her wings, but you will not!

"And now I take leave of you. You have heard my message and have made your decision. Those who have believed my gospel are even now safe within the kingdom of God. To you who have chosen to reject the gift of God, I say that you will no more see me teaching in the temple. My work for you is done. Behold, I now go forth with my children, and your house is left to you desolate!"

And then the Master beckoned his followers to depart from the temple.　∎

FORETELLING THE END OF JERUSALEM

This Tuesday afternoon, as Jesus and the apostles passed out of the temple on their way to the Gethsemane camp, Matthew, calling attention to the temple construction, said: "Master, observe what manner of buildings these are. See the massive stones and the beautiful adornment; can it be that these buildings are to be destroyed?" As they went on toward Olivet, Jesus said: "You see these stones and this massive temple; verily, verily, I say to you: In the days soon to come there shall not be left one stone upon another. They shall all be thrown down." These remarks depicting the destruction of the sacred temple aroused the curiosity of the apostles as they walked along behind the Master; they could conceive of no event short of the end of the world which would occasion the destruction of the temple.

As they turned to leave the road leading on to Bethany, they observed the temple, glorified by the rays of the setting sun; and while they tarried on the mount, they saw the lights of the city appear and beheld the beauty of the illuminated temple; and there, under the mellow light of the full moon, Jesus and the twelve sat down. The Master talked with them, and presently Nathaniel asked this question: "Tell us, Master, how shall we know when these events are about to come to pass?"

In answering Nathaniel's question, Jesus said: "Yes, I will tell you about the times when this people shall have filled up the cup of their iniquity; when justice shall swiftly descend upon this city of our fathers. I am about to leave you; I go to the Father. After I leave you, take heed that no man deceive you, for many will come as deliverers and will lead many astray. When you hear of wars and rumors of wars, be not troubled, for though all these things will happen, the end of Jerusalem is not yet at hand. You should not be perturbed by famines or earthquakes; neither should you be concerned when you are delivered up to the civil authorities and are persecuted for the sake of the gospel. You will be thrown out of the synagogue and put in prison for my sake, and some of you will be killed. When you are brought up before governors and rulers, it shall be for a testimony of your faith and to show your steadfastness in the gospel of the kingdom. And when you stand before judges, be not anxious

beforehand as to what you should say, for the spirit will teach you in that very hour what you should answer your adversaries. In these days of travail, even your own kinsfolk, under the leadership of those who have rejected the Son of Man, will deliver you up to prison and death. For a time you may be hated by all men for my sake, but even in these persecutions I will not forsake you; my spirit will not desert you. Be patient! doubt not that this gospel of the kingdom will triumph over all enemies and, eventually, be proclaimed to all nations."

Jesus paused while he looked down upon the city. The Master realized that the rejection of the spiritual concept of the Messiah, the determination to cling persistently and blindly to the material mission of the expected deliverer, would presently bring the Jews in direct conflict with the powerful Roman armies, and that such a contest could only result in the final and complete overthrow of the Jewish nation.

Then Andrew inquired: "But, Master, if the Holy City and the temple are to be destroyed, and if you are not here to direct us, when should we forsake Jerusalem?" Said Jesus: "You may remain in the city after I have gone, even through these times of travail and bitter persecution, but when you finally see Jerusalem being encompassed by the Roman armies after the revolt of the false prophets, then will you know that her desolation is at hand; then must you flee to the mountains. Let none who are in the city and around about tarry to save aught, neither let those who are outside dare to enter therein. There will be great tribulation, for these will be the days of gentile vengeance. And after you have deserted the city,

SAFEGUARDING THE FLOCK

Since Jerusalem was to become the cradle of the early gospel movement, Jesus did not want its teachers and preachers to perish in the terrible overthrow of the Jewish people in connection with the destruction of Jerusalem; wherefore did he give these instructions to his followers. Jesus was much concerned lest some of his disciples become involved in these soon-coming revolts and so perish in the downfall of Jerusalem.

[FRANCESCO HAYEZ — *The Destruction of the Temple of Jerusalem*]

this disobedient people will fall by the edge of the sword and will be led captive into all nations; and so shall Jerusalem be trodden down by the gentiles. In the meantime, I warn you, be not deceived. If any man comes to you, saying, 'Behold, here is the Deliverer,' or 'Behold, there is he,' believe it not, for many false teachers will arise and many will be led astray; but you should not be deceived, for I have told you all this beforehand."

Even after this explicit warning, in their minds these Jews were determined to connect the destruction of the temple with the "end of the world." They believed this New Jerusalem would fill all Palestine; that the end of the world would be followed by the immediate appearance of the "new heavens

and the new earth." And so it was not strange that Peter should say: "Master, we know that all things will pass away when the new heavens and the new earth appear, but how shall we know when you will return to bring all this about?"

When Jesus heard this, he was thoughtful for some time and then said: "You ever err since you always try to attach the new teaching to the old; you are determined to misunderstand all my teaching; you insist on interpreting the gospel in accordance with your established beliefs. Nevertheless, I will try to enlighten you."

THE SECOND COMING

On several occasions Jesus had made statements

which led his hearers to infer that, while he intended presently to leave this world, he would most certainly return to consummate the work of the heavenly kingdom. The doctrine of the second coming of Christ thus became early incorporated into the teachings of the Christians, and almost every subsequent generation of disciples has devoutly believed this truth and has confidently looked forward to his sometime coming.

If they were to part with their Master and Teacher, how much more did these first disciples and the apostles grasp at this promise to return, and they lost no time in associating the predicted destruction of Jerusalem with this promised second coming. And they continued thus to interpret his words notwithstanding that, throughout this evening of instruction on Mount Olivet, the Master took particular pains to prevent just such a mistake.

In further answer to Peter's question, Jesus said: "Why do you still look for the Son of Man to sit upon the throne of David and expect that the material dreams of the Jews will be fulfilled? Have I not told you all these years that my kingdom is not of this world? The things which you now look down upon are coming to an end, but this will be a new beginning out of which the gospel of the kingdom will go to all the world and this salvation will spread to all peoples. And when the kingdom shall have come to its full fruition, be assured that the Father in heaven will not fail to visit you with an enlarged revelation of truth and an enhanced demonstration of righteousness, even as he has already bestowed upon this world him who became the prince of darkness, and then Adam, who was followed by Melchizedek, and in these days, the Son of Man. And so will my Father continue to manifest his mercy and show forth his love, even to this dark and evil world. So also will I, after my Father has invested me with all power and

[C. MICHAEL DUDASH — *The Master Teacher*]

"BE OF GOOD COURAGE, FOR I WILL SOMETIME RETURN. IN THE MEANTIME, MY SPIRIT OF THE TRUTH OF A UNIVERSE SHALL COMFORT AND GUIDE YOU."

authority, continue to follow your fortunes and to guide in the affairs of the kingdom by the presence of my spirit, who shall shortly be poured out upon all flesh. Even though I shall thus be present with you in spirit, I also promise that I will sometime return to this world, where I have lived this life in the flesh and achieved the experience of simultaneously revealing God to man and leading man to God. Very soon must I leave you and take up the work the Father has intrusted to my hands, but be of good courage, for I will sometime return. In the meantime, my Spirit of the Truth of a universe shall comfort and guide you.

"You behold me now in weakness and in the flesh, but when I return, it shall be with power and in the spirit. The eye of flesh beholds the Son of Man in the flesh, but only the eye of the spirit will behold the Son of Man glorified by the Father and appearing on earth in his own name.

"But the times of the reappearing of the Son of Man are known only in the councils of Paradise; not even the angels of heaven know when this will occur. However, you should understand that, when this gospel of the kingdom shall have been proclaimed to all the world for the salvation of all peoples, and when the fullness of the age has come to pass, the Father will send you another dispensational bestowal, or else the Son of Man will return to adjudge the age.

"And now concerning the travail of Jerusalem, about which I have spoken to you, even this generation will not pass away until my words are fulfilled; but concerning the times of the coming again of the Son of Man, no one in heaven or on earth may presume to speak. But you should be wise regarding the ripening of an age; you should be alert to discern the signs of the times. You know when the fig tree shows its tender branches and puts forth its leaves that summer is near. Likewise, when the world has passed through the long winter of material-mindedness and you discern the coming of the spiritual springtime of a new dispensation, should you know that the summertime of a new visitation draws near.

"But what is the significance of this teaching having to do with the coming of the Sons of God? Do you not perceive that, when each of you is called to lay down his life struggle and pass through the portal of death, you stand in the immediate presence of judgment, and that you are face to face with the facts of a new dispensation of service in the eternal plan of the infinite Father? What the whole world must face as a literal fact at the end of an age, you, as individuals, must each most certainly face as a personal experience when you reach the end of your natural life and thereby pass on to be confronted with the conditions and demands inherent in the next revelation of the eternal progression of the Father's kingdom."

As these thirteen men resumed their journey toward the camp, the apostles were speechless and under great emotional tension. Judas had finally confirmed his decision to abandon his associates. It was a late hour when David Zebedee, John Mark, and a number of the leading disciples welcomed Jesus and the twelve to the new camp, but the apostles did not want to sleep; they wanted to know more about the destruction of Jerusalem, the Master's departure, and the end of the world.

As they gathered about the campfire, some twenty of them, Thomas asked: "Since you are to return to finish the work of the kingdom, what should be our attitude while you are away on the Father's business?" As Jesus looked them over by the firelight, he answered:

"And even you, Thomas, fail to comprehend what I have been saying. Have I not all this time taught you that your connection with the kingdom is spiritual and individual, wholly a matter of personal experience in the spirit by the faith-realization that you are a son of God? What more shall I say? The downfall of nations, the crash of empires, the destruction of the unbelieving Jews, the end of an age, even the end of the world, what have these things to do with one who believes this gospel, and who has hid his life in the surety of the eternal kingdom? You who are God-knowing and gospel-believing have already received the assurances of eternal life. Since your lives have been lived in the spirit and for the Father, nothing can be of serious concern to you. Kingdom builders, the accredited citizens of the heavenly worlds, are not to be disturbed by temporal upheavals or perturbed by terrestrial cataclysms. What does it matter to you who believe this gospel of the kingdom if nations overturn, the age ends, or all things visible crash, since you know that your life is the gift of the Son, and that it is eternally secure in the Father? Having lived the temporal life by faith and having yielded the fruits of the spirit as the righteousness of loving service for your fellows, you can confidently look forward to the next step in the eternal career with the same survival faith that has carried you through your first and earthly adventure in sonship with God.

"Each generation of believers should carry on their work, in view of the possible return of the Son of Man, exactly as each individual believer carries forward his lifework in view of inevitable and ever-impending natural death. When you have by faith once established yourself as a son of God, nothing else matters as regards the surety of survival. But make no mistake! this survival faith is a living faith, and it increasingly manifests the fruits of that divine spirit which first inspired it in the human heart.

"Freely have you received; therefore freely should you give of the truth of heaven, and in the giving will this truth multiply and show forth the increasing light of saving grace, even as you minister it." ∎

ONE DAY ALONE WITH GOD

W hen the work of teaching the people did not press them, it was the custom of Jesus and his apostles to rest from their labors each Wednesday. After breakfast the Master informed Andrew that he intended to be absent for the day and suggested that the apostles be permitted to spend the time in accordance with their own choosing, except that under no circumstances should they go within the gates of Jerusalem.

When Jesus made ready to go into the hills alone, David Zebedee accosted him, saying: "You well know, Master, that the Pharisees and rulers seek to destroy you, and yet you make ready to go alone into the hills. To do this is folly; I will therefore send three men with you well prepared to see that no harm befalls you." Jesus looked over the three well-armed and stalwart Galileans and said to David: "You mean well, but you err in that you fail to understand that the Son of Man needs no one to defend him. No man will lay hands on me until that hour when I am ready to lay down my life in conformity to my Father's will. These men may not accompany me. I desire to go alone, that I may commune with the Father."

THIS EVENT HAS BECOME KNOWN ON HIGH AS "THE DAY
WHICH A YOUNG MAN SPENT WITH GOD IN THE HILLS."
FOREVER THIS OCCASION EXEMPLIFIES THE WILLINGNESS
OF THE CREATOR TO FELLOWSHIP THE CREATURE.

Upon hearing these words, David and his armed guards withdrew; but as Jesus started off alone, John Mark came forward with a small basket containing food and water and suggested that, if he intended to be away all day, he might find himself hungry. The Master smiled on John and reached down to take the basket.

As Jesus was about to take the lunch basket from John's hand, the young man ventured to say: "But, Master, you may set the basket down while you turn aside to pray and go on without it. Besides, if I should go along to carry the lunch, you would be more free to worship, and I will surely be silent. I will ask no questions and will stay by the basket when you go apart by yourself to pray."

While making this speech, the temerity of which astonished some of the near-by listeners, John had made bold to hold on to the basket. There they stood, both John and Jesus holding the basket. Presently the Master let go and, looking down on the lad, said: "Since with all your heart you crave to go with me, it shall not be denied you. We will go off by ourselves and have a good visit. You may ask me any question that arises in your heart, and we will comfort and console each other. You may start out carrying the lunch, and when you grow weary, I will help you. Follow on with me."

Jesus did not return to the camp that evening until after sunset. The Master spent this last day of quiet on earth visiting with this truth-hungry youth and talking with his Paradise Father. This event has become known on high as "the day which a young man spent with God in the hills." Forever this occasion exemplifies the willingness of the Creator to fellowship the creature. Even a youth, if the desire of the heart is really supreme, can command the attention and enjoy the loving companionship of the God of a universe, actually experience the unforgettable ecstasy of being alone with God in the hills, and for a whole day. And such was the unique experience of John Mark on this Wednesday in the hills of Judea.

Jesus visited much with John, talking freely about the affairs of this world and the next. John told Jesus how much he regretted that he had not been old enough to be one of the apostles and expressed his great appreciation that he had been permitted to follow on with them since their first preaching at the Jordan ford near Jericho. Jesus warned the lad not to become discouraged by impending events and assured him he would live to become a mighty messenger of the kingdom.

John Mark was thrilled by the memory of this day with Jesus in the hills, but he never forgot the Master's final admonition, spoken just as they were about to return to the Gethsemane camp, when he said: "Well, John, we have had a good visit, a real day of rest, but see to it that you tell no man the things which I told you." And John Mark never did reveal anything that transpired on this day which he spent with Jesus in the hills.

Throughout the few remaining hours of Jesus' earth life John Mark never permitted the Master for long to get out of his sight. Always was the lad in hiding near by; he slept only when Jesus slept.

Shortly after Jesus and John Mark left the camp, Judas Iscariot disappeared from among his brethren, not returning until late in the afternoon. This confused and discontented apostle, notwithstanding his Master's specific request to refrain from entering Jerusalem, went in haste to keep his appointment with Jesus' enemies at the home of Caiaphas the high priest to arrange for the betrayal.

Judas returned to his associates at the camp intoxicated with thoughts of grandeur and glory such as he had not had for many a day. He had enlisted with Jesus hoping to become a great man in the new kingdom. He at last realized that there

[DEL PARSON — *One Day Alone with God* (detail)]

was to be no new kingdom such as he had anticipated. But he rejoiced in being so sagacious as to trade off his disappointment in failing to achieve glory in an anticipated new kingdom for the immediate realization of honor and reward in the old order, which he now believed would survive, and which he was certain would destroy Jesus and all that he stood for. ■

THE LAST SUPPER

Jesus planned to spend this Thursday, his last free day on earth as a divine Son incarnated in the flesh, with his apostles and a few loyal and devoted disciples. Soon after the breakfast hour on this beautiful morning, the Master led them to a secluded spot a short distance above their camp and there taught them many new truths. Although Jesus delivered other discourses to the apostles during the early evening hours of the day, this talk of Thursday forenoon was his farewell address to the combined camp group of apostles and chosen disciples, both Jews and gentiles. The twelve were all present save Judas. Peter and several of the apostles remarked about his absence, and some of them thought Jesus had sent him into the city to attend to some matter, probably to arrange the details of their forthcoming celebration of the Passover. Judas did not return to the camp until midafternoon, a short time before Jesus led the twelve into Jerusalem to partake of the Last Supper.

PREPARATIONS FOR THE SUPPER

About this time Philip came to the Master and asked: "Master, seeing that the time of the Passover draws near, where would you have us prepare to eat it?" And when Jesus heard Philip's question, he answered: "Go and bring Peter and John, and I will give you directions concerning the supper we will eat together this night. As for the Passover, that you will have to consider after we have first done this."

Said Jesus to the three: "Go immediately into Jerusalem, and as you enter the gate, you will meet a man bearing a water pitcher. He will speak to you, and then shall you follow him. When he leads you to a certain house, go in after him and ask of the good man of that house, 'Where is the guest chamber wherein the Master is to eat supper with his apostles?' And when you have thus inquired, this householder will show you a large upper room all furnished and ready for us."

When the apostles reached the city, they met the man with the water pitcher near the gate and followed on after him to the home of John Mark, where the lad's father met them and showed them the upper room in readiness for the evening meal.

It was about half past four o'clock when the three apostles returned and informed Jesus that everything was in readiness for the supper. The Master immediately prepared to lead his twelve apostles over the trail to the Bethany road and on into Jerusalem. And this was the last journey he ever made with all twelve of them.

Seeking again to avoid the crowds passing through the Kidron valley back and forth between Gethsemane Park and Jerusalem, Jesus and the twelve walked over the western brow of Mount Olivet to meet the road leading from Bethany down to the city. As they drew near the place where Jesus had tarried the previous evening to discourse on the destruction of Jerusalem, they unconsciously paused while they stood and looked down in silence upon the city.

None of the apostles, save three, knew where they were going as they made their way along the narrow streets in the approaching darkness. The crowds jostled them, but no one recognized them nor knew that the Son of God was passing by on his way to the last mortal rendezvous with his chosen ambassadors of the kingdom. And neither did the apostles know that one of their own number had already entered into a conspiracy to betray the Master into the hands of his enemies.

After receiving the greetings of welcome extended by the father and mother of John Mark, the apostles went immediately to the upper chamber while Jesus lingered behind to talk with the Mark family.

It had been understood beforehand that the Master was to celebrate this occasion alone with his twelve apostles; therefore no servants were provided to wait upon them.

When the apostles had been shown upstairs by John Mark, they beheld a large and commodious chamber, which was completely furnished for the supper, and observed that the bread, wine, water, and herbs were all in readiness on one end of the table. Except for the end on which rested the bread and wine, this long table was surrounded by thirteen reclining couches, just such as would be provided for the celebration of the Passover in a well-to-do Jewish household.

As the twelve entered this upper chamber, they noticed, just inside the door, the pitchers of water, the basins, and towels for laving their dusty feet; and since no servant had been provided to render this service, the apostles began to look at one another as soon as John Mark had left them, and each began to think within himself, Who shall wash our feet? And each likewise thought that it would not be he who would thus seem to act as the servant of the others.

As they stood there, debating in their hearts, they surveyed the seating arrangement of the table, taking note of the higher divan of the host with one couch on the right and eleven arranged around the table on up to opposite this second seat of honor on the host's right.

They expected the Master to arrive any moment, but they were in a quandary as to whether they should seat themselves or await his coming and depend on him to assign them their places. While they hesitated, Judas stepped over to the seat of honor, at the left of the host, and signified that he intended there to recline as the preferred guest. This act of Judas immediately stirred up a heated dispute among the other apostles. Judas had no sooner seized the seat of honor than John Zebedee laid claim to the next preferred seat, the one on the right of the host. Simon Peter was so enraged at this assumption of choice positions by Judas and John that, as the other angry apostles looked on, he marched clear around the table and took his place on the lowest couch, the end of the seating order and just opposite to that chosen by John Zebedee. Since others had seized the high seats, Peter thought to choose the lowest, and he did this, not merely in protest against the unseemly pride of his brethren, but with the hope that Jesus, when he should come and see him in the place of least honor, would call him up to a higher one, thus displacing one who had presumed to honor himself.

With the highest and the lowest positions thus occupied, the rest of the apostles chose places, some near Judas and some near Peter, until all were located. They were seated about the U-shaped table on these reclining divans in the following

JOHN MARK'S SECRET

The final meal of Jesus and the apostles at the home of John Mark was the result of an understanding arrived at between the Master and the young disciple during the afternoon of the preceding day when they were alone in the hills. Jesus wanted to be sure he would have this one last meal undisturbed with his apostles, and believing if Judas knew beforehand of their place of meeting he might arrange with his enemies to take him, he made this secret arrangement with John Mark. In this way Judas did not learn of their place of meeting until later on when he arrived there in company with Jesus and the other apostles.

order: on the right of the Master, John; on the left, Judas, Simon Zelotes, Matthew, James Zebedee, Andrew, the Alpheus twins, Philip, Nathaniel, Thomas, and Simon Peter.

They are gathered to celebrate, at least in spirit, an institution which antedated even Moses and referred to the times when their fathers were slaves in Egypt. This supper is their last rendezvous with Jesus, and even in such a solemn setting, under the leadership of Judas the apostles are led once more to give way to their old predilection for honor, preference, and personal exaltation.

They were still engaged in voicing angry recriminations when the Master appeared in the doorway, where he hesitated a moment as a look of disappointment slowly crept over his face. Without comment he went to his place, and he did not disturb their seating arrangement.

They were now ready to begin the supper, except that their feet were still unwashed, and they were in anything but a pleasant frame of mind. When the Master arrived, they were still engaged in making uncomplimentary remarks about one another, to say nothing of the thoughts of some who had sufficient emotional control to refrain from publicly expressing their feelings.

For a few moments after the Master had gone to his place, not a word was spoken. Jesus looked them all over and, relieving the tension with a smile, said: "I have greatly desired to eat this Passover with you. I wanted to eat with you once more before I suffered, and realizing that my hour has come, I arranged to have this supper with you tonight, for, as concerns the morrow, we are all in the hands of the Father, whose will I have come to execute. I shall not again eat with you until you sit down with me in the kingdom which my Father will give me when I have finished that for which he sent me into this world."

After the wine and the water had been mixed, they brought the cup to Jesus, who, when he had received it from the hand of Thaddeus, held it while he offered thanks. And when he had finished offering thanks, he said: "Take this cup and divide it among yourselves and, when you partake of it, realize that I shall not again drink with you the fruit of the vine since this is our last supper. When we sit down again in this manner, it will be in the kingdom to come."

Jesus began thus to talk to his apostles because he knew that his hour had come. He understood that the time had come when he was to return to the Father, and that his work on earth was almost finished. The Master knew he had revealed the Father's love on earth and had shown forth his mercy to mankind, and that he had completed that for which he came into the world, even to the receiving of all power and authority in heaven and on earth. Likewise, he knew Judas Iscariot had fully made up his mind to deliver him that night into the hands of his enemies. He fully realized that this traitorous betrayal was the work of Judas, but that it also pleased Lucifer, Satan, and Caligastia the prince of darkness. But he feared none of those who sought his spiritual overthrow any more than he feared those who sought to accomplish his physical death. The Master had but one anxiety, and that was for the safety and salvation of his chosen followers. And so, with the full knowledge that the Father had put all things under his authority, the Master now prepared to enact the parable of brotherly love.

WASHING THE APOSTLES' FEET

After drinking the first cup of the Passover, it was the Jewish custom for the host to arise from the table and wash his hands. Later on in the meal and after the second cup, all of the guests likewise rose up and washed their hands. Since the apostles knew that their Master never observed these rites of ceremonial hand washing, they were very curious to know what he intended to do when, after they had partaken of this first cup, he arose from

AND THEIR CURIOSITY GREW INTO ASTONISHMENT AS THEY SAW THE MASTER REMOVE HIS OUTER GARMENT, GIRD HIMSELF WITH A TOWEL, AND BEGIN TO POUR WATER INTO A FOOT BASIN.

the table and silently made his way over to near the door, where the water pitchers, basins, and towels had been placed. And their curiosity grew into astonishment as they saw the Master remove his outer garment, gird himself with a towel, and begin to pour water into one of the foot basins. Imagine the amazement of these twelve men, who had so recently refused to wash one another's feet, and who had engaged in such unseemly disputes about positions of honor at the table, when they saw him make his way around the unoccupied end of the table to the lowest seat of the feast, where Simon Peter reclined, and, kneeling down in the attitude of a servant, make ready to wash Simon's feet. As the Master knelt, all twelve arose as one man to their feet; even the traitorous Judas so far forgot his infamy for a moment as to arise with his fellow apostles in this expression of surprise, respect, and utter amazement.

There stood Simon Peter, looking down into the upturned face of his Master. Jesus said nothing; it was not necessary that he should speak. His attitude plainly revealed that he was minded to wash Simon Peter's feet. Notwithstanding his frailties of the flesh, Peter loved the Master. This Galilean fisherman was the first human being wholeheartedly to believe in the divinity of Jesus *and* to make full and public confession of that belief. And Peter had never since really doubted the divine nature of the Master. Since Peter so revered and honored Jesus in his heart, it was not strange that his soul resented the thought of Jesus' kneeling there before him in the attitude of a menial servant and proposing to wash his feet as

would a slave. When Peter presently collected his wits sufficiently to address the Master, he spoke the heart feelings of all his fellow apostles.

After a few moments of this great embarrassment, Peter said, "Master, do you really mean to wash my feet?" And then, looking up into Peter's face, Jesus said: "You may not fully understand what I am about to do, but hereafter you will know the meaning of all these things." Then Simon Peter, drawing a long breath, said, "Master, you shall never wash my feet!" And each of the apostles nodded their approval of Peter's firm declaration of refusal to allow Jesus thus to humble himself before them.

The dramatic appeal of this unusual scene at first touched the heart of even Judas Iscariot; but when his vainglorious intellect passed judgment upon the spectacle, he concluded that this gesture of humility was just one more episode which conclusively proved that Jesus would never qualify as Israel's deliverer, and that he had made no mistake in the decision to desert the Master's cause.

As they all stood there in breathless amazement, Jesus said: "Peter, I declare that, if I do not wash your feet, you will have no part with me in that which I am about to perform." When Peter heard this declaration, coupled with the fact that Jesus continued kneeling there at his feet, he made one of those decisions of blind acquiescence in compliance with the wish of one whom he respected and loved. As it began to dawn on Simon Peter that there was attached to this proposed enactment of service some signification that determined one's future connection with the Master's work, he not only became reconciled to the thought of allowing Jesus to wash his feet but, in his characteristic and impetuous manner, said: "Then, Master, wash not my feet only but also my hands and my head."

As the Master made ready to begin washing Peter's feet, he said: "He who is already clean needs only to have his feet washed. You who sit with me tonight are clean—but not all. But the dust of your feet should have been washed away before you sat down at meat with me. And besides, I would perform this service for you as a parable to illustrate the meaning of a new commandment which I will presently give you."

In like manner the Master went around the table, in silence, washing the feet of his twelve apostles, not even passing by Judas. When Jesus had finished washing the feet of the twelve, he donned his cloak, returned to his place as host, and after looking over his bewildered apostles, said:

"Do you really understand what I have done to you? You call me Master, and you say well, for so I am. If, then, the Master has washed your feet, why was it that you were unwilling to wash one another's feet? What lesson should you learn from this parable in which the Master so willingly does that service which his brethren were unwilling to do for one another? Verily, verily, I say to you: A servant is not greater than his master; neither is one who is sent greater than he who sends him. You have seen the way of service in my life among you, and blessed are you who will have the gracious courage so to serve. But why are you so slow to learn that the secret of greatness in the spiritual kingdom is not like the methods of power in the material world?

"When I came into this chamber tonight, you were not content proudly to refuse to wash one another's feet, but you must also fall to disputing among yourselves as to who should have the places of honor at my table. Such honors the Pharisees and the children of this world seek, but it should

not be so among the ambassadors of the heavenly kingdom. Do you not know that there can be no place of preferment at my table? Do you not understand that I love each of you as I do the others? Do you not know that the place nearest me, as men regard such honors, can mean nothing concerning your standing in the kingdom of heaven? You know that the kings of the gentiles have lordship over their subjects, while those who exercise this authority are sometimes called benefactors. But it shall not be so in the kingdom of heaven. He who would be great among you, let him become as the younger; while he who would be chief, let him become as one who serves. Who is the greater, he who sits at meat, or he who serves? Is it not commonly regarded that he who sits at meat is the greater? But you will observe that I am among you as one who serves. If you are willing to become fellow servants with me in doing the Father's will, in the kingdom to come you shall sit with me in power, still doing the Father's will in future glory."

When Jesus had finished speaking, the Alpheus twins brought on the bread and wine, with the bitter herbs and the paste of dried fruits, for the next course of the Last Supper.

LAST WORDS TO THE BETRAYER

For some minutes the apostles ate in silence, but under the influence of the Master's cheerful demeanor they were soon drawn into conversation, and ere long the meal was proceeding as if nothing out of the ordinary had occurred to interfere with the good cheer and social accord of this extraordinary occasion. After some time had elapsed, in about the middle of this second course of the meal, Jesus, looking them over, said: "I have told you how much I desired to have this supper with you, and knowing how the evil forces of darkness have conspired to bring about the death of the Son of Man, I determined to eat this supper with you in this secret chamber and a day in advance of the Passover since I will not be with you by this time tomorrow night. I have repeatedly told you that I must return to the Father. Now has my hour come, but it was not required that one of you should betray me into the hands of my enemies."

When the twelve heard this, having already been robbed of much of their self-assertiveness and self-confidence by the parable of the feet washing and the Master's subsequent discourse, they began to look at one another while in disconcerted tones they hesitatingly inquired, "Is it I?" And when they had all so inquired, Jesus said: "While it is necessary that I go to the Father, it was not required that one of you should become a traitor to fulfill the Father's will. This is the coming to fruit of the concealed evil in the heart of one who failed to love the truth with his whole soul. How deceitful is the intellectual pride that precedes the spiritual downfall! My friend of many years, who even now eats my bread, will be willing to betray me, even as he now dips his hand with me in the dish."

And when Jesus had thus spoken, they all began again to ask, "Is it I?" And as Judas, sitting on the left of his Master, again asked, "Is it I?" Jesus, dipping the bread in the dish of herbs, handed it to Judas, saying, "You have said." But the others did not hear Jesus speak to Judas. John, who reclined on Jesus' right hand, leaned over and asked the Master: "Who is it? We should know who it is that has proved untrue to his trust." Jesus answered: "Already have I told you, even he to whom I gave the sop." But it was so natural for the host to give a sop to the one who sat next to him on the left that none of them took notice of this, even though the Master had so plainly spoken. But Judas was painfully conscious of the meaning of the Master's words associated with his act, and he became fearful lest his brethren were likewise now aware that he was the betrayer.

Peter was highly excited by what had been said, and leaning forward over the table, he addressed John, "Ask him who it is, or if he has told you, tell me who is the betrayer."

Jesus brought their whisperings to an end by saying: "I sorrow that this evil should have come to pass and hoped even up to this hour that the power of truth might triumph over the deceptions of evil, but such victories are not won without the faith of the sincere love of truth. I would not have told you these things at this, our last supper, but I desire to warn you of these sorrows and so prepare you for what is now upon us. I have told you of this because I desire that you should recall, after I have gone, that I knew about all these evil plottings, and that I forewarned you of my betrayal. And I do all this only that you may be strengthened for the temptations and trials which are just ahead."

When Jesus had thus spoken, leaning over toward Judas, he said: "What you have decided to do, do quickly." And when Judas heard these words, he arose from the table and hastily left the room, going out into the night to do what he had set his mind to accomplish. When the other apostles saw Judas hasten off after Jesus had spoken to him, they thought he had gone to procure something additional for the supper or to do some other errand for the Master since they supposed he still carried the bag.

Jesus now knew that nothing could be done to keep Judas from turning traitor. He started with twelve—now he had eleven. He chose six of these apostles, and though Judas was among those nominated by his first-chosen apostles, still the Master accepted him and had, up to this very hour, done everything possible to sanctify and save him, even as he had wrought for the peace and salvation of the others.

This supper, with its tender episodes and softening touches, was Jesus' last appeal to the deserting Judas, but it was of no avail. Warning, even when administered in the most tactful manner and conveyed in the most kindly spirit, as a rule, only intensifies hatred and fires the evil determination to carry out to the full one's own selfish projects, when love is once really dead.

ESTABLISHING THE REMEMBRANCE SUPPER

As they brought Jesus the third cup of wine, the "cup of blessing," he arose from the couch and, taking the cup in his hands, blessed it, saying: "Take this cup, all of you, and drink of it. This shall be the cup of my remembrance. This is the cup of the blessing of a new dispensation of grace and truth. This shall be to you the emblem of the bestowal and ministry of the divine Spirit of Truth. And I will not again drink this cup with you until I drink in new form with you in the Father's eternal kingdom."

The apostles all sensed that something out of the ordinary was transpiring as they drank of this cup of blessing in profound reverence and perfect silence. The old Passover commemorated the emergence of their fathers from a state of racial slavery into individual freedom; now the Master was instituting a new remembrance supper as a symbol of the new dispensation wherein the enslaved individual emerges from the bondage of ceremonialism and selfishness into the spiritual joy of the brotherhood and fellowship of the liberated faith sons of the living God.

When they had finished drinking this new cup of remembrance, the Master took up the bread and, after giving thanks, broke it in pieces and, directing them to pass it around, said: "Take this bread of remembrance and eat it. I have told you that I am the bread of life. And this bread of life is the united life of the Father and the Son in one gift. The word of the Father, as revealed in the Son, is indeed the bread of life." When they had partaken of the bread of remembrance, the symbol of the living word of truth incarnated in the likeness of mortal flesh, they all sat down.

In instituting this remembrance supper, the Master, as was always his habit, resorted to parables and symbols. He employed symbols because he wanted to teach certain great spiritual truths in such a manner as to make it difficult for his successors to attach precise interpretations and definite meanings to his words. In this way he sought to prevent successive generations from crystallizing

"TAKE THIS BREAD OF REMEMBRANCE AND EAT IT. I HAVE TOLD YOU THAT I AM THE BREAD OF LIFE. AND THIS BREAD OF LIFE IS THE UNITED LIFE OF THE FATHER AND THE SON IN ONE GIFT."

his teaching and binding down his spiritual meanings by the dead chains of tradition and dogma.

This supper of remembrance, when it is partaken of by those who are Son-believing and God-knowing, does not need to have associated with its symbolism any of man's puerile misinterpretations regarding the meaning of the divine presence, for upon all such occasions the Master is *really present*. When you become thus spirit-conscious, the Son is actually present, and his spirit fraternizes with the indwelling fragment of his Father.

After they had engaged in meditation for a few moments, Jesus continued speaking: "When you do these things, recall the life I have lived on earth among you and rejoice that I am to continue to live on earth with you and to serve through you. As individuals, contend not among yourselves as to who shall be greatest. Be you all as brethren. And when the kingdom grows to embrace large groups of believers, likewise should you refrain from contending for greatness or seeking preferment between such groups."

And this mighty occasion took place in the upper chamber of a friend. There was nothing of sacred form or of ceremonial consecration about either the supper or the building. The remembrance supper was established without ecclesiastical sanction.

When Jesus had thus established the supper of the remembrance, he said to the eleven: "And as often as you do this, do it in remembrance of me. And when you do remember me, first look back upon my life in the flesh, recall that I was once with you, and then, by faith, discern that you shall all sometime sup with me in the Father's eternal kingdom. This is the new Passover which I leave with you, even the memory of my bestowal life, the word of eternal truth; and of my love for you, the outpouring of my Spirit of Truth upon all flesh."

THE NEW COMMANDMENT

After a few moments of informal conversation, Jesus stood up and said: "When I enacted for you a parable indicating how you should be willing to serve one another, I said that I desired to give you a new commandment; and I would do this now as I am about to leave you. You well know the commandment which directs that you love one another; that you love your neighbor even as yourself. But I am not wholly satisfied with even that sincere devotion on the part of my children. I would have you perform still greater acts of love in the kingdom of the believing brotherhood. And so I give you this new commandment: That you love one another even as I have loved you. And by this will all men know that you are my disciples if you thus love one another.

LOVE ONE ANOTHER EVEN AS I HAVE LOVED YOU

If you would share the Master's joy, you must share his love. And to share his love means that you have shared his service. Such an experience of love does not deliver you from the difficulties of this world; it does not create a new world, but it most certainly does make the old world new.

Keep in mind: It is loyalty, not sacrifice, that Jesus demands. The consciousness of sacrifice implies the absence of that wholehearted affection which would have made such a loving service a supreme joy. The idea of *duty* signifies that you are servant-minded and hence are missing the mighty thrill of doing your service as a friend and for a friend. The impulse of friendship transcends all convictions of duty, and the service of a friend for a friend can never be called a sacrifice. The Master has taught the apostles that they are the sons of God. He has called them brethren, and now, before he leaves, he calls them his friends.

"When I give you this new commandment, I do not place any new burden upon your souls; rather do I bring you new joy and make it possible for you to experience new pleasure in knowing the delights of the bestowal of your heart's affection upon your fellow men. I am about to experience the supreme joy, even though enduring outward sorrow, in the bestowal of my affection upon you and your fellow mortals.

"When I invite you to love one another, even as I have loved you, I hold up before you the supreme measure of true affection, for greater love can no man have than this: that he will lay down his life for his friends. And you are my friends; you will continue to be my friends if you are but willing to do what I have taught you. You have called me Master, but I do not call you servants. If you will only love one another as I am loving you, you shall be my friends, and I will ever speak to you of that which the Father reveals to me.

"You have not merely chosen me, but I have also chosen you, and I have ordained you to go forth into the world to yield the fruit of loving service to your fellows even as I have lived among you and revealed the Father to you. The Father and I will both work with you, and you shall experience the divine fullness of joy if you will only obey my command to love one another, even as I have loved you."

The Promised Helper

Jesus continued to teach, saying: "When I have gone to the Father, and after he has fully accepted the work I have done for you on earth, and after

SPIRIT OF TRUTH

The new helper which Jesus promised to send into the hearts of believers, to pour out upon all flesh, is the *Spirit of Truth*. This divine endowment is not the letter or law of truth, neither is it to function as the form or expression of truth. The new teacher is the *conviction of truth*, the consciousness and assurance of true meanings on real spirit levels. And this new teacher is the spirit of living and growing truth, expanding, unfolding, and adaptative truth.

I have received the final sovereignty of my own domain, I shall say to my Father: Having left my children alone on earth, it is in accordance with my promise to send them another teacher. And when the Father shall approve, I will pour out the Spirit of Truth upon all flesh. Already is my Father's spirit in your hearts, and when this day shall come, you will also have me with you even as you now have the Father. This new gift is the spirit of living truth. The unbelievers will not at first listen to the teachings of this spirit, but the sons of light will all receive him gladly and with a whole heart. And you shall know this spirit when he comes even as you have known me, and you will receive this gift in your hearts, and he will abide with you. You thus perceive that I am not going to leave you without help and guidance. I will not leave you desolate. Today I can be with you only in person. In the times to come I will be with you and all other men who desire my presence, wherever you may be, and with each of you at the same time. Do you not discern that it is better for me to go away; that I leave you in the flesh so that I may the better and the more fully be with you in the spirit?

"In just a few hours the world will see me no more; but you will continue to know me in your hearts even until I send you this new teacher, the Spirit of Truth. As I have lived with you in person, then shall I live in you; I shall be one with your personal experience in the spirit kingdom. And when this has come to pass, you shall surely know that I am in the Father, and that, while your life is hid with the Father in me, I am also in you. I have loved the Father and have kept his word; you have loved me, and you will keep my word. As my Father has given me of his spirit, so will I give you of my spirit. And this Spirit of Truth which I will bestow upon you shall guide and comfort you and shall eventually lead you into all truth.

"I am telling you these things while I am still with you that you may be the better prepared to endure those trials which are even now right upon us. And when this new day comes, you will be indwelt by the Son as well as by the Father. And these gifts of heaven will ever work the one with the other even as the Father and I have wrought on earth and before your very eyes as one person, the Son of Man. And this spirit friend will bring to your remembrance everything I have taught you."

The Necessity for Leaving

"Now that I am leaving you, seeing that the hour has come when I am about to go to the Father, I am surprised that none of you have asked me, Why do you leave us? Nevertheless, I know that you ask such questions in your hearts. I will speak to you plainly, as one friend to another. It is really profitable for you that I go away. If I go not away, the new teacher cannot come into your hearts. I must be divested of this mortal body and be restored to my place on high before I can send this spirit teacher to live in your souls and lead your spirits into the truth. And when my spirit comes to indwell you, he will illuminate the difference between sin and righteousness and will enable you to judge wisely in your hearts concerning them.

"I have yet much to say to you, but you cannot stand any more just now. Albeit, when he, the Spirit of Truth, comes, he shall eventually guide you into all truth as you pass through the many abodes in my Father's universe.

"This spirit will not speak of himself, but he will declare to you that which the Father has revealed to the Son, and he will even show you things to come; he will glorify me even as I have glorified my Father. This spirit comes forth from me, and he will reveal my truth to you. Everything which the Father has in this domain is now mine; wherefore did I say that this new teacher would take of that which is mine and reveal it to you.

"In just a little while I will leave you for a short time. Afterward, when you again see me, I shall already be on my way to the Father so that even then you will not see me for long.

"But remember my promise: When I am raised up, I will tarry with you for a season before I go to the Father. And even this night will I make supplication to the Father that he strengthen each of you for that which you must now so soon pass through. I love you all with the love wherewith the Father loves me, and therefore should you henceforth love one another, even as I have loved you." ∎

The Last Group Prayer

It was about ten o'clock this Thursday night when Jesus led the eleven apostles from the home of Elijah and Mary Mark on their way back to the Gethsemane camp. Ever since that day in the hills, John Mark had made it his business to keep a watchful eye on Jesus. John, being in need of sleep, had obtained several hours of rest while the Master had been with his apostles in the upper room, but on hearing them coming downstairs, he arose and, quickly throwing a linen coat about himself, followed them through the city, over the brook Kidron, and on to their private encampment adjacent to Gethsemane Park. And John Mark remained so near the Master throughout this

[C. Michael Dudash — *He Lifted His Eyes Toward Heaven*]

night and the next day that he witnessed everything and overheard much of what the Master said from this time on to the hour of the crucifixion.

As Jesus and the eleven made their way back to camp, the apostles began to wonder about the meaning of Judas's prolonged absence, and they spoke to one another concerning the Master's prediction that one of them would betray him, and for the first time they suspected that all was not well with Judas Iscariot. But they did not engage in open comment about Judas until they reached the camp and observed that he was not there, waiting to receive them. When they all besieged Andrew to know what had become of Judas, their chief remarked only, "I do not know where Judas is, but I fear he has deserted us."

A few moments after arriving at camp, Jesus said to them: "My friends and brethren, my time with you is now very short, and I desire that we draw apart by ourselves while we pray to our Father in heaven for strength to sustain us in this hour and henceforth in all the work we must do in his name."

When Jesus had thus spoken, he led the way a short distance up on Olivet, and in full view of Jerusalem he bade them kneel on a large flat rock in a circle about him as they had done on the day of their ordination; and then, as he stood there in the midst of them glorified in the mellow moonlight, he lifted up his eyes toward heaven and prayed:

"Father, my hour has come; now glorify your Son that the Son may glorify you. I know that you have given me full authority over all living creatures in my realm, and I will give eternal life to all who will become faith sons of God. And this is eternal life, that my creatures should know you as the only true God and Father of all, and that they should believe in him whom you sent into the world. Father, I have exalted you on earth and have accomplished the work which you gave me to do. I have almost finished my bestowal upon the children of our own creation; there remains only for me to lay down my life in the flesh. And now, O my Father, glorify me with the glory which I had with you before this world was and receive me once more at your right hand.

"I have manifested you to the men whom you chose from the world and gave to me. They are yours—as all life is in your hands—you gave them to me, and I have lived among them, teaching them the way of life, and they have believed. These men are learning that all I have comes from you, and that the life I live in the flesh is to make known my Father to the worlds. The truth which you have given to me I have revealed to them. These, my friends and ambassadors, have sincerely willed to receive your word. I have told them that I came forth from you, that you sent me into this world, and that I am about to return to you. Father, I do pray for these chosen men. And I pray for them not as I would pray for the world, but as for those whom I have chosen out of the world to represent me to the world after I have returned to your work, even as I have represented you in this world during my sojourn in the flesh. These men are mine; you gave them to me; but all things which are mine are ever yours, and all that which was yours you have now caused to be mine. You have been exalted in me, and I now pray that I may be honored in these men. I can no longer be in this world; I am about to return to the work you have given me to do. I

> "FATHER, I DO PRAY FOR THESE CHOSEN MEN, NOT AS I WOULD PRAY FOR THE WORLD, BUT AS FOR THOSE WHOM I HAVE CHOSEN OUT OF THE WORLD TO REPRESENT ME."

I Am the Way, the Truth, and the Life

The Master, during the course of this final prayer with his apostles, alluded to the fact that he had manifested the Father's *name* to the world. And that is truly what he did by the revelation of God through his perfected life in the flesh. The Father in heaven had sought to reveal himself to Moses, but he could proceed no further than to cause it to be said, "I AM." And when pressed for further revelation of himself, it was only disclosed, "I AM that I AM." But when Jesus had finished his earth life, this name of the Father had been so revealed that the Master, who was the Father incarnate, could truly say:

I am the bread of life.
I am the living water.
I am the light of the world.
I am the desire of all ages.
I am the open door to eternal salvation.
I am the reality of endless life.
I am the good shepherd.
I am the pathway of infinite perfection.
I am the resurrection and the life.
I am the secret of eternal survival.
I am the way, the truth, and the life.
I am the infinite Father of my finite children.
I am the true vine; you are the branches.
I am the hope of all who know the living truth.
I am the living bridge from one world to another.
I am the living link between time and eternity.

Thus did Jesus enlarge the living revelation of the name of God to all generations. As divine love reveals the nature of God, eternal truth discloses his name in ever-enlarging proportions.

must leave these men behind to represent us and our kingdom among men. Father, keep these men faithful as I prepare to yield up my life in the flesh. Help these, my friends, to be one in spirit, even as we are one. As long as I could be with them, I could watch over them and guide them, but now am I about to go away. Be near them, Father, until we can send the new teacher to comfort and strengthen them.

"You gave me twelve men, and I have kept them all save one, the son of revenge, who would not have further fellowship with us. These men are weak and frail, but I know we can trust them; I have proved them; they love me, even as they reverence you. While they must suffer much for my sake, I desire that they should also be filled with the joy of the assurance of sonship in the heavenly kingdom. I have given these men your word and have taught them the truth. The world may hate them, even as it has hated me, but I do not ask that you take them out of the world, only that you keep them from the evil in the world. Sanctify them in the truth; your word is truth. And as you sent me into this world, even so am I about to send these men into the world. For their sakes I have lived among men and have consecrated my life to your service that I might inspire them to be purified through the truth I have taught them and the love I have revealed to them. I well know, my Father, that there is no need for me to ask you to watch over these brethren after I have gone; I know you love them even as I, but I do this that they may the better realize the Father loves mortal men even as does the Son.

"And now, my Father, I would pray not only for these eleven men but also for all others who now believe, or who may hereafter believe the gospel of the kingdom through the word of their future ministry. I want them all to be one, even as you and I are one. You are in me and I am in you, and I desire that these believers likewise be in us; that both of our spirits indwell them. If my children are one as we are one, and if they love one another as I have loved them, all men will then believe that I came forth from you and be willing to receive the revelation of truth and glory which I have made. The glory which you gave me I have revealed to these believers. As you have lived with me in spirit, so have I lived with them in the flesh. As you have been one with me, so have I been one with them, and so will the new teacher ever be one with them and in them. And all this have I done that my brethren in the flesh may know that the Father loves them even as does the Son, and that you love them even as you love me. Father, work with me to save these believers that they may presently come to be with me in glory and then go on to join you in the Paradise embrace. Those who serve with me in humiliation, I would have with me in glory so that they may see all you have given into my hands as the eternal harvest of the seed sowing of time in the likeness of mortal flesh. I long to show my earthly brethren the glory I had with you before the founding of this world. This world knows very little of you, righteous Father, but I know you, and I have made you known to these believers, and they will make known your name to other generations. And now I promise them that you will be with them in the world even as you have been with me—even so."

The eleven remained kneeling in this circle about Jesus for several minutes before they arose and in silence made their way back to the camp.

Resentment of Judas's being a traitor for now eclipsed everything else in the apostles' minds. The Master's comment in reference to Judas, spoken in the course of the last prayer, opened their eyes to the fact that he had forsaken them. ■

ALONE IN GETHSEMANE

After all was still and quiet about the camp, Jesus, taking Peter, James, and John, went a short way up a near-by ravine where he had often before gone to pray and commune. The three apostles could not help recognizing that he was grievously oppressed; never before had they observed their Master to be so heavy-laden and sorrowful. When they arrived at the place of his devotions, he bade the three sit down and watch with him while he went off about a stone's throw to pray. And when he had fallen down on his face, he prayed: "My Father, I came into this world to do your will, and so have I. I know that the hour has come to lay down this life in the flesh, and I do not shrink therefrom, but I would know that it is your will that I drink this cup. Send me the assurance that I will please you in my death even as I have in my life."

The Master remained in a prayerful attitude for a few moments, and then, going over to the three apostles, he found them sound asleep, for their eyes were heavy and they could not remain awake. As Jesus awoke them, he said: "What! can you not watch with me even for one hour? Cannot you see that my soul is exceedingly sorrowful, even to death, and that I crave your companionship?" After the three had aroused from their slumber, the Master again went apart by himself and, falling down on the ground, again prayed: "Father, I know it is possible to avoid this cup—all things are possible with you—but I have come to do your will, and while this is a bitter cup, I would drink it if it is your will." And when he had thus prayed, a mighty angel came down by his side and, speaking to him, touched him and strengthened him.

When Jesus returned to speak with the three apostles, he again found them fast asleep. He awakened them, saying: "In such an hour I need that you should watch and pray with me—all the more do you need to pray that you enter not into temptation—wherefore do you fall asleep when I leave you?"

And then, for a third time, the Master withdrew and prayed: "Father, you see my sleeping apostles; have mercy upon them. The spirit is indeed willing, but the flesh is weak. And now,

O Father, if this cup may not pass, then would I drink it. Not my will, but yours, be done." And when he had finished praying, he lay for a moment prostrate on the ground. When he arose and went back to his apostles, once more he found them asleep. He surveyed them and, with a pitying gesture, tenderly said: "Sleep on now and take your rest; the time of decision is past. The hour is now upon us wherein the Son of Man will be betrayed into the hands of his enemies." As he reached down to shake them that he might awaken them, he said: "Arise, let us be going back to the camp, for, behold, he who betrays me is at hand, and the hour has come when my flock shall be scattered. But I have already told you about these things."

During the years that Jesus lived among his followers, they did, indeed, have much proof of his divine nature, but just now are they about to witness new evidences of his humanity. Just before the greatest of all the revelations of his divinity, his resurrection, must now come the greatest proofs of his mortal nature, his humiliation and crucifixion.

Each time he prayed in the garden, his humanity laid a firmer faith-hold upon his divinity; his human will more completely became one with the divine will of his Father. Among other words spoken to him by the mighty angel was the message that the Father desired his Son to finish his earth bestowal by passing through the creature experience of death just as all mortal creatures must experience material dissolution in passing from the existence of time into the progression of eternity.

Earlier in the evening it had not seemed so difficult to drink the cup, but as the human Jesus bade farewell to his apostles and sent them to their rest, the trial grew more appalling. Jesus experienced that natural ebb and flow of feeling which is common to all human experience, and just now he was weary from work, exhausted from the long hours of strenuous labor and painful anxiety concerning the safety of his apostles. While no mortal can presume to understand the thoughts and feelings of the incarnate Son of God at such a time as this, we know that he endured great anguish and suffered untold sorrow, for the perspiration rolled off his face in great drops. He was at last convinced that the Father intended to allow natural events to take their course; he was fully determined to employ none of his sovereign power as the supreme head of a universe to save himself.

The experience of parting with the apostles was a great strain on the human heart of Jesus; this sorrow of love bore down on him and made it more difficult to face such a death as he well knew awaited him. He realized how weak and how ignorant his apostles were, and he dreaded to leave them. He well knew that the time of his departure had come, but his human heart longed to find out whether there might not possibly be some legitimate avenue of escape from this terrible plight of suffering and sorrow. And when it had thus sought escape, and failed, it was willing to drink the cup. The divine mind of Michael knew he had done his best for the twelve apostles; but the human heart of Jesus wished that more might have been done for them before they should be left alone in the world. Jesus' heart was being crushed; he truly loved his brethren. He was isolated from his family in the flesh; one of his chosen associates was betraying him. His father Joseph's people had rejected him and thereby sealed their doom as a people with a special mission on earth. His soul was tortured by baffled love and rejected mercy. It was just one of those awful human moments when everything seems to bear down with crushing cruelty and terrible agony.

Jesus' humanity was not insensible to this situation of private loneliness, public shame, and the appearance of the failure of his cause. All these sentiments bore down on him with indescribable heaviness. In this great sorrow his mind went back to the days of his childhood in Nazareth and to his early work in Galilee. At the time of this great trial there came up in his mind many of those pleasant scenes of his earthly ministry. And it was from these old memories of Nazareth, Capernaum, Mount Hermon, and of the sunrise and sunset on the shimmering Sea of Galilee, that he soothed himself as he made his human heart strong and ready to encounter the traitor who should so soon betray him.

Before Judas and the soldiers arrived, the Master had fully regained his customary poise; the spirit had triumphed over the flesh; faith had asserted itself over all human tendencies to fear or entertain doubt. The supreme test of the full realization of the human nature had been met and acceptably passed. Once more the Son of Man was prepared to face his enemies with equanimity and in the full assurance of his invincibility as a mortal man unreservedly dedicated to the doing of his Father's will.

Jesus sat down, alone, on the olive press, where he awaited the coming of the betrayer, and he was seen at this time only by John Mark and an innumerable host of celestial observers. ✶

[YONGSUNG KIM — *Gethsemane Prayer*]

CHAPTER XI

"It Is Finished!"

"Father, forgive them; for they know not what they do."

—LUKE 23:34 RSV

THERE IS GREAT DANGER OF MISUNDERSTANDING THE MEANING OF NUMEROUS SAYINGS and many events associated with the termination of the Master's career in the flesh. It was, indeed and in truth, the will of the Father that his Son should drink to the full the cup of mortal experience, from birth to death, but the Father in heaven had nothing whatever to do with instigating the barbarous behavior of those supposedly civilized human beings who so brutally tortured the Master and so horribly heaped successive indignities upon his nonresisting person.

The Father in heaven desired the bestowal Son to finish his earth career *naturally,* just as all mortals must finish up their lives on earth and in the flesh. Accordingly, Jesus elected to lay down his life in the flesh in the manner which was in keeping with the outworking of natural events, and he steadfastly refused to extricate himself from the cruel clutches of a wicked conspiracy of inhuman events which swept on with horrible certainty toward his unbelievable humiliation and ignominious death. And every bit of all this astounding manifestation of hatred and this unprecedented demonstration of cruelty was the work of evil men and wicked mortals. God in heaven did not will it, neither did the archenemies of Jesus dictate it, though they did much to insure that unthinking and evil mortals would thus reject the bestowal Son. Even the father of sin turned his face away from the excruciating horror of the scene of the crucifixion.

Pilate spoke more truly than he knew when, after Jesus had been scourged, he presented him before the multitude, exclaiming, "Behold the man!" Indeed, the fear-ridden Roman governor little dreamed that at just that moment the universe stood at attention, gazing upon this unique scene of its beloved Sovereign thus subjected in humiliation to the taunts and blows of his darkened and degraded mortal subjects. And as Pilate spoke, there echoed throughout a universe, "Behold God and man!"

These are the moments of the Master's greatest victories in all his long and eventful career as maker, upholder, and savior of a vast and far-flung universe. Having lived to the full a life of revealing God to man, Jesus is now engaged in making a new and unprecedented revelation of man to God. The Son of Man has finally achieved the realization of identity as the Son of God.

THE URANTIA BOOK: PAPERS 183–188
THURSDAY, APRIL 6–FRIDAY, APRIL 7, A.D. 30

[RUSS DOCKEN — *Father Forgive Them*]

THE BETRAYAL AND ARREST OF JESUS

After Judas so abruptly left the table while eating the Last Supper, he went directly to the home of his cousin, and then did the two go straight to the captain of the temple guards. Judas requested the captain to assemble the guards and informed him that he was ready to lead them to Jesus. Judas having appeared on the scene a little before he was expected, there was some delay in getting started for the Mark home, where Judas expected to find Jesus still visiting with the apostles. The Master and the eleven left the home of Elijah Mark fully fifteen minutes before the betrayer and the guards arrived. By the time the apprehenders reached the Mark home, Jesus and the eleven were well outside the walls of the city and on their way to the Olivet camp.

When they failed to find Jesus in the upper chamber, Judas asked the captain of the guard to return to the temple. By this time the rulers had begun to assemble at the high priest's home preparatory to receiving Jesus, seeing that their bargain with the traitor called for Jesus' arrest by midnight of that day. Judas explained to his associates that they had missed Jesus at the Mark home, and that it would be necessary to go to Gethsemane to arrest him. The betrayer then went on to state that more than threescore devoted followers were encamped with him, and that they were all well armed. The rulers of the Jews reminded Judas that Jesus had always preached nonresistance, but Judas replied that they could not depend upon all Jesus' followers obeying such teaching. He really feared for himself and therefore made bold to ask for a company of forty armed soldiers.

Accordingly, when Judas Iscariot started out from the temple, about half after eleven o'clock,

he was accompanied by more than sixty persons—temple guards, Roman soldiers, and curious servants of the chief priests and rulers.

As this company of armed soldiers and guards, carrying torches and lanterns, approached the garden, Judas stepped well out in front of the band that he might be ready quickly to identify Jesus so that the apprehenders could easily lay hands on him before his associates could rally to his defense. And there was yet another reason why Judas chose to be ahead of the Master's enemies: He thought it would appear that he had arrived on the scene ahead of the soldiers so that the apostles and others gathered about Jesus might not directly connect him with the armed guards following so closely upon his heels. Judas had even thought to pose as having hastened out to warn them of the coming of the apprehenders, but this plan was thwarted by Jesus' blighting greeting of the betrayer. Though the Master spoke to Judas kindly, he greeted him as a traitor.

As soon as Peter, James, and John, with some thirty of their fellow campers, saw the armed band with torches swing around the brow of the hill, they knew that these soldiers were coming to arrest Jesus, and they all rushed down to near the olive press where the Master was sitting in moonlit solitude. As the company of soldiers approached on one side, the three apostles and their associates approached on the other. As Judas strode forward to accost the Master, there the two groups stood, motionless, with the Master between them and Judas making ready to impress the traitorous kiss upon his brow.

It had been the hope of the betrayer that he could, after leading the guards to Gethsemane, simply point Jesus out to the soldiers, or at most carry out the promise to greet him with a kiss, and then quickly retire from the scene. Judas greatly feared that the apostles would all be present, and that they would concentrate their attack upon him in retribution for his daring to betray their

THERE THE TWO GROUPS STOOD, MOTIONLESS, WITH THE MASTER BETWEEN THEM AND JUDAS MAKING READY TO IMPRESS THE TRAITOROUS KISS UPON HIS BROW.

beloved teacher. But when the Master greeted him as a betrayer, he was so confused that he made no attempt to flee.

Jesus made one last effort to save Judas from actually betraying him in that, before the traitor could reach him, he stepped to one side and, addressing the foremost soldier on the left, the captain of the Romans, said, "Whom do you seek?" The captain answered, "Jesus of Nazareth." Then Jesus stepped up immediately in front of the officer and, standing there in the calm majesty of the God of all this creation, said, "I am he." Many of this armed band had heard Jesus teach in the temple, others had learned about his mighty works, and when they heard him thus boldly announce his identity, those in the front ranks fell suddenly backward. They were overcome with surprise at his calm and majestic announcement of identity. There was, therefore, no need for Judas to go on with his plan of betrayal. The Master had boldly revealed himself to his enemies, and they could have taken him without Judas's assistance. But the traitor had to do something to account for his presence with this armed band, and besides, he wanted to make a show of carrying out his part of the betrayal bargain with the rulers of the Jews in order to be eligible for the great reward and honors which he believed would be heaped upon him in compensation for his promise to deliver Jesus into their hands.

As the guards rallied from their first faltering at the sight of Jesus and at the sound of his unusual voice, and as the apostles and disciples drew nearer, Judas stepped up to Jesus and, placing a kiss upon his brow, said, "Hail, Master and Teacher." And as Judas thus embraced his Master, Jesus said, "Friend, is it not enough to do this! Would you even betray the Son of Man with a kiss?"

The apostles and disciples were literally stunned by what they saw. For a moment no one moved. Then Jesus, disengaging himself from the traitorous embrace of Judas, stepped up to the guards and soldiers and again asked, "Whom do you seek?" And again the captain said, "Jesus of Nazareth." And again answered Jesus: "I have told you that I am he. If, therefore, you seek me, let these others go their way. I am ready to go with you."

Jesus was ready to go back to Jerusalem with the guards, and the captain of the soldiers was altogether willing to allow the three apostles and their associates to go their way in peace. But before they were able to get started, as Jesus stood there awaiting the captain's orders, one Malchus, the Syrian bodyguard of the high priest, stepped up to Jesus and made ready to bind his hands behind his back, although the Roman captain had not directed that Jesus should be thus bound. When Peter and his associates saw their Master being subjected to this indignity, they were no longer able to restrain themselves. Peter drew his sword and with the others rushed forward to smite Malchus. But before the soldiers could come to the defense of the high priest's servant, Jesus raised a forbidding hand to Peter and, speaking sternly, said: "Peter, put up your sword. They who take the sword shall

[WALTER RANE — *I Am He*] OVERLEAF >

perish by the sword. Do you not understand that it is the Father's will that I drink this cup? And do you not further know that I could even now command more than twelve legions of angels and their associates, who would deliver me from the hands of these few men?"

While Jesus thus effectively put a stop to this show of physical resistance by his followers, it was enough to arouse the fear of the captain of the guards, who now, with the help of his soldiers, laid heavy hands on Jesus and quickly bound him. And as they tied his hands with heavy cords, Jesus said to them: "Why do you come out against me with swords and with staves as if to seize a robber? I was daily with you in the temple, publicly teaching the people, and you made no effort to take me."

When Jesus had been bound, the captain, fearing that the followers of the Master might attempt to rescue him, gave orders that they be seized; but the soldiers were not quick enough since, having overheard the captain's orders to arrest them, Jesus' followers fled in haste back into the ravine. All this time John Mark had remained secluded in the near-by shed. When the guards started back to Jerusalem with Jesus, John Mark attempted to steal out of the shed in order to catch up with the fleeing apostles and disciples; but just as he emerged, one of the last of the returning soldiers who had pursued the fleeing disciples was passing near and, seeing this young man in his linen coat, gave chase, almost overtaking him. In fact, the soldier got near enough to John to lay hold upon his coat, but the young man freed himself from the garment, escaping naked while the soldier held the empty coat. ■

BEFORE THE SANHEDRIN COURT

It was about half past three o'clock this Friday morning when the chief priest, Caiaphas, called the Sanhedrist court of inquiry to order and asked that Jesus be brought before them for his formal trial. On three previous occasions the Sanhedrin, by a large majority vote, had decreed the death of Jesus, had decided that he was worthy of death on informal charges of law-breaking, blasphemy, and flouting the traditions of the fathers of Israel.

This was not a regularly called meeting of the Sanhedrin and was not held in the usual place, the chamber of hewn stone in the temple. This was a special trial court of some thirty Sanhedrists and was convened in the palace of the high priest. John Zebedee was present with Jesus throughout this so-called trial.

Jesus appeared before this court clothed in his usual garments and with his hands bound together behind his back. The entire court was startled and somewhat confused by his majestic appearance. Never had they gazed upon such a prisoner nor witnessed such composure in a man on trial for his life.

The Jewish law required that at least two witnesses must agree upon any point before a charge could be laid against the prisoner. Judas could not be used as a witness against Jesus because the

Jewish law specifically forbade the testimony of a traitor. More than a score of false witnesses were on hand to testify against Jesus, but their testimony was so contradictory and so evidently trumped up that the Sanhedrists themselves were very much ashamed of the performance. Jesus stood there, looking down benignly upon these perjurers, and his very countenance disconcerted the lying witnesses. Throughout all this false testimony the Master never said a word; he made no reply to their many false accusations.

The first time any two of their witnesses approached even the semblance of an agreement was when two men testified that they had heard Jesus say in the course of one of his temple discourses that he would "destroy this temple made with hands and in three days make another temple without hands." That was not exactly what Jesus said, regardless of the fact that he pointed to his own body when he made the remark referred to.

Although the high priest shouted at Jesus, "Do you not answer any of these charges?" Jesus opened not his mouth. He stood there in silence while all of these false witnesses gave their testimony. Hatred, fanaticism, and unscrupulous exaggeration so characterized the words of these perjurers that their testimony fell in its own entanglements. The very best refutation of their false accusations was the Master's calm and majestic silence.

Shortly after the beginning of the testimony of the false witnesses, Annas arrived and took his seat beside Caiaphas.

Already had the full Sanhedrin agreed that Jesus was guilty of death-deserving transgressions of the Jewish laws, but they were now more concerned with developing charges regarding his conduct and teachings which would justify Pilate in pronouncing the death sentence upon their prisoner. They knew that they must secure the consent of the Roman governor before Jesus could legally be put to death.

But Caiaphas could not longer endure the sight of the Master standing there in perfect composure and unbroken silence. He thought he knew at least one way in which the prisoner might be induced to speak. Accordingly, he rushed over to the side of Jesus and, shaking his accusing finger in the Master's face, said: "I adjure you, in the name of the living God, that you tell us whether you are the Deliverer, the Son of God." Jesus answered Caiaphas: "I am. Soon I go to the Father, and presently shall the Son of Man be clothed with power and once more reign over the hosts of heaven."

When the high priest heard Jesus utter these words, he was exceedingly angry, and rending his outer garments, he exclaimed: "What further need have we of witnesses? Behold, now have you all heard this man's blasphemy. What do you now think should be done with this lawbreaker and blasphemer?" And they all answered in unison, "He is worthy of death; let him be crucified."

Annas desired that the trial proceed further, and that charges of a definite nature regarding Jesus' relation to the Roman law and Roman institutions be formulated for subsequent presentation to Pilate. The councilors were anxious to carry these matters to a speedy termination, not only because it was the preparation day for the Passover and no secular work should be done after noon, but also because they

FALSE JUDGES

Thirty prejudiced and tradition-blinded false judges, with their false witnesses, are presuming to sit in judgment on the righteous Creator of a universe. And these impassioned accusers are exasperated by the majestic silence and superb bearing of this God-man. His silence is terrible to endure; his speech is fearlessly defiant. He is unmoved by their threats and undaunted by their assaults. Man sits in judgment on God, but even then he loves them and would save them if he could.

SIMON PETER'S TEARS OF AGONY

Before Jesus was taken to the Sanhedrin court at the palace of the high priest Caiaphas, he spent three hours at the palace of Annas on Mount Olivet, not far from Gethsemane. Representatives of Annas had secretly instructed the captain of the Roman soldiers to bring Jesus immediately to him after he had been arrested.

Annas, enriched by the temple revenues, his son-in-law the acting high priest Caiaphas, and with his relations to the Roman authorities, was indeed the most powerful single individual in all Jewry. He had not seen Jesus for several years, not since the time when the Master called at his house and immediately left upon observing his coldness and reserve in receiving him. When Jesus was young, Annas had taken a great interest in him, but now that his revenues were threatened by what Jesus had so recently done in driving the commerce from the temple, his enmity was fully aroused, far more than Jesus' teachings had done.

At the end of his examination, going up to the Master's side, Annas said, "Do you claim to be the Messiah, the deliverer of Israel?" Said Jesus: "Annas, you have known me from the times of my youth. You know that I claim to be nothing except that which my Father has appointed, and that I have been sent to all men, gentile as well as Jew." Then said Annas: "I have been told that you have claimed to be the Messiah; is that true?" Jesus looked upon Annas but only replied, "So you have said."

But this episode is most famous as the scene of Simon Peter's denial. As the band of guards and soldiers approached the entrance to the palace,

John Zebedee was marching by the side of the Roman captain who had granted him something of the status of a Roman counselor designated to act as observer of all these transactions. Peter followed afar off and when he arrived, and as he stood before the gate, John saw him and requested of the portress who kept the gate to let him in.

It was here in this courtyard that Peter thrice denied his Master. And after he had for the last time denied all connection with Jesus, the cock crowed, and Peter remembered the words of warning spoken to him by his Master at their last supper: "Peter, verily, verily, I say to you, this night the cock will not crow until you have denied me three or four times. And thus what you have failed to learn from peaceful association with me, you will learn through much trouble and many sorrows."

As he stood there, heavy of heart and crushed with the sense of guilt, the palace doors opened, and the guards led Jesus past on the way to Caiaphas. As the Master passed Peter, he saw, by the light of the torches, the look of despair on the face of his former self-confident and superficially brave apostle, and he turned and looked upon Peter. Peter never forgot that look as long as he lived. It was such a glance of commingled pity and love as mortal man had never beheld in the face of the Master.

After Jesus and the guards passed out of the palace gates, Peter followed them, but only for a short distance. He could not go farther. He sat down by the side of the road and wept bitterly. And when he had shed these tears of agony, he turned his steps back toward the camp.

feared Pilate might any time return to the Roman capital of Judea, Caesarea, since he was in Jerusalem only for the Passover celebration.

But Annas did not succeed in keeping control of the court. After Jesus had so unexpectedly answered Caiaphas, the high priest stepped

forward and smote him in the face with his hand. Annas was truly shocked as the other members of the court, in passing out of the room, spit in Jesus' face, and many of them mockingly slapped him with the palms of their hands. And thus in disorder and with such unheard-of confusion this

[CARL BLOCH — *Peter's Denial* (detail)]

first session of the Sanhedrist trial of Jesus ended at half past four o'clock.

The Jewish law required that, in the matter of passing the death sentence, there should be two sessions of the court. This second session was to be held on the day following the first, and the intervening time was to be spent in fasting and mourning by the members of the court. But these men could not await the next day for the confirmation of their decision that Jesus must die. They waited only one hour. In the meantime Jesus was left in the audience chamber in the custody of the temple guards, who, with the servants of the high priest, amused themselves by heaping every sort of indignity upon the Son of Man. They mocked him, spit upon him, and cruelly buffeted him. They would strike him in the face with a rod and then say, "Prophesy to us, you the Deliverer, who it was that struck you." And thus they went on for one full hour, reviling and mistreating this unresisting man of Galilee.

During this tragic hour of suffering and mock trials before the ignorant and unfeeling guards and servants, John Zebedee waited in lonely terror in an adjoining room. When these abuses first started, Jesus indicated to John, by a nod of his head, that he should retire.

Throughout this awful hour Jesus uttered no word. To this gentle and sensitive soul of humankind, joined in personality relationship with the

God of all this universe, there was no more bitter portion of his cup of humiliation than this terrible hour at the mercy of these ignorant and cruel guards and servants, who had been stimulated to abuse him by the example of the members of this so-called Sanhedrist court.

At five-thirty o'clock the court reassembled, and Jesus was led into the adjoining room, where John was waiting. Here the Roman soldier and the temple guards watched over Jesus while the court began the formulation of the charges which were to be presented to Pilate. Annas made it clear to his associates that the charge of blasphemy would carry no weight with Pilate. Judas was present during this second meeting of the court, but he gave no testimony.

This session of the court lasted only a half hour, and when they adjourned to go before Pilate, they had drawn up the indictment of Jesus, as being worthy of death, under three heads:

Firstly, that he was a perverter of the Jewish nation; he deceived the people and incited them to rebellion; secondly that he taught the people to refuse to pay tribute to Caesar; and lastly that, by claiming to be a king and the founder of a new sort of kingdom, he incited treason against the emperor.

Jesus did not again appear before the Sanhedrist court. They did not want again to look upon his face as they sat in judgment upon his innocent life. Jesus did not know (as a man) of their formal charges until he heard them recited by Pilate. ∎

THE TRIAL BEFORE PILATE

Shortly after six o'clock on this Friday morning, April 7, A.D. 30, Jesus was brought before Pilate, the Roman procurator who governed Judea, Samaria, and Idumea under the immediate supervision of the legatus of Syria. The Master was taken into the presence of the Roman governor by the temple guards, bound, and was accompanied by about fifty of his accusers, including the Sanhedrist court (principally Sadduceans), Judas Iscariot, and the high priest, Caiaphas, and by the Apostle John. Annas did not appear before Pilate.

Pilate was up and ready to receive this group of early morning callers, having been informed by those who had secured his consent, the previous evening, to employ the Roman soldiers in arresting the Son of Man, that Jesus would be early brought before him. This trial was arranged to take place in front of the praetorium, an addition to the fortress of Antonia, where Pilate and his wife made their headquarters when stopping in Jerusalem.

Though Pilate conducted much of Jesus' examination within the praetorium halls, the public trial was held outside on the steps leading up to the main entrance. This was a concession to the Jews, who refused to enter any gentile building where leaven might be used on this day of preparation for the Passover. Such conduct would not only render them ceremonially unclean and thereby debar them from partaking of the afternoon feast of thanksgiving but would also necessitate their subjection to purification ceremonies after sundown, before they would be eligible to partake of the Passover supper.

Claudia Procula, Pilate's wife, had heard much of Jesus through the word of her maid-in-waiting, who was a Phoenician believer in the gospel of the kingdom. After Pilate's suicide some years later, Claudia became prominently identified with the spread of the good news.

When Jesus and his accusers had gathered in front of Pilate's judgment hall, the Roman governor came out and, addressing the company assembled, asked, "What accusation do you bring against this fellow?" The Sadducees and councilors who had taken it upon themselves to put Jesus

JESUS DID NOT AGAIN APPEAR BEFORE THE SANHEDRIST COURT. THEY DID NOT WANT AGAIN TO LOOK UPON HIS FACE AS THEY SAT IN JUDGMENT UPON HIS INNOCENT LIFE.

out of the way had determined to go before Pilate and ask for confirmation of the death sentence pronounced upon Jesus, without volunteering any definite charge. Therefore did the spokesman for the Sanhedrist court answer Pilate: "If this man were not an evildoer, we should not have delivered him up to you."

When Pilate observed that they were reluctant to state their charges against Jesus, although he knew they had been all night engaged in deliberations regarding his guilt, he answered them: "Since you have not agreed on any definite charges, why do you not take this man and pass judgment on him in accordance with your own laws?"

Then spoke the clerk of the Sanhedrin court to Pilate: "It is not lawful for us to put any man to death, and this disturber of our nation is worthy to die for the things which he has said and done. Therefore have we come before you for confirmation of this decree."

Pilate, being keenly sensitive to the disrespectful manner of the approach of these Jews, was not willing to comply with their demands that Jesus be sentenced to death without a trial. When, therefore, he had waited a few moments for them to present their charges against the prisoner, he turned to them and said: "I will not sentence this man to death without a trial; neither will I consent to examine him until you have presented your charges against him in writing."

When the high priest and the others heard Pilate say this, they signaled to the clerk of the court, who then handed to Pilate the written charges against Jesus.

THE PRIVATE EXAMINATION BY PILATE

Pilate was confused in mind, fearful of the Jews in his heart, and mightily stirred in his spirit by the spectacle of Jesus' standing there in majesty before his bloodthirsty accusers and gazing down on them, not in silent contempt, but with an expression of genuine pity and sorrowful affection.

Pilate took Jesus and John Zebedee into a private chamber, leaving the guards outside in the hall, and requesting the prisoner to sit down, he sat down by his side and asked several questions. Pilate began his talk with Jesus by assuring him that he did not believe the first count against him: that he was a perverter of the nation and an inciter to rebellion. Then he asked, "Did you ever teach that tribute should be refused Caesar?" Jesus, pointing to John, said, "Ask him or any other man who has heard my teaching." Then Pilate questioned John about this matter of tribute, and John testified concerning his Master's teaching and explained that Jesus and his apostles paid taxes both to Caesar and to the temple.

When Pilate had questioned John, he said, "See that you tell no man that I talked with you." And John never did reveal this matter.

Pilate then turned around to question Jesus further, saying: "And now about the third accusation against you, are you the king of the Jews?" Since there was a tone of possibly sincere inquiry in Pilate's voice, Jesus smiled on the procurator and said: "Pilate, do you ask this for yourself, or do you take this question from these others, my accusers?" Whereupon, in a tone of partial indignation, the governor answered: "Am I a Jew? Your own people and the chief priests delivered you up and asked me to sentence you to death. I question the validity of their charges and am only trying to find out for myself what you have done. Tell me, have you said that you are the king of the Jews, and have you sought to found a new kingdom?"

Then said Jesus to Pilate: "Do you not perceive that my kingdom is not of this world? If my kingdom were of this world, surely would my disciples fight that I should not be delivered into the hands of the Jews. My presence here before you in these bonds is sufficient to show all men that my kingdom is a spiritual dominion, even the brotherhood of men who, through faith and by love, have become the sons of God. And this salvation is for the gentile as well as for the Jew."

"Then you are a king after all?" said Pilate. And Jesus answered: "Yes, I am such a king, and my kingdom is the family of the faith sons of my Father who is in heaven. For this purpose was I born into this world, even that I should show my Father to all men and bear witness to the truth of God. And even now do I declare to you that every one who loves the truth hears my voice."

Then said Pilate, half in ridicule and half in sincerity, "Truth, what is truth—who knows?"

Pilate was not able to fathom Jesus' words, nor was he able to understand the nature of his

[HARRY ANDERSON — *Pilate Confronts Christ*]

spiritual kingdom, but he was now certain that the prisoner had done nothing worthy of death. One look at Jesus, face to face, was enough to convince even Pilate that this gentle and weary, but majestic and upright, man was no wild and dangerous revolutionary who aspired to establish himself on the temporal throne of Israel. Pilate thought he understood something of what Jesus meant when he called himself a king, for he was familiar with the teachings of the Stoics, who declared that "the wise man is king." Pilate was thoroughly convinced that, instead of being a dangerous seditionmonger, Jesus was nothing more or less than a harmless visionary, an innocent fanatic.

After questioning the Master, Pilate went back to the chief priests and the accusers of Jesus and said: "I have examined this man, and I find no fault in him. I do not think he is guilty of the charges you have made against him; I think he ought to be set free." And when the Jews heard this, they were moved with great anger, so much so that they wildly shouted that Jesus should die; and one of the Sanhedrists boldly stepped up by the side of Pilate, saying: "This man stirs up the people, beginning in Galilee and continuing throughout all Judea. He is a mischief-maker and an evildoer. You will long regret it if you let this wicked man go free."

Pilate was hard pressed to know what to do with Jesus; therefore, when he heard them say that he began his work in Galilee, he thought to avoid the responsibility of deciding the case, at least to gain time for thought, by sending Jesus to appear before Herod, who was then in the city attending the Passover. Pilate also thought that this gesture would help to antidote some of the bitter feeling which had existed for some time between himself and Herod, due to numerous misunderstandings over matters of jurisdiction.

Pilate, calling the guards, said: "This man is a Galilean. Take him forthwith to Herod, and when he has examined him, report his findings to me." And they took Jesus to Herod. ∎

BEFORE HEROD AND THE RETURN TO PILATE

When they brought Jesus before Herod, the tetrarch was startled by his stately appearance and the calm composure of his countenance. For some fifteen minutes Herod asked Jesus questions, but the Master would not answer. Herod taunted and dared him to perform a miracle, but Jesus would not reply to his many inquiries or respond to his taunts.

Then Herod turned to the chief priests and the Sadducees and, giving ear to their accusations, heard all and more than Pilate had listened to regarding the alleged evil doings of the Son of Man. Finally, being convinced that Jesus would neither talk nor perform a wonder for him, Herod, after making fun of him for a time, arrayed him in an old purple royal robe and sent him back to Pilate. Herod knew he had no jurisdiction over Jesus in Judea. Though he was glad to believe that he was finally to be rid of Jesus in Galilee, he was thankful that it was Pilate who had the responsibility of putting him to death. Herod never had fully recovered from the fear that cursed him as a result of killing John the Baptist. Herod had at certain times even feared that Jesus was John risen from the dead. Now he was relieved of that fear since he observed that Jesus was a very different sort of person from the outspoken and fiery prophet who dared to expose and denounce his private life.

When the guards had brought Jesus back to Pilate, he went out on the front steps of the praetorium, where his judgment seat had been placed, and calling together the chief priests and Sanhedrists, said to them: "You brought this man before me with charges that he perverts the people, forbids the payment of taxes, and claims to be king of the Jews. I have examined him and fail to find him guilty of these charges. In fact, I find no fault in him. Then I sent him to Herod, and the tetrarch must have reached the same conclusion since he has sent him back to us. Certainly, nothing worthy of death has been done by this man. If you still think he needs to be disciplined, I am willing to chastise him before I release him."

Just as the Jews were about to engage in shouting their protests against the release of Jesus, a vast crowd came marching up to the praetorium for the purpose of asking Pilate for the release of a prisoner in honor of the Passover feast. For some time it had been the custom of the Roman governors to allow the populace to choose some imprisoned or condemned man for pardon at the time of the Passover. And now that this crowd had come before him to ask for the release of a prisoner, and since Jesus had so recently been in great favor with the multitudes, it occurred to Pilate that he might possibly extricate himself from his predicament by proposing to this group that, since Jesus was now a prisoner before his judgment seat, he release to them this man of Galilee as the token of Passover good will.

As the crowd surged up on the steps of the building, Pilate heard them calling out the name of one Barabbas. Barabbas was a noted political agitator and murderous robber, the son of a priest, who had recently been apprehended in the act of robbery and murder on the Jericho road. This man was under sentence to die as soon as the Passover festivities were over.

PILATE'S INSULT

By figuratively crowning Jesus the king of the Jews, Pilate made the chief priests furious. The Jews were a proud people, now subject to the Roman political yoke but hoping for the coming of a Messiah who would deliver them from gentile bondage with a great show of power and glory. They resented, more than Pilate could know, the intimation that this meek-mannered teacher of strange doctrines, now under arrest and charged with crimes worthy of death, should be referred to as "the king of the Jews." They looked upon such a remark as an insult to everything which they held sacred and honorable in their national existence, and therefore did they all let loose their mighty shouts for Barabbas's release and Jesus' death.

Pilate stood up and explained to the crowd that Jesus had been brought to him by the chief priests, who sought to have him put to death on certain charges, and that he did not think the man was worthy of death. Said Pilate: "Which, therefore, would you prefer that I release to you, this Barabbas, the murderer, or this Jesus of Galilee?" And when Pilate had thus spoken, the chief priests and the Sanhedrin councilors all shouted at the top of their voices, "Barabbas, Barabbas!" And when the people saw that the chief priests were minded to have Jesus put to death, they quickly joined in the clamor for his life while they loudly shouted for the release of Barabbas.

Pilate was angered at the sight of the chief priests clamoring for the pardon of a notorious murderer while they shouted for the blood of Jesus. He saw their malice and hatred and perceived their prejudice and envy. Therefore he said to them: "How could you choose the life of a murderer in preference to this man's whose worst crime is that he figuratively calls himself the king of the Jews?"

Pilate knew Jesus was innocent of the charges brought against him, and had he been a just and courageous judge, he would have acquitted him and turned him loose. But he was afraid to defy these angry Jews, and while he hesitated to do his duty, a messenger came up and presented him with a sealed message from his wife, Claudia.

Pilate indicated to those assembled before him that he wished to read the communication which he had just received before he proceeded further with the matter before him. When Pilate opened this letter from his wife, he read: "I pray you have nothing to do with this innocent and just man whom they call Jesus. I have suffered many things in a dream this night because of him." This note from Claudia not only greatly upset Pilate and thereby delayed the adjudication of this matter, but it unfortunately also provided considerable time in which the Jewish rulers freely circulated among the crowd and urged the people to call for the release of Barabbas and to clamor for the crucifixion of Jesus.

Finally, Pilate addressed himself once more to the solution of the problem which confronted him, by asking the mixed assembly of Jewish rulers and the pardon-seeking crowd, "What shall I do with him who is called the king of the Jews?" And they all shouted with one accord, "Crucify him! Crucify him!" The unanimity of this demand from the mixed multitude startled and alarmed Pilate, the unjust and fear-ridden judge.

Then once more Pilate said: "Why would you crucify this man? What evil has he done? Who will come forward to testify against him?" But when they heard Pilate speak in defense of Jesus, they only cried out all the more, "Crucify him! Crucify him!"

Then again Pilate appealed to them regarding the release of the Passover prisoner, saying: "Once more I ask you, which of these prisoners shall I release to you at this, your Passover time?" And again the crowd shouted, "Give us Barabbas!"

Then said Pilate: "If I release the murderer, Barabbas, what shall I do with Jesus?" And once more the multitude shouted in unison, "Crucify him! Crucify him!"

Pilate was terrorized by the insistent clamor of the mob, acting under the direct leadership of the chief priests and the councilors of the Sanhedrin; nevertheless, he decided upon at least one more attempt to appease the crowd and save Jesus.

PILATE'S LAST APPEAL
In all that is transpiring early this Friday morning before Pilate, only the enemies of Jesus are participating. His many friends either do not yet know of his night arrest and early morning trial or are in hiding lest they also be apprehended and adjudged worthy of death because they believe Jesus' teachings. In the multitude which now clamors for the Master's death are to be found only his sworn enemies and the easily led and unthinking populace.

Pilate would make one last appeal to their pity. Being afraid to defy the clamor of this misled mob who cried for the blood of Jesus, he ordered the Jewish guards and the Roman soldiers to take Jesus and scourge him. This was in itself an unjust and illegal procedure since the Roman law provided that only those condemned to die by crucifixion should be thus subjected to scourging. The guards took Jesus into the open courtyard of the praetorium for this ordeal. Though his enemies did not witness this scourging, Pilate did, and before they had finished this wicked abuse, he directed the scourgers to desist and indicated that Jesus should be brought to him. Before the scourgers laid their knotted whips upon Jesus as he was bound to

the whipping post, they again put upon him the purple robe, and plaiting a crown of thorns, they placed it upon his brow. And when they had put a reed in his hand as a mock scepter, they knelt before him and mocked him, saying, "Hail, king of the Jews!" And they spit upon him and struck him in the face with their hands. And one of them, before they returned him to Pilate, took the reed from his hand and struck him upon the head.

Then Pilate led forth this bleeding and lacerated prisoner and, presenting him before the mixed multitude, said: "Behold the man! Again I declare to you that I find no crime in him, and having scourged him, I would release him."

There stood Jesus of Nazareth, clothed in an old purple royal robe with a crown of thorns piercing his kindly brow. His face was blood-stained and his form bowed down with suffering and grief. But nothing can appeal to the unfeeling hearts of those who are victims of intense emotional hatred and slaves to religious prejudice. This sight sent a mighty shudder through the realms of a vast universe, but it did not touch the hearts of those who had set their minds to effect the destruction of Jesus.

When they had recovered from the first shock of seeing the Master's plight, they only shouted the louder and the longer, "Crucify him! Crucify him! Crucify him!"

And now did Pilate comprehend that it was futile to appeal to their supposed feelings of pity. He stepped forward and said: "I perceive that you are determined this man shall die, but what has he done to deserve death? Who will declare his crime?"

Then the high priest himself stepped forward and, going up to Pilate, angrily declared: "We have a sacred law, and by that law this man ought to die because he made himself out to be the Son of

[Antonio Ciseri — *Ecce Homo*]

God." When Pilate heard this, he was all the more afraid, not only of the Jews, but recalling his wife's note and the Greek mythology of the gods coming down on earth, he now trembled at the thought of Jesus possibly being a divine personage. He waved to the crowd to hold its peace while he took Jesus by the arm and again led him inside the building that he might further examine him. Pilate was now confused by fear, bewildered by superstition, and harassed by the stubborn attitude of the mob.

PILATE'S LAST INTERVIEW

As Pilate, trembling with fearful emotion, sat down by the side of Jesus, he inquired: "Where do you come from? Really, who are you? What is this they say, that you are the Son of God?"

But Jesus could hardly answer such questions when asked by a man-fearing, weak, and vacillating judge who was so unjust as to subject him to flogging even when he had declared him innocent of all crime, and before he had been duly sentenced to die. Jesus looked Pilate straight in the face, but he did not answer him. Then said Pilate: "Do you refuse to speak to me? Do you not realize that I still have power to release you or to crucify you?" Then said Jesus: "You could have no power over me except it were permitted from above. You could exercise no authority over the Son of Man unless the Father in heaven allowed it. But you are not so guilty since you are ignorant of the gospel. He who betrayed me and he who delivered me to you, they have the greater sin."

This last talk with Jesus thoroughly frightened Pilate. This moral coward and judicial weakling now labored under the double weight of the superstitious fear of Jesus and mortal dread of the Jewish leaders.

Again Pilate appeared before the crowd, saying: "I am certain this man is only a religious offender. You should take him and judge him by your law. Why should you expect that I would consent to his death because he has clashed with your traditions?"

Pilate was just about ready to release Jesus when Caiaphas, the high priest, approached the cowardly Roman judge and, shaking an avenging finger in Pilate's face, said with angry words which the entire multitude could hear: "If you release this man, you are not Caesar's friend, and I will see that the emperor knows all." This public threat was too much for Pilate. Fear for his personal fortunes now eclipsed all other considerations, and the cowardly governor ordered Jesus brought out before the judgment seat. As the Master stood there before them, he pointed to him and tauntingly said, "Behold your king." And the Jews answered, "Away with him. Crucify him!" And then Pilate said, with much irony and sarcasm, "Shall I crucify your king?" And the Jews answered, "Yes, crucify him! We have no king but Caesar." And then did Pilate realize that there was no hope of saving Jesus since he was unwilling to defy the Jews.

PILATE'S TRAGIC SURRENDER

Here stood the Son of God incarnate as the Son of Man. He was arrested without indictment; accused without evidence; adjudged without witnesses; punished without a verdict; and now was soon to be condemned to die by an unjust judge who confessed that he could find no fault in him. If Pilate had thought to appeal to their patriotism by referring to Jesus as the "king of the Jews," he utterly failed. The Jews were not expecting any such a king. The declaration of the chief priests and the Sadducees, "We have no king but Caesar," was a shock even to the unthinking populace, but it was too late now to save Jesus even had the mob dared to espouse the Master's cause.

Pilate was afraid of a tumult or a riot. He dared not risk having such a disturbance during Passover time in Jerusalem. He had recently received a reprimand from Caesar, and he would not risk another. The mob cheered when he ordered the release of Barabbas. Then he ordered a basin and some water, and there before the multitude he washed his hands, saying: "I am innocent of the blood of this man. You are determined that he shall die, but I have found no guilt in him. See you to it. The soldiers will lead him forth." And then the mob cheered and replied, "His blood be on us and on our children." ∎

THE CRUCIFIXION

It was just before nine o'clock this morning when the soldiers led Jesus from the praetorium on the way to Golgotha.

Before leaving the courtyard of the praetorium, the soldiers placed the crossbeam on Jesus' shoulders. It was the custom to compel the condemned man to carry the crossbeam to the site of the crucifixion. Such a condemned man did not carry the whole cross, only this shorter timber. The longer and upright pieces of timber for the three crosses had already been transported to Golgotha and, by the time of the arrival of the soldiers and their prisoners, had been firmly implanted in the ground.

As the Master trudged along on the way to the crucifixion, he was very weary; he was nearly exhausted. He had had neither food nor water since the Last Supper; neither had he been permitted to enjoy one moment of sleep. In addition, there had been one hearing right after another up to the hour of his condemnation, not to mention the abusive scourgings with their

CRUCIFIXION

Crucifixion was resorted to in order to provide a cruel and lingering punishment, the victim sometimes not dying for several days. There was considerable sentiment against crucifixion in Jerusalem, and there existed a society of Jewish women who always sent a representative to crucifixions for the purpose of offering drugged wine to the victim in order to lessen his suffering. But when Jesus tasted this narcotized wine, as thirsty as he was, he refused to drink it. The Master chose to retain his human consciousness until the very end. He desired to meet death, even in this cruel and inhuman form, and conquer it by voluntary submission to the full human experience.

accompanying physical suffering and loss of blood. Superimposed upon all this was his extreme mental anguish, his acute spiritual tension, and a terrible feeling of human loneliness.

Shortly after passing through the gate on the way out of the city, as Jesus staggered on bearing the crossbeam, his physical strength momentarily gave way, and he fell beneath the weight of his heavy burden. The soldiers shouted at him and kicked him, but he could not arise. When the captain saw this, knowing what Jesus had already endured, he commanded the soldiers to desist. Then he ordered a passerby, one Simon from Cyrene, to take the crossbeam from Jesus' shoulders and compelled him to carry it the rest of the way to Golgotha.

This man Simon had come all the way from Cyrene, in northern Africa, to attend the Passover. He was stopping with other Cyrenians just outside the city walls and was on his way to the temple services in the city when the Roman captain commanded him to carry Jesus' crossbeam. Simon lingered all through the hours of the Master's death on the cross, talking with many of his friends and with his enemies. After the resurrection and before leaving Jerusalem, he became a valiant believer in the gospel of the kingdom, and when he returned home, he led his family into the heavenly kingdom. His two sons, Alexander and Rufus, became very effective teachers of the new gospel in Africa. But Simon never knew that Jesus, whose burden he bore, and the Jewish tutor who once befriended his injured son, were the same person.

It was shortly after nine o'clock when this procession of death arrived at Golgotha, and the Roman soldiers set themselves about the task of nailing the two brigands and the Son of Man to their respective crosses.

The soldiers first bound the Master's arms with cords to the crossbeam, and then they nailed his hands to the wood. When they had hoisted this crossbeam up on the post, and after they had nailed it securely to the upright timber of the cross, they bound and nailed his feet to the wood, using one long nail to penetrate both feet. The upright timber had a large peg, inserted at the proper height, which served as a sort of saddle for supporting the body weight. The cross was not high, the Master's feet being only about three feet from the ground. He was therefore able to hear all that was said of him in derision and could plainly see the expression on the faces of all those who so thoughtlessly mocked him. And also could those present easily hear all that Jesus said during these hours of lingering torture and slow death.

It was the custom to remove all clothes from those who were to be crucified, but since the Jews greatly objected to the public exposure of the naked human form, the Romans always provided a suitable loin cloth for all persons crucified at Jerusalem. Accordingly, after Jesus' clothes had been removed, he was thus garbed before he was put upon the cross.

Before Jesus was put on his cross, the two brigands had already been placed on their crosses, all the while cursing and spitting upon their executioners. Jesus' only words, as they nailed him to the crossbeam, were, "Father, forgive them, for they know not what they do." He could not have so mercifully and lovingly interceded for his executioners if such thoughts of affectionate devotion had not been the mainspring of all his life of unselfish service. The ideas, motives, and longings of a lifetime are openly revealed in a crisis.

After the Master was hoisted on the cross, the captain nailed the title up above his head, and it read in three languages, "Jesus of Nazareth—the King of the Jews." The Jews were infuriated by this believed insult. But Pilate was chafed by their disrespectful manner; he felt he had been intimidated and humiliated, and he took this method of obtaining petty revenge. He could have written "Jesus, a rebel." But he well knew how these Jerusalem Jews detested the very name of Nazareth, and he was determined thus to humiliate them. He knew that they would also be cut to the very quick by seeing this executed Galilean called "The King of the Jews."

Many of the Jewish leaders, when they learned how Pilate had sought to deride them by placing this inscription on the cross of Jesus, hastened out to Golgotha, but they dared not attempt to remove it since the Roman soldiers were standing on guard. Not being able to remove the title, these leaders mingled with the crowd and did their utmost to incite derision and ridicule, lest any give serious regard to the inscription.

The Apostle John, with Mary the mother of Jesus, Ruth, and Jude, arrived on the scene just after Jesus had been hoisted to his position on the cross, and just as the captain was nailing the title above the Master's head. John was the only one of the eleven apostles to witness the crucifixion, and even he was not present all of the time since he ran into Jerusalem to bring back his mother and her friends soon after he had brought Jesus' mother to the scene.

As Jesus saw his mother, with John and his brother and sister, he smiled but said nothing. Meanwhile the four soldiers assigned to the Master's crucifixion, as was the custom, had divided his clothes among them, one taking the sandals, one the turban, one the girdle, and the fourth the cloak. This left the tunic, or seamless vestment reaching down to near the knees, to be cut up into four pieces, but when the soldiers saw what an unusual garment it was, they decided to cast

The End of Judas Iscariot

Early this Friday morning as the Romans made preparations to crucify Jesus, the Sanhedrin was meeting at their usual place in the hall of hewn stone in the temple. As Caiaphas was engaged in making his report regarding the trial and condemnation of Jesus, Judas appeared before them to claim his reward for the part he had played in his Master's arrest and sentence of death.

He anticipated suitable honors in token of the great service which he flattered himself he had rendered his nation. Imagine, therefore, the great surprise of this egotistic traitor when a servant of the high priest, tapping him on the shoulder, called him just outside the hall and said: "Judas, I have been appointed to pay you for the betrayal of Jesus. Here is your reward." And the servant of Caiaphas handed Judas a bag containing thirty pieces of silver—the current price of a good, healthy slave.

Judas was stunned, dumfounded. He wanted to appeal to the Sanhedrin, but they would not admit him. He was humiliated, disillusioned, and utterly crushed. He dropped the money bag in that same pocket wherein he had so long carried the bag containing the apostolic funds. And he wandered out through the city after the crowds who were on their way to witness the crucifixions.

From a distance Judas saw them raise the cross piece with Jesus nailed thereon, and upon sight of this he rushed back to the temple and, forcing his way past the doorkeeper, found himself standing in the presence of the Sanhedrin, which was still in session. The betrayer was well-nigh breathless and highly distraught, but he managed to stammer out these words: "I have sinned in that I have betrayed innocent blood. You have insulted me. You have offered me as a reward for my service, money—the price of a slave. I repent that I have done this; here is your money. I want to escape the guilt of this deed."

When the rulers of the Jews heard Judas, they scoffed at him. One of them said: "Your Master has already been put to death by the Romans, and as for your guilt, what is that to us? See you to that—and begone!"

As Judas left the Sanhedrin chamber, he removed the thirty pieces of silver from the bag and threw them broadcast over the temple floor. When the betrayer left the temple, he was almost beside himself. Judas was now passing through the experience of the realization of the true nature of sin. All the glamor, fascination, and intoxication of wrongdoing had vanished. Now the evildoer stood alone and face to face with the judgment verdict of his disillusioned and disappointed soul.

This onetime ambassador of the kingdom of heaven on earth now walked through the streets of Jerusalem, forsaken and alone. His despair was desperate and well-nigh absolute. On he journeyed down into the terrible solitude of the valley of Hinnom, where he climbed up the steep rocks and, taking the girdle of his cloak, fastened one end to a small tree, tied the other about his neck, and cast himself over the precipice. Ere he was dead, the knot which his nervous hands had tied gave way, and the betrayer's body was dashed to pieces as it fell on the jagged rocks below.

[Edward Okuń — *Judas* (detail)]

[PREM MUKHERJEE — *No Greater Love*]

lots for it. Jesus looked down on them while they divided his garments, and the thoughtless crowd jeered at him.

It was well that the Roman soldiers took possession of the Master's clothing. Otherwise, if his followers had gained possession of these garments, they would have been tempted to resort to superstitious relic worship. The Master desired that his followers should have nothing material to associate with his life on earth. He wanted to leave mankind only the memory of a human life dedicated to the high spiritual ideal of being consecrated to doing the Father's will.

At about half past nine o'clock this Friday morning, Jesus was hung upon the cross. Before eleven o'clock, upward of one thousand persons had assembled to witness this spectacle of the crucifixion of the Son of Man. Throughout these dreadful hours the unseen hosts of a universe stood in silence while they gazed upon this extraordinary phenomenon of the Creator as he was dying the death of the creature, even the most ignoble death of a condemned criminal.

Many who passed by wagged their heads and, railing at him, said: "You who would destroy the temple and build it again in three days, save yourself. If you are the Son of God, why do you not come down from your cross?" In like manner some of the rulers of the Jews mocked him, saying, "He saved others, but himself he cannot save." Others said, "If you are the king of the Jews, come down from the cross, and we will believe in you." And later on they mocked him the more, saying: "He trusted in God to deliver him. He even claimed to be the Son of God—look at him now—crucified between two thieves." Even the two thieves also railed at him and cast reproach upon him.

Inasmuch as Jesus would make no reply to their taunts, and since it was nearing noontime of this special preparation day, by half past eleven o'clock most of the jesting and jeering crowd had gone its way; less than fifty persons remained on the scene. The soldiers now prepared to eat lunch and drink their cheap, sour wine as they settled down for the long deathwatch. As they partook of their wine, they derisively offered a toast to Jesus, saying, "Hail and good fortune! to the king of the Jews." And they were astonished at the Master's tolerant regard of their ridicule and mocking.

When Jesus saw them eat and drink, he looked down upon them and said, "I thirst." When the captain of the guard heard Jesus say, "I thirst," he took some of the wine from his bottle and, putting the saturated sponge stopper upon the end of a javelin, raised it to Jesus so that he could moisten his parched lips.

Jesus had purposed to live without resort to his supernatural power, and he likewise elected to die as an ordinary mortal upon the cross. He had lived as a man, and he would die as a man—doing the Father's will.

THE THIEF ON THE CROSS

One of the brigands railed at Jesus, saying, "If you are the Son of God, why do you not save yourself and us?" But when he had reproached Jesus, the other thief, who had many times heard the Master teach, said: "Do you have no fear even of God? Do you not see that we are suffering justly for our deeds, but that this man suffers unjustly? Better that we should seek forgiveness for our sins and salvation for our souls." When Jesus heard the thief say this, he turned his face toward him and smiled approvingly. When the malefactor saw the face of Jesus turned toward him, he mustered up his courage, fanned the flickering flame of his faith, and said, "Lord, remember me when you come into your kingdom." And then Jesus said, "Verily, verily, I say to you today, you shall sometime be with me in Paradise."

The Master had time amidst the pangs of mortal death to listen to the faith confession of the believing brigand. When this thief reached out for salvation, he found deliverance. Many times before this he had been constrained to believe in Jesus, but only in these last hours of consciousness did he turn with a whole heart toward the Master's teaching. When he saw the manner in which Jesus faced death upon the cross, this thief could no longer resist the conviction that this Son of Man was indeed the Son of God.

During this episode of the conversion and reception of the thief into the kingdom by Jesus, the Apostle John was absent, having gone into the city to bring his mother and her friends to the scene of the crucifixion. Luke subsequently heard this story from the converted Roman captain of the guard.

The Apostle John told about the crucifixion as he remembered the event two thirds of a century after its occurrence. The other records were based upon the recital of the Roman centurion on duty who, because of what he saw and heard, subsequently believed in Jesus and entered into the full fellowship of the kingdom of heaven on earth.

Just after the repentant thief heard the Master's promise that they should sometime meet in Paradise, John returned from the city, bringing with him his mother and a company of almost a dozen women believers. John took up his position near Mary the mother of Jesus, supporting her. Her son Jude stood on the other side. As Jesus looked down upon this scene, it was noontide, and he said to his mother, "Woman, behold your son!" And speaking to John, he said, "My son, behold your mother!" And then he addressed them both, saying, "I desire that you depart from this place." And so John and Jude led Mary away from Golgotha. John took the mother of Jesus to the place where he tarried in Jerusalem and then hastened back to the scene of the crucifixion. After the Passover Mary returned to Bethsaida, where she lived at John's home for the rest of her natural life. Mary did not live quite one year after the death of Jesus.

Although it was early in the season for such a phenomenon, shortly after twelve o'clock the sky darkened by reason of the fine sand in the air. The people of Jerusalem knew that this meant the coming of one of those hot-wind sandstorms from the Arabian desert. Before one o'clock the sky was so dark the sun was hid, and the remainder of the crowd hastened back to the city. When the Master gave up his life, less than thirty people were present, only the thirteen Roman soldiers and a group of about fifteen believers.

Shortly after one o'clock, amidst the increasing darkness of the fierce sandstorm, Jesus began to fail in human consciousness. His last words of mercy, forgiveness, and admonition had been spoken. His last wish—concerning the care of his mother—had been expressed. During this hour of approaching death the human mind of Jesus resorted to the repetition of many passages in the Hebrew scriptures, particularly the Psalms. The last conscious thought of the human Jesus was concerned with the repetition in his mind of a portion of the Book of Psalms now known as the twentieth, twenty-first, and twenty-second Psalms. While his lips would often move, he was too weak to utter the words as these passages, which he so well knew by heart, would pass through his mind. Only a few times did those standing by catch some utterance, such as, "I know the Lord will save his anointed," "Your hand shall find out all my enemies," and "My God, my God, why have you forsaken me?" Jesus did not for one moment entertain the slightest doubt that he had lived in accordance with the Father's will; and he never doubted that he was now laying down his life in the flesh in accordance with his Father's will. He did not feel that the Father had forsaken him; he was merely reciting in his vanishing consciousness many Scriptures, among them this twenty-second Psalm, which begins with "My God, my God, why have you forsaken me?" And this happened to be one of the three passages which were spoken with sufficient clearness to be heard by those standing by.

The last request which the mortal Jesus made of his fellows was about half past one o'clock when, a second time, he said, "I thirst," and the same captain of the guard again moistened his lips with

Jesus, with a loud voice, cried out, "It is finished! Father, into your hands I commend my spirit." And he bowed his head and gave up the life struggle.

the same sponge wet in the sour wine, in those days commonly called vinegar.

The sandstorm grew in intensity and the heavens increasingly darkened. Still the soldiers and the small group of believers stood by. The soldiers crouched near the cross, huddled together to protect themselves from the cutting sand. The mother of John and others watched from a distance where they were somewhat sheltered by an overhanging rock. When the Master finally breathed his last, there were present at the foot of his cross John Zebedee, his brother Jude, his sister Ruth, Mary Magdalene, and Rebecca, onetime of Sepphoris.

It was just before three o'clock when Jesus, with a loud voice, cried out, "It is finished! Father, into your hands I commend my spirit." And when he had thus spoken, he bowed his head and gave up the life struggle. When the Roman centurion saw how Jesus died, he smote his breast and said: "This was indeed a righteous man; truly he must have been a Son of God." And from that hour he began to believe in Jesus.

The rulers of the Jews had planned to have Jesus' body thrown in the open burial pits of Gehenna, south of the city; it was the custom thus to dispose of the victims of crucifixion. If this plan had been followed, the body of the Master would have been exposed to the wild beasts.

In the meantime, Joseph of Arimathea, accompanied by Nicodemus, had gone to Pilate and asked that the body of Jesus be turned over to them for proper burial. It was not uncommon for friends of crucified persons to offer bribes to the Roman authorities for the privilege of gaining possession of such bodies. Joseph went before Pilate with a large sum of money, in case it became necessary to pay for permission to remove Jesus' body to a private burial tomb. But Pilate would not take money for this. When he heard the request, he quickly signed the order which authorized Joseph to proceed to Golgotha and take immediate and full possession of the Master's body. In the meantime, the sandstorm having considerably abated, a group of Jews representing the Sanhedrin had gone out to Golgotha for the purpose of making sure that Jesus' body accompanied those of the brigands to the open public burial pits.

When Joseph and Nicodemus arrived at Golgotha, they found the soldiers taking Jesus down from the cross and the representatives of the Sanhedrin standing by to see that none of Jesus' followers prevented his body from going to the criminal burial pits. When Joseph presented Pilate's order for the Master's body to the centurion, the Jews raised a tumult and clamored for its possession. In their raving they sought violently to take possession of the body, and when they did this, the centurion ordered four of his soldiers to his side, and with drawn swords they stood astride the Master's body as it lay there on the ground. The centurion ordered the other soldiers to leave the two thieves while they drove back this angry mob of infuriated Jews. When order had been restored, the centurion read the permit from Pilate to the Jews and, stepping aside, said to Joseph: "This body is yours to do with as you see fit. I and my soldiers will stand by to see that no man interferes."

A crucified person could not be buried in a Jewish cemetery; there was a strict law against such a procedure. Joseph and Nicodemus knew this law, and on the way out to Golgotha they had decided to bury Jesus in Joseph's new family tomb, hewn out of solid rock, located a short distance north of Golgotha and across the road leading to Samaria. No one had ever lain in this tomb, and they thought it appropriate that the Master should rest there. Joseph really believed that Jesus would rise from the dead, but Nicodemus was very doubtful. These former members of the Sanhedrin had kept their faith in Jesus more or less of a secret, although their fellow Sanhedrists had long suspected them,

even before they withdrew from the council. From now on they were the most outspoken disciples of Jesus in all Jerusalem.

At about half past four o'clock the burial procession of Jesus of Nazareth started from Golgotha for Joseph's tomb across the way. The body was wrapped in a linen sheet as the four men carried it, followed by the faithful women watchers from Galilee. The mortals who bore the material body of Jesus to the tomb were: Joseph, Nicodemus, John, and the Roman centurion.

They carried the body into the tomb, a chamber about ten feet square, where they hurriedly prepared it for burial. The Jews did not really

MEANING OF THE DEATH ON THE CROSS

Although Jesus did not die this death on the cross to atone for the racial guilt of mortal man nor to provide some sort of effective approach to an otherwise offended and unforgiving God; even though the Son of Man did not offer himself as a sacrifice to appease the wrath of God and to open the way for sinful man to obtain salvation; notwithstanding that these ideas of atonement and propitiation are erroneous, nonetheless, there are significances attached to this death of Jesus on the cross which should not be overlooked. It is a fact that Urantia has become known among other neighboring inhabited planets as the "World of the Cross."

Jesus desired to live a full mortal life in the flesh on Urantia. Death is, ordinarily, a part of life. Death is the last act in the mortal drama. In your well-meant efforts to escape the superstitious errors of the false interpretation of the meaning of the death on the cross, you should be careful not to make the great mistake of failing to perceive the true significance and the genuine import of the Master's death.

Mortal man was never the property of the arch-deceivers. Jesus did not die to ransom man from the clutch of the apostate rulers and fallen princes of the spheres. The Father in heaven never conceived of such crass injustice as damning a mortal soul because of the evil-doing of his ancestors. Neither was the Master's death on the cross a sacrifice which consisted in an effort to pay God a debt which the race of mankind had come to owe him.

Before Jesus lived on earth, you might possibly have been justified in believing in such a God, but not since the Master lived and died among your fellow mortals. Moses taught the dignity and justice of a Creator God; but Jesus portrayed the love and mercy of a heavenly Father.

The animal nature—the tendency toward evil-doing—may be hereditary, but sin is not transmitted from parent to child. Sin is the act of conscious and deliberate rebellion against the Father's will and the Sons' laws by an individual will creature.

Jesus lived and died for a whole universe, not just for the races of this one world. While the mortals of the realms had salvation even before Jesus lived and died on Urantia, it is nevertheless a fact that his bestowal on this world greatly illuminated the way of salvation; his death did much to make bury their dead; they actually embalmed them. Joseph and Nicodemus had brought with them large quantities of myrrh and aloes, and they now wrapped the body with bandages saturated with these solutions. When the embalming was completed, they tied a napkin about the face, wrapped the body in a linen sheet, and reverently placed it on a shelf in the tomb.

After placing the body in the tomb, the centurion signaled for his soldiers to help roll the doorstone up before the entrance to the tomb. The soldiers then departed for Gehenna with the bodies of the thieves while the others returned to Jerusalem, in sorrow, to observe the Passover feast according to the laws of Moses.

There was considerable hurry and haste about the burial of Jesus because this was preparation day and the Sabbath was drawing on apace. The men hurried back to the city, but the women lingered near the tomb until it was very dark.

The women who thus tarried by the tomb on this Friday evening were: Mary Magdalene, Mary the wife of Clopas, Martha another sister of Jesus' mother, and Rebecca of Sepphoris.

Aside from David Zebedee and Joseph of Arimathea, very few of Jesus' disciples really believed or understood that he was due to arise from the tomb on the third day. ✶

---

forever plain the certainty of mortal survival after death in the flesh.

Though it is hardly proper to speak of Jesus as a sacrificer, a ransomer, or a redeemer, it is wholly correct to refer to him as a *savior*. He forever made the way of salvation (survival) more clear and certain; he did better and more surely show the way of salvation for all the mortals of all the worlds of the universe of Nebadon.

When once you grasp the idea of God as a true and loving Father, the only concept which Jesus ever taught, you must forthwith, in all consistency, utterly abandon all those primitive notions about God as an offended monarch, a stern and all-powerful ruler whose chief delight is to detect his subjects in wrongdoing and to see that they are adequately punished, unless some being almost equal to himself should volunteer to suffer for them, to die as a substitute and in their stead. The whole idea of ransom and atonement is incompatible with the concept of God as it was taught and exemplified by Jesus of Nazareth. The infinite love of God is not secondary to anything in the divine nature.

The sufferings of Jesus were not confined to the crucifixion. In reality, Jesus of Nazareth spent upward of twenty-five years on the cross of a real and intense mortal existence. The real value of the cross consists in the fact that it was the supreme and final expression of his love, the completed revelation of his mercy.

The triumph of the death on the cross is all summed up in the spirit of Jesus' attitude toward those who assailed him. He made the cross an eternal symbol of the triumph of love over hate and the victory of truth over evil when he prayed, "Father, forgive them, for they know not what they do." That devotion of love was contagious throughout a vast universe; the disciples caught it from their Master. Stephen, the very first teacher of his gospel who was called upon to lay down his life in this service, said, as they stoned him to death, "Lay not this sin to their charge."

The cross makes a supreme appeal to the best in man because it discloses one who was willing to lay down his life in the service of his fellow men. Greater love no man can have than this: that he would be willing to lay down his life for his friends—and Jesus had such a love that he was willing to lay down his life for his enemies, a love greater than any which had hitherto been known on earth.

The great thing about the death of Jesus, as it is related to the enrichment of human experience, is not the *fact* of his death but rather the superb manner and the matchless spirit in which he met death.

"I AM THE RESURRECTION AND THE LIFE"

So then the Lord Jesus, after he had spoken to them, was taken up into heaven, and sat down at the right hand of God.

—MARK 16:19 RSV

JUST BEFORE THREE O'CLOCK ON FRIDAY AFTERNOON, JESUS OF NAZARETH LAID DOWN HIS life as a mortal of the realm. Thirty-six hours later on Sunday morning, he took it up again in a higher form. All this power which is inherent in Jesus—the endowment of life—and which enabled him to rise from the dead, is the very gift of eternal life which he bestows upon kingdom believers, and which even now makes certain their resurrection from the bonds of natural death.

Jesus lived a life which is a revelation of man submitted to the Father's will, not an example for any person literally to attempt to follow. This life in the flesh, together with his death on the cross and subsequent resurrection, presently became a new gospel of the ransom which had thus been paid in order to purchase man back from the clutch of the evil one—from the condemnation of an offended God. Nevertheless, even though the gospel did become greatly distorted, it remains a fact that this new message about Jesus carried along with it many of the fundamental truths and teachings of his earlier gospel of the kingdom. And, sooner or later, these concealed truths of the fatherhood of God and the brotherhood of men will emerge to effectually transform the civilization of all mankind.

But these mistakes of the intellect in no way interfered with the believer's great progress in growth in spirit. In less than a month after the bestowal of the Spirit of Truth, the apostles made more individual spiritual progress than during their almost four years of personal and loving association with the Master. Neither did this substitution of the *fact* of the resurrection of Jesus for the saving gospel *truth* of sonship with God in any way interfere with the rapid spread of their teachings; on the contrary, this new gospel of the risen Christ seemed greatly to facilitate the preaching of the good news.

———

THE URANTIA BOOK: PAPERS 189–196
SUNDAY, APRIL 9–THURSDAY, MAY 18, A.D. 30

[J. KIRK RICHARDS — *Garden Tomb*]

THE RESURRECTION

At two minutes past three o'clock, this Sunday morning, April 9, A.D. 30, the resurrected morontia form and personality of Jesus of Nazareth came forth from the tomb.

After the resurrected Jesus emerged from his burial tomb, the body of flesh in which he had lived and wrought on earth for almost thirty-six years was still lying there in the sepulchre niche, undisturbed and wrapped in the linen sheet, just as it had been laid to rest by Joseph and his associates on Friday afternoon. Neither was the stone before the entrance of the tomb in any way disturbed; the seal of Pilate was still unbroken; the soldiers were still on guard. The temple guards had been on continuous duty; the Roman guard had been changed at midnight. None of these watchers suspected that the object of their vigil had risen to a new and higher form of existence, and that the body which they were guarding was now a discarded outer covering which had no further connection with the delivered and resurrected morontia personality of Jesus.

At ten minutes past three o'clock, the chief of archangels—the angels of the resurrection—approached Gabriel and asked for the mortal body of Jesus. Said the chief of the archangels: "It is enough that we have seen the Sovereign live and die on Urantia; the hosts of heaven would be spared the memory of enduring the sight of the slow decay of the human form of the Creator and Upholder of a universe. I ask for

JESUS' MORTAL TRANSIT

Now is the mortal transit of Jesus—the morontia resurrection of the Son of Man—completed. The transitory experience of the Master as a personality midway between the material and the spiritual has begun. And he has done all this through power inherent within himself; no personality has rendered him any assistance.

a mandate giving me the custody of the mortal body of Jesus of Nazareth and empowering us to proceed with its immediate dissolution."

As they made ready to remove the body of Jesus from the tomb preparatory to according it the dignified and reverent disposal of near-instantaneous dissolution, it was assigned the secondary Urantia midwayers to roll away the stones from the entrance of the tomb. The larger of these two stones was a huge circular affair, much like a millstone, and it moved in a groove chiseled out of the rock, so that it could be rolled back and forth to open or close the tomb. When the watching Jewish guards and the Roman soldiers, in the dim light of the morning, saw this huge stone begin to roll away from the entrance of the tomb, apparently of its own accord—without any visible means to account for such motion—they were seized with fear and panic, and they fled in haste from the scene. The Jews fled to their homes, afterward going back to report these doings to their captain at the temple. The Romans fled to the fortress of Antonia and reported what they had seen to the centurion as soon as he arrived on duty.

The Jewish leaders began the sordid business of supposedly getting rid of Jesus by offering bribes to the traitorous Judas, and now, when confronted with this embarrassing situation, instead of thinking of punishing the guards who deserted their post, they resorted to bribing these guards and the Roman soldiers. They paid each of these twenty men a sum of money and instructed them to say to all: "While we slept during the nighttime, his disciples came upon us and took away the body." And the Jewish leaders made solemn promises to the soldiers to defend them before Pilate in case it should ever come to the governor's knowledge that they had accepted a bribe.

The tomb of Joseph was empty, not because the body of Jesus had been rehabilitated or resurrected, but because the celestial hosts had been granted their request to afford it a special and unique dissolution, a return of the "dust to dust," without the intervention of the delays of time and without the operation of the ordinary and visible processes of mortal decay and material corruption.

The mortal remains of Jesus underwent the same natural process of elemental disintegration as characterizes all human bodies on earth except that, in point of time, this natural mode of dissolution was greatly accelerated, hastened to that point where it became well-nigh instantaneous.

The true evidences of the resurrection of Jesus are spiritual in nature, albeit this teaching is corroborated by the testimony of many mortals of the realm who met, recognized, and communed with the resurrected Master. He became a part of the personal experience of almost one thousand human beings before he finally took leave of this world of his bestowal.

DISCOVERY OF THE EMPTY TOMB
At the home of Nicodemus there were gathered together, with David Zebedee and Joseph of Arimathea, some twelve or fifteen of the more prominent of the Jerusalem disciples of Jesus. At the home of Joseph of Arimathea there were some fifteen or twenty of the leading women believers.

Only these women abode in Joseph's house, and they had kept close within during the hours of the Sabbath day and the evening after the Sabbath, so that they were ignorant of the military guard on watch at the tomb; neither did they know that a second stone had been rolled in front of the tomb, and that both of these stones had been placed under the seal of Pilate.

A little before three o'clock this Sunday morning, when the first signs of day began to appear in the east, five of the women started out for the tomb of Jesus. They had prepared an abundance of special embalming lotions, and they carried many linen bandages with them. It was their purpose more thoroughly to give the body of Jesus its death anointing and more carefully to wrap it up with the new bandages.

It was about half past three o'clock when the five women, laden with their ointments, arrived before the empty tomb. As they passed out of the Damascus gate, they encountered a number of soldiers fleeing into the city more or less panic-stricken, and this caused them to pause for a few minutes; but when nothing more developed, they resumed their journey.

They were greatly surprised to see the stone rolled away from the entrance to the tomb, inasmuch as they had said among themselves on the way out, "Who will help us roll away the stone?" They set down their burdens and began to look upon one another in fear and with great amazement. While they stood there, atremble with fear, Mary Magdalene ventured around the smaller stone and dared to enter the open sepulchre. This tomb of Joseph was in his garden on the hillside on the eastern side of the road, and it also faced toward the east. By this hour there was just enough of the dawn of a new day to enable Mary to look back to the place where the Master's body had lain and to discern that it was gone. In the recess of stone where they had laid Jesus, Mary saw only the folded napkin where his head had rested and the bandages wherewith he had been wrapped lying intact and as they had rested on the stone before the celestial hosts removed the body. The covering sheet lay at the foot of the burial niche.

After Mary had tarried in the doorway of the tomb for a few moments (she did not see distinctly when she first entered the tomb), she saw that Jesus' body was gone and in its place only these grave cloths, and she uttered a cry of alarm and anguish. All the women were exceedingly nervous; they had been on edge ever since meeting the panicky soldiers at the city gate, and when Mary uttered this scream of anguish, they were terror-stricken and fled in great haste. And they did not stop until they had run all the way to the Damascus gate. By this time Joanna was conscience-stricken that they had deserted Mary; she rallied her companions, and they started back for the tomb.

As they drew near the sepulchre, the frightened Magdalene, who was even more terrorized when she failed to find her sisters waiting when she came out of the tomb, now rushed up to them, excitedly exclaiming: "He is not there—they have taken him away!" And she led them back to the tomb, and they all entered and saw that it was empty.

All five of the women then sat down on the stone near the entrance and talked over the situation. It had not yet occurred to them that Jesus had been resurrected. They had been by themselves over the Sabbath, and they conjectured that the body had been moved to another resting place.

But when they pondered such a solution of their dilemma, they were at a loss to account for the orderly arrangement of the grave cloths; how could the body have been removed since the very bandages in which it was wrapped were left in position and apparently intact on the burial shelf?

As these women sat there in the early hours of the dawn of this new day, they looked to one side

[WALTER RANE — *He Is Not Here*]

and observed a silent and motionless stranger. For a moment they were again frightened, but Mary Magdalene, rushing toward him and addressing him as if she thought he might be the caretaker of the garden, said, "Where have you taken the Master? Where have they laid him? Tell us that we may go and get him." When the stranger did not answer Mary, she began to weep. Then spoke Jesus to them, saying, "Whom do you seek?" Mary said: "We seek for Jesus who was laid to rest in Joseph's tomb, but he is gone. Do you know where they have taken him?" Then said Jesus: "Did not this Jesus tell you, even in Galilee, that he would die, but that he would rise again?" These words startled the women, but the Master was so changed that they did not yet recognize him with his back

turned to the dim light. And as they pondered his words, he addressed the Magdalene with a familiar voice, saying, "Mary." And when she heard that word of well-known sympathy and affectionate greeting, she knew it was the voice of the Master, and she rushed to kneel at his feet while she exclaimed, "My Lord, and my Master!" And all of the other women recognized that it was the Master who stood before them in glorified form, and they quickly knelt before him.

As Mary sought to embrace his feet, Jesus said: "Touch me not, Mary, for I am not as you knew me in the flesh. In this form will I tarry with you for a season before I ascend to the Father. But go, all of you, now and tell my apostles—and Peter—that I have risen, and that you have talked with me."

After these women had recovered from the shock of their amazement, they hastened back to the city and to the home of Elijah Mark, where they related to the ten apostles all that had happened to them; but the apostles were not inclined to believe them. They thought at first that the women had seen a vision, but when Mary Magdalene repeated the words which Jesus had spoken to them, and when Peter heard his name, he rushed out of the upper chamber, followed closely by John, in great haste to reach the tomb and see these things for himself.

The women repeated the story of talking with Jesus to the other apostles, but they would not believe; and they would not go to find out for themselves as had Peter and John.

John, being younger than Peter, outran him and arrived first at the tomb. John tarried at the door, viewing the tomb, and it was just as Mary had described it. Very soon Simon Peter rushed up and, entering, saw the same empty tomb with the grave cloths so peculiarly arranged. And when Peter had come out, John also went in and saw it all for himself, and then they sat down on the stone to ponder the meaning of what they had seen and heard.

Again they both went back into the tomb more closely to examine the grave cloths. As they came out of the tomb the second time, they found Mary Magdalene returned and weeping before the entrance. Mary had gone to the apostles believing that Jesus had risen from the grave, but when they all refused to believe her report, she became downcast and despairing. She longed to go back near the tomb, where she thought she had heard the familiar voice of Jesus.

As Mary lingered after Peter and John had gone, the Master again appeared to her, saying: "Be not doubting; have the courage to believe what you have seen and heard. Go back to my apostles and again tell them that I have risen, that I will appear to them, and that presently I will go before them into Galilee as I promised."　■

THE WALK WITH TWO BROTHERS

At Emmaus, about seven miles west of Jerusalem, there lived two brothers, shepherds, who had spent the Passover week in Jerusalem attending upon the sacrifices, ceremonials, and feasts. Cleopas, the elder, was a partial believer in Jesus; at least he had been cast out of the synagogue. His brother, Jacob, was not a believer, although he was much intrigued by what he had heard about the Master's teachings and works.

On this Sunday afternoon, about three miles out of Jerusalem and a few minutes before five o'clock, as these two brothers trudged along the road to Emmaus, they talked in great earnestness about Jesus, his teachings, work, and more especially concerning the rumors that his tomb was empty, and that certain of the women had

[MICHAEL MALM — *Two Brothers from Emmaus*]

talked with him. Cleopas was half a mind to believe these reports, but Jacob was insistent that the whole affair was probably a fraud. While they thus argued and debated as they made their way toward home, the morontia manifestation of Jesus, his seventh appearance, came alongside them as they journeyed on. Cleopas had often heard Jesus teach and had eaten with him at the homes of Jerusalem believers on several occasions. But he did not recognize the Master even when he spoke freely with them.

After walking a short way with them, Jesus said: "What were the words you exchanged so earnestly as I came upon you?" And when Jesus had spoken, they stood still and viewed him with sad surprise. Said Cleopas: "Can it be that you sojourn in Jerusalem and know not the things which have recently happened?" Then asked the Master, "What things?" Cleopas replied: "If you do not know about these matters, you are the only one in Jerusalem who has not heard these rumors concerning Jesus of Nazareth, who was a prophet mighty in word and in deed before God and all the people. The chief priests and our rulers delivered him up to the Romans and demanded that they crucify him. Now many of us had hoped that it was he who would deliver Israel from the yoke of the gentiles. But that is not all. It is now the third day since he was crucified, and certain women have this day amazed us by declaring that very early this morning they went to his tomb and found it empty. And these same women insist that they talked with this man; they maintain that he has risen from the dead. And when the women

reported this to the men, two of his apostles ran to the tomb and likewise found it empty"—and here Jacob interrupted his brother to say, "but they did not see Jesus."

As they walked along, Jesus said to them: "How slow you are to comprehend the truth! When you tell me that it is about the teachings and work of this man that you have your discussions, then may I enlighten you since I am more than familiar with these teachings. Do you not remember that this Jesus always taught that his kingdom was not of this world, and that all men, being the sons of God, should find liberty and freedom in the spiritual joy of the fellowship of the brotherhood of loving service in this new kingdom of the truth of the heavenly Father's love? Do you not recall how this Son of Man proclaimed the salvation of God for all men, ministering to the sick and afflicted and setting free those who were bound by fear and enslaved by evil? Do you not know that this man of Nazareth told his disciples that he must go to Jerusalem, be delivered up to his enemies, who would put him to death, and that he would arise on the third day? Have you not been told all this? And have you never read in the Scriptures concerning this day of salvation for Jew and gentile, where it says that in him shall all the families of the earth be blessed; that he will hear the cry of the needy and save the souls of the poor who seek him; that all nations shall call him blessed? That such a Deliverer shall be as the shadow of a great rock in a weary land. That he will feed the flock like a true shepherd, gathering the lambs in his arms and tenderly carrying them in his bosom. That he will open the eyes of the spiritually blind and bring the prisoners of despair out into full liberty and light; that all who sit in darkness shall see the great light of eternal salvation. That he will bind up the brokenhearted, proclaim liberty to the captives of sin, and open up the prison to those who are enslaved by fear and bound by evil. That he will comfort those who mourn and bestow upon them the joy of salvation in the place of sorrow and heaviness. That he shall be the desire of all nations and the everlasting joy of those who seek righteousness. That this Son of truth and righteousness shall rise upon the world with healing light and saving power; even that he will save his people from their sins; that he will really seek and save those who are lost. That he will not destroy the weak but minister salvation to all who hunger and thirst for righteousness. That those who believe in him shall have eternal life. That he will pour out his spirit upon all flesh, and that this Spirit of Truth shall be in each believer a well of water, springing up into everlasting life. Did you not understand how great was the gospel of the kingdom which this man delivered to you? Do you not perceive how great a salvation has come upon you?"

By this time they had come near to the village where these brothers dwelt. Not a word had these two men spoken since Jesus began to teach them as they walked along the way. Soon they drew up in front of their humble dwelling place, and Jesus was about to take leave of them, going on down the road, but they constrained him to come in and abide with them. They insisted that it was near nightfall, and that he tarry with them. Finally Jesus consented, and very soon after they went into the house, they sat down to eat. They gave him the bread to bless, and as he began to break and hand to them, their eyes were opened, and Cleopas recognized that their guest was the Master himself. And when he said, "It is the Master—," the morontia Jesus vanished from their sight.

And then they said, the one to the other, "No wonder our hearts burned within us as he spoke to us while we walked along the road! and while he opened up to our understanding the teachings of the Scriptures!"

They would not stop to eat. They had seen the Master, and they rushed from the house, hastening back to Jerusalem to spread the good news of the risen Savior.

About nine o'clock that evening and just before the Master appeared to the ten, these two excited brothers broke in upon the apostles in the upper chamber, declaring that they had seen Jesus and talked with him. And they told all that Jesus had said to them and how they had not discerned who he was until the time of the breaking of the bread. ∎

APPEARANCES TO THE APOSTLES

Resurrection Sunday was a terrible day in the lives of the apostles; ten of them spent the larger part of the day in the upper chamber behind barred doors. They might have fled from Jerusalem, but they were afraid of being arrested by the agents of the Sanhedrin if they were found abroad. Thomas was brooding over his troubles alone at Bethpage. He would have fared better had he remained with his fellow apostles, and he would have aided them to direct their discussions along more helpful lines.

It was near half past eight o'clock this Sunday evening when Jesus appeared to Simon Peter in the garden of the Mark home as the dejected apostle strolled among the flowers and shrubs.

When Peter thought of the loving look of the Master as he passed by on Annas's porch, and as he turned over in his mind that wonderful message brought him early that morning by the women who came from the empty tomb, "Go tell my apostles—and Peter"—as he contemplated these tokens of mercy, his faith began to surmount his doubts, and he stood still, clenching his fists, while he spoke aloud: "I believe he has risen from the dead; I will go and tell my brethren." And as he said this, there suddenly appeared in front of him the form of a man, who spoke to him in familiar tones, saying: "Peter, the enemy desired to have you, but I would not give you up. I knew it was not from the heart that you disowned me; therefore I forgave you even before you asked; but now must you cease to think about yourself and the troubles of the hour while you prepare to carry the good news of the gospel to those who sit in darkness. No longer should you be concerned with what you may obtain from the kingdom but rather be exercised about what you can give to those who live in dire spiritual poverty. Gird yourself, Simon, for the battle of a new day, the struggle with spiritual darkness and the evil doubtings of the natural minds of men."

Peter and Jesus walked through the garden and talked of things past, present, and future for almost five minutes. Then the Master vanished from his gaze, saying, "Farewell, Peter, until I see you with your brethren."

FIRST APPEARANCE

The Master put off the first appearance to the apostles for a number of reasons. First, he wanted them to have time, after they heard of his resurrection, to think well over what he had told them about his death and resurrection when he was still with them in the flesh. The Master wanted Peter to wrestle through with some of his peculiar difficulties before he manifested himself to them all. In the second place, he desired that Thomas should be with them at the time of his first appearance.

Shortly after nine o'clock that evening, after the departure of Cleopas and Jacob, and as the ten apostles were there assembled in the upper chamber with all the doors bolted for fear of arrest, the Master, in morontia form, suddenly appeared in the midst of them, saying: "Peace be upon you. Why are you so frightened when I appear, as though you had seen a spirit? Did I not tell you about these things when I was present with you in the flesh? Did I not say to you that the chief priests and the rulers would deliver me up to be killed, that one of your own number would betray me, and that on the third day I would rise? Wherefore all your doubtings and all this discussion about the reports of the women, Cleopas and Jacob, and even Peter? How long will you doubt my words and refuse to believe my promises? And now that you actually see me, will you believe? Even now one of you is absent. When you are gathered together once more, and after all of you know of a certainty that the Son of Man has risen from the grave, go hence into Galilee. Have faith in God; have faith in one another; and so shall you enter into the new service of the kingdom of heaven. I will tarry in Jerusalem with you until you are ready to go into Galilee. My peace I leave with you."

"WHY ARE YOU SO FRIGHTENED WHEN I APPEAR, AS THOUGH YOU HAD SEEN A SPIRIT? DID I NOT TELL YOU ABOUT THESE THINGS WHEN I WAS PRESENT WITH YOU IN THE FLESH?"

"I WILL NOT BELIEVE UNLESS I SEE THE MASTER WITH MY OWN EYES AND PUT MY FINGER IN THE MARK OF THE NAILS."

SECOND APPEARANCE TO THE APOSTLES

Thomas spent a lonesome week alone with himself in the hills around about Olivet. During this time he saw only those at Simon's house and John Mark. It was about nine o'clock on Saturday, April 15, when the two apostles found him and took him back with them to their rendezvous at the Mark home. The next day Thomas listened to the telling of the stories of the Master's various appearances, but he steadfastly refused to believe. He maintained that Peter had enthused them into thinking they had seen the Master. Nathaniel reasoned with him, but it did no good. There was an emotional stubbornness associated with his customary doubtfulness, and this state of mind, coupled with his chagrin at having run away from them, conspired to create a situation of isolation which even Thomas himself did not fully understand. He had withdrawn from his fellows, he had gone his own way, and now, even when he was back among them, he unconsciously tended to assume an attitude of disagreement. He was slow to surrender; he disliked to give in. Without intending it, he really enjoyed the attention paid him; he derived unconscious satisfaction from the efforts of all his fellows to convince and convert him. He had missed them for a full week, and he obtained considerable pleasure from their persistent attentions.

They were having their evening meal a little after six o'clock, with Peter sitting on one side of Thomas and Nathaniel on the other, when the doubting apostle said: "I will not believe unless I see the Master with my own eyes and put my finger in the mark of the nails." As they thus sat at supper, and while the doors were securely shut and barred, the morontia Master suddenly appeared inside the curvature of the table and, standing directly in front of Thomas, said:

"Peace be upon you. For a full week have I tarried that I might appear again when you were all present to hear once more the commission to go into all the world and preach this gospel of the kingdom. Again I tell you: As the Father sent me into the world, so send I you. As I have revealed the Father, so shall you reveal the divine love, not merely with words, but in your daily living. I send you forth, not to love the souls of men, but rather to *love men*. You are not merely to proclaim the joys of heaven but also to exhibit in your daily experience these spirit realities of the divine life since you already have eternal life, as the gift of God, through faith. When you have faith, when power from on high, the Spirit of Truth, has come upon you, you will not hide your light here behind closed doors; you will make known the love and the mercy of God to all mankind. Through fear you now flee from the facts of a disagreeable experience, but when you shall have been baptized with the Spirit of Truth, you will bravely and joyously go forth to meet the new experiences of proclaiming the good news of eternal life in the kingdom of God. You may tarry here and in Galilee for a short season while you recover from the shock of the transition from the false security of the authority of traditionalism to the new order of the authority of facts, truth, and faith in the supreme realities of living experience. Your mission to the world is founded on the fact that I lived a God-revealing life among you; on the truth

[J. KIRK RICHARDS — *Jesus Resurrected* (detail)]

that you and all other men are the sons of God; and it shall consist in the life which you will live among men—the actual and living experience of loving men and serving them, even as I have loved and served you. Let faith reveal your light to the world; let the revelation of truth open the eyes blinded by tradition; let your loving service effectually destroy the prejudice engendered by ignorance. By so drawing close to your fellow men in understanding sympathy and with unselfish devotion, you will lead them into a saving knowledge of the Father's love. The Jews have extolled goodness; the Greeks have exalted beauty; the Hindus preach devotion; the faraway ascetics teach reverence; the Romans demand loyalty; but I require of my disciples life, even a life of loving service for your brothers in the flesh."

When the Master had so spoken, he looked down into the face of Thomas and said: "And you, Thomas, who said you would not believe unless you could see me and put your finger in the nail marks of my hands, have now beheld me and heard my words; and though you see no nail marks on my hands, since I am raised in the form that you also shall have when you depart from this world, what will you say to your brethren? You will acknowledge the truth, for already in your heart you had begun to believe even when you so stoutly asserted your unbelief. Your doubts, Thomas, always most stubbornly assert themselves just as they are about to crumble. Thomas, I bid you be not faithless but believing—and I know you will believe, even with a whole heart."

When Thomas heard these words, he fell on

THEN SAID JESUS TO THOMAS: "BLESSED ARE THOSE IN THE AGES TO COME WHO WILL BELIEVE EVEN THOUGH THEY HAVE NOT SEEN WITH THE EYE OF FLESH NOR HEARD WITH THE MORTAL EAR."

his knees before the morontia Master and exclaimed, "I believe! My Lord and my Master!" Then said Jesus to Thomas: "You have believed, Thomas, because you have really seen and heard me. Blessed are those in the ages to come who will believe even though they have not seen with the eye of flesh nor heard with the mortal ear."

And then, as the Master's form moved over near the head of the table, he addressed them all, saying: "And now go all of you to Galilee, where I will presently appear to you." After he said this, he vanished from their sight.

The eleven apostles were now fully convinced that Jesus had risen from the dead, and very early the next morning, before the break of day, they started out for Galilee. ∎

FRIDAY, APRIL 21, A.D. 30

APPEARANCE BY THE LAKE

About six o'clock Friday morning, April 21, the Master made his thirteenth appearance, the first in Galilee, to the ten apostles as their boat drew near the shore close to the usual landing place at Bethsaida.

After the apostles had spent the afternoon and early evening of Thursday in waiting at the Zebedee home, Simon Peter suggested that they go fishing. When Peter proposed the fishing trip, all of the apostles decided to go along. All night they toiled with the nets but caught no fish. They did not much mind the failure to make a catch,

for they had many interesting experiences to talk over, things which had so recently happened to them at Jerusalem. But when daylight came, they decided to return to Bethsaida. As they neared the shore, they saw someone on the beach, near the boat landing, standing by a fire. At first they thought it was John Mark, who had come down to welcome them back with their catch, but as they drew nearer the shore, they saw they were mistaken—the man was too tall for John. It had occurred to none of them that the person on the shore was the Master. They did not altogether understand why Jesus wanted to meet with them amidst the scenes of their earlier associations and out in the open in contact with nature, far away from the shut-in environment of Jerusalem with its tragic associations of fear, betrayal, and death. He had told them that, if they would go into Galilee, he would meet them there, and he was about to fulfill that promise.

As they dropped anchor and prepared to enter the small boat for going ashore, the man on the beach called to them, "Lads, have you caught anything?" And when they answered, "No," he spoke again. "Cast the net on the right side of the boat, and you will find fish." While they did not know it was Jesus who had directed them, with one accord they cast in the net as they had been instructed, and immediately it was filled, so much so that they were hardly able to draw it up. Now, John Zebedee was quick of perception, and when he saw the heavy-laden net, he perceived that it was the Master who had spoken to them. When this thought came into his mind, he leaned over and whispered to Peter, "It is the Master." Peter was ever a man of thoughtless action and impetuous devotion; so when John whispered this in his ear, he quickly arose and cast himself into the water that he might the sooner reach the Master's side.

[DEL PARSON — *Peter Do You Love Me?*]

His brethren came up close behind him, having come ashore in the small boat, hauling the net of fishes after them.

By this time John Mark was up and, seeing the apostles coming ashore with the heavy-laden net, ran down the beach to greet them; and when he saw eleven men instead of ten, he surmised that the unrecognized one was the risen Jesus, and as the astonished ten stood by in silence, the youth rushed up to the Master and, kneeling at his feet, said, "My Lord and my Master." And then Jesus spoke, not as he had in Jerusalem, when he greeted them with "Peace be upon you," but in commonplace tones he addressed John Mark: "Well, John, I am glad to see you again and in carefree Galilee, where we can have a good visit. Stay with us, John, and have breakfast."

As Jesus talked with John, the ten were so astonished and surprised that they neglected to haul the net of fish in upon the beach. Now spoke Jesus: "Bring in your fish and prepare some for breakfast. Already we have the fire and much bread."

While John Mark had paid homage to the Master, Peter had for a moment been shocked at the sight of the coals of fire glowing there on the beach; the scene reminded him so vividly of the midnight fire of charcoal in the courtyard of Annas, where he had disowned the Master, but he shook himself and, kneeling at the Master's feet, exclaimed, "My Lord and my Master!"

Peter then joined his comrades as they hauled in the net. When they had landed their catch, they counted the fish, and there were 153 large ones. And again was the mistake made of calling this another miraculous catch of fish. There was no miracle connected with this episode. It was merely an exercise of the Master's preknowledge. He knew the fish were there and accordingly directed the apostles where to cast the net.

Jesus spoke to them, saying: "Come now, all of you, to breakfast. Even the twins should sit down while I visit with you; John Mark will dress the fish." John Mark brought seven good-sized fish, which the Master put on the fire, and when they were cooked, the lad served them to the ten. Then Jesus broke the bread and handed it to John, who in turn served it to the hungry apostles. When they had all been served, Jesus bade John Mark sit down while he himself served the fish and the bread to the lad. And as they ate, Jesus visited with them and recounted their many experiences in Galilee and by this very lake.

This was the third time Jesus had manifested himself to the apostles as a group. When Jesus first addressed them, asking if they had any fish, they did not suspect who he was because it was a common experience for these fishermen on the Sea of Galilee, when they came ashore, to be thus accosted by the fish merchants of Tarichea, who were usually on hand to buy the fresh catches for the drying establishments.

Jesus visited with the ten apostles and John Mark for more than an hour, and then he walked up and down the beach, talking with them two and two—but not the same couples he had at first sent out together to teach. All eleven of the apostles had come down from Jerusalem together, but Simon Zelotes grew more and more despondent as they drew near Galilee, so that, when they reached Bethsaida, he forsook his brethren and returned to his home.

Before taking leave of them this morning, Jesus directed that two of the apostles should volunteer to go to Simon Zelotes and bring him back that very day. And Peter and Andrew did so.

When they had finished breakfast, and while the others sat by the fire, Jesus beckoned to Peter and to John that they should come with him for a stroll on the beach. As they walked along, Jesus said to John, "John, do you love me?" And when John answered, "Yes, Master, with all my heart," the Master said: "Then, John, give up your intolerance and learn to love men as I have loved you. Devote your life to proving that love is the greatest thing in the world. It is the love of God that impels men to seek salvation. Love is the ancestor of all spiritual goodness, the essence of the true and the beautiful."

Jesus then turned toward Peter and asked, "Peter, do you love me?" Peter answered, "Lord, you know I love you with all my soul." Then said Jesus: "If you love me, Peter, feed my lambs. Do not neglect to minister to the weak, the poor, and the young. Preach the gospel without fear or favor; remember always that God is no respecter of persons. Serve your fellow men even as I have served you; forgive your fellow mortals even as I have forgiven you. Let experience teach you the value of meditation and the power of intelligent reflection."

After they had walked along a little farther, the Master turned to Peter and asked, "Peter, do you really love me?" And then said Simon, "Yes, Lord, you know that I love you." And again said Jesus: "Then take good care of my sheep. Be a good and a true shepherd to the flock. Betray not their confidence in you. Be not taken by surprise at the enemy's hand. Be on guard at all times—watch and pray."

When they had gone a few steps farther, Jesus turned to Peter and, for the third time, asked, "Peter, do you truly love me?" And then Peter, being slightly grieved at the Master's seeming distrust of him, said with considerable feeling, "Lord, you know all things, and therefore do you know that I really and truly love you." Then said Jesus: "Feed my sheep. Do not forsake the flock. Be an example and an inspiration to all your fellow shepherds. Love the flock as I have loved you and devote yourself to their welfare even as I have devoted my life to your welfare. And follow after me even to the end."

Peter took this last statement literally—that he should continue to follow after him—and turning to Jesus, he pointed to John, asking, "If I follow on after you, what shall this man do?" And then, perceiving that Peter had misunderstood his words, Jesus said: "Peter, be not concerned about what your brethren shall do. If I will that John should tarry after you are gone, even until I come back, what is that to you? Only make sure that you follow me."

This remark spread among the brethren and was received as a statement by Jesus to the effect that John would not die before the Master returned, as many thought and hoped, to establish the kingdom in power and glory. It was this interpretation of what Jesus said that had much to do with getting Simon Zelotes back into service, and keeping him at work.

It was almost ten o'clock when Jesus returned from his visit with the Alpheus twins, and as he left the apostles, he said: "Farewell, until I meet you

VISITING WITH THE APOSTLES

Jesus walked up and down the beach talking with these men two and two, and he began by asking each pair a question:

"Andrew, do you trust me?" And Andrew answered, "Yes, Master, of a certainty I trust you, and you know that I do."

"James, do you trust me?" And of course James replied, "Yes, Master, I trust you with all my heart."

"Thomas, do you serve me?" Thomas replied, "Yes, Lord, I serve you now and always."

"Nathaniel, do you serve me?" And the apostle answered, "Yes, Master, and with an undivided affection."

"Philip, do you obey me?" Philip answered, "Yes, Lord, I will obey you even with my life."

"Matthew, do you have it in your heart to obey me?" Matthew answered, "Yes, Lord, I am fully dedicated to doing your will."

"James and Judas, do you believe in me?" And they both answered, "Yes, Master, we do believe."

all on the mount of your ordination tomorrow at noontime." When he had thus spoken, he vanished from their sight. ∎

RESURRECTION APPEARANCES

In the forty days from his resurrection until the hour of his spirit ascension on high, Jesus made nineteen separate appearances in visible form to his believers on earth. He did not appear to his enemies nor to those who could not make spiritual use of his manifestation in visible form. These appearances were corroborated by the testimony of many of those who met, recognized, and communed with the resurrected Master. When the various believers saw Jesus after his resurrection, they really saw him; they were not the self-deceived victims of visions or hallucinations. He became a part of the personal experience of almost one thousand human beings before he finally took leave of this world.

THE THIRD APPEARANCE:
JAMES, THE BROTHER OF JESUS, IN BETHANY

While James stood there in the garden near the tomb of Lazarus, he became aware of a near-by presence, as if someone had touched him on the shoulder; and when he turned to look, he beheld the gradual appearance of a strange form by his side. He was too much amazed to speak and too frightened to flee. And then the strange form spoke, saying: "James, I come to call you to the service of the kingdom. Join earnest hands with your brethren and follow after me." When James heard his name spoken, he knew that it was his eldest brother, Jesus, who had addressed him. They all had more or less difficulty in recognizing the risen form of the Master, but few of them had any trouble recognizing his voice or otherwise identifying his charming personality when he once began to communicate with them.

When James perceived that Jesus was addressing him, he started to fall to his knees, exclaiming, "My father and my brother," but Jesus bade him stand while he spoke with him. And they walked through the garden and talked for almost three minutes; talked over experiences of former days and forecast the events of the near future. As they neared the house, Jesus said, "Farewell, James, until I greet you all together."

THE FIFTH APPEARANCE:
THE WOMEN BELIEVERS, IN JERUSALEM

Mary Magdalene had returned to her sister believers at Joseph's house and was in the very midst of a thrilling recital when a sudden and solemn hush fell over them; they beheld in their very midst the fully visible form of the risen Jesus. He greeted them, saying: "Peace be upon you. In the fellowship of the kingdom there shall be neither Jew nor gentile, rich nor poor, free nor bond, man nor woman. You also are called to publish the good news of the liberty of mankind through the gospel of sonship with God in the kingdom of heaven. Go to all the world proclaiming this gospel and confirming believers in the faith thereof. And while you do this, forget not to minister to the sick and strengthen those who are fainthearted and fear-ridden. And I will be with you always, even to the ends of the earth." And when he had thus spoken, he vanished from their sight, while the women fell on their faces and worshiped in silence.

THE SIXTH APPEARANCE:
THE GREEK BELIEVERS, HOME OF FLAVIUS

While some forty Greek believers were engaged in discussing the reports of the Master's resurrection, he manifested himself in their midst, notwithstanding that the doors were securely fastened, and speaking to them, said: "Peace be upon you. While the Son of Man appeared on earth among the Jews, he came to minister to all men. In the kingdom of my Father there shall be neither Jew nor gentile; you will all be brethren—the sons of God. Go you, therefore, to all the world, proclaiming this gospel of salvation as you have received it from the ambassadors of the kingdom, and I will fellowship you in the brotherhood of the Father's sons of faith and truth." And when he had thus charged them, he took leave, and they saw him no more. They remained within the house all evening; they were too much overcome with awe and fear to venture forth. Neither did any of these Greeks sleep that night; they stayed awake discussing these things and hoping that the Master might again visit them. Among this group were many of the Greeks who were at Gethsemane when Jesus was arrested.

The Twelfth Appearance:
Alexandria

David Zebedee had dispatched his messengers to inform believers scattered far and wide of the tragic word of the crucifixion. The fifth messenger in the Jerusalem-Alexandria relay of runners, one Nathan of Busiris, arrived in Alexandria four days later and appeared before some eighty Greek and Jewish believers who had gathered together to hear his report. Nathan ended his touching recital with these words: "But David, who sends us this word, reports that the Master, in foretelling his death, declared that he would rise again." Even as Nathan spoke, the risen Master appeared there in full view of all. And when Nathan sat down, Jesus said:

"Peace be upon you. That which my Father sent me into the world to establish belongs not to a race, a nation, nor to a special group of teachers or preachers. This gospel of the kingdom belongs to both Jew and gentile, to rich and poor, to free and bond, to male and female, even to the little children. And you are all to proclaim this gospel of love and truth by the lives which you live in the flesh. You shall love one another with a new

and startling affection, even as I have loved you. You will serve mankind with a new and amazing devotion, even as I have served you. And when men see you so love them, and when they behold how fervently you serve them, they will perceive that you have become faith-fellows of the kingdom of heaven, and they will follow after the Spirit of Truth which they see in your lives, to the finding of eternal salvation.

"As the Father sent me into this world, even so now send I you. You are all called to carry the good news to those who sit in darkness. This gospel of the kingdom belongs to all who believe it; it shall not be committed to the custody of mere priests. Soon will the Spirit of Truth come upon you, and he shall lead you into all truth. Go you, therefore, into all the world preaching this gospel, and lo, I am with you always, even to the end of the ages."

When the Master had so spoken, he vanished from their sight. All that night these believers remained there together recounting their experiences as kingdom believers and listening to the many words of Rodan and his associates. And they all believed that Jesus had risen from the dead. Imagine the surprise of David's herald of the resurrection, who arrived the second day after this, when they replied to his announcement, saying: "Yes, we know, for we have seen him. He appeared to us day before yesterday."

The Fifteenth Appearance:
Seaside Gathering, at Bethsaida

Word of the appearances of Jesus was spreading throughout Galilee, and every day increasing numbers of believers arrived at the Zebedee home to inquire about the Master's resurrection and to find out the truth about these reputed appearances. Peter, early in the week, sent out word that a public meeting would be held by the seaside the next Sabbath at three o'clock in the afternoon.

Accordingly, more than five hundred believers from around Capernaum assembled at Bethsaida

CHART OF THE NINETEEN APPEARANCES

No.	Date	Time	Location and Details	People
1	Sun 4–9	3:02 am	**Jerusalem:** At the new family tomb of Joseph of Arimathea where Jesus had been laid to rest; to Mary Magdalene, Mary the mother of the Alpheus twins, Salome the mother of the Zebedee brothers, Joanna the wife of Chuza, and Susanna the daughter of Ezra of Alexandria.	5
	Jesus rises 36 hours from his death on the cross. He appears to the women at dawn.			
2		6:00 am	**Jerusalem:** The tomb; to Mary Magdalene after she returns.	1
3		noon	**Bethany:** The empty tomb of Lazarus; to James, the Master's brother in the flesh. They walked and talked for almost three minutes.	1
4		2:00 pm	**Bethany:** Home of Mary and Martha; to Jesus' earthly family and their friends, including David Zebedee, 20 in all.	20
5		4:15 pm	**Jerusalem:** Home of Joseph of Arimathea; to some 25 women believers. Of the first five appearances of Jesus, Mary Magdalene witnessed four.	25
6		4:30 pm	**Jerusalem:** Home of one Flavius; to some 40 Greek believers.	40
7		5:00 pm	**Emmaus:** Three miles out of Jerusalem on the road to Emmaus; walked with the brothers Cleopas and Jacob to their humble dwelling place.	2
8		8:30 pm	**Jerusalem:** The home of Elijah and Mary Mark; to Simon Peter, alone in the garden, and just as his faith surmounted his doubts.	1
9		9:00 pm	**Jerusalem:** Upper chamber of the Mark home where they had celebrated the last supper; to ten apostles (less Thomas).	10
10	Tue 4–11	8:00 am	**Philadelphia:** Synagogue; to Abner, Lazarus and some 150 associates.	152
11	Sat 4–15	6:00 pm	**Jerusalem:** Upper chamber of the Mark home; to all eleven apostles.	11
12	Tue 4–18	8:30 pm	**Alexandria:** To Rodan and some 80 other believers.	81
13	Fri 4–21	6:00 am	**Bethsaida:** The shores of the Sea of Galilee; to ten apostles (less Simon Zelotes) and John Mark. The first appearance in Galilee.	11
14	Sat 4–22	noon	**Capernaum:** Mount of Ordination; to all eleven apostles.	11
15	Sat 4–29	3:00 pm	**Bethsaida:** Seaside; to more than 500 believers after Peter's sermon.	500
16	Fri 5–5	9:00 pm	**Jerusalem:** Courtyard of Nicodemus; to the apostles, the women's corps and their associates, and about 50 other leading disciples.	74
17	Sat 5–13	4:00 pm	**Sychar:** Near Jacob's well; to Nalda and about 75 Samaritan believers.	76
18	Tue 5–16	9:00 pm	**Tyre:** At the close of a meeting of believers; (no count specified).	
19	Thu 5–18	6:30 am / 7:30 am	**Jerusalem:** Upper chamber of the Mark home; to the eleven apostles. **The Mount of Olives:** Jesus then led them two thirds the way up the mountain where he began the ascent to the right hand of his Father. This so-called ascension of Jesus was in no way different from his other disappearances from mortal vision; he simply vanished from sight.	11

Jesus appeared on 11 separate days over span of 40, in 9 localities, to almost 1,000 eyewitnesses.

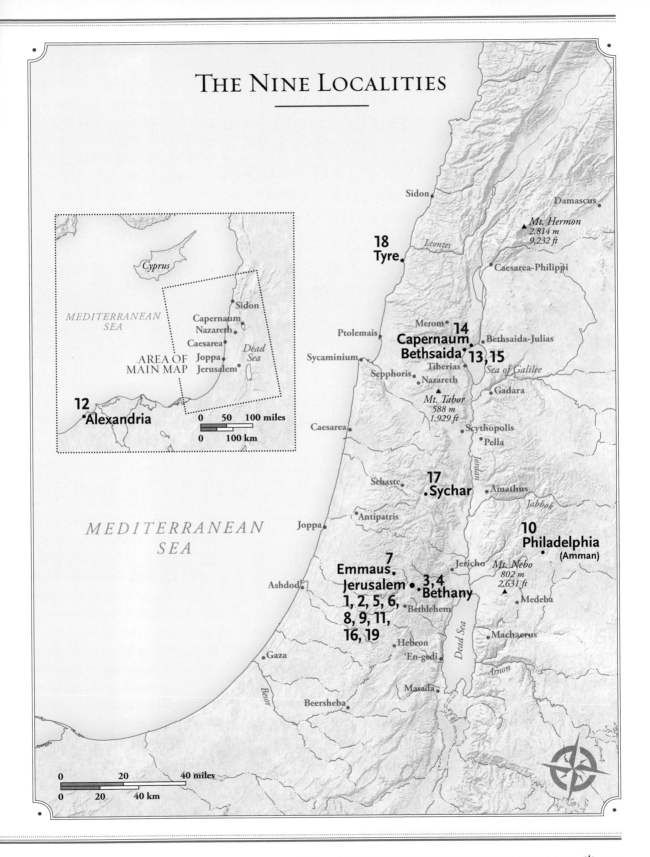

THE NINE LOCALITIES

Cyprus

MEDITERRANEAN
SEA

AREA OF
MAIN MAP

Sidon
Capernaum
Nazareth
Caesarea
Joppa
Jerusalem

Dead
Sea

12
•**Alexandria**

0   50   100 miles

0   100 km

Sidon

Damascus

Leontes

▲ *Mt. Hermon*
2,814 m
9,232 ft

**18
Tyre**•

•Caesarea-Philippi

Merom

**14
Capernaum
Bethsaida**•

•Bethsaida-Julias

13, 15

Sea of Galilee

Ptolemais•

Sycaminium•

Sepphoris•

Tiberias•

Nazareth•

▲ *Mt. Tabor*
588 m
1,929 ft

•Gadara

Caesarea•

Scythopolis•
Pella•

Jordan

Sebaste•

17
•**Sychar**

•Amathus

Jabbok

MEDITERRANEAN
SEA

Joppa•

•Antipatris

**10
Philadelphia**
(Amman)

Ashdod•

**7
Emmaus**•
Jerusalem•
**1, 2, 5, 6,
8, 9, 11,
16, 19**

Jericho•

3, 4
•**Bethany**

Bethlehem•

Mt. Nebo
802 m
2,631 ft ▲

•Medeba

Hebron•

'En-gedi•

Dead Sea

•Machaerus

Gaza•

Besor

Masada•

Arnon

Beersheba•

0   20   40 miles

0   20   40 km

to hear Peter preach his first public sermon since the resurrection. The apostle was at his best, and after he had finished his appealing discourse, few of his hearers doubted that the Master had risen from the dead.

Peter ended his sermon, saying: "We affirm that Jesus of Nazareth is not dead; we declare that he has risen from the tomb; we proclaim that we have seen him and talked with him." Just as he finished making this declaration of faith, there by his side, in full view of all these people, the Master appeared and, speaking to them in familiar accents, said, "Peace be upon you, and my peace I leave with you." When he had thus appeared and had so spoken to them, he vanished from their sight. This group embraced the largest number of mortals who saw him on any single occasion.

THE SEVENTEENTH APPEARANCE: JACOB'S WELL

The Samaritan believers at Sychar were in the habit of meeting near Jacob's well where Jesus had spoken to Nalda concerning the water of life. On this Sabbath afternoon, just as they had finished their discussions of the reported resurrection, Jesus suddenly appeared before them, saying:

"Peace be upon you. You rejoice to know that I am the resurrection and the life, but this will avail you nothing unless you are first born of the eternal spirit, thereby coming to possess, by faith, the gift of eternal life. If you are the faith sons of my Father, you shall never die; you shall not perish. The gospel of the kingdom has taught you that all men are the sons of God. And this good news concerning the love of the heavenly Father for his

> "GO, THEN, INTO ALL THE WORLD TELLING THIS GOOD NEWS TO ALL CREATURES OF EVERY RACE, TRIBE, AND NATION. MY SPIRIT SHALL GO BEFORE YOU, AND I WILL BE WITH YOU ALWAYS."

children on earth must be carried to all the world. The time has come when you worship God neither on Gerizim nor at Jerusalem, but where you are, as you are, in spirit and in truth. It is your faith that saves your souls. Salvation is the gift of God to all who believe they are his sons. But be not deceived; while salvation is the free gift of God and is bestowed upon all who accept it by faith, there follows the experience of bearing the fruits of this spirit life as it is lived in the flesh. The acceptance of the doctrine of the fatherhood of God implies that you also freely accept the associated truth of the brotherhood of man. And if man is your brother, he is even more than your neighbor, whom the Father requires you to love as yourself. Your brother, being of your own family, you will not only love with a family affection, but you will also serve as you would serve yourself. And you will thus love and serve your brother because you, being my brethren, have been thus loved and served by me. Go, then, into all the world telling this good news to all creatures of every race, tribe, and nation. My spirit shall go before you, and I will be with you always."

These Samaritans were greatly astonished at this appearance of the Master, and they hastened off to the near-by towns and villages, where they published abroad the news that they had seen Jesus, and that he had talked to them.

THE EIGHTEENTH APPEARANCE: TYRE IN PHOENICIA

Jesus appeared at the close of a meeting of believers in Tyre as they were about to disperse, saying:

"Peace be upon you. You rejoice to know that the Son of Man has risen from the dead because you thereby know that you and your brethren shall also survive mortal death. But such survival is dependent on your having been previously born of the spirit of truth-seeking and God-finding. The bread of life and the water thereof are given only to those who hunger for truth and thirst for righteousness—for God. The fact that the dead rise is not the gospel of the kingdom. These great truths and these universe facts are all related to this gospel in that they are a part of the result of believing the good news and are embraced in the subsequent experience of those who, by faith, become, in deed and in truth, the everlasting sons of the eternal God. My Father sent me into the world to proclaim this salvation of sonship to all men. And so send I you abroad to preach this salvation of sonship. Salvation is the free gift of God, but those who are born of the spirit will immediately begin to show forth the fruits of the spirit in loving service to their fellow creatures. And the fruits of the divine spirit which are yielded in the lives of spirit-born and God-knowing mortals are: loving service, unselfish devotion, courageous loyalty, sincere fairness, enlightened honesty, undying hope, confiding trust, merciful ministry, unfailing goodness, forgiving tolerance, and enduring peace. If professed believers bear not these fruits of the divine spirit in their lives, they are dead; the Spirit of Truth is not in them; they are useless branches on the living vine, and they soon will be taken away. My Father requires of the children of faith that they bear much spirit fruit. If, therefore, you are not fruitful, he will dig about your roots and cut away your unfruitful branches. Increasingly, must you yield the fruits of the spirit as you progress heavenward in the kingdom of God. You may enter the kingdom as a child, but the Father requires that you grow up, by grace, to the full stature of spiritual adulthood. And when you go abroad to tell all nations the good news of this gospel, I will go before you, and my Spirit of Truth shall abide in your hearts. My peace I leave with you."

And then the Master disappeared from their sight. The next day there went out from Tyre those who carried this story to Sidon and even to Antioch and Damascus. Jesus had been with these believers when he was in the flesh, and they were quick to recognize him when he began to teach them. While his friends could not readily recognize his risen form when made visible, they were never slow to identify his personality when he spoke to them. ∎

THE MASTER'S ASCENSION

Early Thursday morning, May 18, Jesus made his last appearance on earth as a morontia personality. As the eleven apostles were about to sit down to breakfast in the upper chamber of Mary Mark's home, Jesus appeared to them and said:

"Peace be upon you. I have asked you to tarry here in Jerusalem until I ascend to the Father, even until I send you the Spirit of Truth, who shall soon be poured out upon all flesh, and who shall endow you with power from on high." Simon Zelotes interrupted Jesus, asking, "Then, Master, will you restore the kingdom, and will we see the glory of God manifested on earth?" When Jesus had listened to Simon's question, he answered: "Simon, you still cling to your old ideas about the Jewish Messiah and the material kingdom. But you will receive spiritual power after the spirit has descended upon you, and you will presently go into all the world preaching this gospel of the kingdom. As the Father sent me into the world, so do I send you. And I wish that you would love and trust one another. Judas is no more with you because his love grew cold, and because he refused to trust you, his loyal brethren. Have you not read

"Remember all I have taught you and the life I have lived among you. My love overshadows you, my spirit will dwell with you, and my peace shall abide upon you. Farewell."

[Harold Copping — *Come unto Me* (detail)]

in the Scripture where it is written: 'It is not good for man to be alone. No man lives to himself'? And also where it says: 'He who would have friends must show himself friendly'? And did I not even send you out to teach, two and two, that you might not become lonely and fall into the mischief and miseries of isolation? You also well know that, when I was in the flesh, I did not permit myself to be alone for long periods. From the very beginning of our associations I always had two or three of you constantly by my side or else very near at hand even when I communed with the Father. Trust, therefore, and confide in one another. And this is all the more needful since I am this day going to leave you alone in the world. The hour has come; I am about to go to the Father."

When he had spoken, he beckoned for them to come with him, and he led them out on the Mount of Olives, where he bade them farewell preparatory to departing from Urantia. This was a solemn journey to Olivet. Not a word was spoken by any of them from the time they left the upper chamber until Jesus paused with them on the Mount of Olives.

It was almost half past seven o'clock this Thursday morning, May 18, when Jesus arrived on the western slope of Mount Olivet with his eleven silent and somewhat bewildered apostles. From this location, about two thirds the way up the mountain, they could look out over Jerusalem and down upon Gethsemane. Jesus now prepared to say his last farewell to the apostles before he took leave of Urantia. As he stood there before them, without being directed they knelt about him in a circle, and the Master said:

"I bade you tarry in Jerusalem until you were endowed with power from on high. I am now about to take leave of you; I am about to ascend to my Father, and soon, very soon, will we send into this world of my sojourn the Spirit of Truth; and when he has come, you shall begin the new proclamation of the gospel of the kingdom, first

in Jerusalem and then to the uttermost parts of the world. Love men with the love wherewith I have loved you and serve your fellow mortals even as I have served you. By the spirit fruits of your lives impel souls to believe the truth that man is a son of God, and that all men are brethren. Remember all I have taught you and the life I have lived among you. My love overshadows you, my spirit will dwell with you, and my peace shall abide upon you. Farewell."

When the morontia Master had thus spoken, he vanished from their sight. This so-called ascension of Jesus was in no way different from his other disappearances from mortal vision during the forty days of his post-resurrection career on earth.

It was about seven forty-five this morning when Jesus disappeared from the observation of his eleven apostles to begin the ascent to the right hand of his Father, there to receive formal confirmation of his completed sovereignty of the universe of Nebadon. ∎

THURSDAY, MAY 18, A.D. 30

BESTOWAL OF THE SPIRIT OF TRUTH

Acting upon the instruction of Peter, John Mark and others went forth to call the leading disciples together at the home of Mary Mark. By ten thirty, one hundred and twenty of the foremost disciples of Jesus living in Jerusalem had forgathered to hear the report of the farewell message of the Master and to learn of his ascension. Among this company was Mary the mother of Jesus. She had returned to Jerusalem with John Zebedee when the apostles came back from their recent sojourn in Galilee. Soon after Pentecost she returned to the home of Salome at Bethsaida. James the brother of Jesus was also present at this meeting, the first conference of the

Master's disciples to be called after the termination of his planetary career.

Simon Peter took it upon himself to speak for his fellow apostles and made a thrilling report of the last meeting of the eleven with their Master and most touchingly portrayed the Master's final farewell and his ascension disappearance. It was a meeting the like of which had never before occurred on this world.

About one o'clock, as the one hundred and twenty believers were engaged in prayer, they all became aware of a strange presence in the room. At the same time these disciples all became conscious of a new and profound sense of spiritual joy, security, and confidence. This new consciousness of spiritual strength was immediately followed by a strong urge to go out and publicly proclaim the gospel of the kingdom and the good news that Jesus had risen from the dead.

Peter stood up and declared that this must be the coming of the Spirit of Truth which the Master had promised them and proposed that they go to the temple and begin the proclamation of the good news committed to their hands. And they did just what Peter suggested.

These men had been trained and instructed that the gospel which they should preach was the fatherhood of God and the sonship of man, but at just this moment of spiritual ecstasy and personal triumph, the best tidings, the greatest news, these men could think of was the *fact* of the risen Master. And so they went forth, endowed with power from on high, preaching glad tidings to the people—even salvation through Jesus—but they unintentionally stumbled into the error of substituting some of the facts associated with the gospel for the gospel message itself. Peter unwittingly led off in this mistake, and others followed after him on down to Paul, who created a new religion out of the new version of the good news.

The gospel of the kingdom is: the fact of the fatherhood of God, coupled with the resultant truth of the sonship-brotherhood of men. Christianity, as it developed from that day, is: the fact of God as the Father of the Lord Jesus Christ, in association with the experience of believer-fellowship with the risen and glorified Christ.

It is not strange that these spirit-infused men should have seized upon this opportunity to express their feelings of triumph over the forces which had sought to destroy their Master and end the influence of his teachings. At such a time as this it was easier to remember their personal association with Jesus and to be thrilled with the assurance that the Master still lived, that their friendship had not ended, and that the spirit had indeed come upon them even as he had promised.

These believers felt themselves suddenly translated into another world, a new existence of joy, power, and glory. The Master had told them the kingdom would come with power, and some of them thought they were beginning to discern what he meant.

And when all of this is taken into consideration, it is not difficult to understand how these men came to preach a *new gospel about Jesus* in the place of their former message of the fatherhood of God and the brotherhood of men.

The apostles had been in hiding for forty days. This day happened to be the Jewish festival of Pentecost, and thousands of visitors from all parts of the world were in Jerusalem. Many arrived for this feast, but a majority had tarried in the city since the Passover. Now these frightened apostles emerged from their weeks of seclusion to appear boldly in the temple, where they began to preach the new message of a risen Messiah. And all the disciples were likewise conscious of having received some new spiritual endowment of insight and power.

It was about two o'clock when Peter stood up in that very place where his Master had last taught in this temple, and delivered that impassioned appeal

[C. Michael Dudash — *The Comforter*]

which resulted in the winning of more than two thousand souls. The Master had gone, but they suddenly discovered that this story about him had great power with the people. No wonder they were led on into the further proclamation of that which vindicated their former devotion to Jesus and at the same time so constrained men to believe in him. Six of the apostles participated in this meeting: Peter, Andrew, James, John, Philip, and Matthew. They talked for more than an hour and a half and delivered messages in Greek, Hebrew, and Aramaic, as well as a few words in even other tongues with which they had a speaking acquaintance.

The leaders of the Jews were astounded at the boldness of the apostles, but they feared to molest them because of the large numbers who believed their story.

By half past four o'clock more than two thousand new believers followed the apostles down to the pool of Siloam, where Peter, Andrew, James, and John baptized them in the Master's name. And it was dark when they had finished with baptizing this multitude. ■

The Significance of Pentecost

Jesus lived on earth and taught a gospel which redeemed man from the superstition that he was a child of the devil and elevated him to the dignity of a faith son of God. Jesus' message, as he preached it and lived it in his day, was an effective solvent for man's spiritual difficulties in that day of its statement. And now that he has personally left the world, he sends in his place his Spirit of Truth, who is designed to live in man and, for each new generation, to restate the Jesus message so that every new group of mortals to appear upon the face of the earth shall have a new and up-to-date version of the gospel, just such personal enlightenment and group guidance as will prove to be an effective solvent for man's ever-new and varied spiritual difficulties.

The first mission of this spirit is, of course, to foster and personalize truth, for it is the comprehension of truth that constitutes the highest form of human liberty. Next, it is the purpose of this spirit to destroy the believer's feeling of orphanhood. Jesus having been among men, all believers would experience a sense of loneliness had not the Spirit of Truth come to dwell in men's hearts.

The spirit also came to help men recall and understand the words of the Master as well as to illuminate and reinterpret his life on earth.

Next, the Spirit of Truth came to help the believer to witness to the realities of Jesus' teachings and his life as he lived it in the flesh, and as he now again lives it anew and afresh in the individual believer of each passing generation of the spirit-filled sons of God.

Thus it appears that the Spirit of Truth comes really to lead all believers into all truth, into the expanding knowledge of the experience of the living and growing spiritual consciousness of the reality of eternal and ascending sonship with God.

The term "baptism of the spirit," which came into such general use about this time, merely signified the conscious reception of this gift of the Spirit of Truth and the personal acknowledgment of this new spiritual power as an augmentation of all spiritual influences previously experienced by God-knowing souls.

Many queer and strange teachings became associated with the early narratives of the day of Pentecost. In subsequent times the events of this day, on which the Spirit of Truth, the new teacher, came to dwell with mankind, have become confused with the foolish outbreaks of rampant emotionalism. The chief mission of this outpoured spirit of the Father and the Son is to teach men about the truths of the Father's love and the Son's mercy. These are the truths of divinity which men can comprehend more fully than all the other divine traits of character. The Spirit of Truth is concerned primarily with the revelation of the Father's spirit nature and the Son's moral character. The Creator Son, in the flesh, revealed God to men; the Spirit of Truth, in the heart, reveals the Creator Son to men. When man yields the "fruits of the spirit" in his life, he is simply showing forth the traits which the Master manifested in his own earthly life. When Jesus was on earth, he lived his life as one personality—Jesus of Nazareth. As the indwelling spirit of the "new teacher," the Master has, since Pentecost, been able to live his life anew in the experience of every truth-taught believer.

To Jesus, mortal life had dealt its hardest, cruelest, and bitterest blows; and this man met these ministrations of despair with faith, courage, and the unswerving determination to do his Father's will. Jesus met life in all its terrible reality and mastered it—even in death. He did not use religion as a release from life. The religion of Jesus does not seek to escape this life in order to enjoy the waiting bliss of another existence. The religion of Jesus provides the joy and peace of another and spiritual existence to enhance and ennoble the life which men now live in the flesh.

If religion is an opiate to the people, it is not the religion of Jesus.

Do not overlook the fact that the Spirit of Truth was bestowed upon all sincere believers; this gift of the spirit did not come only to the apostles. The one hundred and twenty men and women assembled in the upper chamber all received the new teacher, as did all the honest of heart throughout the whole world. This new teacher was bestowed

FRUITS OF THE DIVINE SPIRIT

In his eighteenth appearance Jesus revealed that the following fruits "are yielded in the lives of spirit-born and God-knowing mortals."

LOVING SERVICE
UNSELFISH DEVOTION
COURAGEOUS LOYALTY
SINCERE FAIRNESS
ENLIGHTENED HONESTY
UNDYING HOPE
CONFIDING TRUST
MERCIFUL MINISTRY
UNFAILING GOODNESS
FORGIVING TOLERANCE
ENDURING PEACE

upon mankind, and every soul received him in accordance with the love for truth and the capacity to grasp and comprehend spiritual realities. At last, true religion is delivered from the custody of priests and all sacred classes and finds its real manifestation in the individual souls of men.

Pentecost, with its spiritual endowment, was designed forever to loose the religion of the Master from all dependence upon physical force; the teachers of this new religion are now equipped with spiritual weapons. They are to go out to conquer the world with unfailing forgiveness, matchless good will, and abounding love. They are equipped to overcome evil with good, to vanquish hate by love, to destroy fear with a courageous and living faith in truth. Jesus had already taught his followers that his religion was never passive; always were his disciples to be active and positive in their ministry of mercy and in their manifestations of love.

Pentecost endowed mortal man with the power to forgive personal injuries, to keep sweet in the midst of the gravest injustice, to remain unmoved in the face of appalling danger, and to challenge the evils of hate and anger by the fearless acts of love and forbearance. Urantia has passed through the ravages of great and destructive wars in its history. All participants in these terrible struggles met with defeat. There was but one victor; there was only one who came out of these embittered struggles with an enhanced reputation—that was Jesus of Nazareth and his gospel of overcoming evil with good. The secret of a better civilization is bound up in the Master's

THE RELIGION OF JESUS IS THE MOST POWERFUL UNIFYING INFLUENCE THE WORLD HAS EVER KNOWN.

teachings of the brotherhood of man, the good will of love and mutual trust.

Up to Pentecost, religion had revealed only man seeking for God; since Pentecost, man is still searching for God, but there shines out over the world the spectacle of God also seeking for man and sending his spirit to dwell within him when he has found him.

Before the teachings of Jesus which culminated in Pentecost, women had little or no spiritual standing in the tenets of the older religions. After Pentecost, in the brotherhood of the kingdom woman stood before God on an equality with man. Among the one hundred and twenty who received this special visitation of the spirit were many of the women disciples, and they shared these blessings equally with the men believers. No longer can man presume to monopolize the ministry of religious service. The Pharisee might go on thanking God that he was "not born a woman, a leper, or a gentile," but among the followers of Jesus woman has been forever set free from all religious discriminations based on sex. Pentecost obliterated all religious discrimination founded on racial distinction, cultural differences, social caste, or sex prejudice. No wonder these believers in the new religion would cry out, "Where the spirit of the Lord is, there is liberty."

Both the mother and brother of Jesus were present among the one hundred and twenty believers, and as members of this common group of disciples, they also received the outpoured spirit.

They received no more of the good gift than did their fellows. No special gift was bestowed upon the members of Jesus' earthly family. Pentecost marked the end of special priesthoods and all belief in sacred families.

Pentecost was the call to spiritual unity among gospel believers. When the spirit descended on the disciples at Jerusalem, the same thing happened in Philadelphia, Alexandria, and at all other places where true believers dwelt. It was literally true that "there was but one heart and soul among the multitude of the believers." The religion of Jesus is the most powerful unifying influence the world has ever known.

Pentecost was designed to lessen the self-assertiveness of individuals, groups, nations, and races. It is this spirit of self-assertiveness which so increases in tension that it periodically breaks loose in destructive wars. Mankind can be unified only by the spiritual approach, and the Spirit of Truth is a world influence which is universal.

The coming of the Spirit of Truth purifies the human heart and leads the recipient to formulate a life purpose single to the will of God and the welfare of men. The material spirit of selfishness has been swallowed up in this new spiritual bestowal of selflessness. Pentecost, then and now, signifies that the Jesus of history has become the divine Son of living experience. The joy of this outpoured spirit, when it is consciously experienced in human life, is a tonic for health, a stimulus for mind, and an unfailing energy for the soul. ✳

[GREG OLSEN — *Peace on Earth*]

"I am with you always, even to the end of the age."

—MATTHEW 28:20 NKJV

Of Jesus it was truly said, "He trusted God." As a man among men he most sublimely trusted the Father in heaven. He trusted his Father as a little child trusts his earthly parent. His faith was perfect but never presumptuous. No matter how cruel nature might appear to be or how indifferent to man's welfare on earth, Jesus never faltered in his faith. He was immune to disappointment and impervious to persecution. He was untouched by apparent failure.

He loved men as brothers, at the same time recognizing how they differed in innate endowments and acquired qualities. "He went about doing good."

Jesus was the perfectly unified human personality. And today, as in Galilee, he continues to unify mortal experience and to co-ordinate human endeavors. He unifies life, ennobles character, and simplifies experience. He enters the human mind to elevate, transform, and transfigure it. It is literally true: "If any man has Christ Jesus within him, he is a new creature; old things are passing away; behold, all things are becoming new."

"The kingdom of God is within you" was probably the greatest pronouncement Jesus ever made, next to the declaration that his Father is a living and loving spirit.

The religious challenge of this age is to those farseeing and forward-looking men and women of spiritual insight who will dare to construct a new and appealing philosophy of living out of the enlarged and exquisitely integrated concepts of cosmic truth, universe beauty, and divine goodness as exemplified in Jesus' life. Such a new and righteous vision of morality will attract all that is good in the mind of man and challenge that which is best in the human soul.

A lasting social system without a morality predicated on spiritual realities can no more be maintained than could the solar system without gravity. Religion is now confronted by the challenge of a new age of scientific minds and materialistic tendencies. But in this gigantic struggle between the secular and the spiritual, the religion of Jesus will eventually triumph.

Christianity is the product of the combined moral genius of the God-knowing men of many races during many ages, and it has truly been one of the greatest powers for good on earth; but what is now most needed is Jesus. Religion does need new leaders, spiritual men and women who will dare to depend solely on Jesus and his incomparable teachings.

Modern culture must become spiritually baptized with a new revelation of Jesus' life and illuminated with a new understanding of his gospel of eternal salvation. And when Jesus becomes thus lifted up, he will draw all men to himself. Jesus' disciples should be more than conquerors, even overflowing sources of inspiration and enhanced living to all men. Religion is only an exalted humanism until it is made divine by the discovery of the reality of the presence of God in personal experience.

The beauty and sublimity, the humanity and divinity, the simplicity and uniqueness, of Jesus' life on earth present such a striking and appealing picture of man-saving and God-revealing that the theologians and philosophers of all time should be effectively restrained from daring to form creeds or create theological systems of spiritual bondage out of such a transcendental bestowal of God in the form of man. In Jesus the universe produced a mortal man in whom the spirit of love triumphed over the material handicaps of time and overcame the fact of physical origin.

The call to the adventure of building a new and transformed human society by means of the spiritual rebirth of Jesus' brotherhood of the kingdom should thrill all who believe in him as men have not been stirred since the days when they walked about on earth as his companions in the flesh.

If the Christian church would only dare to espouse the Master's program, thousands of apparently indifferent youths would rush forward to enlist in such a spiritual undertaking, and they would not hesitate to go all the way through with this great adventure.

The hope of modern Christianity is that it should cease to sponsor the social systems and industrial policies of Western civilization while it humbly bows itself before the cross it so valiantly extols, there to learn anew from Jesus of Nazareth the greatest truths mortal man can ever hear—the living gospel of the fatherhood of God and the brotherhood of man.

The time is ripe to witness the figurative resurrection of the human Jesus from his burial tomb amidst the theological traditions and the religious dogmas of twenty centuries. Jesus of Nazareth must no longer be sacrificed to even the splendid concept of the glorified Christ. What a transcendent service if, through this revelation, the Son of Man should be recovered from the tomb of traditional theology and be presented as the living Jesus to the church that bears his name, and to all other religions! Indeed, the social readjustments, the economic transformations, the moral rejuvenations, and the religious revisions of Christian civilization would be drastic and revolutionary if the living religion of Jesus should suddenly supplant the theologic religion about Jesus.

To "follow Jesus" means to personally share his religious faith and to enter into the

spirit of the Master's life of unselfish service for man. One of the most important things in human living is to find out what Jesus believed, to discover his ideals, and to strive for the achievement of his exalted life purpose.

Jesus led men to feel at home in the world; he delivered them from the slavery of taboo and taught them that the world was not fundamentally evil. He did not long to escape from his earthly life; he mastered a technique of acceptably doing the Father's will while in the flesh. He attained an idealistic religious life in the very midst of a realistic world. The Master looked upon men as the sons of God and foresaw a magnificent and eternal future for those who chose survival. He was not a moral skeptic; he viewed man positively,

not negatively. He saw most men as weak rather than wicked, more distraught than depraved. But no matter what their status, they were all God's children and his brethren.

He taught men to place a high value upon themselves in time and in eternity. Because of this high estimate which Jesus placed upon men, he was willing to spend himself in the unremitting service of humankind. And it was this infinite worth of the finite that made the golden rule a vital factor in his religion. What mortal can fail to be uplifted by the extraordinary faith Jesus has in him?

Be not discouraged; human evolution is still in progress, and the revelation of God to the world, in and through Jesus, shall not fail. ∎

Ch. I   March, 8 BC   (Page #17)
Joseph (21) and Mary are married after a courtship of two years. Caesar Augustus decrees a census of the Roman Empire.

June, 8 BC   (117)
Gabriel's announcement to Elizabeth.

November, 8 BC   (14)
The day following her conception, Gabriel imparts to Mary the glad tidings that she is to bear the promised child.

October, 6 BC   (23)
The family flees to Alexandria after Herod orders the massacre of all boy babies under two in Bethlehem of Judea. Sixteen perish in one day.

April 2, 3 BC   (59)
Birth of James (2nd).

June, 1 BC   (29)
Zacharias, Elizabeth, and their son John visit the Nazareth family.

March 16, AD 1   (59)
Birth of Joseph (4th).

Sept 13, AD 3   (59)
Birth of Martha (6th).

April 17, AD 9   (59)
Birth of Ruth, the last of nine.

January 9, AD 7   (59)
Birth of Amos (8th).

March 20, AD 7   (41)
Jesus graduates the Nazareth synagogue school at twelve.

April 4, AD 7   (42)
Jesus makes a thrilling first visit to Jerusalem but the lad is also shocked and sickened.

April 8, AD 7   (43)
A heavenly messenger from Immanuel appears to Jesus.

April 17, AD 7   (43)
Jesus is left behind as his parents depart Jerusalem.

April 20, AD 7   (47)
Joseph and Mary at last find Jesus teaching in the temple.

September, AD 12   (58)
Jesus and John meet again in Nazareth at 18, never to see each other until the baptism.

December 3, AD 12   (59)
The death of little Amos.

November 3, AD 20   (63)
Jesus formally cedes his position and installs James as "head and protector of my father's house."

December 10, AD 23   (98)
The travelers tearfully part ways at Charax. Gonod and Ganid embark for India. Jesus returns by way of Ur to Babylon, then by caravan to Damascus, and after stopping at Capernaum, on to Nazareth.

See map, page 74:
"Jesus Tours the Mediterranean World."

March, AD 25   (117)
John begins his brilliant career as the herald of the Messiah.

April, AD 25   (106)
Jesus begins five months of solitary wanderings through Palestine and Syria to Antioch.

August, AD 25   (109)
Jesus sojourns alone for six weeks, wet with the dews of Mount Hermon.

September, AD 25   (110)
Jesus triumphs in the great temptation and returns to Galilee to begin the time of waiting for "my hour to come."

January 14, AD 26   (115)
At 31-½ years old, Jesus is baptized by John the Baptist on the river Jordan near Pella. He then retires to the Perean hills near a village sometime called Beit Adis. And no man sees Jesus again for forty days.

Ch. V   February 23, AD 26   (126)
Jesus rejoins John's company at Pella and chooses two pairs of brothers as his first four apostles: Andrew and Peter, then James and John Zebedee.

February 24, AD 26   (127)
Jesus calls Phillip and Nathaniel.

February 27, AD 26   (130)
Jesus attends the wedding at Cana. His sympathy for Mary brings about the transformation of the water to the wine.

June 12, AD 26   (118)
John is arrested and languishes 19 months in Herod's despicable prison at Machaerus until his execution.

June 22, AD 26   (135)
Jesus preaches the sermon on "The Kingdom" at the Capernaum synagogue crowded to overflowing.

July, AD 26   (136)
Each of the first six apostles chooses one man to join them: Jesus calls Matthew, Simon, James and Judas Alpheus, and lastly Thomas and Judas.

8	4	BC	AD	5	7	8	9	12	17	20	21	22	23	24	25	26	27

Ch. II   Sept 25, AD 8 (52)
Joseph is killed by a falling derrick while at work on the governor's residence at Sepphoris. For the next 12 years, Jesus is head of household and raises the children with Mary.

May, AD 5   (39)
Joseph takes Jesus to Scythopolis.

June 24, AD 5   (59)
Birth of Jude (7th).

April 14, AD 2   (59)
Birth of Simon (5th).

February 11, 2 BC   (29)
Jesus makes his first moral decision at 5-½ years old, and the Father's spirit comes to abide in him.

July 11, 2 BC   (59)
Birth of Miriam (3rd).

October, 4 BC   (26)
The family returns to Nazareth after the death of Herod.

March 25, 7 BC   (117)
Birth of John the Baptist.

August 21, 7 BC   (20)
The Babe of Bethlehem is born at noon and laid in a near-by manger. Angels above sing anthems of glory.

January, AD 21   (65)
Jesus takes casual leave of his family and spends a year crafting a new style of far superior boats in Zebedee's shops.

April 17, AD 17   (64)
In Jerusalem, Jesus meets Stephen whose martyrdom leads to the conversion of Saul of Tarsus.

March, AD 22
Jesus journeys to Jerusalem for two months where he meets Gonod and his brilliant son Ganid, wealthy travelers from India who engage him to accompany them as interpreter and tutor.

(68)

Ch. III   April 26, AD 22   (72)
Jesus departs from Jerusalem on a Mediterranean tour which consumes most of the 28th and the entire 29th year of his life on earth. He is known as the *Damascus scribe* and the *Jewish tutor*.

Ch. IV   April 1, AD 24   (102)
Jesus leaves Nazareth as caravan conductor to the Caspian Sea region. On the return trip he tarries over two weeks at Lake Urmia and delivers 24 lectures at Cymboyton's school of religion—the most systematic and formal of all his teachings.

January 12, AD 27   (151)
On the highlands north of Capernaum, Jesus ordains his apostles and delivers the well-known Sermon on the Mount and the Beatitudes.

Ch. VI   Jan 19, AD 27   (158)
Jesus and the twelve depart from their headquarters in Bethsaida. This entire year is spent in quietly taking over John the Baptist's work in Perea and Judea.

April, AD 27   (160)
The first ministry in Jerusalem. Hundreds rejoice in the good news, alarming the Jewish rulers. Annas coldly receives Jesus who takes his immediate leave. Jesus meets Nicodemus.

June, AD 27   (163)
Jesus first proclaims his divine nature to Nalda, a Samaritan woman at Jacob's well, Sychar.

September, AD 27   (169)
Jesus teaches his apostles the Lord's Prayer.

October, AD 27   (170)
A three-week conference is held with John's twelve apostles at the Gilboa camp. Abner becomes a believer.

The Master's Seven Thousand-Mile Journey

The travelers go to Caesarea by way of Joppa; sail to Alexandria; to Lasea in Crete; to Carthage, touching at Cyrene; to Naples, stopping at Malta, Syracuse, and Messina; to Capua; then along the Appian Way to Rome. They have an audience with the emperor Tiberias and spend six months in Rome. They make five side trips including one to the northern Italian lakes and Switzerland.

Jesus prepares 30 Romans for the coming of the gospel.

They return overland to Tarentum; sail to Athens, stopping at Nicopolis and Corinth; to Ephesus by way of Troas; to Cyprus, putting in at Rhodes; to Antioch in Syria; to Sidon and then over to Damascus; to Mesopotamia by caravan, through Thapsacus and Larissa; to Babylon, visiting Ur; to Susa and finally to Charax.

Only Zebedee the boatbuilder of Bethsaida knows the facts about these extensive travels, and he tells no one.

January 16, AD 29 (190)
Jesus announces the formation of the women's evangelistic corps. He commissions ten women and later two more.

March 5, AD 29 (194)
The Nazareth rejection.

March, AD 29 (197)
Jesus heals the Kheresa lunatic and the daughter of Jairus.

March 30, AD 29 (201)
The feeding of the five thousand at Magadan Park is followed by the king-making episode.

Ch. VIII   Apr 30, AD 29 (208)
Jesus preaches his epoch-making sermon in the new Capernaum synagogue to friends and foes.

May 8, AD 29 (213)
The Sanhedrin passes an unprecedented decree closing all synagogues of Palestine to Jesus and his followers.

May 21, AD 29 (214)
Herod Antipas signs a decree authorizing the arrest of Jesus.

May 22, AD 29 (214)
His arrest imminent, Jesus and his party flee Galilee through Batanea and northern Galilee to the Phoenician coast.

January 10, AD 28 (117, 171)
John the Baptist is beheaded.

January 13, AD 28 (171)
Jesus and the twelve return to Capernaum to proclaim the kingdom openly and with power.

Ch. VII   January, AD 28 (174)
The healing at sundown of 683 men, women, and children at the Zebedee home in Bethsaida.

January 18, AD 28 (178)
The first public preaching tour of Galilee lasts through March 17.

March, AD 28 (178)
Jesus cleanses a leper in his first deliberate "miraculous" healing.

April 2, AD 28 (180)
The apostolic party journeys to Jerusalem for the Passover. Jesus visits the Pool of Bethesda alone with John but heals no one.

January 3, AD 30 (254)
The three-month Perean mission begins from Pella and is the last ministry of the Master.

February 19, AD 30 (254)
Jesus heals the ten lepers in Amathus. Only the lone Samaritan returns to give thanks.

February 26, AD 30 (257)
A runner from Bethany arrives at Philadelphia with a message that Lazarus is near death.

March 2, AD 30 (261)
Lazarus is resurrected from the dead around 2:30 p.m. after four days in the tomb.

March 30, AD 30 (271)
Jesus heals the blind beggar Bartimeus on the way into Jericho. Then as he passes under the sycamore tree, he calls down Zaccheus, the hated publican, and he is converted.

March 31, AD 30 (273)
The Master makes his last journey up to Jerusalem in the likeness of mortal flesh and lodges in Bethany with one Simon.

Ch. X   April 1, AD 30 (279)
Mary anoints the Master's head with spikenard.

April 2, AD 30 (280)
Palm Sunday: Jesus enters Jerusalem to the praise and hosannas of the festive multitude.

April 3, AD 30 (285)
Monday: The cleansing of the temple.

April 4, AD 30 (295, 299, 304)
Tuesday: Jesus gives his farewell temple address. That evening on Mt. Olivet he predicts the destruction of Jerusalem (AD 70), and promises, "I will sometime return to this world."

April 5, AD 30 (305)
Wednesday: The day of rest. Judas leaves camp to plot with Jesus' enemies in the city.

April 6, AD 30 (308) (322)
Thursday: The Last Supper. Jesus washes the feet of his apostles and gives us the New Commandment. | He suffers untold sorrow as he prays in the garden of Gethsemane. He is arrested near midnight, bound, and led away. John is allowed at his side.

---

28   **29**   **30**

May, AD 28 (184)
For five months David Zebedee maintains an enormous seaside camp and the kingdom's first hospital nearby the tented city.

September, AD 28 (187)
A spying Pharisee induces a man with a withered hand to seek healing before Jesus on the Sabbath. The man is healed.

October 1, AD 28 (188)
Jesus heals the paralytic lowered through the roof.

October 3, AD 28 (187, 189)
The second public preaching tour of Galilee lasts through December. The widespread fame of Jesus provokes the hostility and hardens the hearts of the religious leaders at Jerusalem.

August 9, AD 29 (220)
Peter's Confession.

August 15, AD 29 (225)
The transfiguration on Mount Hermon.

August 16, AD 29 (228)
Jesus heals the epileptic boy.

August 17, AD 29 (231)
Peter's Protest.

Ch. IX   Sept, AD 29 (236)
Jesus boldly returns to Jerusalem and teaching in the temple, makes the clear and formal announcement of his divinity.

September, AD 29 (239)
The woman taken in adultery is brought before Jesus. He writes three times in the sand.

September, AD 29 (240)
Jesus gives the sermon on the "Light of the World."

November 19, AD 29 (243)
Jesus ordains the seventy evangelists at Magadan.

December, AD 29 (249)
Jesus secretly goes up to Jerusalem at the feast of the dedication. He heals Josiah the blind beggar, anointing his eyes with clay and spittle, issuing an open challenge to the Sanhedrin.

Ch. XI   April 7, AD 30 (332)
Friday, 12:30 am: The examination of Annas. Peter denies Jesus in the palace courtyard.
  3:30 am: In a sordid sham trial, Caiaphas and the Sanhedrist court decree Jesus' death.
  6:00 am: Jesus is brought before Pilate, next to Herod, then back again to Pilate.
  8:00 am: Pilate's tragic surrender: He washes his hands and orders the crucifixion.
  9:30 am: Jesus is hung upon the cross at Golgotha. Judas Iscariot commits suicide.
  Midday : The thief on the cross reaches out for salvation and finds deliverance.
  3:00 pm: Jesus bows his head and gives up the life struggle. The Master's life in the flesh has lasted thirty-six years "lacking a trifle more than four months."
  4:30 pm: Joseph of Arimathea and Nicodemus arrive with Pilate's order granting them the body of Jesus, and along with John Zebedee and the converted Roman centurion, bear it to Joseph's new family tomb across the way and reverently lay him to rest.

Ch. XII   April 9, AD 30 (356)
Sunday, 3:02 am: The resurrected form and personality of Jesus of Nazareth comes forth from the tomb. *See chart and map of all 19 resurrection appearances (pages 374 & 375).*
  3:30 am: Mary Magdalene and four women companions discover the empty tomb.
  4:30 am: Jesus orders the dispensational resurrection: the third planetary roll call.
  Dawn: Jesus appears to the women saying, "... go now and tell my apostles."
  Noon–5 pm: Jesus makes five appearances in and around Jerusalem starting with his brother James in Bethany and finally with the two brothers on the road to Emmaus.
  8:30 pm: Jesus appears to Simon Peter in the garden of the Mark home. After nine o'clock, he makes his first appearance to the apostles in the upper chamber.

April 21, AD 30 (367)
His first in Galilee, Jesus appears to the apostles at dawn as their boat lands at Bethsaida.

April 29, AD 30 (373)
As Peter ends his sermon lakeside at Bethsaida, Jesus appears to more than 500 believers.

May 18, AD 30 (377, 379)
Thursday, 7:30 am: On Mt. Olivet, Jesus begins the ascent to the right hand of his Father. He has made nineteen appearances over forty days and become part of the personal experience of almost one thousand human beings; but not to even one of his enemies.
  1:00 pm: Pentecost. The Spirit of Truth, the Comforter, is bestowed upon the world.

STORY	PG	UB REF	NEW TESTAMENT VERSE
Gabriel's Announcement to Mary	14	122:3.1	Luke 1:26–38
Joseph's Dream	16	122:4.1	Matthew 1:20–25
Joseph and Mary	16	122:5.1	
The Trip to Bethlehem for the Census	19	122:7.1	Luke 2:1–5
The Birth of Jesus	20	122:8.1	Matthew 2:1–12, Luke 2:6–20
The Presentation in the Temple	21	122:9.1	Luke 2:22–38; 1:67–80
The Escape from Herod	23	122:10.1	Matthew 2:7–8, 13–16
Sojourn in Alexandria	25	123:0.1	
Back in Nazareth	26	123:0.6	Matthew 2:19–23, Luke 2:39–40
Life in Nazareth, Ages Four to Five	27	123:1.4	
Life in Nazareth, Ages Six to Seven	30	123:1.4	
School Days	31	123:5.1	
The Invitation to Jerusalem	34	123:6.1	
Trouble at School	35	124:0.1	
Sabbath Walks with Joseph	36	123:5.12	
The Trip with Joseph to Scythopolis	39	124:2.9	
The Twelfth Year	40	124:4.1	
The Trip to Jerusalem	41	124:5.1	Luke 2:41–42
Young Jesus Teaching in the Temple	43	125:3.1	Luke 2:43–45
Mary and Joseph Find Jesus	47	125:6.1	Luke 2:46–52
The Death of Joseph	52	126:2.1	
The Son of Man	53	126:3.6	
The Financial Struggle	54	126:5.1	
Head of Household	55	127:0.1	
Rebecca's Undying Love	60	127:5.1	
The Visit with Lazarus, Martha, & Mary	62	127:6.3	
James Installed as Head of the Family	63	128:7.1	
Jesus Leaves His Family	65	129:1.1	
The Wealthy Travelers from India	68	129:2.1	
Embarking from Caesarea	72	130:2.1	
The Lighthouse at Alexandria	77	130:3.1	
The Alexandrian Library	78	130:3.4	
The Young Man Who Was Afraid	79	130:6.1	
The Sojourn at Rome	82	132:0.1	
The Thoughtless Pagan	85	132:7.1	
The Return from Rome	85	133:0.1	
The Two Courtesans	88	133:3.6	
Personal Work in Corinth	90	133:4.1	
Ministry to Hungry Souls	92	133:4.9	
The Conclusion of the Tour	95	133:7.1	
The Three Friends Part	98	133:9.4	
Managing a Caravan to the Caspian Sea	102	134:1.1	
The Urmia Lectures	104	134:2.5	
The Year of Solitary Wanderings	106	134:7.1	
The Great Temptation	109	134:7.6	Matthew 4:1–11, Mark 1:12–13, Luke 4: 1–13
The War in Heaven (sidebars)	111	53 / 67	Isaiah 14:12–15, Luke 10:18, John 8:44, 12:30–31|Revelation 12: 7–9
The Time of Waiting	111	134:9.6	Matthew 4:13
The Baptism in the Jordan	114	135:8.1	Matthew 3:13–17, Mark 1:9–11, Luke 3:21–22
John the Baptist	116	135:9.2	Mt 14:3–4, Lk 3:19– 20, Jn 1:15, 29–32 | Mt 11:2–6, Lk 7:18–23, Jn 3:25–36 | Mt 14:6–12
			(Cont): Mk 6:21–29
Forty Days in the Perean Wilderness	122	136:3.3	
Choosing the First Six Apostles	125	137:0.1	Matthew 4:18–22, Mark 1:16–18, Luke 5:10, John 1:35–51
The Wedding at Cana	130	137:4.1	John 2:1–12
Introducing the Kingdom of Heaven	135	137:8.1	Matthew 4:17, Mark 1:14–15
Choosing the Final Six Apostles	136	138:1.1	Matthew 9:9, Mark 2:14, Luke 5:10, 27
Fishers of Men	138	138:7.1	Matthew 4:19, Mark 1:17, Luke 5:10
First Work of the Twelve	139	138:8.1	
Five Months of Testing	142	138:9.1	
The Twelve Apostles	142	139:0.1	Matthew 10:1–4, Mark 3:13–19, Luke 6:12–16
The Ordination of the Twelve	151	140:0.1	Matthew 5:1–16, 43–45, 48; 7:1–6, 15–23 | Mark 9:50 | Luke 6:20–28, 35–45; 11:33–36
Leaving Galilee	158	141:0.1	*(Cont):* Luke 14:34–35
The Passover at Jerusalem	160	142:0.1	John 2:23; 3:1–9
Nalda, the Woman at Jacob's Well	163	143:0.1	John 4:1–42
The Lord's Prayer	169	144:0.1	Matthew 6:9–13, Luke 11:1–4

The Missing Years

STORY	PG	UB REF	NEW TESTAMENT VERSE
Conference with John's Apostles	170	144:6.1	Matthew 11:1–5, 7–11; 14:1–12 | Mark 6:17–29 | Luke 7:18–22, 24–28
The Healing at Sundown	174	145:3.1	Matthew 8:14–17, Mark 1:29–34; 6:14–16, Luke 4:38–41
The Leper at Iron	178	146:4.1	Matthew 8:1–4, Mark 1:40–45, Luke 5:12–15
At the Pool of Bethesda	180	147:2.1	John 5:2–9, 24, 28
The Penitent Woman	181	147:5.1	Luke 7:36–50
The Six Jerusalem Spies	183	147:6.2	Matthew 12:1–8, Mark 2:23–27, Luke 6:1–5
The Kingdom's First Hospital	184	148:0.1	
The Man with the Withered Hand	187	148:7.1	Matthew 12:9–14, Mark 3:1–6, Luke 6:6–11
Healing the Paralytic	188	148:9.1	Mark 2:1–12, Luke 5:17–26
The Women's Evangelistic Corps	190	150:1.1	Luke 8:1–3
The Nazareth Rejection	194	150:6.3	Matthew 13:54–58, Mark 6:1–4, Luke 4:16–24, 28–30
Jairus and His Daughter	197	152:0.1	Matthew 9:18–26, Mark 5:21–43, Luke 8:40–56
Feeding the Five Thousand	201	152:2.1	Matthew 14:13–21, Mark 6:30–44, Luke 9:10–17, John 6:1–14
The King-Making Episode	203	152:3.1	John 6:15
The Epochal Sermon	208	153:1.1	Matthew 12:22–28, 30–40 | Mark 3:22–30; 8:11–12 | Luke 11:14–20, 29–30 |
			(Cont): John 6:28–59
Last Days at Capernaum	212	153:5.1	John 6:60–70
The Hasty Flight	214	154:5.1	Matthew 12:46–50, Mark 3:31–35, Luke 8:19–21
Teaching at Tyre	217	156:4.1	Matthew 15:21, Mark 7:24 | cf. 1 Kings 7:13 | cf. 1 Corinthians 13:1–8 | cf. Galatians 6:9
Peter's Confession	220	157:3.1	Matthew 16:13–20, Mark 8:27–30, Luke 9:18–20
The Transfiguration	225	158:0.1	Matthew 17:1–8, Mark 9:2–8, Luke 9:28–36
The Epileptic Boy	228	158:4.1	Matthew 17:14–20, Mark 9:14–29, Luke 9:37–43
Peter's Protest	231	158:7.1	Matthew 16:21–28; 17:22–23, Mark 8:31–33, Luke 9:21–27, 43–45
Public Announcement of Divinity	236	162:1.1	John 7
The Woman Taken in Adultery	239	162:3.1	John 8:2–11
"I Am the Light of the World"	240	162:5.1	John 8:12–30
The Truth Will Set You Free	242	162:7.1	John 8:31–59
The Seventy Evangelists	243	163:0.1	Luke 10:1–23
The Rich Young Man	244	163:2.1	Matthew 19:16–22, Mark 10:17–22, Luke 18:18–23
The Good Samaritan	247	164:0.1	Luke 10:25–37
An Open Challenge to the Sanhedrin	249	164:2.1	John 9:1–12
The Good Shepherd	251	165:2.1	John 10:1–21
The Ten Lepers	254	166:2.1	Luke 17:11–19
The Sermon at Gerasa	255	166:3.1	Matthew 7:13–24; 19:30, Mark 10:31
The Message from Bethany	257	167:4.1	John 11:1–16
Blessing the Little Children	258	167:6.1	Matthew 19:13–15, Mark 10:13–16, Luke 18:15–17
The Resurrection of Lazarus	261	168:0.1	John 11:17–44
Meeting of the Sanhedrin	266	168:2.10	John 11:45–53
The Prodigal Son	268	169:1.1	Matthew 18:12–14, Luke 15:8–32
"Make Haste Zaccheus"	271	171:5.1	Matthew 20:29–34, Mark 10:46–52, Luke 18:35–43; 19:1–10
Judas Turns Traitor	278	172:0.1	Matthew 26:6–13, Mark 14:3–9, John 11:55–56; 12:1–11
Your King Comes As the Lowly One	280	172:3.1	Matthew 21:1–11, Mark 11:1–11, Luke 19:28–44, John 12:12–19
Cleansing the Temple	285	173:0.1	Matthew 21:12–17, Mark 11:15–19, Luke 19:45–48, John 2:13–16, 23
Challenging the Master's Authority	288	173:2.1	Matthew 21:23–27, Mark 11:27–33, Luke 20:1–7
Tuesday Morning in the Temple	290	174:0.1	Matthew 22:15–22, 34–46; Mark 12:13–17, 28–37; Luke 20:20–26, 41–44
The Inquiring Greeks	292	174:5.1	John 12:20–36
The Last Temple Discourse	295	175:0.1	Matthew 23, Mark 12:38–40, Luke 11:42–52
Foretelling the End of Jerusalem	299	176:0.1	Matthew 24:1–24, 32–36; Mark 13:1–13, 21–23, 28–33; Luke 21:5–21, 29–31
One Day Alone with God	305	177:0.1	
The Last Supper	308	178:0.1	Matthew 26:17–30, Mark 14:12–20, 22–25, Luke 22:7–27, John 13 (cf. John 14)
The Last Group Prayer	318	182:0.1	John 17
Alone in Gethsemane	322	182:3.1	Matthew 26:36–46, Mark 14:32–42, Luke 22:39–46
The Betrayal and Arrest of Jesus	328	183:2.1	Matthew 26:47–56, Mark 14:43–52, Luke 22:47–53, John 18:1–9
Before the Sanhedrin Court	332	184:3.1	Matthew 26:57–67, Mark 14:53–65, Luke 22:69–71
Simon Peter's Tears of Agony	334	184:1.1	Matthew 26:69–75, Mark 14:66–72, Luke 22:55–62, John 18:15–18, 25–28
The Trial Before Pilate	336	185:0.1	Matthew 27:1–2, 11–14; Mark 15:1–5, Luke 23:1–5, John 18:28–38
Before Herod and the Return to Pilate	339	185:4.2	Matthew 27:15–31, Mark 15:6–20, Luke 23:7–25, John 18:38–40; 19:1–16
The Crucifixion	345	187:0.4	Matthew 27:32–50, 54–56; Mark 15:21–37, 39–41; Luke 23:26–43; John 19:17–30
The End of Judas Iscariot	347	186:1.1	Matthew 27:3–10
The Resurrection	356	189:1.1	Matthew 28:1–15, Mark 16:1–11, Luke 24:1–11, John 20:1–18
The Walk with Two Brothers	360	190:5.1	Mark 16:12–13, Luke 24:13–35
Appearances to the Apostles	363	191:0.1	Mark 16:14–15, Luke 24:36–38, 44–49; John 20:19–21, 24–29
Appearance by the Lake	367	192:1.1	John 21
Resurrection Appearances	372	190–193	1 Corinthians 15:6–7
The Master's Ascension	377	193:3.1	Matthew 28:16–20, Mark 16:19, Luke 24:50–51, John 20:30–31
Bestowal of the Spirit of Truth	379	194:0.1	Matthew 3:11, Mark 1:8, Luke 3:16; 24:49 | John 1:33; 14:16–18, 26; 16:7, 13–14 |
The Significance of Pentecost	382	194:2.1	cf. Ezekiel 36:26–27 | cf. Acts 1:8
			(Cont): Acts 2:1–4

CREATOR SON OF GOD *(See Jesus of Nazareth)*

GABRIEL
(Hebrew: *Gavri'el* "God is my strength")
Known in the Abrahamic religions as an archangel who typically serves as God's messenger, Gabriel is in fact the chief executive of the universe of Nebadon and the arbiter of all executive appeals respecting its administration. Also known as the Bright and Morning Star, he was a prominent player in many of the pivotal events in the life of Jesus, beginning most famously with the annunciation to Mary and later in converse with Jesus on the Mount of Transfiguration.

FATHER MELCHIZEDEK
The first-born of the Melchizedek order, he acts as the first executive associate of Gabriel. *(See also Melchizedek)*

IMMANUEL
The Paradise brother of Michael of Nebadon.

JESUS OF NAZARETH
The Urantia Book also refers to Jesus of Nazareth by his celestial titles of Michael, Christ Michael, and Michael of Nebadon—the Creator Son of God in whose universe (Nebadon) our world (Urantia) exists. Christ derives from the Greek *Christós:* the anointed one. The name Michael springs from the Latin *micare:* to shine, glitter. Michael means literally and interrogatively: "who is like God" in the Hebrew. So Christ Michael translates as "the anointed one who is like God."

The name Jesus of Nazareth (or simply the Master), designating the human hero who we know, now takes its rightful place alongside these noble titles that designate the sovereign Creator of the universe whose monumental mission to our seemingly insignificant planet changed the course of human history and continues to influence it today.

MELCHIZEDEK
(mel'kizədek; Hebrew: *malkı̄-sedeq*, "king of righteousness") **Machiventa** (maki'ventə)
Known from the Book of Genesis as the king of Salem and priest of El Elyon, he brings out bread and wine and blesses Abram and El Elyon. Hebrews 7:3 (KJV) describes him as, "Without father, without mother, without descent, having neither beginning of days, nor end of life; but made like unto the Son of God; abideth a priest continually."

That individual, **Machiventa Melchizedek**, lived on Earth in human form during the times of Abraham around 2000 B.C. The term "Melchizedek" more broadly refers to a distinct order of descending Sons of God in the local universe. They are a self-governing group and are primarily devoted to education and experiential training even to the mortal worlds. Their stationary number is upwards of ten million.

MICHAEL (OF NEBADON) *(See Jesus of Nazareth)*

MIDWAYERS
These creatures appear on most inhabited worlds and exist and function in the realm "midway" between humans and angels. Midwayers are native permanent inhabitants of a world and are invaluable to the seraphim in their work for the races of mankind as well as to the guardian angels. The generations of humans forget; the corps of midwayers remembers; and in proper circumstances treasured memories of past events are made available, even as the story of the

life and teachings of Jesus has been given by the midwayers of Urantia to their cousins in the flesh.

MORONTIA
(mō'ränshə)
The soul-like state of being. That phase of universe reality intervening and bridging the gulf between the material and spiritual. As Mary Magdalene sought to embrace his feet after the resurrection, Jesus said: "Touch me not, Mary, for I am not as you knew me in the flesh. In this form will I tarry with you for a season before I ascend to the Father." He was referring to this morontia state of being through which he was passing, and in which form he was able to appear and disappear throughout all his resurrection appearances.

Jesus was unique in this regard as people do not resurrect on this world as he did. Nevertheless, the morontia estate is that to which we will be resurrected on the next world. Paul learned of the existence of the morontia worlds and of the reality of the morontia estate, for he wrote, "ye have in heaven a better and an enduring substance." (Hebrews 10:34 KJV). And these morontia materials are real, literal, even as in "a city which hath foundations, whose builder and maker is God." (Hebrews 11:10 KJV).

NEBADON
('nebədän)
The name of our local universe of which Christ Michael is the Sovereign Son and our world is located. Nebadon will eventually comprise ten million mortal inhabited worlds.

PERSONALIZED THOUGHT ADJUSTER
Sometimes when Thought Adjusters are subject to extraordinary circumstances of their indwelling, they become personalized by the Universal Father; that is to say, they enjoy a distinct personal existence apart from their normal indwelling of a mortal mind. *(See also Thought Adjuster)*

SALVINGTON
The architectural headquarters world of Nebadon.

SATANIA
(sə'tān(ē)ə)
The administrative system of approximately one thousand inhabitable planets to which Earth (Urantia) belongs. It is one of ten thousand such systems in Nebadon.

THOUGHT ADJUSTER
The spirit of God that lives within us. Ezekiel teaches that God says, "And I will put my spirit within you, and cause you to walk in my statutes..." (36:27 KJV). It is through this direct gift of a fragment of his eternal spirit that the Father is able to guide his mortal children Godward. Also known as his "indwelling presence," the inner "divine spark," and the "divine light which illumines the mind."

The degree to which a human mind chooses to accept the Adjuster's guidance becomes the degree to which that person's soul grows and becomes a reality that can survive death. The soul is in essence an embryonic spiritual development—a joint creation of the divine Adjuster and the human mind. They are also known as Mystery Monitors.

URANTIA
(yü'ranshə; Greek: *Urania,* muse of astronomy, personalized to mean "our heavenly place in the cosmos")
The name by which our planet is known in the universes.

[INDEX]

Page numbers in **bold italic** indicate illustrations. Painting titles are *italicized*.

A

Aaron, stone mason 189
Abner 170–171, 188, 243, 244, 254, 265, 291, 374
Abraham 79, 97, 224, 242, 243, 292, 296, 299
Abraham of the Sanhedrin 188, 189
Adam 302
Agaman 194
Agondonters 367
Alexander, the Great 77, 78, 217
Alexander, son of Simon of Cyrene 345
Alexandria 20, 26, 35, 64, *70*, 72, 77–79, 86, 95, 102, 150, 373, 384
Alpheus twins. *See* James Alpheus; Judas Alpheus.
Amatha 174
Amathus 158, 254, 255
Amos, brother of Jesus 59
Amos, the prophet 160
Anaxand 73, 76
Anderson, Harry
  John the Baptist Baptizing Jesus **115**
  Pilate Confronts Christ **338**
  Suffer Little Children to Come to Me **259**
  The Tribute Coin **290**
Andrew (apostle) 126–128, 133, 137, 139, 143–145, 147, 149, 151, 158, 160, 161, 166, 183–185, 194, 202, 203–205, 216, 228–229, 232, 244, 245, 279, 289, 290, 292, 300, 305, 310, 320, 370, 371, 382
angels 45, 91, 260, **261**, 268, 294, 304, 322, 323, ***324–325***, 332, 356, 260
Anna (poetess) 21–22
Annas 67, 68, 160, 285, 333, 334, 336, 370
The Annunciation (Carl Bloch) **15**
Antioch 83, 95, 97, 106, 377
Appearance Before Tiberius (Slawa Radziszewska) **83**
Archelaus 26, 42
ascension 170, 280, 372, 377, *378*, 379, 380
At the Genisaret Lake (Vasily Polenov) **208**
Augustus Caesar 19, 72, 116

B

The Babe of Bethlehem (Jeremy Winborg) **12**
Baptism II (J. Kirk Richards) **100**
Barabbas 340, 341, 344
Bartimeus 271, **272**
Bartolo, Taddeo di: *The Twelve Apostles* **143**
beatitudes 155
Beside Quiet Waters (Yongsung Kim) **252–253**
Bethany 42, 45–47, 63, 109, 158, 160, 163, 180, 185, 236, 239, 243, 249, 257, 260–267, 271, 273, 278, 280–285, 289, 300, 308, 372
Bethesda, pool of 180–181, **181**
Bethlehem 13, 16, 17, 19, 20, 21, 23–26, 106, 142, 243
Bethsaida 65, 67, 69, 128, 133, 135, 145, 158, 174, 177, 184, 187–190, 197, 203, 205, 212, 217, 350, 367, 368, 373, 379
Bethsaida-Julias 142, 201, 202, 231
Bida, Alexandre: *The Priests Take Counsel with the Herodians* **214**
Bloch, Carl
  The Annunciation **15**
  Jesus Clears the Temple **287**
  Peter's Denial **335**
  Transfiguration of Christ **227**
"The Brotherhood of Men" lectures 105
The Burial of Joseph (Russ Docken) **50**

C

Caesarea-Philippi 109, 197, 222, 223, 231
Caiaphas 267, 307, 332–334, 336, 344, 347
Caligastia 110, 111, 122, 310
Calvary 124. *See* Golgotha.
Cana wedding 130–133, **131**
Capernaum 62, 65, 67, 68, 71, 102, 104, 105, 106, 109, 111, 112, 114, 116, 126, 128, 135, 137, 138, 142, 143, 145, 147, 150, 151, 155, 171, 174, 177, 187, 195, 208, 212, 281, 373
The Caravan Conductor (Gerry Metz) **102–103**
Celsus 222, 231
Celta 194
centurion at the cross (*also* Roman captain) 163, 329, 334, 345, 350, 351, 352, 353, 356
Chang, the Chinese Merchant (Slawa Radziszewska) **93**
The Chief Priests Take Counsel Together (James Tissot) **266**
Christ among the Lepers (J. Kirk Richards) **179**
Christ and the Rich Young Ruler (Heinrich Hofmann) **245**
City of Judah 14,117
Ciseri, Antonio: *Ecce Homo* **342–343**
Claudia Procula 336, 340
Cleopas of Emmaus 360, 362, 363, 364
Come unto Me (Harold Copping) **378**
The Comforter (C. Michael Dudash) **381**
Commissioning the Women's Corps (J. Kirk Richards) **192–193**
Copping, Harold
  Come unto Me **378**

The Healing of Blind Bartimeus **272**
Jesus Heals the Epileptic Boy **230**
The Pool of Bethesda **181**
Corinth 68, 88, 89, 91, 94
Cornelius 76
courtesans 88–91, **90–91**
Creator Son 111, 175, 177, 298, 383
Crispus 88
crucifixion
  as act of love, meaning 352
  address to family of Jesus 350
  audience of 346, 348, 349
  carriage of crossbeam 346
  clothing and 346
  cruelty of 345
  derision toward Jesus 346, 349
  exhaustion of Jesus 345
  forgiveness by Jesus during 346
  inscription on cross 346
  moment of physical death 351
  nailing to cross 346
  narcotized wine and 345
  possession of body 351–353
  repetition of Psalms 350
  sandstorm during 350
  soldiers and 346, 348, 349
  thief on the cross 349
  thirst of Jesus 349
Cymboyton 105
Cynics 82, 86
Cyprus 95, 149

D

Damascus 34, 64, 68, 72, 83, 102, 194
Damascus gate (of Jerusalem) 357, 358
David (king) 16, 25–26, 49, 121, 207, 217, 291, 302
David, son of Zebedee 67, 138, 184–185, 201, 214, 217, 244, 282, 305, 353, 357, 373
The Destruction of the Temple of Jerusalem (Francesco Hayez) **301**
Deuteronomy, Book of 208
Docken, Russ
  The Burial of Joseph **50**
  Father Forgive Them **326**
  The Kingdom's First Hospital **186**
  The Master Boatbuilder **66**
  Leave No Writings Behind **129**
  My Hour Has Come **112–113**
  Rebecca's Marriage Proposal **61**
  The Young Man Who Was Afraid **81**
Dreams (On the Hill) (Vasily Polenov) **168**
Dudash, C. Michael
  The Comforter **381**
  Fishers of Men **140–141**
  Follow Me **388–389**
  He Lifted His Eyes Toward

Heaven **319**
Light of the World 2, 241
Living Water **164–165**
The Master Teacher **302–303**
Not by Bread Alone **108–109**
On the Way to Bethlehem **18–19**
Peter's Confession **220–221**

E

Eber 238, 249
Ecce Homo (Antonio Ciseri) ***342–343***
Elijah 38, 117, 222, 226, 228
Elijah Mark 318, 328, 360, 327
Elizabeth, mother of John the Baptist 14, 24, 29, 47, 58, 117
Elizabeth (evangelist) 194
Elman (Syrian physician) 185, 187, 194
Enoch, Book of 53
epochal sermon 208–211
Esta 65
Ezra (father of Rebecca) 60
Ezra (deciple of John) 127, 128
Ezraeon 25

F

Facing Eternity (Del Parson) **120**
The Family Garden (Michael Malm) **56**
Father Forgive Them (Russ Docken) **326**
Father Melchizedek 226, **226**
feast of tabernacles 235, 236, 249, 251
feast of the dedication 247, 249, 251
feeding the five thousand ***200–201***, 201–202
Feeding the Five Thousand (Walter Rane) ***200–201***
Fishers of Men (C. Michael Dudash) ***140–141***
Flavius, Greek Jew 160, 161, 162, 372
The Flight into Egypt (Eugene Girardet) **24**
Follow Me (C. Michael Dudash) ***388–389***
Follow Me (Vasily Polenov) **125**
Fontainne, Andon
  Serendipity **69**
  The Son of Peace Enters Jerusalem **282**
Forbidden Art (Slawa Radziszewska) **35**
Forgiven (Daniel Gerhartz) **172**
Forgiven (Yongsung Kim) **239**
Fortune 80, **81**

G

Gabriel 14, **15**, 16, 52, 116, 117, 215, 226, **226**, 264, 265, 356
Gaius 81
Ganid 63, **64**, 66, 67, **67**, **68–69**, 70–71, 74, **75**, 76, 77, 79, 81, 82, 84, **86–87**, 87, 88, **89**
Garden Tomb (J. Kirk Richards) **354**
General View of Tyre (David

Roberts) 218
Gerhartz, Daniel: *Forgiven* 172
Gethsemane Prayer (Yongsung
Kim) 324–325
Girardet, Eugene: *The Flight
into Egypt* 24
God
as Yahweh 78
cause of natural events 29
concept of as Father 158,
160–161
kingdom of 135–136
one day alone with 305–307
personality of 13
within 92
Golgotha 345, 346, 350, 351,
352
Gonod 69, *70*, 72, 78, *83*, 85,
86, 88, 94, 95, *96*, 97, *98*,
102
The Good Samaritan (Vincent
Willem van Gogh) 248
"Good Samaritan" parable
247–249, *248*, 271
"Good Shepherd" sermon/
parable 251–254, 268
"Grace of Salvation" sermon
268
The Great Lighthouse of Pharos
(Slawa Radziszewska) 78
Great Commandment 291
Greek believers 292–295,
372, 373

H

Hall of Hewn Stones 163
Hayez, Francesco: *The
Destruction of the Temple of
Jerusalem* 301
The Healing at Sundown (J.
Kirk Richards) *176–177*
The Healing of Blind Bartimeus
(Harold Copping) *272*
Healing the Blind Man
(Yongsung Kim) *250*
Hebrews, Book of 71
Hebrew nation. *See* Jewish
nation.
Hebron 106, 213–214
He Is Not Here (Walter Rane)
358–359
*He Lifted His Eyes Toward
Heaven* (C. Michael
Dudash) *319*
Herod Agrippa 145
Herod Antipas 19, 23–25, 26,
38, 42, 54–55, 117, 118, 135,
158, 171, 177, 188, 194, 208,
214, 217, 228, 231, 235, 339
Herodians 188, *214*, 295
Herodias 117
Hildana 239–240, *239*
Hofmann, Heinrich
*Christ and the Rich Young
Ruler* 245
Jesus in the Temple 44–45
Hole, William
Jesus as a Boy in Nazareth
28
The Wedding at Cana 131

I

I Am He (Walter Rane) *330–331*

Ikhnaton 25
Immanuel 43
In Joseph's Woodshop (Michael
Malm) *32–31*
In Remembrance of Me (Walter
Rane) *314–315*
The Intervention (Del Parson)
87
In the World, Not of the World
(Greg Olsen) *106–107*
Iron 178–179, 286
Isaiah 32, 54, 160, 222, 292
I Stand at the Door and Knock
(J. Kirk Richards) *234*

J

Jacob of Emmaus 360, 362,
364
Jacob, friend of Jesus 27, 32,
34, 39, 65
Jacob, husband of Miriam 65
Jacob, prophet 166, 296
Jacob, trader from Crete
160–161
Jacob's well 163–169, *164–165*,
376
Jairus 197–198, *199*, 208
Jairus's Daughter (Jeremy
Winborg) *199*
James Alpheus (apostle) 137,
143, 144, 149–150, 185, 202,
231, 283, 284, 290, 310,
312, 371
James Zebedee (apostle) 67,
114, 122, *125*, 126, 127, 128,
137, 138, 139, 144, 145, 146,
151, 160, 161, 169, 181, 183,
184, 197, 204, 225, 226, 229,
233, 258, 290, 310, 322, 328,
371, 382
James, brother of Jesus 30, 34,
52, 54, 55, 57, 58, 59, 60, 63,
64, 65, 102, 104, 105, 112,
114, 115, 116, 130, 134, 215,
217, 246, 372, 379
James of Safed 228, 229
Jeremiah, Book of 208
Jerusalem 10, 13, 14, 20, 21, 26,
31, 34, 39, 40–49, *48*, 52,
53, 57, 59, 62–64, 67, 68, 72,
104, 109, 112, 138, 144, 145,
148, 150, 158, 160, 163, 167,
180–185, 187–189, 191, 197,
202, 205, 208, 210–217, 228,
232, 235, 236, 238–240, 242,
243, 245–247, 249, 251, 254,
257, 258, 265, 266, 271–273,
277, 278, 280–286, *282*,
288, 290, *294*, 295, 299,
300–308, *301*, 320, 329, 332,
334, 336, 344–437, 350, 352,
353, 357, 360, 362, 363, 364,
368, 370, 372, 373, 376, 377,
379, 380, 384
Jerusalem, Jerusalem (James
Tissot) *294*
Jerusalem (Herod's) Temple
41, 42, 163, 288
Jesus
on accusations against
236–237, 249–250, 267
adolescence of 40–41, 43,
49, 55

on angels 260
animal sacrifice and 42
apostle selection by
125–128, 137
apostles of John the Baptist
and 170
appeal by Pilate for 341,
342–343, 344
appeal to Herod 54–55
appearance at Alexandria
373
appearance at Bethsaida
373, 376
appearance at Jacob's well
376
appearance to apostles
363–367, 367–372, *368–369*,
377–379
appearance to brothers
from Emmaus 360–363, *361*
appearance to Greek
believers 372–373
appearance to James 372
appearance to Mary
Magdalene 359–360
appearance to Simon Peter
alone 364
appearance to women
believers 372
appearances (chart and
map of all) *374–375*
arrest of 185, 214–217, 236,
238, 243, 281, 328, *330–331*,
332
as artist 32–34, *35*, 36
ascension of 377–379
baptism of 52, 58, *100*, 111,
112, 114–116, *115*, 122
"before Abraham was, I
am" proclamation 224, 243
betrayal of 151, 307, 310, 313,
328–332, *330–331*, 347
"birthday text" 32
birth of *12*, 13, 20–21
blessing of children by *259*,
261–228
blind beggar and 271–273,
272
as boatbuilder, *66*, 67,
111–112, 139
burial of 163, 352–353
burial bandages of 358,
358–359, 360
at Capernaum synagogue
143, 174, 187, *206*, 207, 208
as caravan conductor
101–104, *102–103*
as carpenter 39, 40, 51, 52,
54, 55, 57, 67
carriage of crossbeam by
345
on casting out evil 211–212
centurion and 91
challenge to authority of
288–289
challenge to Sanhedrin
249–251, 221
childhood of 26–39, 195
Chinese merchant Chang
and 92, *93*, 94
cleansing of temple
285–288, *287*
closing of synagogues to

213
commandment of love
(new) 155, 316–317
competitive games and 39
condemned criminal and
94
courtesans and 88–91,
90–91
as Creator Son 111, 175, 177,
298, 383
crucifixion of 346–351, *348*
cup of blessing and 314
as Davidic type of Messiah
134
day with John Mark
305–307, *306*
death of 351
death of Joseph and 52
on definition of "neighbor"
247
denial by Peter 334, *335*
departure from home 65
departure from Rome 85
on destruction of Jerusalem
299–301
dissolution of mortal
remains 356
divinity of 223–224
early adulthood of 64
education of 29–42
emergence from tomb 356
on entrance into Kingdom
255–257
entrance into Jerusalem
280–284, *282*
Epicurean teacher and 92
epileptic boy and 228–231,
230
epochal sermon *206*,
201–211
examination by Annas 334
examination by Herod 339
examination by Pilate
336–345, *338*, *342*
family financial struggle
and 54–55
on Father's character
160–161
fearful young man and
79–80, *81*
feast of tabernacles and
235, 236, 249, 251
feast of the dedication and
247, 249, 251
feeding of five thousand
200–201, 201–202
final address to temple *294*,
295–299
final departure from
apostles 323–324
final message to family 216
final prayer with apostles
318, *319*, 320–322
at first hospital 184–187, *186*
as fisherman 67, 139
on forgiveness 145
Gerasa sermon 255–257
Gethsemane prayer
322–324, 324–325
"Good Samaritan" sermon
247–249, *248*, 271
"Good Shepherd" sermon
251–254, 268

"Grace of Salvation"
sermon 268
on gratitude 255
on Great Commandment
291
Great Temptation of
109–111
Greek believers and
292–295, 372, 373
hasty flight of 214–217, 235
hem of garment 197
hostile husband and 86, *87*,
88, 191
infancy of 24, 25
invitation from Nahor 34
isolation of 203
at Jacob's well 163–169,
164–165, 376
Jairus's daughter and
197–198, *199*, 208
Jerusalem spies and
183–184
at Jerusalem temple 236
"Joys of Righteous Living"
sermon 187
Judas and 328–329
on kingship 203, 204
languages of 31
lepers and 178–179, *179*,
254–255
at Library of Alexandria *70*,
78–79
at Lighthouse of Alexandria
77, *78*
"light of the world"
proclamation 240–242, *241*
lost child and 84
on love of mankind 155,
316–317
on love of wealth 246
loyalty and 316
on manifestation of love 155
man with withered hand
and 187–188
as Messiah 134
on Messiah 237
miller and 91
miracle of loaves and fishes
200–201, 201–202
mistress of Greek inn and
92
Mithraic cult and 92
money-changers and
285–286, *287*, 295
at Mount Hermon *108–109*,
109–111, 114, 220, 225–228,
227
music and 34
Nalda and 163–169,
164–165, 376
name of the Father and 321
on neighborly love 291
Nicodemus and 161–163,
162
on welfare of God's children
73
ordination of apostles by
151
on origin of teachings 236
pagan and *84*, 85
paralytic man and 188–189
parenting style of 58–60, 64
as Passover prisoner

340–341
penitent woman and *172*,
181
in Perean wilderness 122,
122–123, 124–125
Personalized Thought
Adjuster of 175
personality of 17, 157, 212,
274
Peter's confession 220,
220–221, 222–223
Peter's protest and 231–233,
232
physical appearance of
13, 55
at pool of Bethesda
180–181, *181*
on prayer 168, 170, 267–268
presentation at temple 21
presentation by Pilate 342,
342–343
Priests of Ur and 21, 23–24
"prodigal son" parable
268–271, *270*
pursuit by Herod 24
Rebecca and 60–62, *61*
refusal to join Zealots 57–58
rejection at Nazareth
194–196
relationship with John the
Baptist 58
repetition of Psalms 350
resurrection of Lazarus
258, 261–265, *261–262*, 278,
280, 372
resurrection of self *354*, 355,
356–360, *366*
rich young man and
244–246, *245*
Roman judge and 92
romantic love and 62
runaway and 94
on the Sabbath 183, 184, 187
on second coming
301–302, 304
sentencing of 333
sermon at Gerasa 255–257
Sermon on the Mount
152–155, *153*
siblings of 59, 64
on sign of authority 212
silence toward Sanhedrin
court 333
Six Great Decisions of
124, 132
solitary time of 106,
106–107, 109, 305, 322–324,
324–325
as "Son of Man" 53
souls of animals and 76–77
spies of Herod and 24, 135
spies of Jerusalem and
183–184
on spirit of Father 162
on Spirit of Truth 111, 135,
314, 316, 317, 318, 363, 365,
373, 377, 379
on spiritual healing 180
stages of life 223
at synagogue of Nazareth
195–196
teachings at Tyre 217–220
at temple of Jerusalem 21,

41–49, *44–45*, 63, 160, 180,
235–243, *241*, 249, 284,
285–290, *287*, 290–292,
290, *294*, 295–299
ten lepers and 254–255
thief on the cross and 349
thoughtless pagan and
84, 85
Tiberius and 82, *83*
tomb of *354*, 355, 356–360,
358–359
tour of Mediterranean
71–99
transfiguration of 225–228,
227
traveler from Britain and 94
trial before Pilate 336–345
trial before Sanhedrin court
332–336
tribute coin and *290*, 291
as tutor 68, 76, 88, 98, 345
Urmia lectures 104
Veronica of Caesarea-
Philippi and 197
walk on water 205
washing of feet by *276*,
310–312
washing of feet for *172*, 181,
279, 279
water into wine 130–133, *131*
wedding at Cana and
130–133, *131*
witnesses against 333
woman taken in adultery
and 239–240, *239*
women evangelists and
190–194, *192–193*
women's emancipation and
142, 191
writings of 128, *129*
Jesus (Akiane Kramarik) *275*
Jesus as a Boy in Nazareth
(William Hole) *28*
Jesus Clears the Temple (Carl
Bloch) *287*
Jesus in the Synagogue (Greg
Olsen) *206*
Jesus in the Temple (Heinrich
Hofmann) *44–45*
Jesus Resurrected (J. Kirk
Richards) *366*
Jewish nation 20, 36, 214, 238,
277, 296, 298, 300, 336
Jews, status of 298
Joab 213
Joanna 190, 194, 358
Johab (groom at Cana) 130
John, Book of 111, 146, 207, 277
John Zebedee (apostle) 8, 9,
67, 102, 111, 122, 126, 127,
128, 137, 139, 143, 143, 144,
145–146, 149, 151, 160, 161,
163, 180, 181, 183, 184, 197,
205, 207, 225, 226, 227, 229,
233, 277, 281, 290, 308, 309,
310, 131, 322, 328, 332, 334,
335, 336, 337, 346, 350, 351,
352, 360, 368, 368–369, 370,
371, 379, 382
John Mark 205, 304, *306*,
307–309, 318, 324, 332, 365,
368, 370, 379
John the Baptist 14, 21, 23, 29,

47, 52, 58, *100*, 101, 112, 114,
115, *115*, 116–119, *119*, 121,
124, 126, 128, 130, 134–136,
138, 141, 150, 158, 160,
169–171, 177, 222, 289, 295,
299, 339
John the Baptist (Louis Tiffany)
119
John the Baptist Baptizing Jesus
(Harry Anderson) *115*
Joseph, brother of Jesus 59,
60, 64, 65, 68, 102, 104,
128, 158
Joseph, earthly father of Jesus
appearance of Gabriel and
14, 16
as carpenter 17, 21, 24, 25,
26, 27, *32–33*
census and 16, 19, 20
as contractor 17, 25
death of 17, *50*, 51, 52
dream of 16
education of 17
education of Jesus 29, 30,
31, 39
escape from Herod 23, 24,
24, 25
journey to Bethlehem
18–19, 19, 20
journey to Nazareth 26
marriage to Mary 17
physical appearance of 17
presentation at temple 21,
22, 23
relationship with Jesus 17,
27, 29, *37*, 38, 39, 40, 49
temperament of 16, 39
Joseph of Arimathea 163, 194,
249, 295, 351–353, 357
Joseph of Tyre 217
Josiah the blind beggar 250,
250, 251, 271
Josiah, disciple of Abner 291
Jotapata 142, 194
Joy of the Lord (Greg Olsen)
156
"Joys of Righteous Living"
sermon 187
Judah 14, 47
Judas Alpheus (apostle) 137,
143, 144, 149–150, 185, 202,
231, 283, 284, 290, 310,
312, 371
Judas (Edward Okuń) *347*
Judas Iscariot (apostle) 137,
138, 139, 142, 144, 147, 150–
151, 163, 166, 180, 190, 202,
208, 228, 235, 278–280, *279*,
285, 304, 307–313, 320, 322,
328, 329, *330–331*, 336, 347,
347, 377
Jude, brother of Jesus 58, 59,
60, 68, 102, 114, 115, 116,
130, 133, 134, 194, 215, 346,
350, 351
Justus 88, 89, 91

K
Kheresa 137, 149
Kidron 308, 318
Kim, Yongsung
Beside Quiet Waters *252–253*
Forgiven *239*

Gethsemane Prayer *324–325*
Healing the Blind Man *250*
Washing of the Feet *276*
"The Kingdom" sermon
135–136
The Kingdom's First Hospital
(Russ Docken) *186*
Kramarik, Akiane: Jesus *275*

L

Lake Urmia 104–105
Last Supper
arrival of Jesus 310
bread of remembrance 314
cup of blessing 314
journey to 308–309
location of 308, 309
preparations for 308–309
remembrance supper
314–316
seating of apostles 309–310
washing of feet 310–312
words to betrayer 312–313
Lazarus 42, 47, 62, 63, 163,
243, 257, 258, 261, 262,
262–263, 264–265, 266,
267, 278–281, 290, 372
Lazarus, Come Forth! (Walter
Rane) *262–263*
Leave No Writings Behind
(Russ Docken) *129*
Lebbeus. See Judas Alpheus.
The Library of Alexandria
(Slawa Radziszewska) *70*
A Light to the Gentiles (Greg
Olsen) *22*
Lighthouse of Alexandria
(Pharos) 77, *78*
Light of the World (C. Michael
Dudash) *2, 241*
Living Water (C. Michael
Dudash) *164–165*
Lord's Prayer 169
Lucifer 110, 111, 225, 226, 260,
310
Luke, Book of 13, 111, 116, 155,
173, 205, 327, 350

M

Magadan 228, 231, 233, 243,
244
Magdala 34, 65, 109, 142, 194
Malchus 329
Malm, Michael
The Family Garden *56*
In Joseph's Woodshop *32–33*
Sabbath Walks with Joseph
37
Two Brothers from Emmaus
361
mansions, celestial 160, 161
maps
Mediterranean Tour *74–75*
Resurrection Localities *375*
Palestine *159*
Mark, Book of 355
Mark (chore lad). See John
Mark.
Martha, sister of Andrew and
Peter 194
Martha, sister of Jesus 27, 59
Martha, sister of Lazarus 342,
62, 63, 243, 249, 257, 260,

261, 262, 264, 265, 278, 280
Martha, wife of Justus 89, 91
Mary Magdalene 194, 351, 353,
357, 359, 360, 372
Mary, mother of Alpheus
twins 374
Mary, mother of Jesus
appearance of Gabriel to
14, *15*, 16
birth of Jesus 20
Cana wedding 130–133, *131*
crucifixion of Jesus and
346, 350
death of Joseph and 52
dovecote of 30, 54
education of 17
education of Jesus *28, 29*, 31
escape from Herod 23,
24, 25
journey to Bethlehem
18–19, 19–20
journey to Nazareth 26
marriage to Joseph 17
physical appearance of 17
presentation at temple 21,
22, 23
purification of 21
relationship with Jesus 17,
30, *31*, 38, 40, 49, 57, 58, 65,
215–216, *215*, 217, 350
Spirit of Truth and 379
temperament of 17
Mary, sister of Lazarus 42, 62,
63, 243, 257, 261, 262, 264,
265, 278, 279, *279*, 280
Mary, wife of Ezra 61
The Master Boatbuilder (Russ
Docken) *66*
The Master Teacher (C.
Michael Dudash) *302–303*
Matadormus 245–246, *245*,
249
Matthew, Book of 101, 121, 148,
155, 157, 386
Matthew Levi (apostle) 137,
139, 144, 147–148, 183, 194,
202, 298, 299, 310, 371, 382
Melchizedek 79, 226, *227*, 302
Messiah 14, 16, 19, 20, 21, 23,
25, 34, 53, 57, 59, 60, 65,
116–119, 121, 128, 132, 134,
203, 207, 210, 223, 224, 232,
236–239, 267, 281–283, 291,
292, 300, 334, 340, 377, 380
messenger service 184, 185,
190, 214–217, 244, 257, 261,
262, 267, 282, 373
Metz, Gerry: The Caravan
Conductor *102–103*
Michael (of Nebadon) 111, 124,
202, 226, 323
midwayers 228, 356
Milcha 194
Miriam, sister of Jesus 54, 59,
60, 62, 64, 65
Mithraic group 82, 83, 92
money-changers 285–286, *287*,
289, 295
morontia 356, 362, 329, 363,
364, 365, 367, 377, 379
Moses 16, 24, 63, 121, 160, 179,
210, 222, 226, 237, 239, 240,
296, 310, 321, 352

Mother's Love (Slawa
Radziszewska) *31*
Mount Hermon 38, 101,
109–111, *108–109*, 114, 122,
125, 220, 225, 226, *227*, 324
Mount Olivet (Mount of
Olives) 41, 42, 46, 47, 49,
273, 277, 282, 283, 285, 289,
290, 299, 302, 308, 320,
328, 334, 365, 379
Mukherjee, Prem: No Greater
Love *348*
My Hour Has Come (Russ
Docken) *112–113*
mystery cults 79, 82, 86

N

Nahor (evangelist) 196
Nahor (teacher) 34
Nalda 163–169, *164–165*, 376
Naomi (bride at Cana) 130
Nasanta 194
Nathan (potter) 32
Nathaniel (apostle) 128, 137,
138, 144, 147, 150, 228, 247,
249–251, 260, 300, 310,
365, 371
Nathan of Busiris (messenger)
373
Nazareth (life in) 26–32, *28*
Nazareth 13, 17, 20, 21, 24, 25,
34, 35, 38, 39, 41–43, 45,
46, 49, 51, 52, 53, 54, 57, 58,
60, 62, 64, 65, 67, 68, 71,
102, 103, 104, 106, 128, 147,
158, 176, 194–196, 240, 281,
324, 346
Nebadon 111, 174, 226, 353, 379
New Commandment 312,
316–317
Nicodemus 157, 161–163, *162*,
185, 249, 293, 351–353, 357
Nicodemus (J. Kirk Richards)
162
No Greater Love (Prem
Mukherjee) *348*
Not by Bread Alone (C.
Michael Dudash) *108–109*

O

O Jerusalem (Greg Olsen)
10–11
O Jerusalem, Jerusalem
(Jeremy Winborg) *48*
Okuń, Edward: Judas *347*
Olsen, Greg
In the World, Not of the
World *106–107*
Jesus in the Synagogue *206*
Joy of the Lord *156*
A Light to the Gentiles *22*
O Jerusalem *10–11*
Peace on Earth *385*
Worlds Without End *122–123*
One Day Alone with God (Del
Parson) *306*
On the Way to Bethlehem (C.
Michael Dudash) *18–19*
Ordination sermon 152–155,
153

P

Palestine 13, 16, 25, 53, 62, 69,

72, 73, 78, 87, 98, 101, 106,
114, 118, *159*, 173, 185, 213,
243, 301
parable 142, 158, 232, 251–254,
286–271, 310, 312
Parson, Del
Facing Eternity *120*
The Intervention *87*
One Day Alone with God
306
Peter Do You Love Me?
368–369
Passover celebrations 42, 43,
59, 63, 68, 160, 180, 205,
273, 308, 310, 314, 316, 334,
340, 353
Paul 64, 72, 76, 83, 88, 95, 106,
194, 265, 380
Peace on Earth (Greg Olsen)
385
Pentecost 111, 211, 379–382,
382–384
Personalized Thought Adjuster
115, 175, 293
Peter (apostle) 72, 76, 83, 84,
126, 128, 133, 135, 137–139,
143, 144, 145, 149, 151, 160,
161, 166, 175, 178, 181, 185,
189, 194, 197, 203–205, 213,
220–224, *220–221*, 225–228,
227, 231–233, *232*, 281, 301,
309, 311, 313, 329, 334, *335*,
360, 363–364, 367–371,
368–369, 376, 380, 382
Peter Do You Love Me? (Del
Parson) *368–369*
Peter's Confession (C. Michael
Dudash) *220–221*
Peter's Denial (Carl Bloch) *335*
Pharisees 57, 163, 181–183,
187–189, 191, 208, 211, 212,
214–215, *214*, 236, 238–239,
247, 250, 251, 254, 257, 266,
266, 273, 278, 283, 291,
295–298, 305, 312
Phasaelis (wife of Herod
Antipas) 117
Phasaelis (Greek city) 166
Philip the Curious (apostle)
76, 127–128, 137, 144,
146–147, 166, 170, 201, 202,
208, 289, 292, 298, 308,
310, 371, 382
Philip, brother of Herod
Antipas 117, 208, 228
Pilate, Pontius 116, 163, 327,
333, 336–345, *338, 342–343*,
351, 356, 357
Pilate Confronts Christ (Harry
Anderson) *338*
Playing with the Shepherd Dog
(Slawa Radziszewska) *77*
Polenov, Vasily
At the Genisaret Lake *208*
Dreams (On the Hill) *168*
Follow Me *125*
Pontius Pilate. See Pilate,
Pontius.
The Pool of Bethesda (Harold
Copping) *181*
prayer
effective 170

Jesus' childhood 30
last group 318–322
Lord's 170
meant to Jesus 168
The Priests Take Counsel with the Herodians (Alexandre Bida) 214
Priests of Ur 21, 23–24
The Prodigal Son (Liz Lemon Swindle) 270
"prodigal son" parable 268–271, 270
The Protestations of Saint Peter (James Tissot) 232
Proverbs, Book of 51
Psalms 350

R

Rachel 194
Radziszewska, Slawa
  Appearance Before Tiberius 83
  Chang, the Chinese Merchant 93
  Forbidden Art 35
  The Great Lighthouse of Pharos 78
  The Library of Alexandria 70
  Mother's Love 31
  Playing with the Shepherd Dog 77
  Tender Loving Care 96–97
  The Thoughtless Pagan 84
  Trek Across the Desert Sands 98–99
  The Turning Point (with Stephen Sawyer) 279
  The Two Courtesans 90–91
Rane, Walter
  Feeding the Five Thousand 200–201
  He Is Not Here 358–359
  I Am He 330–331
  In Remembrance of Me 314–315
  Lazarus, Come Forth! 262–263
Rebecca (daughter of Ezra) 60–62, 61, 351, 353
Rebecca (daughter of Joseph of Arimathea) 194
Rebecca's Marriage Proposal (Russ Docken) 61
Rembrandt van Rijn: *The Storm on the Sea of Galilee* 204
remembrance supper 277, 314–316, 314–315
resurrection
  angels of 356
  discovery of empty tomb 357
  dissolution of mortal remains 356
  emergence from tomb 356
  seals of Pilate and 356
Revelation, Book of 111, 146, 235
Richards, J. Kirk
  Baptism II 100
  Christ among the Lepers 179
  Commissioning the Women's Corps 192–193

Garden Tomb 354
The Healing at Sundown 176–177
I Stand at the Door and Knock 234
Jesus Resurrected 366
Nicodemus 162
Small Angel in White 261
Roberts, David: *General View of Tyre* 218
Rodan 373
Rome 36, 57, 68, 72, 78, 82–85, 85–86, 88, 94, 145, 146, 292
Rufus, son of Simon of Cyrene 82, 345
Ruth, sister of Jesus 59, 64, 102–105, 142, 158, 185, 215, 346, 351

S

Sabbath Walks with Joseph (Michael Malm) 37
Sadducees 150, 163, 208, 260, 295, 336, 339, 344
Salome, wife of Zebedee 67, 133, 138, 160, 379
Salvington 43
Samaritans 163, 166, 169, 191, 247–249, 248, 254–255, 271, 296, 376
Sanhedrin 161–163, 181, 183, 188, 189, 197, 208, 210, 213–215, 214, 216, 217, 236, 238–240, 243, 245, 247, 249, 251, 265–267, 278, 280, 281, 284, 286, 288, 289, 292, 332–334, 340, 347, 351, 352, 363
Satan 110, 111, 212, 289, 310
Satania 110, 111
Saul. See Paul.
Sawyer, Stephen: *The Turning Point* (with Slawa Radziszewska) 279
Scythopolis 26, 38–39, 171, 184
Sea of Galilee 34, 65, 148, 149, 204, 217, 324, 370
Sebaste (home of Abner) 171
Sepphoris 26, 38, 52, 54, 62, 64, 65, 133, 194, 195, 351, 353
Serendipity (Andon Fontainne) 69
Sermon on the Mount 151–155, 153
The Sermon on the Mount (James Tissot) 153
Seventy Evangelists 170, 243–244, 246, 255
Sidon 97, 106, 377
Silas 88
Siloam, pool of 188, 250, 251, 382
Simeon (singer) 21, 23, 24
Simon (of Bethany) 278, 280, 284, 285, 290, 365
Simon, brother of Jesus 59–60, 64, 102
Simon, father of Mary, Martha, and Lazarus 42, 45, 46, 47
Simon of Cyrene 82, 345
Simon Peter (apostle) 72, 76, 83, 84, 126, 128, 133, 135, 137–139, 143, 144, 145,

149, 151, 160, 161, 166, 175, 178, 181, 185, 189, 194, 197, 203–205, 213, 220–224, 220–221, 225–228, 227, 231–233, 232, 281, 301, 309, 311, 313, 329, 334, 335, 360, 363–364, 367–371, 368–369, 376, 380, 382
Simon the Pharisee 181–183
Simon Zelotes (apostle) 126–127, 137, 144, 150, 196, 228, 255, 310, 370, 371, 377
Six Great Decisions 124, 132
Small Angel in White (J. Kirk Richards) 261
The Son of Peace Enters Jerusalem (Andon Fontainne) 282
Song of Solomon 62
soul (nature of) 29, 76, 77, 86, 94, 161, 167, 191, 211, 218, 219, 233, 250, 257, 260, 277, 318, 352, 376, 383, 384
spies 24, 135, 183–184, 187, 188, 189, 260
Spirit of Truth 111, 135, 314, 316, 317, 318, 355, 363, 365, 373, 377, 379–384, 381
Stephen 64, 353
Stoics 82, 86, 339
The Storm on the Sea of Galilee (Rembrandt van Rijn) 204
Suffer Little Children to Come to Me (Harry Anderson) 259
Susanna 190, 194
Swindle, Liz Lemon: *The Prodigal Son* 270
Sychar 109, 166, 169, 184, 376

T

Taricheia 137, 148, 370
Tender Loving Care (Slawa Radziszewska) 96–97
Thaddeus. See James Alpheus.
Thomas Didymus (apostle) 137, 144, 148–149, 158, 169, 194, 195, 228, 231, 247, 250, 251, 258, 289, 305, 310, 363, 364, 365, 367, 371
Thought Adjuster 29, 109, 175
The Thoughtless Pagan (Slawa Radziszewska) 84
Thrace 148
Tiberius Caesar 82, 83, 116
Tiffany, Louis: *John the Baptist* 119
Tiglath 109, 110, 111, 225
Timothy 88
Tissot, James
  The Chief Priests Take Counsel Together 266
  Jerusalem, Jerusalem 294
  The Protestations of Saint Peter 232
  The Sermon on the Mount 153
Titus 80
Transfiguration 225–228, 227
Transfiguration of Christ (Carl Bloch) 227
Trek Across the Desert Sands (Slawa Radziszewska)

98–99
The Tribute Coin (Harry Anderson) 290
Truth, Spirit of 111, 135, 314, 316, 317, 318, 355, 363, 365, 373, 377, 379–384, 381
The Turning Point (Stephen Sawyer and Slawa Radziszewska) 279
The Twelve Apostles (Taddeo di Bartolo) 143
Two Brothers from Emmaus (Michael Malm) 361
The Two Courtesans (Slawa Radziszewska) 90–91
Tyre 106, 217–220, 218, 376, 377

U

Ur 21, 23, 97, 102
Urantia 8, 9, 11, 21, 43, 52, 53, 55, 69, 104, 105, 109, 111, 122, 124, 142, 225, 226, 265, 352, 356, 379, 383
Urmia 104–105

V

van Gogh, Vincent Willem: *The Good Samaritan* 248
Veronica of Caesarea-Philippi 197

W

Washing of the Feet (Yongsung Kim) 276
The Wedding at Cana (William Hole) 131
Winborg, Jeremy
  The Babe of Bethlehem 12
  Jairus's Daughter 199
  O Jerusalem, Jerusalem 48
wine
  at Cana wedding 131–133, 135, 174
  for crucifixion 345, 349, 351
  Last Supper 309, 310, 312, 314
Wise Men. See Priests of Ur.
women, emancipation of 142, 190, 191, 384
women's corps 190–194, 192–193, 194, 243, 254, 283, 290
Worlds Without End (Greg Olsen) 122–123

Y

The Young Man Who Was Afraid (Russ Docken) 81

Z

Zaccheus 271–273
Zacharias 21, 23, 24, 25, 29, 34, 47
Zadoc 16
Zealots 57–58, 137, 150
Zebedee 65, 67, 68, 69, 102, 105, 111, 126, 133, 134, 138, 151, 158, 160, 171, 174, 184, 203, 205, 215, 367, 373
Zebedee boatshop 102, 112, 114, 134, 135
Zechariah, Book of 281
Zechariah, times of 299

THE UNTOLD STORY OF JESUS

Urantia Press is a publisher of secondary works related to *The Urantia Book* and its teachings. Urantia Foundation (urantia.org) first published *The Urantia Book* in 1955. Today there are more than eight hundred thousand copies in print and twenty-five translations. The book consists of four parts, the last of which is a narrative of the life and teachings of Jesus. This book is excerpted entirely from that narrative.

533 West Diversey Parkway
Chicago, IL 60614 USA
urantiapress.org

PRODUCERS
Mo Siegel, *Executive Producer*
Jim English, *Producer; Designer*
MaryJo Garascia, *Senior Editor*
Jennifer Siegel, *Senior Advisor*

ASSOCIATE EDITORS

David Kantor	Lucretia Schanfarber
Stuart Kerr	Paula Thompson

BOOK PRODUCTION TEAM (FIRST PRINTING)
Carol Farrar Norton, *Designer*
Kevin Mulroy, *Project Consultant*
Barbara Brownell Grogan, *Editor*
Heather McElwain, *Contributing Editor*
Ed Merritt, *Cartographer*
Timothy Griffin, *Indexer*
Matt Propert, *Illustrations Consultant*

ADVISORS & CONTRIBUTORS

Byron Belitsos	Anna Rahe
Eric Cosh	Joanne Strobel
Meinhardt Greeff	Tamara Strumfeld
Brad Heckenberg	Nick Tamm
Gard Jameson	Carla Tomson
Susi Juckas	Judy Van Cleave
Marilynn Kulieke	Jim Zigarelli

PUBLISHER'S CATALOGING-IN-PUBLICATION DATA
Names: Siegel, Morris, producer. | English, James G., producer.
Title: The untold story of Jesus: a modern biography from the Urantia Book.
Description: Includes index. | Chicago, IL: Urantia Press, 2019.
Identifiers: LCCN: 2019900346 | ISBN: 978-0-9974049-1-3 (hardcover) | 978-0-9974049-2-0 (paperback)
Subjects: LCSH: Urantia book. | Jesus Christ--New Age movement interpretations. | Spiritual life--New Age movement. | BISAC RELIGION / General | BODY, MIND & SPIRIT / General
Classification: LCC BT304.93 .U7 2019| DDC 232.9--dc23

DEDICATION
This book is dedicated to Jesus of Nazareth and his lifesaving gospel: the fatherhood of God and the brotherhood of man. Forever we shall love, trust, serve, obey, and believe you.

ACKNOWLEDGMENT
We most gratefully acknowledge our indebtedness to all human and superhuman sources of record and concept which have been utilized in this restatement of Jesus' life on earth.

EDITOR'S NOTES
The Urantia Book was first published in 1955, but the text had been completed some twenty years earlier. As *The Untold Story of Jesus* was taken nearly verbatim from that text, it also follows the style and convention of the early twentieth century. In chapter introductions, sidebars, and illustrated boxes, the editors have taken greater liberty to abridge or add to the text to create our most effective arrangement of these stories and teachings.

Whenever possible we have reproduced artwork to show the entire painting, but occasionally works have been somewhat cropped to best fit the design and layout of the book. When a painting is reproduced as a significantly smaller detail of the original, it is so noted in the caption.

NOTICES AND CREDITS
All originally commissioned paintings:
©2019 Mo and Jennifer Siegel

44	"Jesus in the Temple," bpk Bildagentur/Art Resource, NY
125	"Follow Me," Mariano Garcia / Alamy Stock Photo
153	"The Lord's Prayer," The Picture Art Collection / Alamy Stock Photo
314	"In Remembrance of Me," Collection of Church of Jesus Christ of Latter Day Saints, 1997 Intellectual Reserve
342	"Ecce Homo," Alinari/Art Resource, NY
358	"He Is Not Here," © 2004 by Walter Rane
pp.	38, 82, 146, 202, 211, 282, 317, 333, 340, 356: images used under license from Shutterstock.com
pp.	259, 291, 338: GoodSalt.com

LICENSED ART WEBSITES
Russ Docken, russdockenoriginals.com; **C. Michael Dudash,** cmdudash.com; **Daniel Gerhartz,** danielgerhartz.com; **Yongsung Kim,** yongsungkimart.com; **Akiane Kramarik,** akiane.com; **Michael Malm,** mikemalm.com; **Greg Olsen,** gregolsen.com; **Del Parson,** delparson.com; **Slawa Radziszewska,** Instagram @slawa.rad; **Walter Rane,** walterrane.com; **J. Kirk Richards,** jkirkrichards.com; **Stephen Sawyer,** sawyerportraits.com; **Liz Lemon Swindle,** lizlemonswindle.com; **Jeremy Winborg,** jeremywinborg.com

First Printing, 2019
Second Printing, 2020
Third Printing (paperback, 2024)
Printed in China
RR Donnelley Asia

URANTIA PRESS